THE SCIENTIFIC DIALOGUE

Annual Series of
European Research in Behavior Therapy
5

Series Editors

P.M.G. Emmelkamp, I. Florin, I.M. Marks

THE SCIENTIFIC DIALOGUE: FROM BASIC RESEARCH TO CLINICAL INTERVENTION

Editors

H.G. Zapotoczky
T. Wenzel

SWETS & ZEITLINGER B.V. AMSTERDAM / LISSE

SWETS & ZEITLINGER INC. ROCKLAND, MA / BERWYN, PA PUBLISHING SERVICE

Library of Congress Cataloging-in-Publication Data

The Scientific Dialogue : from basic research to clinical intervention \ editors, H.G. Zapotoczky, T. Wenzel.
p. cm. -- (Annual series of European research in behavior therapy, ISSN 0921-9439 ; 5)
Based on papers from the 19th Congress of the European Association of Behaviour Therapy held in Vienna, Austria.
Includes bibliographical references.
ISBN 902651106X
1. Behavior Therapy -- Congresses. I. Zapotoczky, H.G. (Hans-Georg), 1932- II. Wenzel, T. (Thomas), 1960- III. European Association of Behaviour Therapy. Congress (19th : 1989 : Vienna, Austria) IV. Series.
[DNLM: 1. Behavior Therapy--Congresses. 2. Neurotic Disorders--therapy--congresses. 3. Research--congresses. W1 AN78PQ v.5 / WM 425 S416 1989]
RC489.B4S39 1990
616.89'142--dc20
DNLM/DLC
for Library of Congress 90-10087
CIP

CIP-gegevens Koninklijke Bibliotheek, Den Haag

Scientific

The scientific dialogue : from basic research to clinical intervention / eds. : H.G. Zapotoczky, T. Wenzel. - Amsterdam [etc] : Swets & Zeitlinger - (Annual series of European research in behavior therapy, ISSN 0921-9439 ; 5)
Met lit. opg.
ISBN 90-265-1106-X geb.
SISO 607.33 UDC 615.851 NUGI 713
Trefw.: gedragstherapie.

Printed in the Netherlands by Offsetdrukkerij Kanters B.V., Alblasserdam

ISBN 90 265 1106 X
ISSN 0921-9439
NUGI 713

CONTENTS

PREFACE

In the fifth volume of the Annual Series of European Research in Behavior Therapy papers you will find a selection of the most interesting symposia from the 19th Congress of the European Association of Behaviour Therapy held in Vienna (Austria). The general line which dictated the selection of the papers is characterized by the search leading from theoretical considerations to clinical practice, a way which should be carried out in permanent dialogue.

It is a tradition in this country to emphasize the vicinity of science and art in their various associations. Following this tradition we like to offer as introduction Professor Tunners' reflections about links between anxiety and society.

The first part consists of four articles which show some guidelines for future developments. The second part will offer information on the basic research on affective disorders, the third part includes articles on panic disorder, anxiety States and obsessive-compulsive disorder. The fourth part is concerned with the problem of eating disorders.

The fifth part brings new results on the possible role of pharmacotherapy in behavioral treatment. In the sixth part you will find papers on different topics in behavioral medicine. The subject of part VII is research with HIV-positive patients. The eighth part on treatment programms for schizophrenic patients is followed by papers on behaviour therapy with children and the elderly. Last, but not least- part X offers a paper by Keijsers, Schaap and Hoogduin on the factors influencing the therapeutic relationship.

It is the purpose of conferences and therefore of this book to stimulate our scientific knowledge which may help men and women with psychic disturbances. Also we understand this publication as an attempt to intensify our readiness for increasing and clarifying our human dialog.

H.G. Zapotoczky
T. Wenzel

INTRODUCTION

ANXIETY AND SOCIETY

W. Tunner

University of Munich, Institute of Psychology/Clinical Psychology.

Anxiety arises out of the expectation of approaching danger. This danger is not always clearly recognizable. Fantasy and concrete reality often intertwine with each other.

Our first illustration is a detail from Albrecht Altdorfer's masterful portrayal of Alexander the Great's battle against Dareos III, the King of Persia (see Figure 1). It was created in 1529, the first year the Turkish army besieged Vienna. Fear and aggression, both on an individual and a group level are depicted here. This painting not only captures the specific by its exacting detail, but also the general by the way it is composed.

Figure 1: **Altdorfer's Alexanderschlacht (1529)**

The battle is at an end. Alexander and his army have won. The fate of the individual is hardly recognizable in the mass. By attending to detail, we see the meaning of the individual in the mass. Dareos is escaping, but his chariot driver has fallen and the horses are beyond control. Alexander is closing in with his lance. This strongest moment of individual tension is also the tragedy and triumph of the mass. The king could escape. *Death is certain, but the moment remains uncertain* . This is an important quality of anxiety. Even though Dareos was fully aware of an actual danger, he still could not be certain of what would happen at the next moment.

Figure 2: **Picasso's Guernica (1937)**

A further example (see Figure 2), painted some 400 years later by Picasso in reaction to the Spanish civil war, expresses individual anxiety within the masses.

The anxiety of an individual within the mass is not necessarily equivalent to the mean sum of anxiety that an individual would experience outside the mass. Emotions are exaggerated within the mass *by* the mass. They can also be weakened within the mass or changed in quality. That is, their quality might be simplified or complicated. The panic, for example, at the outbreak of a fire varies as a function of group cohesiveness. If the cohesiveness of the group is weak, the panic reaction is hightened. This is to be seen in many catastrophe reports.

Individuals tend to lose their ability to criticize the actual reality of the situation within groups. The readiness to assume individual responsibility also diminishes within group situations. Furthermore, the individual's tendency to support and justify public opinion inreases within group settings and this leads to an overestimation of the group's strengths and qualities. The foregoing, coupled with group rigidity (or perhaps the foregoing brings about group rigidity), produces a readiness for group behaviour to change rapidly from general anxiety to ecstatic enthusiasm or from jubilation to mob violence.

War and the preparation for war are an example for this observation. In wartime the masses are controlled by orders given by the highest authority. This authority justifies its priorities with statements regarding the social, political, and economic needs of the state. The behaviour of the individual is defined. He or she is informed exactly how one must behave in order to maintain social order. As plausible as these justifications seem to be, the ideology they express is irrational. Just as irrational as the methods used to stir up the anxiety needed to motivate the decision for warlike aggression. Aggression relieves, at least temporarily, the feeling of anxiety. Propaganda instigates fear and anxiety which establishes the foundation for aggression. Anxiety leads to resentment, which overcomes anxiety, and this resentment is channelled into rigid order. *Possibly, the degree of obsessive compulsive order demanded by society is a measure of the readiness for warlike aggression.*

In politics, anxiety is rarely mentioned. The political expression is rather an atmosphere of threatened security. Security, in this sense, refers to the predictability of events which guarantee the control and gratification of everyday needs. If the predictability is uncertain and control lost, security is threatened and anxiety is released.

The French historian Jean Delumeau, in his two volume work " Anxiety in the Occident ", relates a history of the reasons for anxiety in our cultural development and the varied methods that have been employed to combat it: threats of catastrophe, ghosts, eternal darkness, plague, hunger, war, irresponsible leaders, taxes, crime, the apocalypse, the devil and his agents, etc. As an example, the eclipse of August 12th, 1654 occurred just a few years after the ravages of the thirty years war and released a wave of tremendous panic. Grim prophecies were supported by astrological readings. The plague, another example, ravaged Europe with such an impact that a large part of the population died of it. As late as the 17th century, more than half of Vienna's population died of the plague within a year. The fear of this horrible disease led to the consequences it had. The attempt was made to delay recognizing the presence of the plague as long as it was possible. The doctors and authorities tried to keep the public quiet. After examining many documents, Delumeau has concluded that, "when the plague threatened a city, the city officials generally behaved this way: They allowed the doctors to examine the suspected cases of bubonic plague, the doctors often announced a quieting diagnosis which appealed to the wishes of the authorities, if they did not, other doctors were called in who questioned their colleagues' fears. The assessors and health officials thereby closed their eyes to the coming danger" (1985, p. 155). "Whoever mentioned the danger of the plague on the piazza, in the stores, while visiting friends," Manzoni wrote in the year 1630 in Lombardy, "encountered unbelievably strong ridicule and angry disgust." Heinrich Heine described similar collective behaviour in the 1832 cholera epidemic in Paris. Supported by theories that stated that anxiety increases the threat of becoming infected and therefore one should remain in good humour in times of epidemics, extravagant revelry spread throughout Parisian society as the threat of the epidemic increased.

On August 5th, 1989, a Munich medical journal (nr. 32 of Münchner Ärztliche Anzeigen) published a report on the increase in air pollution in Germany and the destructive effects it has on our organism. "Nitrogen Dioxide pollution has been steadily increasing through the 60's und the 70's. This tendency has carried on to the 80's. Studies conducted in Mannheim and Karlsruhe illustrate this clearly. Nitrogen dioxide emissions were nationally higher in 1986 than ever before. On the average, traffic produces about 60% of this poison; in S. Germany it is closer to 75%. Nitrogen dioxide emissions from traffic have increased 16% since 1983 and are therefore about 48% higher than the government predicted 3 years ago for 1988. The causes are excessive emission levels and an increase in car performance and speed in the lasÄ two years" (1989, p. 8). Nitrogen dioxide is a pungent smelling brownish gas. Like ozone, it reaches into the minutest parts of the respiration system and causes a lowering of our bodily resistance against a number of serious diseases, especially in children. The perceptual threshold for this poisonous irritant increases already after a few minutes exposure. After 15 minutes exposure it is no longer perceived, even if it is present in higher concentrations. This gas is only one of many pollutants we inhale. Emotions are set free by the immediate impressions of the senses. However, if one relies only on the senses, one underestimates the danger and considers others who are anxious to be insane. The clicks of a geiger counter have no emotional effect or in reference to the danger of radioactivity, only slightly. *An understanding is weak when it is not grounded in perceptual experience.* We have the ability to move away from it. Science is an example for this in itself. One of its basic laws is that the scientist removes his personal feelings from the object of research and that he works solely with his quantitative intellect. Curiosity and the interest arising from the tension betkeen the pro's and con's should motivate scientific work. This attitude has encouraged unbelievable achievement. However, when its hidden sides are no longer covered by shadows, it becomes clear that the application of scientific knowledge demands other psychological requirements than does research alone. As a result, today's scientist is caught in the same double binds as we all are. Scientific research methods require emotional distance in order to fulfil the goals of investigation. The application of the results requires the sensors of emotionality. The scientist requires emotion to bridge the distance between the intellect and perceptual reality. *Rational distance reduces anxiety. It overcomes this danger, but creates new dangers and we lack the organs to react to these new dangers with anxiety.*

Hans Jonas recently reflected that, "my pessimistic theory is that what wisdom and political understanding have not achieved, might be realized as a result of fear. We are being warned by nature and I hope that a series of minor catastrophes will awaken our reason, so that we will avoid the great catastrophe" (1989, p. 9). So, is it fear that will lead to reason. What is reason after all? One searches in vain in texts on psychology. Reason is not the same thing as understanding. Nature does not provide reason as it does emotions. Reason, and especially collective reason is achieved only by the uncompromising decision, an individual makes to deal with the life of the community in a correct way. On June the 17th, 18th, and 30th, as well as on July 2nd, 1989, ships armed with atomic weapons were blocked by

Greenpeace members in inflatable rubber boats. I don't have any definition of what reason is, but I have no doubt that it was reason what these seemingly unreasonable people were doing as they blocked those ships.

The path leading from Alexander's battle up to modern times is long. The determinants of anxiety in the individual and in society have certainly changed. *It would seem to me that currently, it's not so much anxiety, but rather worry, that anxiety is missing today and if it weren't, it could possibly motivate us towards more reasonable behaviour.*

A clinician is unreasonable if he only busies him or herself with the question of how to eliminate anxiety with medication or psychotherapy as quickly as possible.

REFERENCES

Delumeau, J. (1985) *Angst im Abendland - Die Geschichte kollektiver Ängste im Europa des 14. bis 18. Jahrhunderts (Vol. I and II).* Hamburg: Rowohlt.

Jonas, H. (1989) Gespräch mit dem Moralphilosophen über Euthanasie und Ethik. *Die Zeit, 35*, 9. *Münchner Ärztliche Anzeigen, Nr. 31*, 5. August 1989, p. 8-9.

PART I:

LECTURES

CURRENT STATUS OF BEHAVIOUR THERAPY IN EUROPE

P.M.G. Emmelkamp

Department of Clinical Psychology, Academic Hospital, Oostersingel 59, 9713 EZ Groningen, The Netherlands

When the European Association of Behaviour Therapy was founded in 1971 few would have prophesied that nearly two decades later 22 associations would have become an affiliate of the EABT. The EABT has now approximately 6000 members and is much larger than the American Association of Behavior Therapy and is actually the largest behaviour therapy organization in the world. So at least in terms of members behaviour therapy has been quite successful in Europe. But what has been achieved? To answer that question an inquiry was held among the European behaviour therapy associations that are affiliated with the EABT, the results of which will be discussed.

THE RELATIVE SIZE OF BEHAVIOUR THERAPY ORGANIZATIONS

One of the questions concerned the relative size of the behaviour therapy organization in comparison with other psychotherapy organizations in each country. This information may give a raw figure of the influence of behaviour therapy in the mental health field in each country. As compared with experiential and rogerian organizations, in most countries the behaviour therapy organization is larger and in Holland and France even much larger. In Italy and Spain the size of the behaviour therapy organization is comparable to that of the experiential therapy association. Only in Denmark and Sweden we seem to have lost the battle: here the experiential organization appears to be larger than the behaviour therapy organization. The situation in Germany is a little bit complex, since they have a number of different behaviour therapy organizations: so it is difficult to estimate the relative size of the behaviour therapy organization versus other therapy organizations.

With respect to the psychoanalytic psychotherapy, the situation looks less bright for behaviour therapy. In most european countries psychoanalysis has still more followers than behaviour therapy. Only in Holland and in Norway behaviour therapists outnumber their psychoanalytic colleagues. There is still along way to go!

BACKGROUND PROFESSION

In nearly all countries most members of behaviour therapy organizations are psychologists (70%). The second largest group (20%) is comprised of psychiatrists. Only ten percent of behaviour therapists are neither psychologists nor psychiatrists. This group includes social workers, psychiatric nurses, remedial teachers and physicians. Of course this pattern differs from country to country. For example, in the french behaviour therapy organization psychiatrists outnumber psychologists; in Norway where the emphasis is on applied behavioural analysis only 15% of the behaviour therapists are psychologists. Here most members are either teacher, nurse or social worker. In Britain, also a large number of behaviour therapists are neither psychologist nor psychiatrist. There are a number of organizations (in Germany, Austria, Belgium and Finland) that register only psychologists, psychiatrists or physicians as behaviour therapist. The background profession of behaviour therapists is shown in Table 1.

Table 1. **Background profession of behaviour therapists**

Association	Psychologists	Psychiatrists	Others
Swedish	90%	5%	5%
Finnish	98%	2%	---
Norwegian	15%	1%	84%
Danish	80%	10%	10%
Icelandic	95%	??	??
German (DGVM)	70%	---	30% (physicians)
German (FKV)	75%	25%	---
Austrian	65%	35%	---
Italian (AIAMC)	70%	15%	15%
Italian (SITCC)	60%	40%	---
Spanish (SCRITC)	80%	8%	12%
Dutch	89%	5%	6%
Belgian (flemish)	80%	20%	---
Belgian (AEMTC)	70%	20%	10%
French	30%	60%	10%
Greek	45%	38%	17%
British	52%	6%	42%

In which settings are behaviour therapists employed? The results are presented in Table 2. Most behaviour therapists (33%) work in an outpatient clinic or community health center. The second largest group of behaviour therapists are employed in a hospital, mostly in a psychiatric hospital; approximately 15% works with mental retardates; 9% is involved in school and child guidance; 8%works at a university; and another 6% has a private practice.

Table 2. **Percentage of behaviour therapists employed in**

Outpatient clinic	33%
(Psychiatric) hospital	25%
University	8%
Private practice	6%
Mental retardates	15%
School/child guidance	9%
Penal institutions	2%
Geriatric institutions	2%

Only a few behaviour therapists are employed across the different countries. To give just a few examples: in Holland the largest group of behaviour therapists are working with outpatients; in contrast, in Austria the largest group of behaviour therapists are working in psychiatric hospitals; in Norway most behaviour therapists are either working in schools or with mental retardates. This suggest that in most European countries there is still an as yet hardly unexploited market for behaviour therapists, which market differs from country to country.

Obviously, whether behaviour therapy can be conducted in private practice or not depends in the first place on whether this will be paid by third party payers as insurance companies and social or skilfunds. In a number of European countries this is indeed the case, but - unfortunately in most countries therapy conducted in private practice is only reimbursed by third party payers when conducted by a psychiatrist. Here is an importa:t task for the EABT inthe near future, provided that we can agree upon a formalized curriculum for registration as behaviour therapist.

PUBLICATIONS

In table 3 a number of journals is presented in the area of behaviour therapy and behavioural medicine are listed. Probably, there will be even more of them. Apart from the journal of the British association "Behavioural Psychotherapy" and the "Scandinavian Journal of Behavioural Therapy" all other journals are published in languages that are difficult to read for many Europeans, including Danish, Norwegian, German, Italian, Spanish and dutch. While these journals apparently have a function in communicating research findings within a specific language area, it obviously is not the best way to communicate with other Europeans.

Table 3. **Behaviour therapy and behavioural medicine journals**

Scandinavian Journal of Behaviour Therapy
Discriminant
Dansk Adfaerdstherapeutisk Forening
Praxis der Klinischen Verhaltensmedizin und Rehabilitation
Verhaltensmodifikation und Verhaltensmedizin
Verhaltenstherapie
Therapia del Comportamento
Behavioural Psychotherapy
Gedragstherapie
Revista Espanola de Terapia del Comportamiento
Annual Series of European Research in Behaviour Therapy

Therefore - just a few years ago - the "Annual Series of European Research in Behaviour Therapy " was founded. This series is meant to facilitate communication among behaviour therapist within Europe and across the ocean.

TRAINING IN BEHAVIOUR THERAPIST

How is the training of behaviour therapists organized in the various organizations? Of the 20 associations that completed our inquiry, 8 admitted that they had no formal curriculum.

Table 4. **Characteristics of behaviour therapy courses**

Hours		Theory : Practice
Swedish	500	30 : 70
Finnish	?	60 : 40
German (FKV)	500	50 : 50
Austrian	510	30 : 70
Italian (AIAMC)	200	50 : 50
Italian (SITCC)	400	20 : 80
Dutch	75	70 : 30
Belgian (AEMTC)	225	30 : 70
Belgian (flemish)	75	40 : 60
French	80	40 : 60
British	-	50 : 50
Swiss	450	--: --

Some of the characteristics and requirements of the curricula of those associations that have a formal training programme are summarized in Table 4.

The minimum number of hours of the various courses varies from 75 (dutch and flemish association) till 500 hours. However, in the dutch and flemish courses students receive much more homework assignments than in most other courses,so the hours the students spend on these courses do not differ as much as it may look at first sight.

Training programs can vary in terms of intensity of the professional training experience. Some programs may give the students background knowledge about theory, research and therapeutic skills by means of didactic material but provide less opportunity to practice the skills during the course. Other programs emphasize more the directly teaching of therapeutic skills whereby the student is explained the steps of the skills, shown examples (by transcripts, modeling or video) and practices the skills in role play with performance feedback. In Table 4 the mean ratio between theory and practice in the various courses is shown. In most programs the practice component is slightly more emphasized than the theoretical component, although in most programs at least 30 percent of the time is devoted to theory and research.

The mean percentage of time devoted to a number of topics in these courses is shown in Table 5. Although their are some differences among the various courses, in fact the consensus on the main themes is striking. First of all, in all courses quite a lot of attention is paid to cognitive techniques. This means that in Europe cognitive interventions are seen as an integral part of behaviour therapy. Although there is a lot of turmoil in a few associations with respect to this issue, I am in-clined to see these figures as highly encouraging for an integrative cognitive-behavioural approach.

Table 5. **Mean percentage of hours devoted to specific topics**

(Social) learning theory	10%	(5% - 15%)
Functional behavioural Analysis	12%	(0% - 20%)
Behavioural technique	26%	(15% - 50%)
Cognitive technique	18%	(10% - 25%)
Behavioural medicine	11%	(0% 20%)
Specific disorders	7%	(5% - 30%)
Therapeutic relationship	15%	(5% - 50%)

I don’t think we should teach students one particular - orthodox - religion, be it either radical behaviourism or cognitivism. It is reassuring to see that this is also the opinion of those who are responsible for the various behaviour therapy courses in Europe.

It is also encouraging to see that all programs devote part of the course to the therapeutic relationship. Was this topic a few years ago almost taboo in behaviour therapy circles, now the therapeutic relationship forms a substantial part of most courses.

In addition to successful completion of the behaviour therapy course a number of other requirements have to be met before a trainee can be registered as behaviour therapist. In a number of associations only clinical psychologists or physicians (mostly psychiatrist) are admitted as behaviour therapists. In all associations, however, additional requirements include adequate knowledge of psychopathology and learning theories and most associations also demand from the trainee that they have successfully completed courses in psychopharmacology and interviewing skills.

In addition to following a course in behaviour therapy trainees have to treat a number of patients under supervision. The actual number of patients that have to be treated and the number of supervision sessions differ among the associations.

In Table 6 an overview is given of the requirements of a number of behaviour therapy associations.

Table 6. **Requirements with respect to supervision**

	Number of patients	Therapy-sessions	Supervision-sessions
Swedish	7	---	165
Finnish	2-4	---	150
German (FKV)	20	400	120
Austrian	4	---	120
Italian (AIAMC)	10	---	200
Italian (SITCC)	2	---	100
Dutch	4	120	50
Belgian (AEMTC)	4	Not formalized	
Belgian (flemish)	4	120	50
French	2	20	9
Swiss	8	---	200

The average number of patients to be treated is 7, but this figure varies widely, ranging from 2 patients to 20 patients. Trainees have to conduct on the average 170 sessions under supervision; the average number of supervision sessions is approximately 120. But again, there is a large variance among the behaviour therapy organizations with respect to their requirements.

Personal therapy or alternatively called trainee-psychotherapy is a conditio sine qua non before a trainee can be registered as psychotherapist in a number of psychotherapy schools. To date, only three behaviour therapy organization (the dutch, the swiss and the finnish) require a personal therapy of their trainees. However, in a few other curricula trainees undergo a kind of behaviour therapy as part of the training course, which is called alternatively self-experience or self-modification.

Finally, a number of associations require that the trainees are employed in a mental health setting, but this can be a minimum requirement of 1,5 day a week during the training (as the dutchmen require) to 3 years full-time as is required by the austrian association.

Taken together, there is a large variety in the requirements that behaviour therapy organizations demand before they register a trainee as behaviour therapist. Indeed there are a number of organizations that don't have a formal training programme or requirements at all. In my view the current status of the training of behaviour therapists in Europe is alarming. When in 1992 the boundaries of the countries in the European Economic Community will disappear this means that behaviour therapists within the EEC may apply for jobs in other EEC countries without having fulfilled the necessary requirements in that particular country. It seems timely to come to a standardization of curricula requirements and to reach consensus within the EABT on the necessary components of a behaviour therapy training programme.

PROPOSAL FOR A CURRICULUM

The components of such a training programme are summarized in Table 7. They consist of requirements with respect to:
(1) previous training or background profession,
(2) theoretical and practical training course,
(3) treatment of patients under supervision,
(4) conducting of a research study.

Table 7. **Curriculum proposal**

Previous training: Clinical psychology or psychiatry.

Theoretical/practical training course: Min. 300 hrs; Min. 100 hrs class work (attendance), Min. 150 hrs literature study.

Supervision: Min. 100 sessions; Treatment of 8 patients (min. 200 sessions). Research study, N=1 study.

1. Previous training

Only clinical psychologist and psychiatrist are admitted to the behaviour therapy training programmes that eventually lead to registration as behaviour therapist. Only so is guarantied that prospective behaviour therapists will have adequate knowledge of psychopathology and sufficient experience with psychiatric patients. Only under exceptional circumstances may other professionals be admitted provided that they have successfully completed courses in abnormal psychology, psychopathology, psychopharmacology, and interviewing skills and have the necessary experience in mental health settings. Of course training in behaviour therapy of nurses, social workers and teachers remains important, but should not lead to a formal registration as behaviour therapist.

2. Theoretical and practical training course

In this category a minimum of 300 hours is required. These must minimally consist of 100 hours course work with an emphasis on practical training such as modeling by the teacher or showing of techniques by video and role play of the trainee with performance feedback. A minimum of 150 hours (= 1500 pages) is required for reading relevant behaviour therapy literature. Since all trainees must have enough opportunity to practice the techniques the group of trainees should not be larger than 12. Self-experience or self-modification may be part of this training course.

3. Treatment of patients under supervision

Trainees have to treat a minimum of 8 patients under supervision. The type of problems treated should vary widely as should the treatment techniques used. A minimum of 200 therapy sessions should be conducted under supervision. A minimum of 100 supervision sessions (of one hour) is required. Group supervision is allowed provided that the supervision group is not larger than 4 trainees. With group supervision twice as much supervision sessions are required than in the case of individual supervision. At least half of the supervision sessions should be individual supervision.

4. Research study

Finally, it may be a good idea if behaviour therapy trainees would conduct a small research study. Although this could be a controlled between-group study with a umber of patients, a controlled n = 1 study would also do and is presumably more realistic. Given the strong emphasis in behaviour therapy on research it seems only naturally to require from prospective behaviour therapists that they have some experience in conducting a small research study. I am well aware of the gap that exists between behavioural researchers on the one side and the practitioners on the other side. It seems to me that prospective behaviour therapists should be trained in applied research in order to become data-based practitioners.

CONCLUDING REMARKS

My proposals are only minimum requirements for certification as an EABT behaviour therapist. Each national association -of course- is free to require additional matters. But I hope that we can reach consensus about the minimum requirements for a standard training programme.

One of the clearest trends in the past few years is a greater concern for accountability in mental health services. This trend seems to be due in large part to the greatly increased costs of mental health services in general and psychotherapy in particular and to the growing need for reimbursement of psychotherapy by either government, or third party payers as insurance companies. There have been demands from funding sources and legislators for demonstrations that psychotherapy is effective. In the United States this has even led to legislation in 1981, requiring the clear demonstration of efficacy, and safety of psychotherapy before reimbursement would be forthcoming. No doubt European countries will follow in the near future with establishing standards for quality assurance for provision of psychotherapy. Here is an important task for the European Association of Behaviour Therapy and a challenge for the future. Therefore it is important that we reach as soon as possible consensus on the minimum requirements for a behaviour therapy training programme. Only if we have adequately trained behaviour therapists are we in a position to convince governments and insurance companies that behaviour therapy is in many cases the most effective treatment.

RESEARCH AND THEORY AS GUIDES FOR THERAPEUTIC STRATEGIES

F.H. Kanfer

University of Illinois at Urbana, Champaigne, Department of Psychology

Today, I would like to review briefly the progress in our work that has lead from a simple linear conditioning model to a complex tri-level behavioral approach. I now stress the motivational aspect of the self-regulation system, particularly in non-psychotic patients, because I believe that harnessing motivation and emotions for a maximizing the involvement and effort of clients can greatly facilitate the therapeutic process. The utility of behavior therapy is expanded when we look at the data and theories of cognitive, social and physiological psychology as a basis for the treatment of behavior therapy. However, they do *not* signify a break with the basic methodological and substantive postulates that have been proposed by the founders of the behavior therapy movement. Instead of a learning-based approach, we should now speak of a psychological-science-based approach that retains the same emphasis on verification of knowledge by empirical methods and that presumes the plasticity of human organisms which permits changing and shaping through environmental, biological and self-generated interventions. Although I emphasize intra-personal factors that regulate behavior, this is not to deny the importance of environmental contingencies and biological events that also shape a person's history and individual characteristics. It is the joint effect of interactions at all three levels that determines behavior.

My presentation at the first meeting of this group was an attempt to extend a Skinnerian learning approach to the many clients who are seen weekly for one or two hours and whose behavior could not be systematically shaped by environmental contingency management methods. In this approach, which we called *instigation therapy*, I hypothesized that clients can be taught to take responsibility for becoming their own agents of change. The research and clinical applications of this work have been widely described as self-control or self-management therapy. In contrast to previous behavioral approaches, self-management therapy makes more demands on the client and requires more skills than passive adherence to environmental control. Specifically, to reinforce a new response, such as delaying an anger outburst or approaching a phobic object, the client must develop criteria for when the reinforcement is to be administered. He has to set a clear goal and define precisely the response on which the consequences are contingent and has to monitor his own performance, since there is no clinician to signal that a response has just met the reinforcement criteria. The client also has to compare her actions to the established criteria and finally to deliver the reinforcing event, assuming that it is easily available and that she has delayed delivery of the reward until the proper response had occurred. Thus, the paradigm of a linear model in which a subject simply takes the place of a therapist may seem plausible, but it necessitates further inquiry of how to motivate such self-started actions and leads to an examination of what skills are necessary for self-management.

The shift from external to personal control raises the serious problem of providing incentives and channelling motivation so that (1) the client can move from statements of intention to actual execution of desired behavior, (2) is sufficiently motivated to take responsibility for the change process and (3) carries out the necessary steps in therapy. The allotment of motivational resources to therapy is not a *prerequisite* but a primary goal of therapy. This view puts the burden of furthering motivation on the therapist. It no longer enables clinicians to attribute therapeutic failures primarily to a lack of client motivation.

I do not consider motivation as a unitary concept but ask specific questions about what incentives or commitments are required, for example, just for returning to sessions, what incentives are needed to meet the requirements for the execution of assigned tasks, or the change of the many cognitive and emotional reactions that make up the therapeutic process. The therapist serves as an initial source of motivation, as a partner who gives social support in a joint enterprise. The focus on motivation has led us to emphasize the need for negotiations to set up therapy goals and procedures *jointly* with the client. Early stages of treatment are devoted to motivating clients to collaborate and to work toward change. Goal clarification facilitates goal-setting, strengthens commitment and prepares the client to execute the program. The change program must be designed to make the steps sufficiently easy for the client so that he can do what is required and experience some success. Later, the client is prepared for transfer and generalization of self-regulatory skills and for maintenance of improvements without relapse. Eventually the client's increased capacity for autonomy should assist him in resumption of full personal responsibility and disengagement from the therapy process.

The recent analysis by various European action theorists, particularly by Heckhausen and Kuhl (1985) provides a convenient framework to describe the role of self-regulatory processes in the development and maintenance of various motivations in therapy. Heckenhausen and Kuhl have segmented the motivational processes into two critical stages. In the first or predecisional stage a vague wish of desirable future states is transformed into an *intention*. Once a decision has been made to pursue a goal, the person focuses on stabilizing this decision, facilitating its enactment and attaining the goal. Heckhausen and Kuhl have called the second stage the *volitional* portion of the sequence. The analysis of various motivational stages is parallel to our own work and also to the model Prochaska and DiClemente (1986) who differentiate between the contemplation stage, the determination stage, the action stage and the maintenance stage as distinct sequences in therapy. These approaches suggest that we deal differently with motivational factors in therapy at various points in therapy. The conceptual framework is also iterative. It is similar both for the overall process of therapy and for sections of the therapy hour. While the primary emphasis in many schools of therapy has been on the client's motivation to reduce distress or to eliminate symptoms, the full spectrum of motivational analysis requires equal attention to strategies that enhance the attractiveness of therapeutic goals, facilitate behavior change, encourage the client to proceed toward a goal state and prepare for maintenance by focusing on post-therapy lifestyles.

When viewed in this light, a new world of possibilities opens up. When motives are not linked only to stress reduction and biological survival, many theories from cognitive and social psychology appear relevant, and their findings suggest new strategies or the refinement of existing cognitive behavioral techniques. This perspective also places the role of emotions in psychotherapy in a different light.

Most clients go through several stages on the way to a lasting behavior change: A need exists, an intention is formed, the goal state is imagined and its components are anticipated. A commitment follows, leading to steps toward behavioral enactment. Attainment of the goal state is bolstered by maintenance strategies. First, dissatisfaction with the current state must give rise to a clear specification of a desired goal. Helping the client to develop an intention is the first challenging task of the therapist. Available theories of communication and persuasion can be of help. Fishbein, Petty and Cacioppo, Fazio, Ajzen, among others, have presented work that suggests how attitudes and intentions can be changed. Modeling techniques and information exposure are examples of methods used at this point. Due to time limits I cannot discuss further the implications and use of these theories and methods for therapy.

Once an intention has been formed, the individual focuses on anticipating more precisely how the goal state would be and its consequences. I have called this process *anticipatory self-regulation*. Future behaviors and their outcomes are cognitively rehearsed, prior to choosing among various alternatives. Possible actions, expected outcomes, necessary efforts and costs to attain the goal are rehearsed, with a bias toward the positive side. During this stage the client imagines a situation shaped by his personal experiences, anticipates the reaction of others and the effect of his actions. For example, with the intention to be more assertive with a partner the person imagines a series of events in which such assertiveness is attempted. The partner's reactions, the emotional components, the possible success or failure and the best ways to achieve success are all tried out in imagination an role-play. But, because realistic feedback cannot be attained in imagining future events, biases and distortions can seriously affect conclusions on how to cope best with the situation and they can discourage the client. The therapist, by providing impartial and more realistic feedback, by cueing more effective alternatives, and emphasis on the benefits of the new behaviors, can shape anticipatory self-regulation. By rehearsing various coping strategies the client is better prepared for stressful encounters with problem situations. Among many techniques, cognitive restructuring, stress-inoculation, role-play and cognitive rehearsal can be used.

Considering the research on explanatory style (Peterson and Seligman) the client's position on the optimism-pessimism continuum is also important. In most cases it needs to be shifted toward greater optimism. The client's judgment of his ability to carry out the intended act further influences the process. The anticipatory process also prepares a client for execution of a therapy assignment, such as doing relaxation exercises at home. Simply put, instead of waiting until a problem situation occurs in order to shape effective behaviors, a repertoire can be pre-shaped by anticipatory rehearsal.

When the client has a reasonably accurate picture of what life would be like after a therapeutic change, he needs to make a commitment to this goal and to shift attention to actions that facilitate its attainment. Our goal and value clarification procedures (Kanfer and Schefft, 1988), Klinger's method for ascertaining current concerns, reduction of dysfunctional self-attitudes such as low self-confidence and the emphasis of the utility (i.e., positive consequences) of the intended behavior change can fortify this decision. After commitment, therapeutic work shifts from building positive expectations of the goal state to dealing with the obstacles and costs to achieve it.

As the client moves to behavioral enactment, the desired instrumental behavior must be practiced in everyday situations. This stage is described by our model on self-regulation; the psychological processes involve the self-monitoring of the person's behavior and evaluation of it. Faced with an actual situation, the client now tests his skills, experiences the relevant emotions and gets feedback from his actions and the environment. We have described and studied some of the many vari-ables that influence this process. Since I have published this model in several papers and in our recent book, I will not go into further detail here.

The last two steps of the model concern the immediate and long-term consequences of the client's progress in attaining the goal. To ensure better readiness for coping with difficulties, various techniques are applied in preparation. Both generalization of newly acquired skills and their long-term maintenance, even in the case of recurrent or new conflicts or stresses, are the focus in the last section of therapy.

During the entire sequence, the client's emotional state influences momentary and long-range behavior patterns. Emotions serve as potent motivational agents. Yet they have rarely been used as deliberate tools in therapy.

Until recently, most theories of therapy have focussed on emotions as primarily disruptive states that need to be controlled or removed. Recent research has suggested that both positive and negative moods and emotions can be introduced in therapy as independent variables, as helpful tools for change. Several recent theorists, for example Frijda, Greenberg and Safran, Leventhal have suggested that emotions represent an integrated human experience that changes a person's readiness to act toward a specifiable end. Three aspects of the role of emotions in therapy are especially worth noting: First, the common practice of centering therapy interactions almost exclusively on discussion of problems, conflicts and distress. Secondly, the ever-present effect of mood as a means to facilitate change, and thirdly, the implications of current research for the utilization of catharsis.

In the light of current research it is astounding that therapeutic sessions emphasize negative emotions almost exclusively. Positive moods have been shown to facilitate a person's willingness to negotiate goals, to increase openness to persuasion by others, to increase risk-taking of moderate severity, to recall positive material that can influence self-evaluations and decisions, with higher expectation of success, to encode new experiences as relatively happy, to increase creativity and self-efficacy and to use intuitive rather than logical strategies in problem-solving with greater self-confidence. These statements are broad summaries of findings and are modified by various parameters. However they clearly suggest a completely different view on how to use emotions in therapy. For example, since pessimistic and negative self-reactions are fairly common among neurotic patients, the introduction of positive moods, by inquiring about the client's positive experiences, assets or emotionally satisfying fantasies, can be used to increase the client's willingness to engage in therapeutic tasks and to have greater positive expectations about the outcome of his efforts. Such utilization of emotions would be appropriate in all of the stages that we have described, although for different purposes and to a different degree. The deliberate utilization of affective states does not mitigate the utility of various techniques for reducing affective reaction tendencies that encourage dysfunctional self-reactions and behaviors. But we make it a rule to introduce discussion and assignments of assessing and strengthening the client's assets whenever possible. No session should ever end on a focus on problems rather than solutions, nor leave the client without hope for some improvement.

The effects of mood on memory have been repeatedly demonstrated, both for recall and encoding. Feeling good makes people remember positive experiences more easily, judge current events as more pleasant, if the recall is vivid, and increase success expectations. Although other variables may modify such effects, the results of numerous studies suggest a robust effect across a wide range of situations.

In our laboratory, two recent studies showed transitory effects, such as the above noted, and also effects on such self-reactions as goal-setting, self-efficacy and assessment of somatic well-being. The work of Seligman and his coworkers on the role of optimism, a more trait-like effect of mood, is too well-known to require more than mention here.

These findings suggest the need for more specific research for developing techniques to harness mood and emotion for facilitation of change. But enough work has accumulated so that even today it should alert clinicians to the dangers of treating emotions only, as social norms suggest, as disruptive, in need of control, or as dangerous material that needs to be exposed and expressed.

The public as well as many psychotherapists consider catharsis as a critical ingredient of psychotherapy and curative on its own. Recent research and current theorizing paint a completely different picture. As early as 1973, Frank has suggested that emotional arousal is a precondition for attitude change. But he also warned, that the release of emotion has only temporary effects, unless it also modifies cognitive structures.

Frank's statement summarizes years of research that has brought many of us to a similar view. The popularity of catharsis and the continued belief in its utility (when used alone) is probably due to the differences between its short term and long term effects. Intense emotional arousal is usually followed by exhaustion and temporary relief. Depending on the contents of the experience, the client may also feel relief having shared a long-hidden secret or, in state of helplessness due to the disabling effects of the experience, may be open to the therapist's suggestions. Catharsis may also inform of previously unrecognized feelings and behavioral dispositions. There is no general agreement on the processes by which intense emotional arousal influences attitudes and behaviors. There is agreement that catharsis has utility only if the therapist follows up with strategies that produce cognitive and behavioral changes as a result of the emotional expression. These and other recent insights and data on emotion and motivation promise to be the next breakthrough in the progress toward therapeutic effectiveness.

REFERENCES

Frank, J.D. (1973) *Persuasion and healing: A Comparative Study of Psychotherapy.* New York: Schocken Books.

Heckhausen, H.H., Kuhl, J. (1985) From wishes to action: The deadends and shortcuts on the long way to action. In Frese, M. & Sabini, J. (Eds.) *Goal-directed Behavior: The Concept of Action in Psychology.* Hillsdale, NJ: Erlbaum.

Kanfer, F.H. & Schefft, B.K. (1988) *Guiding the Process of Therapeutic Change.* Champaign, IL: Research Press.

Prochaska, J.O. & DiClemente, C.C. (1986) Toward a comprehensive change model. In Miller, W.R., & Heather, N. (Eds) *Treating Addictive Behaviors.* New York: Plenum.

EMOTION, PSYCHOPATHOLOGY AND THE STARTLE REFLEX

P.J. Lang, B.N. Cuthbert and M.M Bradley

Department of Clinical and Health Psychology and The Center for Research in Psychophysiology, University of Florida

A theoretical model is presented for the analysis of emotion, prompted by studies of attention and fear conditioning that use the startle probe methodology. It is intended to provide an organizing framework for future research on emotional perception, imagery, and memory. In this view, emotions are classified biphasically, based on a centrally determined appetitive or aversive (defensive) orientation. Emotional valence is considered to be a basic, organizing parameter of memory, linking the complex processing of affective judgments to simple exteroceptive reflexes. Thus, the startle reflex (an aversion response) evoked in the context of an on-going aversive emotion (e.g., fear) should be enhanced, whereas the same reflex evoked in an appetitive emotional context should be inhibited. This hypothesis has been confirmed in a number of recent studies (Varna, Spence, & Lang, 1988; Bradley, Cuthbert, & Lang, 1988). The affect-startle effect is independent of general arousal, attention, or the stimulus modality of the emotional foreground and is obtained regardless of whether affects are prompted by pictures or memory images.

One of the paradigms used to substantiate this view is similar to one employed by Anthony and Graham (1985) and Simons and Zelson (1985). Visual stimuli were photographic slides of various contents, and the blink component of the reflex was measured with either a cross-modality (a loud noise) or same-modality (a bright light flash) probe. The emotional stimulus values of the slides were determined by prior affective rating obtained from a large sample of college student subjects (see *The International Affective Picture System,* Lang, Öhman, & Vaitl, 1988; Greenwald, Cook, & Lang, 1989). The slides were rated on valence (e.g., pleasure-displeasure) and arousal (e.g., excited-calm), using bipolar graphics scales (Hodes, Cook, & Lang, 1985; Lang, 1980) derived from work on the semantic differential by Mehrabian and Russell (1974). Negatively valent slides included pictures of victims of violent death, snakes, bloody wounds or burns, disaster, aimed guns, medical injection, and angry, destitute, or starving people, neutral slides were generally common household objects, such as a hairdryer, a book, shoes; positively valent pictures included opposite-sex nudes, romantic couples, babies, cuddly animals, sports scenes, and appetizing food.

Vrana, Spence, and Lang (1988) addressed the prediction that acoustic startle probes would be augmented during a negatively valent slide foreground, relative to neutral slides, and reduced during positively valent slides. Twenty undergraduates (10 male and 10 female) viewed 36 slides, divided into three equal groups based on independent rating of positive, neg-ative, and neutral valence. Slides were exposed for six second, with 16 to 24 seconds between slides. Acoustic startle probes were binaurally presented 50-ms., 95 dB white noise bursts, with instantaneous rise-time. They occurred unpredictable during the course of slide exposure and between slides. The pattern of means is consistent with the hypothesis of an affect-reflex relationship. Blink magnitude increased significantly from pleasant to neutral to unpleasant slides. Furthermore, this pattern was exactly replicated in a second experiment (Bradley, Cuthbert, & Lang, 1988) using a new group of 36 subjects, a new 54 slide set that was again categorized according to valence, and monaural probes of 105 dB, presented with equal frequency to both the left and right ears.

Bradley, Cuthbert, & Lang (1989) demonstrated that the same pattern of reflex modulation was obtained regardless of whether the blink reflex was elicited using an acoustic startle stimulus or a visual startle stimulus. In this study, blink responses during the viewing of pleasant slides was smaller than those occurring during unpleasant slides, regardless of whether the startle probe was a loud noise or a bright light flash. These data suggest that the affect- startle effect is general, and not dependent on a cross modality startle paradigm.

The affect-startle effect also appears to be independent of arousal. This conclusion is warranted whether activation is defined by subjective report or by physiological measurement. In both experiments, subjects judged that the pleasant and unpleasant slides prompted an equal arousal experience, greater than for neutral slides. Furthermore, in the Bradley et al. experiment (1988), skin conductance was measured during initial slide viewing.

Conductance change is a near-direct measure of general sympathetic nervous system activity (i.e., physiological arousal). Nevertheless, conductance responses to the positive and neg-ative slides did not differ, and were each significantly greater in amplitude than the response to neutral slides. This pattern was also obtained with ratings of how interesting the slides were to the subject. These data suggest that the valence/reflex relationship is not fundamentally attentional, but also that it is not a non-specific effect of drive or activation, as hypothesized in the original probe reflex studies of classical fear conditioning (e.g., Brown et al., 1951; Ross, 1961; Spence & Runquist, 1958).

PROCESSING CATEGORIES: MODALITY AND AFFECT

Organisms are always processing information - generated both internally and externally, varying continually in content and organization. From an empirical perspective, attention might be defined as the information that is being processed at a given period in time (presumably, organisms are always attending to something). If multiple time samples were obtained, clearly specifying information content and organization (no simple task), the primary attention question would become, what aspects of such information show either significant continuity or reliable patterns of change? To take the analysis a step farther, are there *a priori* categories of information content (in terms of both on-going processing and input) which describe these stable or repeatable changes in information patterns?

Work on the blink reflex in auditory and visual foregrounds, and with instructions specifying the modality of expected stimuli (see Anthony, 1985), suggests that sensory modality is one such category, i.e., a classification parameter according to which the brain habitually organizes information. Thus, when input within a modality is being processed, responses to startle probes in the same category (modality) are larger, relative to probes presented in a different modality. This analysis implies that the brain operates on a broad principle of associative match, and that the categories of information currently active help determine what new information will be most easily integrated into current processing.

Similarities between these attention studies and the emotion experiments presented here, in both their logic and result, suggest that affective valence, as well as modality, is a basic category of human information processing. It is clear that the modality bias in reflex response does not depend on an active sensory foreground. Several experiments have shown modality determined reflex changes simply with verbal instructions to attend to the auditory or visual channel (see Anthony, 1985). Similarly, Varna and Lang (in press) demonstrated that valence modulation of the startle reflex occurs without affective stimuli being physically present, i.e., the affect-startle effect is obtained during imaginal recall. Anthony and Graham (1985) point out that the "modality-match effects could not have been the result of a general, non-specific activation process" (p. 54). The same conclusion was drawn here for the valence-reflex relationship, i.e., that it is not an artifact of differences in arousal level. In experiments where emotional excitation is controlled or minimized, modality appears to determine significant response variance. In effect, both parameters (modality and affect) may be natural categories into which the brain organizes information and according to which responses are deployed.

SUMMATION AND DIRECTIONS FOR RESEARCH

It is proposed here that emotional valence is a general information processing category with sensory, central, and response processing implications. A very broad associative link is suggested - from abstract affective judgments and memory retrieval to obligatory reflex. The reflex priming noted here does not appear to be based on processing specific emotion schema (e.g., a particular context related information network as described by Lang, 1985), nor on a tactical response match between the blink reflex and either an attentional response to external stimuli or the specific facial configuration in fear or distress. It is in this sense that the organism's valence disposition is seen to be strategic, representing a general response disposition.

The heuristic value of this view depends on obtained specific, supporting data. Neither the mechanism by which common valence information is integrated centrally nor the paths of signal conditioning or reflex control are presently clear. In this regard, the importance of studying the interaction of strategic valence and arousal, and using probes to assess affects that show different tactical response patterns has already been noted. It will also be necessary to confirm that reflexes other than the startle blink are modulated by valence. Finally, the present view implies overlap between independent neuro-motivational systems in the brain - for example, between the fear, rage and social loss systems described by Panksepp (1982). The search for an overall biphasic level of neurophysiological integration is encouraged by the present reflex analysis.

In bringing this discussion to an end, several promising clinical applications of probe-reflex analysis merit listing. First, the methodologies described here could be of a particular value in assessing pathological distortions of emotional reactivity: For example, psychopaths have been viewed as affectively under-responsive (Cleckley, 1976), particularly when anticipating *negatively valent*, aversive stimuli (Hare, 1978); Anhedonics on the other hand - in the context of schizotypy, depressive pathology, or as a consequence of the aging process - are described as under-responsive to *positively valent* stimuli (Chapman, Chapman, & Raulin, 1976; Simons & Russo, 1987). Probe analysis of these populations, in affective imagery and perception, could provide an illuminating test of both hypotheses. Secondly, the reflex probe could be of considerable value in the nosological analysis of anxiety disordered patients (exaggerated startle is one of the diagnostic signs of post-traumatic stress disorder, DSM-IIIR, 1987), and in evaluating fear responses to phobic material before and after therapy. Finally, these methods have application in behavioral medicine. Pain, for example, involves both sensory (attentional) and affective components (Tursky, 1976) and should systematically modulate probe responses. The present approach offers a new tool for analyzing all these phenomena, and for monitoring pertinent aspects of treatment progress.

A main promise of the present formulation, however, is in basic research on emotion. Its strength rests on a foundation of quantitative measurement of obligatory reflexes. It is thus easily related to both ontogenetic analysis (already shown in the "attention" studies of young infants), and to the phylogenetic study of animal models of emotion. Because of this measurement orientation, the approach is on the one hand less vulnerable to subjectivist error, and on the other, demonstrably useful for the study of "soft" phenomena, such as "feeling states," moods, or mental images. Finally, the theory shows promise for integrating the often conflicting affective dimension and state views of emotion, accommodating results from cognitive, behavioral, and psychophysiological research, and suggesting a link to the neurophysiological study of the brain.

REFERENCES

Anthony, B.J. (1985) In the blink of an eye: Implications of reflex modification for information processing. In Ackles, P.K., Jennings, J.R. Coles, M.G.H. (Eds.) *Advances in Psychophysiology.* Greenwich CT: JAI Press (Vol. 1, pp. 167-218).

Anthony, B.J., Graham, F.K. (1985) Blink reflex modification by selective attention: Evidence for the modulation of 'automatic' processing. *Biological Psychology, 21,* 43-59.

Bradley, M.M., Cuthbert, B.N., Lang, P.J. (1988) Lateral presentation of acoustic startle stimuli in a varying af-fective foreground. *Psychophysiology, 25,* 436.

Bradley, M.M., Cuthbert, B.N., Lang, P.J. (in press). Startle reflex modification: Attention or emotion? *Psychophys-iology.*

Brown, J.S., Kalish, H.I., Farber, I.E. (1951) Conditioned fear as revealed by magnitude of startle response to an auditory stimulus. *Journal of Experimental Psychology, 41,* 317-328.

Chapman, L.J., Chapman, J.P., Raulin, M.L. (1976) Scales for physical and social anhedonia. *Journal of Abnormal Psychology, 85,* 374-382.

Cleckley, H. (1976). *The mask of sanity* (5th ed.). St. Louis, MO: Mosby.

Greenwald, M.K., Cook, E.W., Lang, P.J. (1989). Affective judgment and psychophysiological response: Dimensional covariation in the evaluation of pictorial stimuli. *Journal of Psychophysiology, 3,* 51-64.

Hare, R.D. (1978) Electrodermal and cardiovascular correlates of psychopathy. In Hare, R.D., & Schalling, D. (Eds.) *Psychopathic behavior: Approaches to research.* Chichester, England: Wiley (pp. 107-143).

Hodes, R.L., Cook, E.W., Lang, P.J. (1985) Individual differences in autonomic response: Conditioned association or conditioned fear? *Psychophysiology, 22,* 545-560.

Lang, P.J., Öhman, A., Vaitl, Dt (1988) *The International Affective Picture System [Photographic Slides].* Gaineville, FL: Center for Research in Psychophysiology, University of Florida.

Lang, P.J. (1985) The cognitive psychophysiology of emotion: Fear and anxiety. In Tuma, A.H., & Maser, H.D. (Eds.) *Anxiety and the anxiety disorders.* Hillsdale, NJ: Erlbaum (pp. 131-170).

Mehrabian, A., & Russell, J.A. (1974) *An Approach to Environmental Psychology.* Cambridge, MA: MIT.

Panksepp, J. (1982) Toward a general psychobiological theory of emotions. *The Behavioral and Brain Sciences, 5,* 407-467.

Simons, R.F., Russo, K.R. (1987) Event-related potentials and continuous performance in subjects with physical anhedonia or perceptual aberrations. *Journal of Psychophysiology, 4,* 401-410.

Simons, R.F., Zelson, M.F. (1985) Engaging visual stimuli and reflex blink modification. *Psychophysiology, 22,* 44-49.

Spence, K.W., Runquist, W.N. (1958) Temporal effects of conditioned fear on the eyelid reflex. *Journal of Experimental Psychology, 55,* 613-616.

Tursky, B. (1976) The development of a pain perception profile: A psychophysical approach. In Weisenberg, M., & Tursky, B. (Eds.) *Pain: New Perspectives in Therapy and Research.* New York: Plenum.

Vrana, S.R., Spence, E.L., Lang, P.J. (1988) The startle probe response: A new measure of emotion? *Journal of Abnormal Psychology, 97,* 487-491.

Vrana, S.R., Lang, P.J. (in press) Fear imagery and the startle probe reflex. *Journal of Abnormal Psychology.*

THE APPROACH-AVOIDANCE PARADOX IN PERSONAL CONSTRUCT

I.H. Oestrich

Municipality of Glostrup, Dept. of Health and Social Services, Rådhusvej 5, DK-2600, Glostrup, Denmark

The subject I am going to touch upon is social skills -training and the relevance or rather necessity of using cognitive strategies, ending with the presentation of a model I am working on: the approach-avoidance paradox in personal construct.

SST forms a bridge between education and therapy, teachers must be good learners too and I believe that we are all in the school of nourishing human resources through learning.

From the beginning I have seen a variety of clients , with different difficulties, different diagnoses , the whole psychiatric repertoire actually, mostly centered around phobias and anxiety disorders, but paranoid cases are also referred to. One thing, however, they all have in common is the deficiency in using their social repertoire. This led me to the construction of a therapeutic platform, where the core of the process is social skills training and it is fortunately still developing.

When the social repertoire suffers from deficiencies, it is not enough just to talk about it. Psychological problems are not solved through talking alone, neither through rehearsal or role-playing alone. Therapeutic change takes place in psychological complexity, which we are just beginning to appreciate and understand. My model is partly based on the work of others and adjusted to the conditions I work under, my own preferences and last but not least my clients needs. It is also based upon the belief that therapy is actively teaching how to use coping strategies rather than passively receiving a cure. And on the belief that changes occur only when the organism in change is treated in it's complexity; skills do not develop very well in humans without the so-called higher functions being taken into consideration and learning of functional skills certainly implies cognition and emotion.

The difficulties lie in getting the process started and keeping it going; there are reasons why the clients have not developed the necessary skills, reasons beyond lack of stimulation and appropriate models. Sometimes it is simple, but most of the time it is not, and the confrontation with the critical situations can be a tremendous strain.

A lot of clients start out disturbed by a certain syndrome, I would call it learning-frigidity : they want the joy so much, but they don't want to do the hard work or rather they don't know how to do it and instruction and modelling are not enough. It takes a more holistic elaboration. The findings from studies in Glostrup (Oestrich, I.H. & Nielsen, A.) indicate that Social Skills Training seems to be an appropriate treatment for clients in the Social Health Sector, but there is more than just the problem solving and rehearsal.

Change develops in several dimensions, at least five levels are taken into consideration here, leading our thoughts to Lazarus' multi-modal approach, which has also been my inspiration on the way.

SENSORY LEVEL	- PERCEPTUAL & CHEMICAL OPERATIONS
EMOTIONAL LEVEL	- AFFECTIVE OPERATIONS
BEHAVIOURAL LEVEL	- CONCRETE OPERATIONS
COGNITIVE LEVEL	- FORMAL OPERATIONS
INTERPERSONAL LEVEL	- SOCIAL OPERATIONS

Making this distinction here one should not neglect that these components of human reaction patterns are interrelated and are forever influencing each other, and when they are analysed in the problem-solving situations that come up in the groups, we cannot discuss or define one without the others.

The sensory level often bridges to the others which I shall return to later in a case description. On the behavioural level we find the more visible reactions and on the cognitive and emotional level the less accessible, often tacit processes. Most of the SST work takes place on the interpersonal level in a social context.

Sensory apparatus

We start where the world comes in through the senses: eyes, ears, mouth, nose and skin, the basis of how we perceive the world. Psychological self-focus and self-awareness lead , I believe , to social sensitivity and active self-care starts with increase in knowledge. Many clients have enormous difficulties in identifying their own body-signals, not to mention the connection between the senses and the brain.

Knowing well what is going on in the sensory apparatus and learning to define those signals from the senses is essential. Some of the senses are directly used in the group sessions, as for example sensitivity to tension and relaxation, when systematic relaxation training takes place usually in the end of each two hour session. All of the senses are used in identification of body signals in critical situations.

Reinforcement and stimulation are important aspects. Anytime you pay attention to a person as a person, his or her arousal and activity level will increase, of course, an important basis for change and growth. Change is however mostly initiated by emotional intensity and the intellectual and the emotional content generates autonomic arousal during exposure and activity.

The cooperation between body and mind is important for analyzing one's own reaction patterns. What is the brain actually? - much more than a computer indeed. a unique bunch of neurons creating art, science, war and peace - not to mention love, the eternal dilemma of being. No computer so far can catch up with the human brain; the holistic functioning is of such genius, that it can not be replaced or artificially developed. For example - it takes a human brain to create a placed or artificially developed. For example - it takes a human brain to create a strophe of Johann Strauss, but how it does so is still a mystery.

The most visible part : behaviour

Clients who don‘t want to move are impossible. And seen from a therapeutic point of view, disturbed behaviour is better than no behaviour at all . I am not talking about death here, though it could seem so, but about the passive, avoidant client who prefers to observe, rather than to live his or her live. The rule is that humans are responding. In memory our response patterns are stored, and they automatically come forward, when activated. Sometimes it is fairly simple to analyse, take a look at what the bodies do. The video used in the group sessions reveals a lot, and it is a way to begin to make bridges in therapy. Look at all the things that are not working interpersonally. During the physical interaction the clients mirror each other . On that point the choreography is very simple getting bodies organized, when they move, the healing starts . Therapy is an opportunity to come back to life, to move.

But we are also dealing with boundaries all the time, finding them and overcoming them or learning to live with them is what it is also about.

After the specific skills are achieved, we need to forget about them. We cannot walk around for the rest of our lives openly self-instructing and occupied with how we perform, the skills need to be integrated naturally into our being. We live and breathe them, while they are serving our purpose. Many of our skills develop automatically and become part of us, others don‘t develop as easily, and then hard personal work is needed.

Cognitions (which are more difficult to deal with)

After the recent world congress in cognitive therapy, so many important things were said about cognition and we all know how what we think is often a very private matter, and our "private monologues" are not easily shared with anybody. Many people share private thoughts with nobody .

Using a number of techniques here, I allow private selftalk to be seen and heard in the group, in order to work on the cognitive level. Asking questions during the role-plays like "what are you saying to yourself"? ," What rules are you operating under?" , "How do you suppose this way of thinking came about to you ?" , "How do your beliefs affect your attitude ?". Those questions lead to the revealing of thinking patterns. Teaching the criteria for self-destructive and constructive thinking and how to restructure self-destructive and irrational ideas, increase the probability to react appropriately according to personal goals.

The cognitions interfere with reality. We experience the world, but it is never pure reality - our personal evaluations get in the way. Humans have a system of rules or codes, according to which they evaluate experiences and regulate their own behaviour and that of others. These rules often operate without one being aware of them. We react without articulating to ourselves the rules and assumptions underlying our actions. Personal construction is not only a broad behavioural repertoire, it is organized at the deep levels of cognitive operations.

Emotions

The emotional part is much neglected. I believe it has long been a condemned and tabooed subject in the behavioural sciences, but times are changing. Emotions show themselves automatically during the sometimes dramatic critical situations which are shown in roleplays in the group. Communicating emotions clearly, sensitively and in a no-nonsense way is a goal in social skills training.

When emotions are painful, we find ourselves in an intensified sensational state, sometimes so unusually intense, that nothing else is "visible" and disturbances like "I am my feelings- I feel stupid, therefore I am stupid", develop and take over in the repertoire. In the psychotic state the emotions we all know are amplified a hundred times, placing the person into the captivated state that is so hard to reach therapeutically. In that case emotions can be enemies. In all other cases I agree with the constructivists when they say that psychotherapists are often too keen on supporting the clients demand when they want their strong emotions to disappear. Emotions are not dangerous they are only enemies if we don‘t know how to express them, which also takes skills (rather differentiated and many-facetted skills actually). It is necessary to express emotions entirely ,which is certainly not easy for the anxious client in crisis and the therapist is an explorer too in this field, we all are at this evolutionary level. When the client first visits the therapist, the main focus is often emotional , chaotically emotional, and psychotherapy is motivated by the desire of ordering, giving structure also gives meaning, making the untold and not clearly told clearer through expression, definition, awareness, understanding and acceptance. Dealing intensely with feelings, is a peculiar experience not following rational rules. Feelings from the past are rushing to the present during therapy ; outside and inside reality meet. Many clients have a history of being deprived, dropped, violated in different ways. They build up anger, and if it is not expressed and elaborated, it leaves them as caged animals. In some ways the therapist acts a part, another role for the client to follow instead of the rejecting mother or father, but the therapist-client relationship is more equal than that between parent and child and it does not ask for the same attachment. The client becomes his own parent in time. Sometimes we interfere so much with a client‘s schemes, that he wants to destroy the relationship, fights to destroy you though he really needs you and also wants to stay in the relationship.

We need to build up trust, but trust has a completely different meaning to someone who is safe, loved and taken care of than to someone who is rejected, hurt, in pain and expecting the worst. Emotions are defined as bodily dispositions for actions and we are dealing with a circular process as actions are not only based on emotions, they also create them. Problems arise when we have contradictory emotions and experience ambivalence.

So the goal is not to take all the problems away or to show how brilliant a therapist you are, but rather to understand the constellation and allow it to be the way it is and then to give the client the necessary support and therapeutic help to change in a continuous process.

Process also runs-

From instruction to self-instruction
From external locus of control to internal locus of control
From reinforcement to self-reinforcement.

It is necessary to become one's own parent and to be able to move on to look at patterns, rather than specific situations, though we start there. In this developmental approach we are dealing with a repeating process of movement or change. Asking questions like "Is this a pattern ?", "Do you often do that ?", "Do you recognize this reaction pattern from earlier experiences?" often highlights the personality style and personal construct. Sometimes there is a tendency to overintellectualize in therapy and we need more awareness of sensory-motor skills and concrete reality. Higher functions are not necessarily better. After the increase in self-awareness, action will be based on this new awareness and changes take place.

I would also like to touch upon a more rare subject in connection with social skills training, namely the therapeutic use of metaphors. We use metaphors in daily life to express something, that is inexpressible in it's essence. When using metaphors an image is created and the interpretation follows the image and the image then symbolizes much more than the actual content and meaning.

When someone tells a story, there is always yet another version. The part that is not expressed in words (call it repressed, unconscious or whatever) are parts of the personal history intruding in its absence and insisting on its organization and meaning. The underlying history can show itself for example in figurative language, imagery, metaphors, pauses and omissions , "empty spaces" etc. What I am talking about here, is the formation of meaning in the dynamic interaction between sender and receiver; it takes much more than verbal and non-verbal reaction patterns to deal with it.

It also takes more than just empathy, it takes what I would call musicality to catch the meaning of the "other" history or of what is written "between the lines", not to mention reacting adequately in relation to the deeper structures. Interpretations, prophecies, guessing, especially misinterpretations are quite different from what I am talking about here, and in the name of psychoanalysis and transference many crucial mistakes have been made in psychotherapy , I think. Therapy demands a receptive therapeutic mind and heart, using the term of musicality the therapist becomes an instrument for the client. Through this instrument the client learns to express even very difficult and painful things. Using the clients images and metaphors in their verbal reactions, the therapist and client together create music and the foundation for a therapeutic meeting between the two of them.

and metaphors in their verbal reactions, the therapist and client together create music and the foundation for a therapeutic meeting between the two of them.

Images and metaphors also create sensuality, when touching the deeper structures as well as stimulating the sensory apparatus. This creates more activity than the concrete language. Behaviourists used to say (in the old days): "There go fish in deep ponds, let them go". But there are still aspects of complexity, where the usual assessment is not enough. We need to get in touch with the deeper structures, and when the connection is made it enhances mutual awareness and emotional depths in the conversation.

A metaphor creates its own meaning by virtue of its contextual quality; using it takes well-developed empathy, readiness and openness to one‘s own associations and willingness to play with the conceptions and ideas. Metaphors can also get you back to process, when you are stuck in the therapeutic work.

Here is a metaphoric example from a group session stagnating, when clients are avoiding "real work" using up the time on irrelevant topics: suddenly one client who has observed a bee coming in through the window as well as another client tensing up, says: "Bees are OK, they don‘t prick you, if you understand them" -It attracts the attention and the therapist picks up the hidden meaning and answers: "Do You wonder, if humans are like that ?" and we are back to work !.

There are many examples of how to use therapeutic metaphors rather than interpretation, and metaphors add another dimension to therapy: in the more creative, spontaneous and intuitive case, new experiences are welcome in therapy as in a healthy life.

METHODOLOGY

1. Anxiety reducing techniques
2. Self-control techniques
3. Cognitive restructuring
4. Challenge of irrational believes , RET-techniques
5. Assertiveness training
6. Self-awareness exercises
7. Identification of underlying patterns and systems
8. Play & creative activities.

This is a survey showing some of the major techniques which I will not go into deeper here. I only want to mention that during social skills training, there is a constant exposure going on first in the group and then in the home work assignments and it is well known how effective exposure is in anxiety reduction and relearning.

Understanding the psychological disturbances is sometimes quite a detective work, which I would like to describe in the following case, a behavioural approach to disclosure in the treatment of incest. In this case, I want to underline how the use of nonverbal cues provided by the client is of utmost importance for the therapeutic progression. I also hope to show that "unconscious" communicative patterns can be used rather simply, direct,to the point and very parsimonious and still have a very complex meaning. Using the signals from the sensory apparatus and the non-verbal gestures sometimes reveals more than words, and non-verbal interactions sometimes work better than any self-talk methodology.

My client is a woman of 47, who has been working as a secretary all her life until she had a psychotic breakdown 4 years ago. She has been exposed to extensive and intensive treatment in the established health system: hospitalization, many classes of psychotropic medication, long term sick-leave , private psychotherapeutic intervention etc. , and when I first see her, she is considered mentally disabled and ready for a disability pension.

When her husband brings her to me, she has a generalized phobia and is, due to suicidal plans, supervised 8 hours a day by a hired hand, while he is at work . In the introductory sessions she could do nothing but cry and shake as well as worry about psychotic episodes, where she would crawl around on the floor talking like a baby. Gradually we identified the anxiety as being especially connected to two situations: her taking a shower or using the washing machine. She exposed herself to those situations, even though her husband had to hold her while she was shaking and crying under the shower. Exposure alone made no difference.In the beginning I was mostly interested in her selftalk which was not easy for her to identify. She was blaming herself "you are too stupid..." etc. But her own observations in the specific situations revealed more and in the third or fourth session she arrived excited, not crying, but eager to tell me that she had discovered, what it was all about. She said to herself: " I am scared, because, if I am able to wash or tidy myself, I must go back to work".

It was not the whole explanation of the extremely disturbed pattern of course, and in the time that followed many more destructive ideas, expectations and irrational rules were revealed and restructured, but the enormous pressure and threat was still there and I decided to go deeper and work on the connection between the sensory apparatus and the behavioural pattern, asking her to identify body-signals during exposure. She also started to keep a diary.

She came to the next session very excited with a piece of paper saying "Last time when I stood under the shower, I suddenly noticed that I held my own hand ; it wanted to tell me something. I felt like having received a hard slap over the hand....I actually felt the pain". Her next homework assignment was to remember episodes of slaps over the hand. It provoked resistance for a while, then she came with a piece of paper telling: "..suddenly I was back home on the farm with my mother and baby brother in the kitchen...." and she told me how they were bathing the baby, and the client, 4 years old, reached out to touch his genitals. Her mother reacted violently, hit her hand extremely hard and pushed her away, yelling at her. The client spent the afternoon at the bottom of a cupboard thinking "she does not like me, she never did...why is he so angry, why can't I do to my baby brother, what my father tells me to do with him".

And this was the beginning of a long line of painful memories, where sexual abuse and threats were the core of her life. She also revealed that she had worn a wig for 17 years, same colour and style as her real hair underneath, and she felt extremely uncomfortable and anxious without it, as it appeared,that her father had threatened to cut off all her hair, if she ever told anyone what was going on. It was during the war and cutting off the hair had a special humiliating meaning.

She was gradually able to confront it all, repeating to herself sentences like "It is not dangerous to remember", "I can confront it all as I am now forty-seven years old" and the panic attacks disappeared. After this phase of therapy, she still lacked self protective skills and her repertoire was rebuild in an SST group, where she especially worked on her personal rights to say NO, recognizing and setting boundaries and giving up the submissive role and excessive desire to please everybody all the time which was hard for her, but she ended therapy with prospects better than a disabled pension.

We all want effective treatment of complex clinical problems and in behaviour therapy the strength has especially been the close relationship between research and clinical praxis, in earlier days the relationship was closer than now. The more we deal with cognitive abstract questions, the harder it is to maintain the relationship. However, the complexity is inevitable, and the superficial use of techniques is not enough, the question is how to retain our basic experimental research and still keep up with development.

Life is full of paradoxes

As I already said before, when we approach, the healing starts and this model has to do with the basic scenary in life. Getting together and coming apart, coming and going. Emotions are involved and change at each moment, choices are made, those choices are created by our body and mind in cooperation. It is good to have choices, with no choices at all, we are victims. In our coming and going we find all the complexity of our being. Everytime we come and go, we relive a story from our past. Sometimes we use outdated skills, because past is not present and skills can develop, even though it once hurt.

These things work out pretty natural and sometimes they don't. We all have a built - in disposition, as we are almost instinctively able to recognize what Martin Seligmann calls "the word in our heart". In any given situation we immediately "feel" whether we need an approach or an avoidance reaction. a YES or a NO. Intuition is like recognition of facial expression, a reaction that comes with lightning speed and cannot be stopped. Intuition also accounts for fast solutions in complex problem situations and some are more skilled in decisiveness than others. Ambivalence and indecisiveness can be crucial and prevent us from reacting according to our best interest and self-protection.

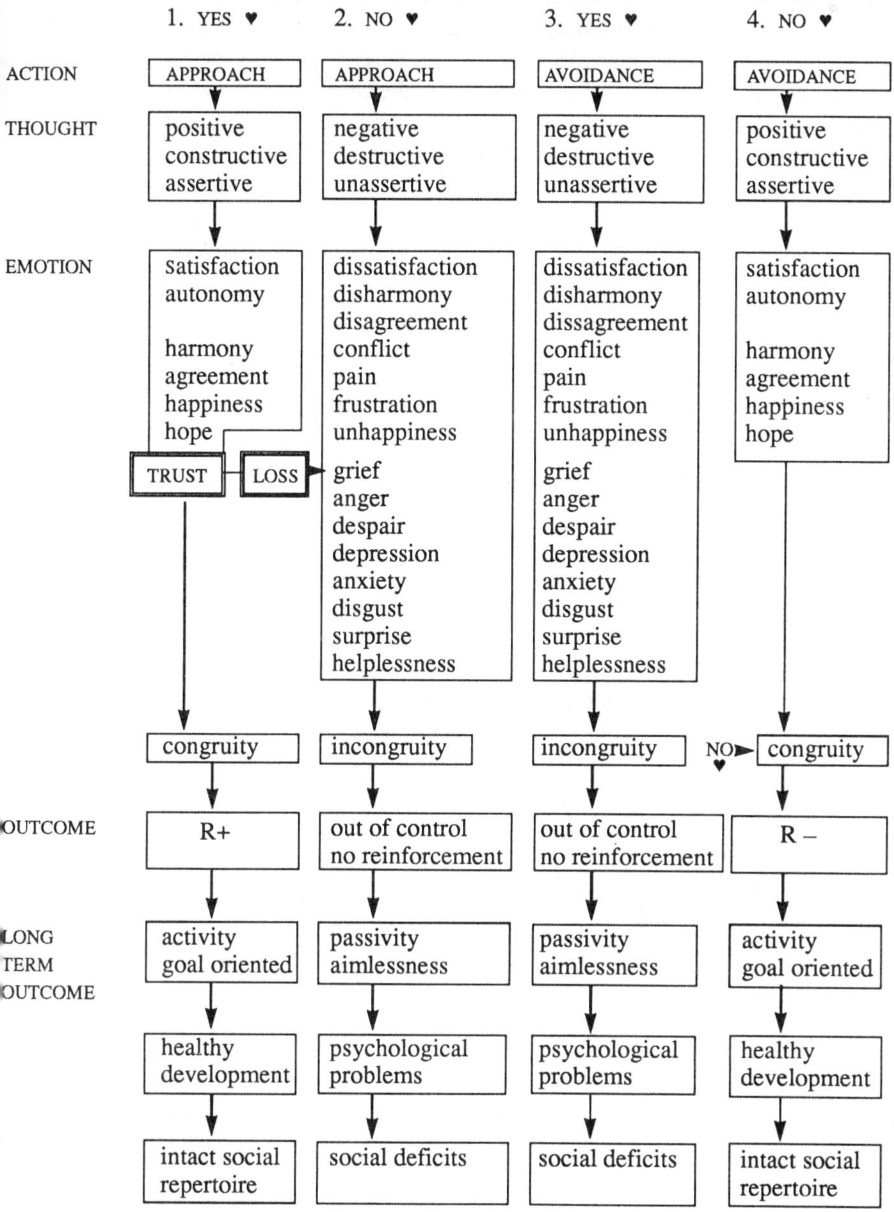

Table 1. **Model for the Development of the Personal Construct**

We all have a contract with ourselves about the direction of our lives. We live with ourselves "for better and for worse" always hoping and working for the better.

Sometimes, however, there is a breach of the contract, often exaggerated by conflict, ambivalence, doubt, frustration and anxiety. This happens recurrently over a life-span, and it is how we learn to deal with these critical situations that decides our psychological well-being and develops our higher levels of functioning.

Basically there are only two possibilities: when we like something, we approach if possible and when we dislike something we avoid, either in flight or attack (make the other disappear). Even very simple organisms have this ability. Sometimes our cognitive functions regulate our actions away from our basic needs and it can be of advantage, but it can also be crucial to health and well-being on longer terms. The model illustrates, that the main reasons for whether our behaviour will serve our best interests and lead us to a happy and healthy development on longer terms (maybe prevent us from developing severe disturbances or physical disease), lies in the cognitive processes and our fundamental personal constructs. The inner processes can either work for us, or against us, and therapeutic changes cannot take place, unless we are aware of what is going on.

In the first column we find the situation that leads to positive reinforcement and active, healthy goal-oriented behaviour - the kind of reaction pattern that is more likely to allow us to stay in control and feel successful.

In the second column, where a No is intuited and the natural response would be avoidance, we still approach. The outcome is dissatisfactory and frustrating. In this category we find all the people with excessive desires to please, working against their own best interest , leading to disturbance in the social repertoire.

In the third column we find avoidance in spite of the YES, meaning a number of destructive thoughts and emotions are elicited, negative energies are bound, and in a way wasted. There are no resources left for development and construction of a healthy and intact social repertoire. We find most skill deficits in this category and the established health system can often do nothing but add another failure to their experiences.

In the fourth column we find the better integrated self protective behavioural pattern, the intuitive reaction is NO and the natural response is avoidance, leading to long term consequences of actively protecting ourselves and our best interests.

I am in the middle of an empirical study on this and the results are very preliminary, but considering a large number of clients response patterns over the years, I find that the type of reaction pattern, that is seen in the third column, is the most dangerous for health and well-being. It heightens vulnerability and pain and leads to more and more passivity and unhappiness (many clients compensate for the lack of sensory and emotional stimulation with abuse of drugs and alcohol) and the social repertoire is strongly disturbed. In the next years I will examine this in more detail.

I would like to close with a few remarks on the current situation in our mutual profession. I am very much aware of the hot debate going on in our circles about what is "right and wrong" and who has the most valid ideas, with the obvious danger of getting trapped with so called eternal truths. And with full respect to those that are leading our way, I also want to say that right and wrong in a profession in continuous change and development does not really make sense and what is even more important, my clients don‘t care, if I call myself a constructivist, a rationalist, just a cognitive therapist or whatever. What they care about, is whether my way is actually helpful to them in their struggle. That was also my main reason for choosing a behaviouristic platform in the first place. The simple request that what I was doing actually has to work, therefore the first criteria comes from my zest for effectiveness (Albert Ellis has a gene for effectiveness, he claims, I am only talking about a strong wish here, that I think we all share). The second criteria has not been there from the start, but it has grown stronger in importance over time, namely that since I am using so much time at work, I prefer to use methods and techniques that are amusing and enjoyable in the daily use, playful, if you wish. And at last I would like to stress that the methods used have to be in congruence with the conditions I work under now and in the future.

REFERENCES

Bellack, H., Hersen, M (1979) *Research and Practice in Social Skills Training.* New York, Plenum.

Cox. M., Theilgaard, A (1987) *Mutative Metaphors in Psychotherapy. The Aeolian Mode.* Tavistock Publications , London.

Ellis, A., Bernard, M.E. (1985) *Clinical Applications of Rational-emotive Therapy.* New York: Plenum Press.

Guidano, V.F. (1987) *Complexity of the Self. A Developmental Approach to Psychopathology and Therapy.* New York. Guilford.

Kelly, J.A. (1982) *Social Skills Training: a Practical Guide for Interventions.* New York. Springer.

Lazarus, A. (1978) *In the Mind‘s Eye: The Power of Imagery for Personal Enrichment.* New York, Rawson.

Mahoney.M.(1976) *Scientist as Subject: The Psychological Imperative.* Ballinger. Cambridge.

Oestrich. I.H., Nielsen. A. (1987) A Short-term Program for Social Skills Training. *Scandinavian Journal of Behaviour Therapy, 16,* 191-207.

Oestrich. I.H. (1989) A Behavioural Approach to Disclosure in the Treatment of Incest: A case Study. *(in press).*

Oestrich, I.H. (1989) The Approach-Avoidance Paradox in Personal Construct *(in press).*

Spence. S., Shepherd. G. (1983) *Development in Social Skills Training,* London. Plenum.

Trower. P., Bryant. B, Argyle M. (1978) *Social Skills & Mental Health.* London. Methuen & Co.

PART II:

PROGRESS IN BASIC RESEARCH ON AFFECTIVE DISORDERS

SOCIAL-BEHAVIOURAL ASPECTS OF MANIC EPISODES AND BIPOLAR AFFECTIVE DISORDER

L. Blöschl

Department of Educational Psychology, University of Graz, Austria; A 8010 Graz, Hans-Sachs-Gasse 3/II

INTRODUCTION

During the past two decades, a considerable amount of clinical-psychological research work has been devoted to the role of behavioural and cognitive factors in affective disorders. Most of this work refers, however, to unipolar depression while relevant research on bipolar affective disorder - on mood disturbances characterized by alternating depressive and manic episodes - and especially on manic episodes themselves is till now comparatively sparse. This state of affairs seems understandable taking into account the lower frequency of these forms of mood disturbances as well as their presumably rather pronounced genetic-biological components (Perris, 1982, Zerbin-Rüding, 1987, Charney & Weissman, 1988). Nevertheless, it should not be overlooked that the phenomenon of bipolarity in affective disorders raises a number of intriguing problems also from a psychological point of view. The purpose of this paper is to draw attention to some of these issues focusing, due to time limitations, primarily on the role of social-behavioural factors in mania.

In analogue to relevant research on depression, there are two major questions emerging in this context: first, the question for social-interactional features and consequences of the manic episode itself, and second, the question for social-environmental stress events anteceding the onset of manic episodes.

CLINICAL AND EMPIRICAL FINDINGS

To begin with, let us take a look at the psychiatric-diagnostic criteria used to define a manic syndrome. According to the Diagnostic and Statistical Manual of Mental Disorders (DSM-III-R, American Psychiatric Association, 1987), these criteria include, besides the essential feature of an elevated, expansive, or irritable mood, several associated symptoms at the behavioural, the cognitive and the somatic level. Among these associated symptoms, social-interactional features hold a prominent place. In particular, emphasis is given to the excessive engagement in social contacts and pleasurable social-environmental activities, often carried out in a domineering and demanding manner and without concern for potential painful consequences. Signs of hostility and anger may occur, especially when the person is thwarted.

Additionally, most of the remaining symptoms obviously will manifest themselves with high probability within the course of interpersonal communication; so, for instance, inflated self-esteem or grandiosity, and flight of ideas. Marked impairment in usual social or occupational functioning as an outcome of manic disturbance is explicitly mentioned as a further defining feature. In agreement with these diagnostic guide-lines, the strong social components of manic behaviour as well as its negative social-environmental implications, particularly although by no means exclusively in the area of marital and family relationships, have been pointed out in numerous case studies and clinical reports (Fitzgerald, 1972, Ludwig & Ables, 1974, Kraus, 1977, Lesser, 1983, Davenport & Adland, 1988). Likewise, observer-rating scales for assessing manic symptomatology in hospitalized patients on the ward or during clinical interviews include, as a rule, items related to social hyperactivity and hostile-angry behaviour (Beigel, Murphy & Bunney, 1971, Blackburn, Loudon & Ashworth, 1977, Brierley, Szabadi, Rix & Bradshaw, 1988; see also Carlson & Goodwin, 1973).

This distinct clinical picture is supplemented by a small number of findings from controlled empirical studies dealing with specific interpersonal features of manic ward behaviour on the base of ratings by staff members. Janowsky, El-Yousef and Davis (1974) found significantly more pronounced signs of hostile-manipulative behaviour in manic patients compared to excited schizoaffective patients and agitated schizophrenic patients. In the study carried out by Klein (1982), the level of physical, verbal and social activity was shown to be significantly higher in acute manics than in acute schizophrenics. The use of selfreport measures in this context is, understandably, rather problematic taking into account the heightened distractibility of the manic as well as potential biases in percepting and/or reporting due to mood elation and inflated self-esteem. Accordingly, results from the few investigations of this kind are rather inconclusive. With regard to outward-directed hostility, Platman, Plutchik, Fieve and Lawlor (1969) found that manic patients judged as highly aggressive by staff members rated themselves as very low in aggression. On the other hand, Blackburn (1974) found a significantly higher level of self-reported extrapunitiveness in manic patients not only compared to depressive patients, recovered depressives and recovered manics but also to normal controls.

The assumption that social-environmental stress events and stress situations may act in some cases as precipitants of manic episodes in biologically vulnerable persons has also been repeatedly discussed in clinical psychiatry. Some evidence in this direction stems from a considerable number of case reports as well as from several clinical and epidemiological surveys (Blankenburg, 1964, Tellenbach, 1965,

Bunney, Murphy, Goodwin & Borge, 1972, Leff, Fischer & Bertelsen, 1976, Dunner, Patrick & Fieve, 1979, Rosenman & Tayler, 1986). Controlled empirical research work on this methodologically very complicated topic is, however, again only in its beginning. In a few contributions, the occurrence of life-change producing events prior to hospital admission for mania was determined by expert ratings on the base of case notes and clinical interviews; the independence of events from pathological development itself (a point especially important with regard to manic episodes) was carefully examined. Ambelas (1979, 1987) found that significantly more manic patients than medical controls had experienced an independent critical life event during a four week period before admission; in patients with first manic admission, this tendency was distinctly stronger than in patients with manic repeat admissions. Kennedy, Thompson, Stancer, Roy and Persad (1983) found in a group of manic patients a significantly greater number of independent critical life events during a four month period before admission than in a control group of medical patients; in addition, significantly fewer manics than controls were rated as having a close confidant available in their personal social network during this time period.

In all three investigations, critical life events anteceding manic episodes were preponderantly of an unpleasant kind. With regard to the question of whether specific types of stressful life changes are particularly prominent prior to mania, no firm statements are possible at present. While Ambelas (1979, 1987) has found a relatively high frequency of bereavement and separation events, Kennedy et al. (1983) have pointed to the relatively pronounced role of work-related stress events in this context. Taken as a whole, the results of these studies seem to be rather similar to results from relevant studies on depression (Paykel, 1987); although clearly in need of further replication, they suggest that there may be a moderate but significant association between the occurrence of social-environmental stressors and the onset of a manic episode.

THEORETICAL CONSIDERATIONS

Turning to the possibilities of integrating these findings and tendencies tentatively into a coherent theoretical framework, it becomes apparent that, like controlled empirical research work in this field, also relevant conceptual approaches are to date rather scarce. Some attempts to deal in a specific manner with the theoretical implications of social-behavioural factors in mania and bipolar disorder have been undertaken on the basis of role-orientated concepts (Kraus, 1977, 1985, Glassner, Haldipur & Dessauersmith, 1979) and on the basis of social-evolutionary concepts (Price, 1967, Gardner, 1982). In the following, I should like to add to this discussion some further theoretical considerations referring to behaviourally orientated concepts as they have been developed with regard to psychosocial aspects of depression in clinical-psychological research during the past years (Lewinsohn, 1974, Blöschl, 1986).

Within such a theoretical frame of reference, the social-interactional features of manic episodes may be regarded as manifestations of an excessive search for positive reinforcement. In contrast to the reduction of reinforcer-directed behaviour in depression, behaviour in mania appears to be extremely reinforcer-directed: the unceasing and expansive initiation of social contacts and pleasurable social-environmental activities results inevitably in a large amount of attention and stimulation and represents, at first, obviously a very effective way of enhancing the rate of positive environmental feedback from the manic's point of view. The problem is only that the concerned members of the manic's social network are not willing or not able to accept this sthenic-reckless search for reinforcement for a longer period of time: at least in severe cases, there is soon increasing resistance against this style of behaviour and its damaging effects and aftereffects. This resistance is answered, in turn, with hostility and anger on the part of the manic. As a consequence, massive social conflicts arise and eventually, help from experts is requested (characteristically, as a rule, from the side of the concerned network members and not from the side of the manic).

Considering from this perspective the relation between stressful life changes and the onset of manic episodes indicated in the foregoing, it seems conceivable that, in some cases, manic behaviour patterns as well as depressive behaviour patterns might reflect pathologically exaggerated coping processes developing in biologically vulnerable persons in response to a loss or a threatening loss of substantial sources of positive reinforcement in central areas of life. In depressive states, the person reacts to this loss of reinforcement with retreat and submission at the behavioural, the emotional and the cognitive level. In manic states, the person reacts to this loss of reinforcement with excessive efforts to reverse it and to compensate for it by means of goal-directed hyperactivity, again associated with corresponding emotional and cognitive features. With repeated episodes, smaller amounts of stress may be sufficient to provoke such pathological response patterns in favour of a more autonomous course. Parenthetically, it should be noted in this context that the borders between both forms of pathological coping processes may be not as rigid as sometimes assumed. That mixed affective pictures, including manic as well as depressive elements, are to be found not infrequently has been documented in several symptomatological studies (Kotin & Goodwin, 1972, Secunda et al., 1987).

Finally, let me comment very briefly upon the question of why some people, when responding along the pathway of affective disorder under the circumstances suggested here, should develop mania or bipolar disorder while others should develop unipolar depression. Again, in this regard, besides the potential impact of specific predisposing factors at the biological level, or rather in close interaction with them, the potential impact of predisposing social-behavioural factors should not be neglected. That the form of manifestation of pathological coping processes in response to a substantial loss of positive life resources will be influenced, to a certain degree, by longstanding features related to the life style and the reinforcement history of the individual, appears to be highly probable from a learning- and reinforcement-orientated perspective. Some preliminary clues in this direction arise from a number of empirical results indicating a higher degree of extraversion and other personality traits connected with outward-directed activity in persons prone to bipolar disorder compared to persons prone to unipolar depression; in persons with predominantly manic episodes, premorbid characteristics of this kind have been reported to be particularly pronounced (Frey, 1977, Strandman, 1978, Matussek & Feil, 1983, Czernik, Steinmeyer & Samen, 1986; v. Zerssen, 1980, 1988). Although empirical evidence and theoretical conceptualization with respect to these tendencies is by not means unequivocal (Angst & Clayton, 1986, Tölle, 1987, Akiskal, 1988), they represent at least interesting starting points for further more detailed research in the coming years.

CONCLUDING REMARKS

In conclusion, it should be underlined once again that the aim of such attempts as outlined above is certainly not to suggest a "psychogenic" theory of mania and bipolar affective disorder. Rather, the aim is to stimulate efforts toward a more precise empirical and theoretical analysis of those psychological factors interplaying, to some extent and in various ways, with genetic-biological factors in the phenomenology and the development of these complex clinical pictures. That enhanced efforts of this kind are needed not only with regard to the social-behavioural variables addressed in the foregoing but also with regard to other psychological variables, particularly in the cognitive field (Solovay, Shenton & Holzman, 1987, Leahy & Beck, 1988), should also be repeated here.

The relevance of such strivings toward a stronger inclusion of problems of mania and bipolar disorder into the mainstream of current clinical-psychological research must be seen chiefly under two aspects. First, while the cornerstone of treatment of manic episodes and bipolar affective disorder obviously lies at the somatic-pharmacotherapeutic level, the value of adjunctive psychological interventions, especially with respect to the combination of lithium therapy with partner- and family-orientated treatment, has been pointed out in numerous clinical studies (Fitzgerald, 1972, Mayo, O'Connell & O'Brien, 1979, Davenport & Adland, 1988; see also O'Connell, Mayo, Eng, Jones & Gabel, 1985). A more systematic use of cognitive-behavioural strategies in this context, as recently suggested by Leahy and Beck (1988), could contribute to further refinement of such adjunctive psychological interventions, until now in the initial stages. Beyond these applied aspects, however, increased attention to the psychological components of mania and bipolar disorder seems also to be necessary with respect to progress in basic research, i.e. in advancing thinking and inquiring on the nature of affective disorders in general.

That there exists a connection between manic and depressive disturbances at least in some cases of affective disorder must be regarded as a substantial and challenging problem in itself at the psychological as well as at the biological level. Possibly, in the long run, an improved understanding of the role of psychological factors in mania will also improve our understanding of the role of psychological factors in depression with a more comprehensive psychobiological framework.

REFERENCES

Akiskal, H.S. (1988) Cyclothymic and related disorders. In A. Georgotas & R. Cancro (Eds.), *Depression and mania* (pp. 86-95). New York: Elsevier.

Ambelas, A. (1979) Psychologically stressful events in the precipitation of manic episodes. *British Journal of Psychiatry, 135,* 15-21.

Ambelas, A. (1987) Life events and mania. A special relationship? *British Journal of Psychiatry, 150,* 235-240.

American Psychiatric Association (Ed.), (1987) *Diagnostic and Statistical Manual of Mental Disorders (DSM-III-R)* (Third Edition-Revised). Washington, D.C.: American Psychiatric Association.

Angst, J. & Clayton, P. (1986) Premorbid personality of depressive, bipolar, and schizophrenic patients with special reference to suicidal issues. *Comprehensive Psychiatry, 27,* 511-532.

Beigel, A., Murphy, D.L. & Bunney, W.E., Jr. (1971) The Manic State Rating Scale. Scale construction, reliability, and validity. *Archives of General Psychiatry, 25,* 256-262.

Blackburn, I.M. (1974) The pattern of hostility in affective illness. *British Journal of Psychiatry, 125, 141-145.*

Blackburn, I.M., Loudon, J.B., Ashworth, C.M. (1977) A new scale for measuring mania. *Psychological Medicine, 7,* 453-458.

Blankenburg, W. (1964) Lebensgeschichtliche Faktoren bei manischen Psychosen. *Nervenarzt, 35,* 536-539.

Blöschl, L. (1986) Verhaltenstherapie. In S.K.D. Sulz (Ed.), *Verständnis und Therapie der Depression* (pp. 105-121). München: Reinhardt.

Brierley, C.E., Szabadi, E., Rix, K.J.B., Bradshaw, C.M. (1988) The Manchester Nurse Rating Scale for the daily simultaneous assessment of depressive and manic ward behaviours. *Journal of Affective Disorders, 15,* 45-54.

Bunney, W.E., Jr., Murphy, D.L., Goodwin, F.K., Borge, G.F. (1972) The "switch process" in manic-depressive illness. I. A systematic study of sequential behavioral changes. *Archives of General Psychiatry, 27,* 295-302.

Carlson, G.A., Goodwin, F.K. (1973) The stages of mania. A longitudinal analysis of the manic episode. *Archives of General Psychiatry, 28,* 221-228.

Charney, E.A., Weissman, M.M. (1988) Epidemiology of depressive and manic syndromes. In A. Georgotas & R. Cancro (Eds.), *Depression and mania* (pp. 26-52). New York: Elsevier.

Czernik, A., Steinmeyer, E.M., Samen, A. (1986) Objektivierende Untersuchungen über Unterschiede der Intervallpersönlichkeit monopolar und bipolar depressiver Patienten unter Lithiumbehandlung. *Nervenarzt, 57,* 517-525.

Davenport, Y.B., Adland, M.L. (1988) Management of manic episodes. In J.F. Clarkin, G.L. Haas & I.D. Glick (Eds.), *Affective disorders and the family. Assessment and treatment* (pp. 173-195). New York: Guilford.

Dunner, D.L., Patrick, V., Fieve, R.R. (1979) Life events at the onset of bipolar affective illness. *American Journal of Psychiatry, 136*, 508-511.

Fitzgerald, R.G. (1972) Mania as a message. Treatment with family therapy and lithium carbonate. *American Journal of Psychotherapy, 26*, 547-554.

Frey, R. (1977) Die prämorbide Persönlichkeit von monopolar und bipolar Depressiven. Ein Vergleich aufgrund von Persönlichkeitstests. *Archiv für Psychiatrie und Nervenkrankheiten, 224*, 161-173.

Gardner, R., Jr. (1982) Mechanisms in manic-depressive disorder. An evolutionary model. *Archives of General Psychiatry, 39*, 1436-1441.

Glassner, B., Haldipur, C.V., Dessauersmith, J. (1979) Role loss and working-class manic depression. *Journal of Nervous and Mental Disease, 167*, 530-541.

Janowsky, D.S., El-Yousef, M.K., Davis, J.M. (1974) Interpersonal maneuvers of manic patients. *American Journal of Psychiatry, 131*, 250-255.

Kennedy, S., Thompson, R., Stancer, H.C., Roy, A., Persad, E. (1983) Life events precipitating mania. *British Journal of Psychiatry, 142*, 398-403.

Klein, D.N. (1982) Activity-withdrawal in the differential diagnosis of schizophrenia and mania. *Journal of Abnormal Psychology, 91*, 157-164.

Kotin, J., Goodwin, F.K. (1972) Depression during mania: Clinical observations and theoretical implications. *American Journal of Psychiatry, 129*, 679-686.

Kraus, A. (1977) *Sozialverhalten und Psychose Manisch-Depressiver. Eine existenz- und rollenanalytische Untersuchung*. Stuttgart: Enke.

Kraus, A. (1985) Praktische Konsequenzen des rollentheoretischen Ansatzes am Beispiel der manisch-depressiven Psychosen. In W. Janzarik (Ed.), *Psychopathologie und Praxis* (pp. 88-100). Stuttgart: Enke.

Leahy, R.L., Beck, A.T. (1988) Cognitive therapy of depression and mania. In A. Georgotas & R. Cancro (Eds.), *Depression and mania* (pp. 517-537). New York: Elsevier.

Leff, J.P., Fischer, M., Bertelsen, A. (1976) A crossnational epidemiological study of mania. *British Journal of Psychiatry, 129*, 428-442.

Lesser, A.L. (1983) Hypomania and marital conflict. *Canadian Journal of Psychiatry, 28*, 362-366.

Lewinsohn, P.M. (1974) A behavioral approach to depression. In R.J. Friedman & M.M. Katz (Eds.), *The psychology of depression: Contemporary theory and research* (pp. 157-185). New York: Wiley.

Ludwig, A.M., Ables, M.F. (1974) Mania and marriage: The relationship between biological and behavioral variables. *Comprehensive Psychiatry, 15*, 411-421.

Matussek, P.,Feil, W.B. (1983) Personality attributes of depressive patients. Results of group comparisons. *Archives of General Psychiatry, 40*, 783-790.

Mayo, J.A., O'Connell, R.A.,O'Brien, J.D. (1979) Families of manic-depressive patients: Effect of treatment. *American Journal of Psychiatry, 136*, 1535-1539.

O'Connell, R.A., Mayo, J.A., Eng, L.K., Jones, J.S., Gabel, R.H. (1985) Social support and long-term lithium outcome. *British Journal of Psychiatry, 147*, 272-275.

Paykel, E.S. (1987) Psychosoziale Faktoren. In K.P. Kisker, H. Lauter, J.-E. Meyer, C. Müller & E. Strömgren (Eds.), *Affektive Psychosen. Psychiatrie der Gegenwart 5* (3. neubearbeitete Aufl.) (pp. 181-201). Berlin: Springer.

Perris, C. (1982) The distinction between bipolar and unipolar affective disorders. In E.S. Paykel (Ed.), *Handbook of affective disorders* (pp. 45-58). Edinburgh: Churchill Livingstone.

Platman, S.R., Plutchik, R., Fieve, R.R., Lawlor, W.G. (1969) Emotion profiles associated with mania and depression. *Archives of General Psychiatry, 20*, 210-214.

Price, J. (1967) The dominance hierarchy and the evolution of mental illness. *Lancet, 2*, 243-246.

Rosenman, S.J., Tayler, H. (1986) Mania following bereavement: A case report. *British Journal of Psychiatry, 148*, 468-470.

Secunda, S.K., Swann, A., Katz, M.M., Koslow, S.H., Croughan, J., Chang, S. (1987) Diagnosis and treatment of mixed mania. *American Journal of Psychiatry, 144*, 96-98.

Solovay, M.R., Shenton, M.E., Holzman, P.S. (1987) Comparative studies of thought disorders. I. Mania and schizophrenia. *Archives of General Psychiatry, 44*, 13-20.

Strandman, E. (1978) "Psychogenic needs" in patients with affective disorders. *Acta Psychiatrica Scandinavica, 58*, 16-29.

Tellenbach, H. (1965) Zur situationspsychologischen Analyse des Vorfeldes endogener Manien. *Jahrbuch für Psychologie, Psychotherapie und Medizinische Anthropologie, 12*, 174-191.

Tölle, R. (1987) Persönlichkeit und Melancholie. *Nervenarzt, 58*, 327-339.

Zerbin-Rüdin, E. (1987) Genetik. In K.P. Kisker, H. Lauter, J.-E. Meyer, C. Müller & E. Strömgren (Eds.), *Affektive Psychosen. Psychiatrie der Gegenwart 5* (3. neubearbeitete Aufl.) (pp. 137-164). Berlin: Springer.

Zerssen, v., D. (1980) Persönlichkeitsforschung bei Depressionen. In H. Heimann & H. Giedke (Ed.), *Neue Perspektiven in der Depressionsforschung* (pp. 155-178). Bern: Huber.

Zerssen, v., D. (1988) Der "Typus manicus" als Gegenstück zum "Typus melancholicus" in der prämorbiden Persönlichkeitsstruktur affektpsychotischer Patienten. In W. Janzarik (Ed.), *Persönlichkeit und Psychose* (pp. 150-171). Stuttgart: Enke.

PEER RELATIONS AND DEPRESSED MOOD IN CHILDREN AND EARLY ADOLESCENTS: A CRITICAL REVIEW OF RECENT RESEARCH

E. Ederer

Department of Educational Psychology, A 8010 Graz, Hans Sachs-Gasse 3

INTRODUCTION

During the last decade, the associations between deficiencies in social-environmental involvement and depressive disturbances have found considerable interest in clinical psychology and personality psychology. Within the framework of research on social networks and social support, significant connections of this kind have been pointed out in numerous empirical studies (for overviews see Leavy, 1983; Blöschl, 1987). Most of this research work, however, has concentrated on adults while corresponding research in children has been intensified only in recent years.

The paper deals with one special aspect of this complex field, namely with the relationships between deficient peer relations and depressed mood in children and early adolescents, an issue which must be considered of particular interest under developmental aspects. It is generally assumed that the level of integration within the peer group is of importance for the psychological well-being of children and early adolescents. The aim of this review is to examine to what extent the present state of empirical knowledge may confirm this assumption and what implications for further basic and applied psychological research can be derived.

For reasons of time limitation, I shall restrict myself to investigations dealing with the connections between peer relations and self-reported depressed mood in non-clinical samples.

EMPIRICAL STUDIES

The review covers nine correlational studies (see <u>Table 1</u>) and four comparisons of extreme groups (see <u>Table 2</u>). From the broad spectrum of data reported in these studies, only those findings are included in the tables which are immediately relevant for the objective of this review.

Starting with the correlational studies, Jacobsen, Lahey and Strauss (1983) investigated the associations between self-reported depressed mood as measured

Table 1: Results of the correlational studies

authors	composition of sample	correlated variables: depression	correlated variables: peer relations	correlational coefficients: mixed sample	correlational coefficients: boys	correlational coefficients: girls
Jacobsen et al. (1983)	N=109 (50 boys, 59 girls) grade: 2-7	CDI CDI	peer rating teacher rating	$.30^{++}$ $.20^{+}$	$.31^{+}$ n.s.	$.28^{+}$ $.38^{++}$
Saylor et al. (1984)	N=111 (57 boys, 54 girls) grade: 2-7	CDI	popularity items of the Peer Nomination Inventory of Depression	n.s.		
Faust et al. (1985)	N=216 boys and girls grade: 6-7; $\overline{X}$=13;1 years	CDI CDI CDI CDI CDI CDI	positive peer nomination child-estimated positive peer nomination negative peer nomination child-estimated negative peer nomination peer rating child-estimated peer rating	n.s. $.15^{+}$ $.26^{++}$ $.25^{++}$ $.23^{++}$ $.30^{++}$		
Fauber et al. (1987)	N=89 (39 boys, 50 girls) age: 11-15; $\overline{X}$=13;1 years	CDI CDI	social subscale of the Competence Scale for Children: child-completed social subscale of the Teacher's Rating Scale of Child's Actual Competence: mother-completed father-completed teacher-completed	$.58^{++}$ $.46^{++}$ $.45^{++}$ $.26^{+}$		
Slotkin et al. (1988)	N=85 (35 boys, 50 girls) age: 11-15; $\overline{X}$=13;4 years	CDI	social subscale of the Teacher's Rating Scale of the Child's Actual Competence: teacher-completed	$.27^{+}$		
Wierzbicki and McCabe (1988)	N=46 (22 boys, 24 girls) age: 8-14; $\overline{X}$=9;9 years	CDI	social subscale of the Child Behavior Checklist: parent-completed	n.s.		
Blöschl and Ederer (1986)	N=117 boys grade: 7-8; $\overline{X}$=13;2 years	QCD-GD	self-reported number of close friends		$.29^{++}$	
Roschitz (1987)	N=56 boys grade: 3-4; $\overline{X}$=9;6 years	QCD-GD	self-reported number of close friends		n.s.	
Egger (1988)	N=224 (127 boys, 97 girls) grade: 4; $\overline{X}$=10;4 years	QCD-GD	self-reported number of close friends		n.s.	n.s.

CDI = Child Depression Inventory
QCD-GD = General Depression subscale of the Questionnaire in Child Depression

$^{+}p<.05$ (in the expected direction) $^{++}p<.01$ (in the expected direction)

Table 2: Results of extreme group comparisons

authors	formation of extreme groups	measures of dependent variables	direction and significance of mean differences
Strauss et al. (1984)	N=252, grade: 2-5	peer rating and nomination	
	depressed group: N=15 (6 boys, 9 girls)	peer rating	$<^{++}$
	non-depressed group: N=15 (5 boys, 10 girls)	positive peer nomination: whole class	n.s.
		same sex	$<^{++}$
	based on the Child Depression Inventory	negative peer nomination: whole class	$>^{+}$
		same sex	$>^{+}$
		nomination as withdrawn	$>^{+}$
		nomination as aggressive	n.s.
		teacher nomination	
		nomination as withdrawn	$>^{+}$
		nomination as aggressive	n.s.
		self-report popularity subscale of the Piers-Harris Self-Concept Scale	$<^{++}$
Altmann and Gotlib (1988)	N=310, grade: 4-5	observational categories	
	depressed group: N=20 (10 boys, 10 girls)	being alone	$>^{++}$
	non-depressed group: N=20 (10 boys, 10 girls)	playing alone	$>^{+}$
		initiates interactions	$>^{+}$
	based on a combination of the Child Depression Inventory and the Peer Nomination Inventory of Depression	other initiates interactions	$>^{+}$
		in process of interacting	$<^{++}$
		in process of interacting, but alone	n.s
		negative/aggressive behavior	$>^{+}$
		self-report social subscale of the Self-Perception Profile for Children[1)]	$<^{++}$
Vosk et al. (1982)	N=101, grade: 3-4 *unpopular group*: N=12 (8 boys, 4 girls) *popular group*: N=16 (8 boys, 8 girls) based on peer nomination and rating	score of the Child Depression Inventory	$>^{+}$
Strauss et al. (1986)	N=640, grade: 2-5 *withdrawn group*: N=48 (20 boys, 28 girls) *outgoing group*: N=72 (36 boys, 36 girls) based on teacher nomination	score of the Child Depression Inventory	$>++$

$^{+}p<.05$ $^{++}p<.01$ [1)] group by gender interaction significant by the Child Depression Inventory (CDI; Kovacs 1980/1981) and peer ratings of likeability as well as teacher ratings of peer popularity for boys and girls from grade two to seven. Whereas for boys only the correlation between the CDI and the peer rating of likeability reached significance, for the mixed sample as well as for girls both connections were significant, indicating that depressed mood was a correlate of unpopularity with peers.

Saylor et al. (1984) correlated in a mixed sample of second to seventh graders the CDI with the two combined popularity items of the Peer Nomination Inventory of Depression (PNID; Lefkowitz & Tesiny, 1980), asking for the favourite neighbour in class and for the children whom the subject would like most to have for best friends. The authors found no significant connection between these two variables.

In the investigation by Faust, Baum and Forehand (1985), the CDI was correlated with positive and negative peer nominations (children in the class he or she would like respectively would not like to work with on a group project) and with peer ratings of likeability in a mixed sample of sixth and seventh graders. Additionally, the connections between the children‘s estimations of the nominations and ratings they would receive on the one hand and the CDI on the other hand were investigated. The correlations between the CDI and the actual and self-estimated positive nominations were weaker (being not significant or significant only at the .05 level) than the highly significant associations between CDI and both - actual as well as self-estimated - negative nominations and peer ratings. These results seem to suggest that depressed mood is more strongly associated with rejection or general dislike by others than with not being selected as a favourite peer.

Fauber, Forehand, Long, Burke and Faust (1987) examined the correlations between the CDI and the social subscale of the Perceived Competence Scale for Children (PCSC; Harter, 1982) as well as the social subscale of the Teacher‘s Rating Scale of Child‘s Actual Competence (TRS; Harter, 1982). Both measures address popularity and likeability with regard to peers. The TRS was not only completed by teachers but also by mothers and fathers of the subjects. Subjects were boys and girls ranging in age from 11 to 15 years. Calculated for the mixed sample, all correlational coefficients were significant, indicating that adolescents with high CDI scores see themselves as less popular and are also perceived by teachers, mothers and fathers as having problems with peer relations.

Essentially the same sample was used by Slotkin, Forehand, Fauber, McCombs and Long (1988) in correlating the CDI with the teacher-completed social subscale of the TRS. The correlational coefficient was again significant.
Wierzbicki and McCabe (1988) applied the social subscale of the Social Competence Scales of the Child Behavior Checklist (CBCL; Achenbach, 1978) to obtain parents' ratings of their children's involvement in social relationships primarily with regard to peers (e.g. number of friends and contacts with them). In a mixed sample with age ranging from 8 to 14, no significant association between this measure and the CDI could be found.

In the other three correlational studies, carried out at our department, depressed mood was assessed by means of the General Depression subscale of the Questionnaire in Child Depression (QCD-GD; Lienert & Kohnen, 1978). As an index of peer contact, the self-reported number of close friends (i.e. of friends to whom a trustful confidential relation exists) was used. Blöschl and Ederer (1986) found a highly significant correlation in a male sample of seventh to eight graders, implying that male early adolescents with fewer close friends are more depressed. However, in two studies conducted in younger children these results could not be replicated (Roschitz, 1987, using a male sample from grade three and four, and Egger, 1988, using a male and a female sample of fourth graders).

Let me proceed now to the four studies based on extreme group comparisons with respect to either depression or deficient peer relations. Strauss, Forehand, Frame and Smith (1984) compared 15 second to fifth graders having extremely high CDI scores with a control group of 15 children with low CDI scores. As mean comparisons showed, the two groups differed significantly in the expected direction regarding the following variables: peer ratings of likeability; positive peer nominations by the same sex; negative peer nominations by the same sex and the whole class; nominations as withdrawn by peers as well as by teachers; scores of the self-report popularity subscale of the Piers-Harris Self-Concept Scale measuring children's perceptions of their own popularity (PH; Piers & Harris, 1964).

Altmann and Gotlib (1988) compared extreme groups of CDI- and PNID-identified depressed and non-depressed children. Each group was composed of 20 children from grades four and five. By means of behavioral observations in a free-play situation it was shown that depressed children spent significantly more time playing alone and less time interacting with others, and were more negative/aggressive when interacting with their peers. Somewhat surprisingly, however, the depressed children initiated a greater number of interactions with other children and were approached by others more frequently. With regard to the social subscale of the Self-Perception Profile for children (Harter, 1983; see Altmann & Gotlib, 1988), the depressed children perceived themselves as more negative. Furthermore, there was one significant group by gender interaction: The social self-perception of depressed boys was more negative than that of depressed girls; this was not the case for the non-depressed group.

Vosk, Forehand, Parker and Rickard (1982) formed extreme groups of 12 unpopular and 16 popular third and fourth graders based on positive peer nominations and peer ratings. Unpopular children were shown to have significantly higher CDI scores than their popular controls. The extreme groups differed also in the expected direction with respect to teacher ratings of popularity and behavioral observations of negative interactions. With respect to behavioral observations of positive interactions there were no significant differences.

Strauss, Forehand, Smith and Frame (1986) formed extreme groups of second to fifth graders on the base of teacher nominations. The first group included 48 children who were judged as most socially withdrawn and not interacting very much with their peers. The control group consisted of 72 children who were nominated as most outgoing and interacting frequently with other children. The social withdrawn group reported significantly more depressive features on the CDI than the outgoing group. Simultaneously, it was shown that the groups also differed significantly with respect to positive and negative peer nominations and to peer ratings of likeability.

DISCUSSION

Taken as a whole, the overview of the empirical investigations shows clearly that there are - rather moderate but significant associations - between deficient peer relations and depressed mood already in children and early adolescents. This appears to confirm the results found in adults and, additionally, may supplement them in so far as these findings were derived not only from self-reports but also from reports by peers, teachers and parents. In those papers measuring peer relations simultaneously by self-reports and by reports from other persons (Faust et al., 1985; Fauber et al., 1987; Strauss et al., 1984; Altmann & Gotlib, 1988), both kinds of measures were significantly associated with depressed mood. This concordance supports the assumption that the self-perception of social deficiencies in depression has an equivalent in the externally evaluated social reality (see for a discussion on this topic Blöschl, 1988). Notwithstanding the general tendency respecting the association between social integration and psychological well-being of children, it should not be ignored, however, that some of the studies reviewed above failed to find significant connections. This divergence may be caused, of course, by a multiplicity of factors. Some of them shall be briefly discussed here as variables of potential interest for further investigations.

At first, it should be pointed to the measures used to investigate the place of the child within the peer group. As has been shown, these measures vary widely, including, among other indices, subscales of questionnaires, behavioral observations, and manifold sociometric methods in the form of positive as well as negative peer nominations and peer ratings. Furthermore, data were gained from subjects themselves as well as from other persons. This variety of methods for assessing peer relations certainly must be seen as one factor reducing the comparability of the studies. The question which of these numerous measures are suited best for investigating friendship relations within depression is still open. Some preliminary clues for more detailed analyses can be possibly derived from those findings suggesting that negative peer nominations, i.e. rejection, might be more strongly connected to depressed mood than positive peer nominations, i.e. not being selected as a favourite peer (Strauss et al., 1984; Faust et al., 1985). Presumably, these tendencies should be seen in relation to findings from behavioral observations pointing to a higher frequency of negative/aggressive behavior in depressed children (Vosk et al., 1982; Altmann & Gotlib, 1988). In any case, it seems to be worthy of further consideration whether respectively under what circumstances positive or negative indices of social integration and social behavior are more appropriate measures for assessing the relations between peer contacts and psychological well-being.

Other factors being presumably of influence on the connections between peer relations and depressed mood are age and gender of the subjects. While no investigation was aimed specifically to analyse the influence of the age and, moreover, the age of subjects within samples often ranged very widely, one tendency deserves to be mentioned: The connections in the correlational studies were nearly always significant in early adolescents (mean age about 13 years) whereas in younger children (mean age about 10 years) they were not significant, with the only exception of the study carried out by Jacobsen et al. (1983). This seems to suggest that the developmental stage of the child, especially with regard to cognitive-perceptual structure, should be considered more carefully in the selection of measures in this context (see Ederer, 1988). With regard to gender, several findings from the general literature on peer relations in childhood support the assumption that friendship patterns are different for boys and girls (Dickens & Perlman, 1981; see also Ederer, 1989). For example, girls are presumed to rely more on intimacy in contacts while for boys a wider range of contacts may be more important. Against this background it could be expected that the connection between friendship relations and depressed mood is also moderated to some degree by the gender of the subjects (with regard to this issue see Blöschl, Ederer & Rossmann, 1987). However, since in most of the studies reviewed above there was not made reference to gender as a separate factor and the remaining ones were inconsistent about gender effects (Jacobsen et al., 1983; Altmann & Gotlib, 1988; Egger, 1988), the investigations do not allow a conclusion with respect to this question.

CONCLUSIONS

To summarize, the systematic investigation of the associations between deficient peer relations and depressed mood in children and early adolescents opens a fruitful field for future research. Especially, the parallel application of self-reports and reports from other persons which is usually more practicable with children should be intensified, representing an interesting complementation to research in adults. For further progress, however, it will be necessary to develop more comprehensive multidimensional measures which permit to cope, in a more adequate way, with the multitude of facets of peer relations and which are taking into account more specifically age and gender of the subjects as potential moderating variables.

Although nothing can be said on the base of the results presented above about the direction of the associations between peer relations and depressed mood, most authors advocate the possibility that depression is, to a certain degree, derived from or maintained by negative social-environmental conditions. Among the various areas constituting the social environment of children, the field of social contacts within the peer group probably holds an important place. In this sense, children with severely deficient peer relations may be regarded as an at-risk population in need of intervention. To assess more exactly the respective deficiencies would enable us to offer more specific help for improving the psychological well-being of these children by a training of social skills.

REFERENCES

Achenbach, T.M. (1978) The Child Behavior Profile: I. Boys aged 6-11. *Journal of Consulting and Clinical Psychology, 46*, 478-488.

Altmann, E.O., Gotlib, I.H. (1988) The social behavior of depressed children: An observational study. *Journal of Abnormal Child Psychology, 16*, 29-44.

Blöschl, L. (1987) Soziales Netzwerk / Soziale Unterstützung, Lebensbelastung und Befindlichkeit. Eine Standortbestimmung aus psychologischer Sicht. *Zeitschrift für Klinische Psychologie, 16*, 311-320.

Blöschl, L. (1988) Die sozialen Umweltbeziehungen Depressiver im Spiegel "subjektiver" und "objektiver" Kontaktmaße. *Psychologische Beiträge, 30*, 9-17.

Blöschl, L., Ederer, E. (1986) Zusammenhänge zwischen Depressivität und selbstberichteten Aktivitäts- und Kontaktdefiziten in der frühen Adoleszenz. *Zeitschrift für Klinische Psychologie, Psychopathologie und Psychotherapie, 34*, 32-40.

Blöschl, L., Ederer, E., Rossmann, P. (1987) Dysthyme Persönlichkeitstendenzen und "close confidents". Zur Frage geschlechtsspezifischer Zusammenhänge zwischen Depressivität und selbstberichtetem Sozialkontakt. In E. Raab & G. Schulter (Eds.), *Perspektiven psychologischer Forschung. Festschrift zum 65. Geburtstag von Erich Mittenecker* (pp. 107-118). Wien: Deuticke.

Dickens, W.J., Perlman, D. (1981) Friendship over the life-cycle. In S. Duck & R. Gilmour (Eds.), *Personal relationships 2: Developing personal relationships* (pp. 91-122). London: Academic Press.

Ederer, E. (1988) *Personality and network correlates of depression in children: Findings, problems, perspectives.* Arbeitsbericht 2/1988 aus der Abteilung für Pädagogische Psychologie, Karl-Franzens-Universität Graz.

Ederer, E. (1989) Friendship relations and social-environmental activities in male and female early adolescents. *Psychologische Beiträge, 31*, in press.

Egger, R. (1988) *Freundeskontakte, Selbstkonzept und Depressivität. Eine empirische Untersuchung an zehnjährigen Knaben und Mädchen*. Unveröff. Diss., Naturwissenschaftliche Fakultät der Universität Graz.

Fauber, R., Forehand, R., Long, N., Burke, M., Faust, J. (1987) The relationship of young adolescent Children's Depression Inventory (CDI) scores to their social and cognitive functioning. *Journal of Psychopathology and Behavioral Assessment, 9*, 161-172.

Faust, J., Baum, C.G., Forehand, R. (1985) An examination of the association between social relationships and depression in early adolescence. *Journal of Applied Developmental Psychology, 6,* 291-297.

Harter, S. (1982) The Perceived Competence Scale for Children. *Child Development, 53,* 87-97.

Jacobsen, R.H, Lahey, B.B., Strauss, C.C. (1983) Correlates of depressed mood in normal children. *Journal of Abnormal Child Psychology, 11,* 29-39.

Kovacs, M. (1980/1981) Rating scales to assess depression in school-aged children. *Acta Paedopsychiatrica, 46,* 305-315.

Leavy, R.L. (1983) Social support and psychological disorder: A review. *Journal of Community Psychology, 11,* 3-21.

Lefkowitz, M.M., Tesiny, E.P. (1980) Assessment of childhood depression. *Journal of Consulting and Clinical Psychology, 48,* 43-50.

Lienert, G.A., Kohnen, R. (1978) *Questionnaire in child depression (Further results).* Paper presented at the 10th Meeting of the International Group for the Study of Affective Disorders (IGSAD), Nürnberg, FRG.

Piers, E.V., Harris, D.B. (1964) Age and other correlates of self-concept in children. *Journal of Educational Psychology, 55,* 91-95.

Roschitz, D. (1987) *Potentiell verstärkende Aktivitäten, selbstberichtete Sozialkontakte und Depressivität. Eine empirische Untersuchung an 10-jährigen Knaben.* Unveröff. Diplomarbeit, Geisteswissenschaftliche Fakultät der Universität Graz.

Saylor, C.F., Finch, JR., A.J., Baskin, C.H., Saylor, C.B., Darnell, G., Furey, W. (1984) Children's Depression Inventory: Investigation of procedures and correlates. *Journal of the American Academy of Child Psychiatry, 23,* 626-628.

Slotkin, J., Forehand, R., Fauber, R., McCombs, A., Long, N. (1988) Parent-completed and adolescent-completed CDIs: Relationship to adolescent social and cognitive functioning. *Journal of Abnormal Child Psychology, 16,* 207-217.

Straus, C.C., Forehand, R., Frame, C., Smith, K. (1984) Characteristics of children with extreme scores on the children's depression inventory. *Journal of Clinical Child Psychology, 13,* 227-231.

Strauss, C.C., Forehand, R., Smith, K., Frame, C.L. (1986) The association between social withdrawal and internalizing problems of children. *Journal of Abnormal Child Psychology, 14,* 525-535.

Vosk, B., Forehand, R., P*arker, J.B., Rickard, K. (1982) A multimethod comparison of popular and unpopular children. Developmental Psychology, 18,* 571-575.

Wierzbicki, M., McCabe, M. (1988) Social skills and subsequent depressive symptomatology in children. *Journal of Clinical Child Psychology, 17,* 203-208.

NEW CHANCES FOR LEWINSOHN'S SOCIAL REINFORCEMENT THEORY OF DEPRESSION

J. Hoevenaars and M.J.M. van Son

Department of Clinical Psychology and Health, University of Utrecht, Utrecht, the Netherlands

INTRODUCTION

In the seventies Lewinsohn and his colleagues (Lewinsohn, 1975; Lewinsohn, Youngren and Grosscup, 1980) developed their social reinforcement theory of depression. The theory is well elaborated, has given rise to much empirical research, and has been extensively used in therapeutical practice. The phrase 'reinforcement theory' is only partly correct. To explain depression Lewinsohn not only uses the principle of reinforcement, but also the operant principles of punishment and extinction. Even classical conditioning plays a part in his theory on depression.

The theory states that depression is caused by a reduction in the level of (positive) reinforcement and/or an increase in the level of (positive) punishment. In a second phase depression is intensified by the social environment through the mechanism of positive reinforcement. In this phase any expression of depression is followed by positive reactions from the social environment, thus intensifying the depression. In a third and last phase, the social environment withdraws any reaction to any behavior of the depressed person. According to Lewinsohn this intensifies the depression, because in this phase all behaviours are put on an extinction schedule.

From 1970 on at least fifty empirical studies have been published on the relation between reinforcement or punishment and depression (for an survey see Hoevenaars, 1987). Almost without exception the level of reinforcement has been operationalized by means of scores on questionnaires of common pleasant events and the level of punishment by means of scores on questionnaires of common unpleasant events. And again, almost without exception, a significant correlation has been found between pleasant or unpleasant events and depression. These results are considered by Lewinsohn as a support for his theory, but a correlation is of course no proof for a causal relation and that is what Lewinsohn assumes: a causal relation between pleasant or unpleasant events and depression.

There are only a few studies published which examine directly the "causal" relation between pleasant events and depression. In seven studies the level of pleasant events was systematically varied to investigate the effects on the level of depression. The results are confusing. Some results confirmed Lewinsohn's hypothesis, but other results did not and in an experiment by Hammen and Glass

(1975) even the opposite was found: higher levels of pleasant events were followed by higher levels of depression. This finding contradicts Lewinsohn's hypothesis.

The Utrecht study

We studied the causal relation between pleasant events (andunpleasant ones) and depression in a longitudinal study using the quasi-experimental cross-lagged panel correlation technique (Kenny, 1979) to analyze our data.

METHOD

Subjects were university students in psychology. 124 students completed several times three questionnaires on depression, Beck's Depression Inventory (BDI), Zung's Self-rating Depression Scale (SDS) and the Depression Adjective Checklist (DACL), together with two questionnaires to measure the level of pleasant and unpleasant events, known as the Pleasant Events Schedule (PES) and the Unpleasant Events Schedule (UES). There was an interval of three months between each completion. The subjects completed seven times all the questionnaires, thus covering a period of almost two years.

The cross-lagged panel correlation technique (figure 1) is a quasi-experimental technique in which two variables (A and B)each are measured on two different points in time (moment 1 and moment 2).

When we suppose that variable B (for example depression) is a function of variable A (for example the amount of pleasant events) one would expect the correlation between A on time 1 and B on time 2 (r A1 B2) to be greater than the reverse correlation (r B1 A2). What one looks for is the difference between the correlations of the so called cross-lags.

Figure 1. **Cross-lagged panel correlation paradigm for variables A and B, measured on two moments (1 and 2)**

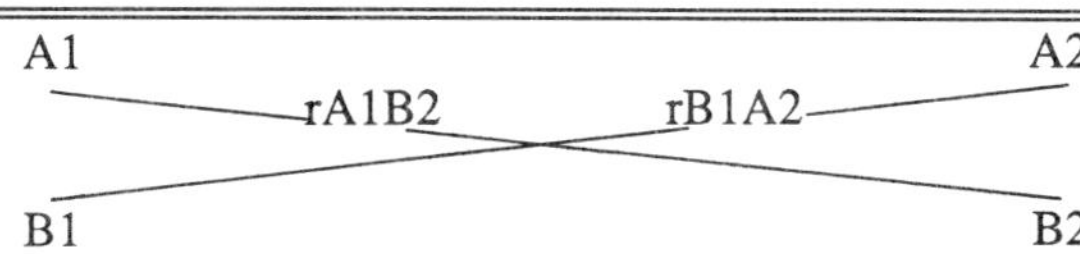

In the interpretation of the cross-lagged differential all other possible correlations (for example r A1 A2 , r A1 B1) should be taken into account. Up to now six studies have been published on the relation between pleasant events and depression using this technique.(for a survey: Hoevenaars, 1987). In these studies very different time-lags were used : one day, two days and even one month.

The results did not support Lewinsohn's assumption that changes in the amount of pleasant events are followed by changes in the amount of depression.

The results of the six studies were, in terms of the cross-lagged panel correlation technique: r A1 B2 - r B1 A2 = 0.

RESULTS

We reasoned that it might take a much longer time than a few days or even a month before changes in the level of pleasant events would result in changes in the level of depression. We chose a time-lag of three months. As we used three different measurements of depression and as we repeated the measurement seven times, we were able to analyze a great amount of cross-lagged differentials. Of the more than fifty differentials only one differed significantly from zero in a direction in accordance with Lewinsohn's hypothesis. The best interpretation of this one significant differential is that it is caused by chance. And so we have to conclude that our study does not support Lewinsohn's theory.

DISCUSSION

This leaves however one problem unsolved. How does ne account for the significant correlation between pleasant events and depression? Significant correlations were reported in more than fifty studies and our data confirmed these findings. One possible explanation is that the correlation is caused by a third variable. Cognitive variables are frequently mentioned in the literature as a supposed third variable, but up to now we don't have knowledge of any publication that implies the influence of cognitive variables on the relation between pleasant events and depression. We had the possibility to do so as our subjects not only completed seven times the three depression inventories and the Pleasant and Unpleasant Events Schedules, but also a completed questionnaire on attributional style. To eliminate the influence of attributional style on the relation between pleasant events and depression we used the partial correlation technique. After removing in this way the influence of attributional style we reanalyzed the relation between pleasant events and depression. The results show that the relation between pleasant events and depression was not affected by attrbutional style. There were only minor differences in the correlation-coefficients between pleasant events and depression before and after removing the influence of attributional style. So we are left with the problem I mentioned before : how does one account for the significant correlation between pleasant events and depression ?

Response bias is another possibility to explain the relation between pleasant events and depression. It has often been suggested that depressed persons simply don't remember pleasant events but do remember well unpleasant events. If this were true, one should obtain a correlation between depression and reported pleasant and unpleasant events. It is however unlikely that this is true. We have two arguments. First of all there is the validity of the Pleasant and Unpleasant Events Schedule. Lewinsohn has studied this validity and has reported that both schedules are valid instruments, even when they are used with depressed persons (Lewinsohn and Amenson, 1978). Our second argument is based upon the relevant literature. From about 1980 a vast body of research has been published on the information processing and the memory of depressed persons. It is clear by now that depressed persons do not distort the information they give about past pleasant and unpleasant events in a way that has often been suggested. In other words, there is no response bias and this rules out another possible explanation about the observed relation between pleasant events and depression. So we are still left with our problem how to explain the positive correlation between pleasant/unpleasant events and depression.

We studied another possible explanation for the correlation. We analyzed the correlation of the individual items of the Pleasant and Unpleasant Events Schedule with the depression-scores. Especially in the Pleasant Events Schedule we found two groups of items. One group that correlated highly with the depression scores and one group that didn't correlate at all. A closer inspection of the items that correlated highly with the depression-scores made us wonder if we were not looking at a depression inventory. Some examples of the items are:

Table 1: **Some PES-items which resemble depression-items.**

-feeling relaxed
-being calm and satisfied
-laughing
-having a good night's rest
-being praised
-just sitting and thinking
-having sexual contact

What we suggest is that the Pleasant Events Schedule is nothing else but a depression inventory, even may be not such a good one. If this is true, we have a very simple explanation for the reported significant relations between the Pleasant Events Schedules depression inventories, both being instruments to measure depression. What we did next was removing those items from the Pleasant Events Schedule that resembled very much items on depression inventories or were the opposite of them. In doing so the correlation between the resulting events and depression was lowered considerably, but it was still significant. We concluded that at least a part of the correlation between pleasant events and depression was due to overlap in item-content and that Lewinsohn's social reinforcement theory lacked any proof, even after twenty years of research.

Reformulation of Lewinsohn's theory

From 1969 up to 1985 Lewinsohn and his colleagues published at least forty articles on their social reinforcement theory, but the last four years no study on this particular issue has been published by them so that it looked as if the theory was abandoned.

In 1988 Barnett and Gotlib published an article on antecedents, concomitants and consequences of depression. They reviewed the research literature and concluded that disturbances in intimate personal functioning in particular should be considered as an antecedent of depression. Unpleasant events, or a reduction of pleasant events, in the primary social environment are an antecedent of depression especially when a person is socially isolated and when the primary social environment is main source of gratification of ones needs. In reviewing the research literature Barnett and Gotlib conclude that variables such as cognitive style, personality characteristics, stress and life events can not be considered to be antecedents of depression,only marriage conflicts can be considered as such. The authors point out that there is no explanation for this relation, it is just a fact. And it is here where Lewinsohn comes in again.

A drop in positive reinforcement causes depression and this depression is intensified by the reactions of the social environment. That is, in a nutshell, Lewinsohn's theory. Research didn't support the theory, but there are new chances if one reformulates the theory.

A loss of social reinforcement causes depression, if the loss is considerable and if there are no other ways to compensate theloss. This loss acts as an unconditioned stimulus. The unconditioned responses to this stimulus are some symptoms of depression. These symptoms are intensified by the reaction of the primary social environment. A further reduction in social reinforcement and an increase in punishment intensifies the depression.

It should be clear that considerable loss of social reinforcement is only possible when a person has only one or very few sources of (social) reinforcement. That is for example the case, if a person has few social contacts and if the person is mainly dependent on his or her partner for need gratification, that is for reinforcement. In this case serious conflicts with the partner would cause a considerable drop in reinforcement, thus starting a depressed episode.

Reformulated in this way, Lewinsohn's social reinforcement theory could explain depression and the fact that marriage conflicts are often followed by depression.

REFERENCES

Barnett, P.A. J.H. Gotlib (1988) Psychological functioning and depression: distinguishing among antecedents, concomittants, and consequences. *Psychological Bulletin, 104*, 97-126.

Hammen, C.L. D.R. Glass (1976) Depression, activity, and evaluation of reinforcement. *Journal of Abnormal Psychology, 84*, 718-721.

Hoevenaars, J. (1987) *Operante visies op depressiviteit*. Utrecht: Elinkwijk. (with a summary in English).

Kenny, D.A. (1979) *Correlation and causality.* New York: Wileyand Sons.

Lewinsohn, P.M. (1975) The behavioral study and treatment of depression. In: M. Hersen, R.M. Eisler and R.M. Miller (Eds.), *Progress in behaviour modification*. New York: Academic Press, 193.

Lewinsohn, P.M. en C.S. Amenson (1978) Some relations between pleasant and unpleasant mood-related events and depression. *Journal of Abnormal Psychology, 87*, 644-654.

Lewinsohn, P.M., M.A. Youngren and S.J. Grosscup (1980) Reinforcement and depression. In: R.A. Depue (ed.), *"The Psychobiology of the depressive disorders:implications for the effects of stress."* New York: Academic Press, 291-316.

PSYCHOPHYSIOLOGICAL RESPONDENCY OF HOSPITALIZED NEUROTIC DEPRESSIVES

M. Kessler (1), D. Munz (2), and H.C. Traue (1)

(1) Department of Medical Psychology, University of Ulm, F.R.G.,
(2) Center for Psychotherapy Research, Stuttgart, F.R.G.

INTRODUCTION

Several psychophysiological investigations demonstrate differences in various central and autonomic measures between depressive patients and healthy controls (e.g. Shagass et al., 1989; Ward & Doerr, 1986; Timsit-Berthier et al., 1984). According to these studies depressives exhibit a decreased electrodermal activity, reduced slow brain potentials, but increased reaction time. In general depressive patients show a lower arousal level of the autonomic and central nervous system. Howeverd the patients studied were mostly confined to psychiatric hospitals and suffered either from endogenous of cyclical depression. That means that there is a considerable lack of comparable research in homogeneous samples of neurotic depressives up to now. This study was designed to investigate possible differences between a homogeneous group of hospitalized neurotic depressives and healthy controls on the subjective motoric and physiological data level.

METHODS

Subjects

The clinical sample comprised 30 patients who had been diagnosed as neurotic depressives according to the ICD-9 and were hospitalized in the psychotherapeutic clinic in Stuttgart. The patient sample consisted of 24 females and 6 males. The mean age was 31.5 years (range 23-48 years). The mean hospital stay was about 6.5 months with a range from 3 months to 10 months. The examination took place one to two weeks after admittance. The control group consisted of 30 healthy normals matched for age and sex. All subjects were free from medication.

Design and procedure

The experimental procedure can be described as following:
The depressive symptoms of the patients were assessed by the Hamilton-Depression-Scale (Hamilton, 1960). Then the patients and the controls were given the Zerssen-Depression-Scale (v. Zerssen, 1976). The psychophysiological assessment was proceeded under a mental arithmetic task, in addition the reaction time was

recorded. Thereafter the subjects had to listen to 10 neutral tones without responses, while electrodermal activity (SCL, SCR, Habituation) was recorded. Finally a 2-stimulus-reaction-time-experiment was presented. A warning tone (S1) announced a second tone (S2) (ISI 2sec) upon which the subject had to press a button. Slow brain potentials (contigent negative variation, CNV; PINV) and reaction time were recorded.

RESULTS

Psychological measures

As expected the patients had significant higher scores in the Zerssen-Depression-Scale compared to the controls (t = 11.31. p = .000)(Figure 1). The mean of the Hamilton-Depression-Scale, as indicator for severity of depression, was 18.

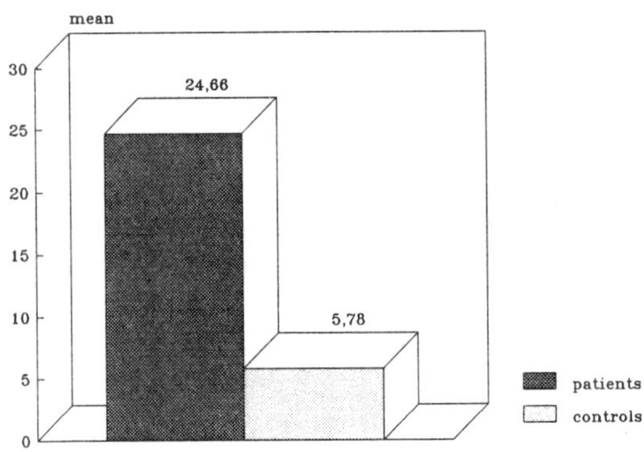

Figure 1: **Means of Zerssen-Depression-Scale**

Physiological measurements

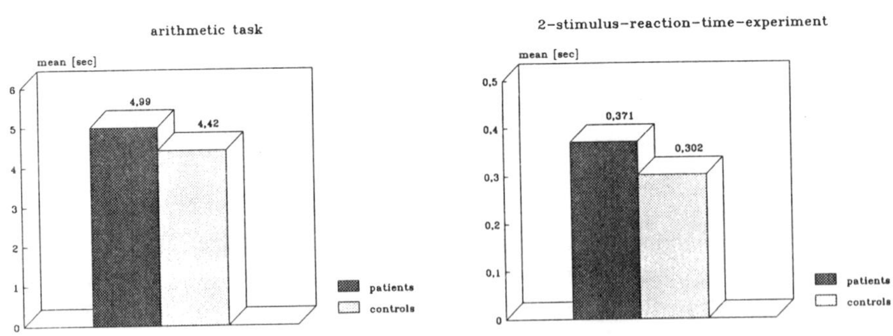

Figure 2: **Reaction time for the arithmetic task and for the 2-stimulus-reaction-time-experiment**

a) Reaction time

The patients had a slightly longer reaction time for the mental arithmetic problem. However, the difference was very small. In the reaction latency for the 2-stimulus-reacton-time-experiment there was also no difference between both groups (p = .13, see figure 2).

b) Electrodermal activity

The mean SCL of the patients during the ten neutral tones and the mean SCR following the tones were significantly lower than the mean SCL and SCR of the controls (t(SCL) = -2.87, p = .006, t(SCR) = -2.09, p = .043 (figure 3)).

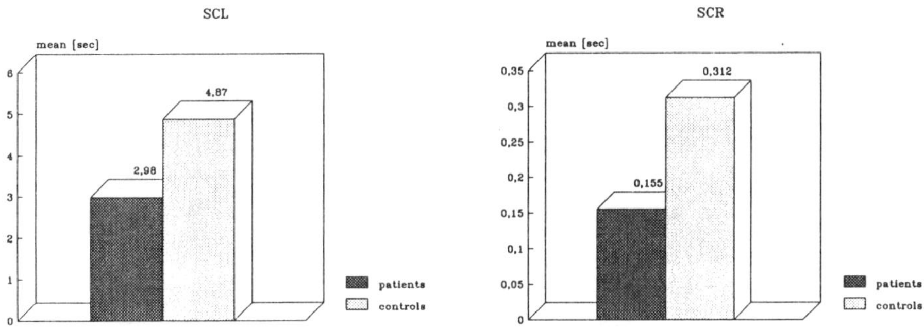

Figure 3: **SCL (left) during the ten tones and SCR (right) following the ten tones**

The course of the habituation of the electrodermal orienting response according to the ten tones is given in Figure 4. Within the patient group 8 subjects showed no orienting response (non-responder) in contrast to 3 subjects in the control group (Chi2 = 3.54, p = .07).

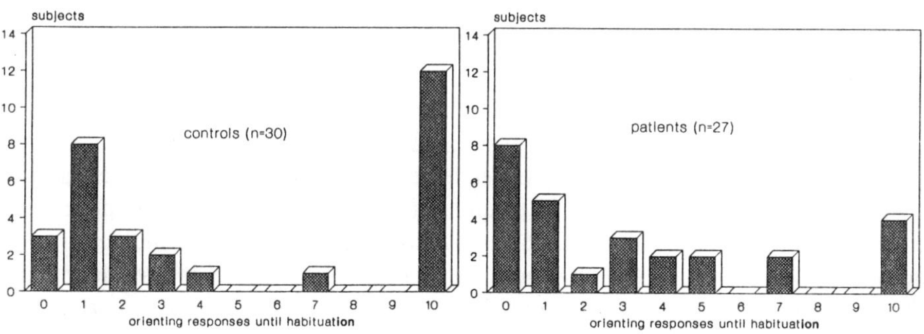

Figure 4: **Course of electrodermal habituation**

A Mann-Whitney-Test measuring the amount of orienting responses until habituation indicated that the patients have a faster habituation rate. But again this difference was not significant on the 5% level (U = 302.5, p = .094).

c) Slow brain potentials

Figure 5 shows the mean curves of the event-related potentials from the five lead on the head (median, FZ, CZ, Pz lateral C3 and C4) during the 2-stimulus-reaction-time-experiment. As was already noted previously both groups did not differ in the reaction time for the second tone. In the slow brain potentials the patients showed a more pronounced CNV and PINV in all measures. A two-factorial group by topography analysis of variance verified these group differences (p(CNV) = .000, p(PINV) = .000).

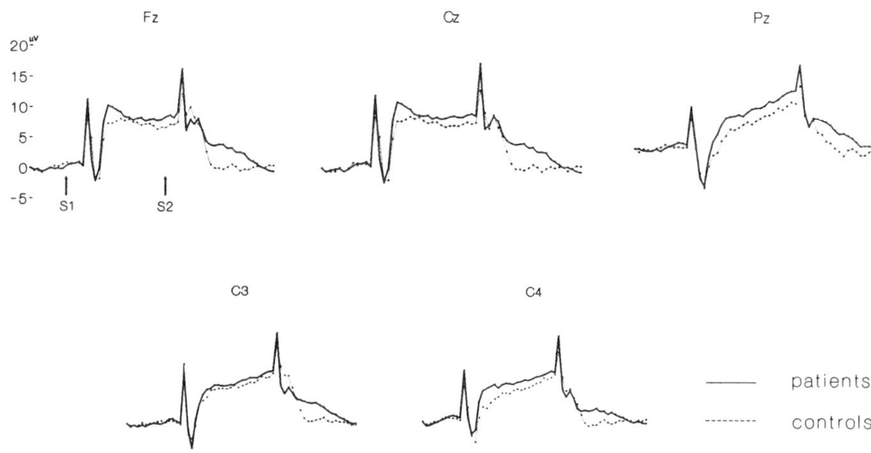

Figure 5: **Mean average of the slow brain potentials between the two tones (S2, S2), separately for both groups**

DISCUSSION

This experimental study shows that a homogeneous group of neurotic depressives can be differentiated from normals in various psychophysiological variables, however no differences could be observed in reaction time tasks. Under the task of passive stimulus processing such as listening to ten tones the neurotic depressives exhibited a reduced SCL and SCR in comparison to normals. These findings are in accordance to the results in endogenous depressives. Thus one could speculate that this electrodermal phenomenon could eventually be considered as a marker or trait variable in depressives.

Regarding the activity of the central nervous system the neurotic depressives in comparison to normals seemed to exhibit higher cortical arousal. This increased cortical arousal level is in contradiction to findings from endogenous depressives, who normally show a reduced CNV (Shagass et al., 1978). But this result is very similar to results from our earlier study (Munz et al, 1984) and data found by Plooij van Gorsel (1984): In these studies event-related potential components were significantly increased and thus supporting the notion of an increased cortical activation in neurotic depressives. Nevertheless, the more pronounced (PINV) was also observed in endogenous depressives and can be interpreted as an indicator for active inhibition, i.e. depressive patients continue to occupy themselves with an already executed response and thus protect themselves against new incoming stimuli (Heinemann, 1979).

Acknowledgements
Research was supported by the Deutsche Forschungsgemeinschaft.

REFERENCES

Hamilton, M. (1960) A rating scale for depression. *Journal for Neurology, Neurosurgery and Psychiatry, 23*, 56-62.

Heinemann, H. (1979) Auf dem Weg zu einer einheitlichen psychophysiologischen Theorie depressiver Syndrome. Praxis der Psychotherapie und Psychosomatik, 24, 281-297.

Munz, D., Ehlers, W., Czogalik, D. (1984) Änderungen der Reaktionspotentiale bei der neurotischen Depression. *Zeitschrift für Elektroenzephalographie, Elektromyographie und verwandte Gebiete, 15*, 105-110.

Plooij-van Gorsel, E. (1984) Evoked potential correlates of information processing and habituation in depressive illness. *Annals of the New York Academy of Sciences, 425*, 609-616.

Shagass, C., Ornitz, E.M., Sutton, S., & Tueting, P. (1978b) Event-related potentials and psychopathology. In Callaway, E., Tueting, P., & Koslow, S. (Eds.) *Event-related brain potentials in man*. New York: Academic Press (pp. 443-496).

Timsit-Berthier, M., Gerono, A., Rousseau, J.C., Mantanus, H., Abraham, P., Verhey, F.H.M., Lamers, T., & Emonds, P. (1984) An international pilot study of CNV in mental illness. Second report. *Annals of the New York Academy of Sciences, 425*, 629-637.

Ward, N.G., Doerr, H.O. (1986) Skin conductance: A potentially sensitive and specific marker for depression. *Journal of Nervous and Mental Disease, 174*, 553-559.

Zerssen, D.v., unter Mitarbeit von Koeller, D.-M. (1976) *Klinische Selbstbeurteilungsskalen (KSb-S) aus dem Münchner psychiatrischen Informations-System* (PSYCHIS München).

ANXIETY LEVEL IN WOMEN SUFFERING FROM UNIPOLAR AFFECTIVE DISORDERS - EXAMINATION CARRIED OUT WITHIN REMISSION PERIOD

M. Majkowicz, J. Jakitowicz, and K. de Walden-Galuszko

I Department of Psychiatry, Medical Academy, Gdansk, Poland

INTRODUCTION

Anxiety is one of the basic symptoms in psychiatric diseases. It is present at a different intensity in affective disorders, particularly in the unipolar form. Scientifically this phenomenon has already been satisfactorily tested. However, the question still remains whether patients continue to differ from healthy people (i.e. those who have never suffered from any mental disorders) during the remission period.

The answers to this question are far from equivocal. Some authors such as Hirschfeld (1983) and Puzynski (1979) try to interpret the discrepancies in the results obtained by the heterogeneous character of the material tested, by the different diagnostic criteria adopted, the lack of homogeneous comparative groups and the lack of precision in research equipment when selecting the study group. We tried to avoid these mistakes by means of stringent diagnostic criteria.

Apart from current clinical criteria the requirement of at least three depressive phases without manic episode was imposed. In order to provide maximum homogeneity of the group and to reduce sex-originated variance of the results, the examination comprised of women only.

Our aim was to determine the anxiety level in women who had been hospitalized in the past due to unipolar affective disease and then compare the results with the anxiety level in women who had never been treated psychiatrically, in order to find the correlation between anxiety level and clinical symptoms during the period of intensified disease, the number of disease phases, the duration of the disease and the age of the patient.

MATERIAL AND METHODS

The examination comprised 72 women aged 27-60. The tested group consisted of 36 women who had been hospitalized in the past due to affective unipolar disorders but showing no symptoms at the time of the test. The control group consisted of 36 women who had never been treated for mental disease. The groups compared did not differ much as to their age, education, marital status, place of residence etc.. All of them came from Gdansk. The selection was based on anamnesis, psychiatric examination and the Beck's scale. The basic examination was performed by means of the MAS scale (Manifest Anxiety Scale).

RESULTS

The results obtained were interpreted in one scale (mean standard deviation 10). According to our data a score of 40-60 was achieved by no more than 22.2% people suffering from the unipolar form of affective disorder. Almost 64% had results over the average (over 60 points). In about 14% of cases, results lower than average were obtained. The distribution of the results in the experimental group was bimodal. The difference between the experimental and control groups the groups is distinctly clear.

On analysis of the case histories it was concluded that in 19 cases intensified anxiety prevailed among other clinical symptoms. In 7 cases this anxiety consisted of depression and in 10 cases of reduced psychomotor activity. The people who showed intensified anxiety or depression during the disease period had a higher anxiety level than the control group during remission (Mean level in the MAS amounted to 66.8 points and 63.9 points). The average anxiety level comparable to the control group was observed in those people whose clinical symptoms were dominated by reduced psychomotor activity (the average in the MAS was 54.5 points). In regard to the correlation between the anxiety level and the number of disease phases no significant correlation was found between the variables analyzed. The correlation coefficient between the disease duration (in years) and the anxiety level is significant yet very low. In this case it is difficult to discuss real correlations between the variables analyzed.

No significant correlation between the age of patient and anxiety level was observed here either.

CONCLUSIONS

1. The anxiety level in women who had been hospitalized in the past for affective unipolar disease in the period of remission is significantly higher than in the control group (healthy women).
2. The anxiety level in this group of patients does not depend on the number of phases, duration of disease or the age of falling ill.
3. A mutual interrelation between the anxiety level and clinical symptoms in the disease period was observed in the people who showed symptoms of anxiety and depression previously. These patients had an anxiety level significantly higher than the control group or those patients who had reduced psychomotor activity.

4. The people who, in the course of unipolar affective disease, suffered depressive phases when free from clinical symptoms should be subjected to therapy directed at anxiety reduction.

REFERENCES

Bilikiewicz, T. (1973) *Psychiatria Kliniczna.* Warszawa: PZWL.

Blöschl, L. (1980) Depressive Störungen. In Wittling, W. *Handbuch der Klinischen Psychologie.* Hamburg: Hoffman und Campe.

Blöschl, L. (1981) Psychodiagnostik depressiver Zustände. *Zeitschrift für Differentielle und Diagnostische Psychologie, 2,* 7-30.

Coryell, W. (1981) Obsessive-compulsive disorder and primary unipolar depressions. Comparisons of background, family history, course and morality. *Journal of Nervous and Mental Diseases, 169,* 220-224.

Donnely, E.F., Murphy, D.L., Goodwin, F.K. (1976) Cross sectional and longitudinal comparisons of bipolar and unipolar depressed groups on the MMPI. *Journal Consult. Clinical Psychology, 44,* 233-237.

Hirschfeld, R.M.A., Klerman, G.L., Clayton, P.J., Keller, M.B. (1983) Personality and depression: Empirical findings. *Archives of General Psychiatry, 40,* 888-983.

Puzynski, S. (1979) *Depresje.* Warszawa: PZWL.

DEPRESSION IN CHILDREN: SELF-REPORTS AND REPORTS FROM PEERS AND TEACHERS IN A NORMAL ELEMENTARY SCHOOL POPULATION

C. Nevermann

Freie Universität Berlin, Institut für Psychologie

INTRODUCTION

Research on depressive disorders in children is done to a larger part within the clinical setting. The present investigation concentrates on aspects of symptomatology and assessment of childhood depression in non-clinical elementary school population. The aspect of relevance to be discussed here concerns the source of information about the child's functioning and the degree of correspondence between different sources. Following an approach of multisource methodology the present study will discuss the following cluster of questions:

- Are there prepubertal children in normal elementary school population who report upon themselves in a negative way on a self-report measure of depression? - How is the prevalence rate of depression? Are there any significant differences in general?
- Are the classroom-teachers able to correspond in their reports on depressed behaviour with the self-reports of the children?
- Are the peers in class just as able as the classroom-teachers to correspond in their reports on classmates with the self-reports?

The investigation of correspondence between self-reports of depression and reports from teachers and peers is based on the assumptions that

- teachers, at least in elementary school, are in general quite familiar with most of the behaviour symptoms defining childhood depression and that
- peers, who spend a wide span of time daily in a variety of interactions together can be looked upon as participating observers, being able therefore to give informations nobody else may possess.

It is of course possible to contradict the above assumptions by asserting just the opposite. Whether teachers and peers are able to perceive children with symptoms of depression in their schoolclasses and how these perceptions correspond with the individual self-reports of depression will be subject of the following discussion.

METHOD

Subjects

A total of 629 prepubertal children (305 boys and 324 girls) aged 11 to 14 years (mean age = 12.2 years, SD = 10.2 month) out of 30 fifth- and sixth-grade classes of different elementary schools in Berlin (West) were recruited together with 30 classroom-teachers to participate in the study.

Measures and Procedure

Only those measures relevant to the actual discussion are mentioned here.

Children's Depression Inventory (CDI) The CDI (Kovacs 1980/1981) is a 27-item self-report scale developed from the Beck Depression Inventory (BDI) to assess the extent of depressive complaints (Kovacs,1983). In the present study CDI-scores were taken as the criterion for the existence of symptoms of depression in children. The scale was translated into German by the author of this study.

The **Peer Nomination Inventory of Depression** (PNID; Lefkowitz & Tesiny, 1980; Lefkowitz & Tesiny, 1985). It is a questionnaire in peer nomination technique, where peers are asked about the characteristics of their classmates. The PNID was administered in a German translation. In the context of the present discussion only the subscale measuring Depressive Symptomatology (PNID-D) is considered.

The **Teacher Nomination Inventory of Depression** (TNID). This is a teacher version of the PNID developed for the present investigation. Classroom-teachers were asked to nominate relevant pupils on the different items of the subscale Depressive Symptomatology (TNID-D).

The **Self Nomination Inventory of Depression** (SNID-D). It is a self-report version of the PNID developed in the context of this investigation to get an additional self-report measure directly comparable with the peer- and teacher-report measures.

Group testing took place in the children's ows classrooms. Each child completed the series of self-report and peer-report measures self-paced within a time limit.

RESULTS

The CDI was taken as the criterion for the existence and intensity of depressive symptomatology.

Table 1 summarizes the mean CDI scores and standard deviations as well as the median for each sex and combined. 71 children (11.3% of the sample) had to be neglected because of missing values.

Table 1. **Children's Depression Inventory: Mean, Standard Deviation, Median**

Sex	n	M	SD	MD
Girls	286	11.22	6.12	10.39
Boys	272	10.43	5.67	9.35
Combined	558	10.83	5.91	9.35

The overall mean for the combined sample ($M = 10.83, SD = 5.91$) is somewhat higher than that of other samples (e.g.Kovacs, 1983b). Boys' and girls' means were not significantly different on the CDI self-report measure ($t(556) = -1.57, p < 0.11$). Neither were there age-specific differences.

Referring to the initial question of the present study regarding the prevalence of childhood depression subjects were divided into "none-to-low"- versus "moderate"- versus "severe"-depression groups on the basis of their total CDI scores. Criteria for inclusion in one of the groups were taken from the normative data (cut-off scores) given by Kovacs (1980; 1983b).

Differences between the three groups of depression, examined by Kruskal-Wallis 1-Way ANOVA were highly significant ($p < .001$). Moreover, there was a significant gender difference concerning the distribution in the three depression groups. There were significantly more girls then boys in the "moderate"- and in the "severe" depression group ($t = -2.15, p < .03$).

The analyses on the existence and severity of depressive symptoms in a sample of elementary school children indicated that there were indeed children reporting from themselves negatively in the sense of symptoms of depression. According to the CDI distribution there were 60 children out of 558 in normal population who, according to CDI-norms, might be regarded as severely depressed. This would mean a prevalence of severe depression of around 9.4% in a population of 5th- and 6th-graders attending regular public elementary school classes. Differences of statistic significance between genders were only found in the subgroups of intensity of depressive symptoms

The question arises , how these self-reports agree with reports from "relevant others" out of the social environment. This aspect of multisource-multimethod approach has found growing interest in recent literature (e.g., Fergusson & Horwood, 1987).

In the context of the present study self-reports on depression were correlated with peers' and teacher reports. For reasons of higher comparability of data an identical scale of measurement - that means, different versions of the Peer Nomination Inventory of Depression - was admimistered to all sources of report. The correlations (Spearman correlation coefficients) of depression between the two self-report measures CDI and SNID-D, between CDI self-report and reports from peers (PNID-D) and teachers (TNID-D), and between the set of SNID-D, PNID-D, and TNID-D are as follows:

Regarding the self-report measures a strong positive correlation (r = .67, p= 0.001) was found between the total depression score of the SNID-D and the CDI total score.

The peer report measure correlated much higher with the CDI self-report measure (r= .43, p= 0.001) than the teacher report measure (r= .27, p= 0.001). The self-report version of the PNID-D, the SNID-D did not correlate higher with the PNID-D (r= .40, p=0.001) than the CDI self-report did.

High correlations were found between the PNID-D total score (r=.50, p= 0.001) and the TNID-D total score.

In contrast low correlations were found between the TNID-D score and the CDI self-report score (r = .27, p= 0.001) as well as between the TNID-D score and the SNID-D self-report score.

Focusing on the aspect of gender, there were differences in the direction that girls had higher correlations on all measures than the total score correlations and the correlations for boys. The boys' correlations were extremely low (the lowest of all correlations in the matrix) between the TNID-D score and the CDI self-report score (r= .15,p= 0.01) as well as between the TNID-D score and the SNID-D self-report score (r= .19, p= 0.001).

Taken together, the results of the correlational analyses indicate that (i) the children in this sample were quite consistent in their reports of symptoms of depression across the two different self-report measures, that (ii) the teacher reports reached low agreement with the self-reports of depression of their children in class and that (iii) the peer reports showed greater correspondence with the self-reports than the teachers' reports.

DISCUSSION

The results of the present study demonstrated that the degree of correspondence between self-reports of depression in prepubertal children and reports of their dysfunction from other sources was only low to moderate. Moreover there was evidence that agreement between reports from the same sources of information was higher. These findings are consistent with other studies in the literature indicating also that one of the additional influential variables of the degree of correspondence might be the kind of dysfunction to report on.

REFERENCES

Blöschl, L., Ederer, E., Linhart, B. (1981) Extraversion, Neurotizismus und potentiell verstärkende Aktivitäten. Eine empirische Untersuchung an 10- bis 14jährigen Kindern. In: Janke, W. (Hrsg.) *Beiträge zur Methodik in der differentiellen diagnostischen und klinischen Psychologie. Festschrift zum 60. Geburtstag von G.A. Lienert.* Königstein, Ts: Hain (S. 104-115).

Blöschl, L, Ederer, E. (1986) Zusammenhänge zwischen Depressivität und selbstberichteten Aktivitäts- und Kontaktdefiziten in der frühen Adoleszenz. *Zeitschrift für Klinische Psychologie, Psychopathologie und Psychotherapie, 34,* 32-40.

Blöschl, L., Ederer, E., Rossmann, P. (1987) Dysthyme Persönlichkeitstendenzen und "close confidants": Zur Frage geschlechtsspezifischer Zusammenhänge wischen Depressivität und selbstberichtetem Sozialkontakt. In: Raab, E., Schulter, G. (Eds.) *Perspektiven psychologischer Forschung. Festschrift zum 65. Geburtstag von Erich Mittenecker.* Wien: Deuticke (S. 107-118).

Fergusson, D.M., Horwood, L.J. (1986) The trait and method components of ratings of conduct disorder - Part I. Maternal and teacher evaluations of conduct disorder in young children. *Journal of Child Psychology and Psychiatry, 28,* 249-260.

Kazdin, A.E., Esveldt-Dawson, K., Unis, A.S., Rancurello, D. (1983a) Child and parent evaluations of depression and aggression in psychiatric inpatient children. *Journal of Abnormal Child Psychology, 11,* 401-413.

Kazdin, A.E., French, N., Unis, A.S. (1983b) Child, mother and father evaluations of depression in psychiatric inpatien children. *Journal of Abnormal Child Psychology, 11,* 167-180.

Kovacs, M. (1983) Definition and assessment of childhood depressions. In Ricks, D., Dohrenwend, B. (Eds.) *Origins of Psychopathology.* New York: Cambridge University Press.

Kovacs, M. (1983b) *The Children's Depression Inventory: A Self-rated Depression Scale for School-aged Youngsters*. University of Pittsburgh School of Medicine. Unpublished manuscript.

Kovacs, M. (1985) The Children's Depression Inventory (CDI). *Psychopharmacology Bulletin, 21,* 995-998.

Lefkowitz, M.M, Tesiny, E.P. (1980) Assessment of childhood depression. *Journal of Consulting and Clinical Psychology, 48,* 43-50.

Lefkowitz, M.M., Tesiny, E.P. (1985) Depression in children: prevalence and correlates. *Journal of Consulting and Clinical Psychology, 53,* 647-656.

Saylor, C.F., Finch, A., Baskin, C., Furey, W., Kelly, M. (1984) Construct validity for measures of childhood depression: application of multitrait-multimethod methodology. *Journal of Consulting and Clinical Psychology, 52,* 977-985.

THE INDIVIDUAL ANALYSIS OF RULE-ORIENTED BEHAVIOR BY DEPRESSED PERSONS

M. Reicherts and M. Perrez

University of Fribourg, Switzerland

THE CONCEPT OF BEHAVIOR RULES (BR) FOR ADEQUATE COPING BEHAVIOR AND THEIR EMPIRICAL FOUNDATION

In the recent research literature, many references are made to the fact that depressed persons may be characterized by specific types of behavior while coping with stressful situations, i.e. with events demanding in a specific way the person's psychological resources (Blöschl, 1982; Billings & Moos, 1982, Fisher, 1984, 1986; Folkman & Lazarus, 1986; Mitchell et al., 1983; Parker et al., 1985).

Many depressed persons practice a dysfunctional coping style which is rather inappropriate for effective adaptation to the characteristics of the situation. Assuming such a hypothesis, we have - at least - an *implicit* idea of functional coping, i.e. of *adequate behavior in view of specific features of the situation*. The question of "What does adequate coping mean?" has been discussed in the past under the denomination of "maturity". According to Vaillant (1976), an "immature" coping style, for example, would be "acting out" or "denial". Antonovsky (1979) delineated three criteria for mature behavior: rationality, flexibility, and farsightedness. Menaghan (1983) criticizes the maturity approach by pointing out that it tells us nothing about real behavior in stressful situations. In addition, such general criteria don't account for the broad range of possible situations.

We assume that the ruling out of criteria for adequate coping behavior is possible if the problem to solve is reformulated in more precise terms of a behavior problem, which allows an empirically founded solution. Instead of asking "What is appropriate or mature behavior?" we ask "What are the features of appropriate action or behavior if a person intends to reach a specific goal under specific internal and external conditions (i.e. the situation)?". This question can be answered - at least for some types of behavior tasks (problems). We refer the answer of this question to a *behavior rule* (BR), which underlies functional coping modalities appropriate for effective adaptation. According to this, depressive behavior can be described as violating specific BR in a specific way. BR's are hypothetical imperatives with a conditional-normative structure: "If a situation has the characteristics c, and if goal G is to be reached within time t, then behavior b is to realize!"

We formulated BR's for a small number of situational features. The types of behavior tasks consider especially situations with moderate to high versus low controllability, situations with high vs low changeability and situations with high vs low ambiguity. The BR are proposed for some typical configurations of these situational features.

How to find behavior rules

Everyone disposes of a set of private BR's acquired in his learning history. How to distinguish rationally, objectively founded BR's from private BR only subjectively based? The first criterion to meet is that of the *effectiveness* of the recommended behavior (other criteria not discussed here, are its efficiency in relation to its "costs" and its compatibility with social norms). The supposition that a certain type of behavior is appropriate to master a certain type of situation must be empirically confirmed. Additionally, we may analyze, if the persons who use these BR's in every day life differ in desirable characteristics from persons not using them.

Rule-oriented behavior is to be analysed in two forms: *Rule-conform* behavior and *rule-guided* behavior, the latter implying the former. If a person behaves in a certain way in a given situation, her behavior may be conform (or not) to rules which are rationally founded (or not). Her behavior is considered as rule-directed only if it refers intentionally and consciously to BR's.

How do depressed people violate behavior rules?

Our rule system (Reicherts, Käslin & Perrez, 1984) contains BR's like

"If a stressful situation is characterized by controllability, then try to influence the situation, - if reduction of stress is your goal!" or

"If a stressful situation is characterized by high negative valence then try at first to palliate your negative emotions, if a reduction of stress is your goal!"

We also formulated some hypotheses about coping tendencies by depressed persons which violate our proposed BR's (Perrez, 1984). The hypotheses concern especially BR's for instrumental behavior in controllable situations and BR's for palliation in situations with highly negative emotional reactions. In a study we compared n=30 patients with major depression with n=30 matched normal controls by a *process-oriented questionnaire* (Perrez & Reicherts, 1986; Reicherts et al., 1987). The depressive persons reacted with less instrumental coping, more avoidance behavior and more passivity. Another correlational study based on computer-aided self-observation confirmed some basic elements of our hypotheses also for depressed persons as observed within a normal sample (Perrez, 1988; Reicherts, 1988).

ASSESSING RULE-ORIENTED BEHAVIOR: THE METHOD OF RULE CONFIRMATION ANALYSIS

For the assessment of rule-oriented behavior we developed a method we called confirmation analysis. Confirmation analysis is a contingency based procedure which assesses how often a person's observed behavior is conform to a given, rationally and intersubjectively founded BR.

Rule conformity of the subject is analyzed on the basis of a number of stressful episodes of his everyday life. The subject is instructed to observe himself in the stressful episodes he experiences during several weeks by means of our pocket-computer recording system (COMRES; Perrez & Reicherts, 1987)): Immediately after every episode he records (1) the characteristics of the situation as perceived by himself, (2) his coping efforts (self-directed and environment-directed) and (3) the outcome of his coping effort. The self-observational variables are presented by the program on the computer display and are to be answered by rating keys. Additionally the subject rates his emotions and he describes in a few words his most relevant coping intention.

Two of those rules we proposed in our earlier research are exemplified here and then analyzed in a single case:

Rule-B concerns environment-directed behavior:

"The higher the controllability of the situation, the less try to evade or avoid - if reduction of stress is your goal".

Rule-E concerns self-directed behavior:

"The more stressful the situation (negative valence), the more try to palliate (smooth) your negative emotions - if reduction of stress is your goal".

Each rule is translated into a contingency table containing valid and not valid cells, which represent the if-then patterns of the rules in detail. The subject's observations of his behavior in his stressful encounters have to be conform to that contingency table (if the individual behaves according to the rule). The two rules are formalized as follows (see table 1).

Table 1. **Behavior rules (BR) for coping with stressful situations formalized for confirmation analysis**

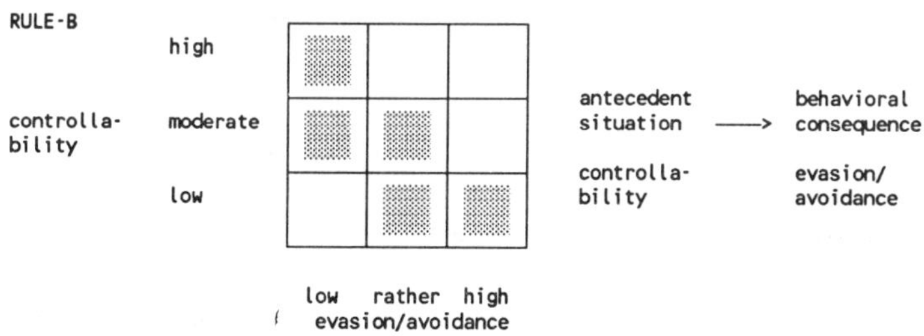

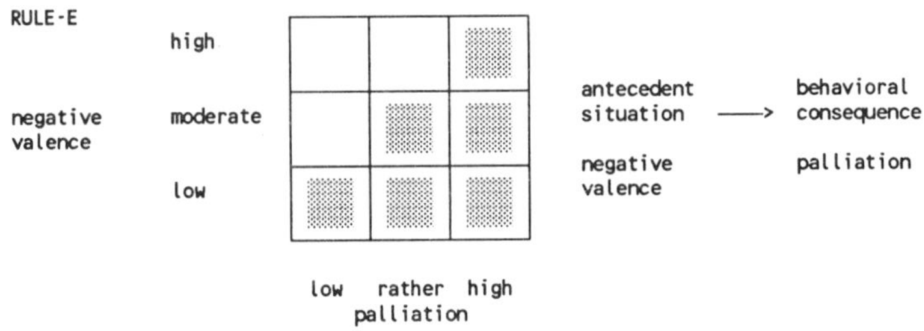

CASE STUDY

We demonstrate the rule confirmation analysis in reference to an individual case of a depressed young man. In the beginning of the therapy this patient had typical symptoms of a reactive depression. Also his BDI-score (24), FPI-scores (depression, irritability augmented), and other inventory data (e.g. real-ideal description, polarity profile) clearly indicated a depression.

The analysis of his rule-oriented coping behavior with daily life stressors took place in the second phase of the therapy. In a self-observational period of two weeks the patient recorded 19 stressful episodes with our COMRES system (Perrez & Reicherts, 1987) using a programmed pocket computer.

Analyzing the patient's self-observational data we first aggregated the stressful events he had recorded and we computed gross means (averages) for the total of his 19 episodes: E.g. his global mean of controllability of the experienced situations, his global strain (negative valence), his global effort to cope with the stress by evasion/avoidance or by palliating his actual stress emotions, and so on. Then we checked the following diagnostical questions, comparing the measures of this patient with a reference group (N=40 students; as a norm):

1) Are his coping efforts globally effective? - Answer: No!
2) Do his global coping tendencies differ from coping tendencies of other people? For example: Does he evade/withdraw more from stressful events or does he smooth his stress emotions less than others? (That are the questions other instruments normally answer to). The answer is: No! Neither does he evade more than others do nor does he smooth his emotions less - globally taken.
3) Does he cope with stress according to the proposed rules of adequate coping? Does he behave according to rule-B, which recommends the degree (intensity) of evasion or avoidance given the controllability of the situation? Answer: No! He is definitively below the average of the confirmation index of the reference group! Is his behavior conform to rule-E? Answer: Not fully! He is somewhat below the confirmation index of the reference group!

A closer look at the contingency table containing the patient's stressful episodes reveals his "violations" of the proposed coping rules (Table 2). The short-comings of his coping tendencies lead to the following hypothesis about actual conditions of his ineffective coping behavior, which is probably related to his depressive symptoms: (i) In situations of high valence the patient does not sufficiently smooth his negative emotions. (ii) In situations of low controllability he doesn't try to evade/ avoid from stress as rule-B recommends to do. But he also tries to evade when there is some controllability (perceived by him) instead of influencing the stressor.

Table 2. **Confirmation index CON of coping behavior rule-B and rule-E by a depressed patient**

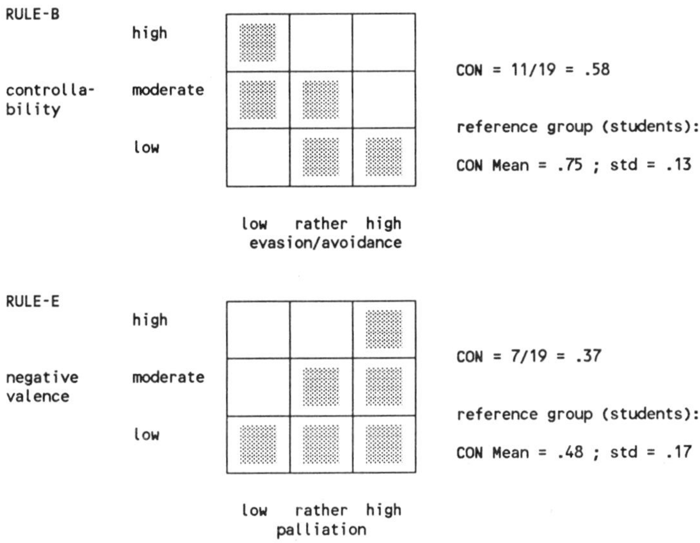

The confirmation index:

$$\text{CON} = \frac{\text{observations in cells covered by the rule}}{\text{total number of observations}}$$

Our patient does not generally evade/avoid too much - but he evades the wrong situations! And he does not generally palliate his stress emotions too little - but he does it in the wrong moment! - This is a very important information to understand the *actual conditions of ineffective coping* with stress (and for planning interventions). Rule confirmation analysis provides us with that information and gives us the hint about what are the probable deficits and where to direct our therapeutic efforts.

The way he violated the two BR leads to the following *treatment hypotheses*: First we have to help this patient to realize his "strategic errors". For that we should use his self-observational data to illustrate his inadequate tendencies. Then we have to verify if he has the behavioral skills to evade or avoid an uncontrollable situation and the skills to smooth his negative emotional reactions - right in the moment when they are straining him and probably hindering effective instrumental behavior. This specific intervention program was one element of a treatment package for coping with depression. The treatment is ongoing and an evaluation of his competence for coping with stress is provided in the next future.

CONCLUDING REMARKS

We started from the notion that dysfunctional coping behavior of the depressed person reveals "strategic errors" in violating behavior rules, which are supposed to be effective. We discussed the idea of such behavior rules, which are hypothetical imperatives recommending specific behavior in view of specific situational characteristics to reach certain goals, like the reduction of strain in stressful encounters. We developed a simple method to analyze the degree to which the coping behavior is conform with proposed and founded BR's, which are of major interest for depressed people. We conducted an individual analysis of a depressed patient, who revealed typical violations of BR's in his self-observation of a number of stressful episodes. The results show the diagnostical value of behavior rule analysis and the hints delineated for individual intervention.

Coping behavior conform to the proposed BRs seems well related to different indicators of coping effectiveness and psychic health showing its external *validity* (Reicherts, 1988). Confirmation index CON is correlated with reported *coping effectiveness* (goal attainment r=.38 to r=.55; perceived behavior discrepancies r=-.28 to r=-.38). Concerning *psychic health*, rule conform behavior is negatively related to depression (BDI) (r=-.32 to r=-.48), positively related to affective well-being according to Becker's SD-SG-scale (r=.36; r=.41) and also to a positive life perspective according to Becker's version of Crumbaugh & Maholick's PIL (r=.29; r=.33). Also reliability of rule confirmation index is quite satisfying (rtt=.78 to rtt=.85 for the rule clusters).

There are some problems still unresolved: We should know more about other criteria the proposed rules have to meet (e.g. behavior economy) and more about the general and the individual repertories to realize the behavior more in detail. But the concept seems to be fruitful for different behavior problems, as for social fears, type-A behavior or chronic illness.

REFERENCES

Antonovsky, A. (1979) *Health, Stress, and Coping.* San Francisco: Jossey-Bass.

Billings, A.G., Moos, R.H. (1982) Psychological theory and research on depression: In integrative framework and review. In *Clinical Psychology Review, 2,* 213-237.

Blöschl, L. (1982) Stress and stress-reducing factors in depression: A reinforcement-oriented analysis. In J. Boulougouris (Ed.), *Learning theory approaches to psychiatry* (pp. 231-236). New York: Wiley.

Fisher, S. (1984) *Stress and the perception of control*. London: Erlbaum.

Fisher, S. (1986) *Stress and strategy*. London: Erlbaum.

Folkman, S., Lazarus, R.S. (1986) Stress processes and depressive symptomatology. *Journal of Abnormal Psychology, 95,* 107-113.

Menaghan, E.G. (1983) Individual coping efforts: Moderators of the relationship between life stress and mental health outcomes. In H.B. Kaplan (Ed.), *Psychological stress: Trends in theory and research* (pp. 157-191). New York: Academic Press.

Mitchell, R.E., Cronkite, R.C. & Moos, R.H. (1983). Stress, coping, and depression among married couples. *Journal of Abnormal Psychology, 92,* 433-448.

Parker, G., Brown, L., Blignault, I. (1986) Coping behaviors as predictors of the course of clinical depression. *Archives of General Psychiatry, 43,* 561-565.

Vaillant, G.E. (1976) Strategies of adaptation: An attempt at systematic description. In G.V. Coelho, D.A. Hamburg & J.E. Adams (Eds.), *Coping and Adaptation* (pp. 47-68). New York: Basic Books.

Perrez, M. (1988) Bewältigung von Alltagsbelastungen und seelische Gesundheit. Zusammenhänge auf der Grundlage computer-unterstützter Selbstbeobachtungs- und Fragebogendaten. *Zeitschrift für Klinische Psychologie, 17,* 292-306.

Perrez, M. (1984) *Stressverarbeitung bei neurotisch Depressiven (Wie sie handeln und wie sie handeln sollten). Theorie und empirische Befunde* (Forschungsbericht Nr. 50). Fribourg/ Switzerland, University, Institute of Psychology.

Perrez, M., Reicherts, M. (1986) Appraisal, coping, and attribution processes by depressed persons: An S-R-S-R approach. *The German Journal of Psychology, 10,* 315-326.

Perrez, M., Reicherts, M. (1987) Coping behavior in the natural setting: A method of computer-aided self-observation. In J.-P. Dauwalder, M. Perrez & V. Hobi (Eds.), *Controversial issues in behavior modification. Annual series of european research in behavior therapy, Vol. 2* (pp.127-137). Lisse: Swets & Zeitlinger.

Reicherts, M., Käslin, S., Perrez, M. (1984) *Stressbewältigung.* Erster Arbeitsbericht der Entwicklung eines kriteriumsorientierten psychodiagnostischen Verfahrens zur theoriegeleiteten Analyse sozialängstlichen und depressiven Verhaltens (Forschungsbericht Nr. 45). Fribourg/Switzerland, Institute of Psychology.

Reicherts, M., Käslin, S., Scheurer, F., Fleischhauer, J., Perrez, M. (1987) Belastungsverarbeitung bei endogen Depressiven. In *Zeitschrift für Klinische Psychologie, Psychopathologie und Psychotherapie, 35,* 197-210.

Reicherts, M. (1988) *Diagnostik der Belastungsverarbeitung. Neue Zugänge zu Stress-Bewältigungs-Prozessen*. Freiburg: Universitätsverlag und Bern: Huber.

SYMPTOMS OF DEPRESSION IN CHILDHOOD AND THE INTERNAL STRUCTURE OF A RECENTLY DEVELOPED AUSTRIAN DEPRESSION SCALE FOR CHILDREN

P. Rossmann

Department of Educational Psychology, Karl Franzens University, Graz, Austria

INTRODUCTION

On more than one occasion in history the progress of science has been hindered by prevailing theoretical dogmas which have biased scientists against believing their own eyes. To some extent this has also been the case in the study of depressive disorders in children. In this context two theoretical beliefs must be mentioned.

Firstly, for a long time it was the prevalent belief of prominent psychoanalytic authorities that an adult-type depressive syndrome simply is not possible in children because of the lack of a well-developed and well-internalized superego (e.g. Rochlin 1959, Rie 1966).

Secondly, another quite influential group of scientists (e.g. Glaser 1968, Cytryn & McKnew 1972) has asserted that depression in children would of course exist but would not express itself by the same clinical features that are indicative for depression in adults. According to this second view, depression in children would often be masked by various other symptoms, so-called depressive equivalents. An underlying, unexpressed depressed affect was postulated to be responsible for manifest behaviour that may include nearly all psychopathological symptoms that are observable in children, e.g. symptom of conduct disorder, hyperactivity, enuresis, learning disabilities, somatic complaints and so forth. The underlying depression has to be largely inferred by the clinician from other diagnostic measures that are able to detect depressive signs e.g. from depressive themes in projective tests. The concept of masked depression has proven to be a very difficult and controversial issue for several reasons. When adopting the concept, the boundaries between well-defined psychopathological syndromes are going to get dissolved. For the clinician it becomes more and more unclear, as Vermilyea, Heimberg & Silverman (1985, p. 125) have put it "when is a conduct disorder a conduct disorder and when isn't it? ... If, for instance, a child presents with aggressive behavior, when is the aggressive behavior the legitimate focus and when is it hiding something else?" The only way to resolve this issue is by conducting broad-based interviews and a careful assessment of the child which may lead to the finding that the initially presented symptoms are not the signs upon which the diagnosis should be based. This solution however, reduces the concept of masked depression to the question whether or not the initially presented symptoms are those that are most important for forming the diagnosis (see also Carlson & Cantwell 1980, Kolvin, Berney & Bhate 1984 and Harper & Kelly 1985).

The position adopted nowadays by virtually all the leading child psychiatrists is that depression in childhood exists and that the essential features of the disorder are very similar in childhood, adolescence and adulthood. However, the controversial discussion still centers around two issues, namely the question *what should the operational diagnostic criteria be* and the question which symptoms are to be viewed as essential and which are only to be seen as age-specific associated features. The two most widely accepted answers to these questions shall be shortly reviewed here.

Diagnostic Criteria:

Table 1. **Definition of Major Depressive Syndrome according to DSM-III-R (American Psychiatric Association 1987)**

At least five of the following symptoms have been present during the same two-week period and represent a change from previous functioning; at least one of the symptoms is either (1) depressed mood, or (2) loss of interest or pleasure. (Do not include symptoms that are clearly due to a physical condition, mood incongruent delusions or hallucinations, incoherence, or marked loosening of associations.)

(1) depressed mood (or can be irritable mood in children and adolescents) most of the day, nearly every day, as indicated either by subjective account or observation by others,
(2) markedly diminished interest or pleasure in all, or almost all, activities most of the day, nearly every day (as indicated either by subjective account or observation by others of apathy most of the time),
(3) significant weight loss or weight gain when not dieting (e.g., more than 5% of body weight in a month), or decrease or increase in appetite nearly every day (in children consider failure to make expected weight gains),
(4) insomnia or hypersomnia nearly every day,
(5) psychomotor agitation or retardation nearly every day (observable by others, not merely subjective feelings of restlessness or being slowed down),
(6) fatigue or loss of energy nearly every day,
(7) feelings of worthlessness or excessive or inappropriate guilt (which may be delusional) nearly every day (not merely self-reproach or guilt about being sick),
(8) diminished ability to think or concentrate, or indecisiveness, nearly every day (either by subjective account or as observed by others),
(9) recurrent thoughts of death (not just fear of dying), recurrent suicidal ideation without a specific plan, or a suicide attempt or a specific plan for committing suicide.

The approach taken in DSM-III-R (American Psychiatric Association 1987), which is today by far the most influential psychiatric classification system, is that the criteria for the diagnosis of major depression as well as for dysthymic disorder are, except for some minor variations, the same in infants, children, adolescents and adults. The definition of a major depressive syndrome according to that approach is shown in Table 1.

Prior to the development of DSM-III, the formulation of separate criteria for childhood depression had been proposed by Weinberg, Rutman, Sullivan, Penick & Dietz (1973). The set of criteria that was published by the authors has together with DSM-III dominated research on childhood depression.

Table 2. **Diagnostic criteria for childhood depression according to Weinberg et al. (1973)**

A. The presence of both symptoms (1) and (2):
(1) dysphoric mood, (2) self-deprecatory ideation
B. Two or more of the following eight symptoms
(3) aggressive behavior (agitation), (4) sleep disturbance, (5) a change in school performance, (6) diminished socialization, (7) change in attitude toward school, (8) somatic complaints, (9) loss of usual energy, (10) unusual change in appetite and/or weight.
C. These symptoms have to represent a change in the child's usual behavior.
D. These symptoms have to be present for a period of more than one month.

When DSM-III-R and Weinberg criteria are compared (e. g. Carlson & Cantwell 1982, see also Cantwell 1983, Kazdin 1988) we find that the Weinberg criteria are less selective for reaching a diagnosis of depression. They require a fewer number of symptoms and permit a broader range of symptoms to be counted as signs of depression. This leads to higher prevalence rates in empirical studies in which the Weinberg criteria were used. The DSM-III-R criteria are currently in greater use than are the Weinberg criteria.

In this report empirical evidence shall be presented that stems from a completely different methodological tradition, namely the attempt to develop psychometric instruments for the quantitative scaling of depressive states in childhood. A first impression of similarities and differences between the above-mentioned symptom lists of diagnostic criteria and the structure of a recently developed austrian self-report questionnaire is given.

DEVELOPMENT OF THE "DEPRESSIONSTEST FÜR KINDER"

At the Karl Franzens University of Graz, our research group is currently developing a self-report depression questionnaire for prepubertal children aged 8 to 12 years. The construction of the test was based on a pool of 107 questions, most of which were translated and reformulated items from comparable questionnaires in English language. In order to obtain a basis for item analysis the questionnaire was administered to a sample of 1450 third to sixth grade children in 15 Austrian schools. Their ages ranged from 9 to 13 years with only a few outliers who were older. About half of the children were boys and half were girls.

Table 3: Oblimin factor loadings[1)] and item-total correlations for all items of the 'Depressionstest für Kinder' (DTK)

	F1	F2	F3	r_{it}
Factor 1: Depressed mood and low self-esteem				
34. Fühlst Du Dich oft wertlos?	.67	--	--	.57
18. Denkst Du oft, daß Du ein schlechter Mensch bist?	.67	--	--	.59
35. Bist Du oft unglücklich?	.65	--	--	.59
42. Bist Du oft so traurig, daß Du es kaum aushalten kannst?	.62	--	--	.53
19. Findest Du, daß Du häßlich aussiehst?	.56	--	--	.49
54. Hast Du mehr Sorgen als andere Kinder?	.56	--	--	.51
21. Weinst Du oft?	.53	--	--	.45
13. Wirst Du oft von anderen Kindern verspottet?	.53	--	--	.44
55. Fühlst Du Dich oft einsam?	.52	--	--	.52
43. Möchtest Du manchmal tot sein?	.50	--	--	.49
51. Findest Du, daß das Leben traurig ist?	.49	--	--	.44
52. Schämst Du Dich oft?	.49	--	--	.45
36. Möchtest Du manchmal von zu Hause weglaufen?	.47	.29	--	.49
49. Bist Du sehr schnell gekränkt?	.46	--	--	.40
4. Ärgerst Du Dich oft über Dich?	.45	--	--	.49
40. Hast Du mehr Schmerzen als andere Kinder?	.45	--	--	.43
31. Bist Du manchmal ohne besonderen Grund traurig?	.44	--	--	.48
33. Hast Du oft Angst, etwas falsch zu machen?	.43	--	--	.46
20. Denkst Du oft, daß andere Kinder besser sind als Du?	.43	--	--	.43
50. Machst Du Dir Sorgen über Deine Zukunft?	.42	--	--	.34
23. Tun Dir manchmal andere Kinder absichtlich weh?	.42	--	--	.38
14. Weinst Du oft nur aus Zorn?	.39	--	--	.44
24. Bist Du oft unglücklich wegen der Schule?	.38	.27	--	.47
48. Bist Du oft mit Dir unzufrieden?	.32	--	--	.36
44. Hast Du oft das Gefühl, eine Strafe zu verdienen?	.29	--	--	.37
Factor 2: Agitation and problems of norm integration				
15. Gibst Du manchmal in der Schule freche Antworten?	--	.66	--	.52
30. Wirst Du in der Schule oft ermahnt, ruhig zu sein?	--	.65	--	.54
29. Beklagt sich manchmal ein Lehrer über Dich?	--	.63	--	.52
6. Schwätzt Du oft?	--	.59	--	.46
5. Denkst Du in der Schule gerne an andere Dinge?	--	.52	--	.52
2. Macht Dir die Schule Spaß? [2)]	--	.50	--	.43
3. Gibst Du zu Hause manchmal freche Antworten?	--	.50	--	.46
11. Würdest Du gerne von der Schule zu Hause bleiben?	--	.48	--	.43
16. Sagst Du Deinen Eltern immer, wohin Du gehst? [2)]	--	.48	--	.35
17. Bist Du zu Hause oft unfreundlich?	--	.41	--	.44
41. Spielst Du in der Klasse oft den Clown?	--	.41	--	.31
32. Wirst Du zu Hause oft ermahnt, brav zu sein?	--	.38	--	.41
12. Mußt Du Dich zwingen, Deine Hausaufgaben zu machen?	--	.37	--	.43
27. Möchtest Du manchmal jemandem sehr weh tun?	--	.34	--	.31
37. Wirfst Du oft aus lauter Wut Dinge auf den Boden?	--	.32	--	.39
39. Streitest Du viel mit anderen Kindern?	--	.32	--	.34
Factor 3: Psychosomatic problems and tiredness				
10. Bist Du oft den ganzen Tag müde?	--	--	.64	.48
25. Bist Du oft ohne Grund müde?	--	--	.57	.47
46. Stehst Du am Morgen schwer auf?	--	--	.54	.42
38. Bist Du öfter müde als Deine Mitschüler	--	--	.52	.48
45. Kannst Du manchmal nur sehr schwer einschlafen?	--	--	.51	.46
26. Hast Du oft Bauchweh?	--	--	.49	.41
53. Bleibst Du am liebsten den ganzen Tag im Bett?	--	--	.47	.33
47. Bist Du oft zum Spielen zu müde?	--	--	.46	.42
1. Bist Du morgens meistens gut ausgeschlafen? [2)]	--	.27	.46	.41
28. Fühlst Du Dich oft krank?	.28	--	.41	.45
9. Hast Du oft Kopfschmerzen?	--	--	.39	.35
22. Wachst Du in der Nacht oft auf?	--	--	.37	.39
7. Schläfst Du in der Nacht immer sehr gut? [2)]	--	--	.37	.34
8. Hast Du manchmal schreckliche Träume?	--	--	.35	.38

1) Loadings less than .25 have been blanked out
2) Scoring of item reversed

The item analysis was based on the 1175 questionnaires (81%) which had been completed by the subjects without any missing data. The process of item selection was as follows:

In a first step a principal components analysis of all 107 items was performed. The number of factors was determined by means of Cattells scree test (see Cattell 1988). Four factors were extracted, three of which were easily interpretable: (1) depressed mood and low self-esteem, (2) agitated behaviour and problems of norm-integration and (3) psychosomatic problems and tiredness.

The fourth factor was a combined item difficulty and response set factor in which items having very low response rates were grouped together with nearly all items with reversed scoring. We dealt with the problems imposed by this fourth factor in the most radical and effective way by simply eliminating all its 12 items together with further 21 items that had low factor loadings after an oblique (oblimin) rotation. The analysis of the remaining 74 items was repeated in the same way by principal components analysis, Scree-Test and oblimin rotation. As expected, the already mentioned three factors were extracted again.

For the last step of item selection the corrected item-total correlations were computed for all questions (whereby "total" refers to the subscore of the scale the item belongs to). Three items were deleted because of their low item-total correlations. Further 10 items were eliminated in order to reduce redundancy of questions (there were for instance no less than 12 variations of the question "Are you sad?" in the pool of items). Four questions containing the words "parents" and "fear" were eliminated in order to secure the applicability of the test to parentless children and in order to avoid artefactual correlations with scales measuring anxiety and phobia. At last one item of the first factor was removed, because it represented the only "masked" symptom of depression in that scale and another was removed, because its formulation appeared to be too childish compared with the rest of the selected items. The resulting pattern is shown in Table 3.

RESULTS

The items were empirically grouped in three correlating scales: (1) depressed mood and low self-esteem, (2) agitated behaviour and problems of norm-integration and (3) psychosomatic problems and tiredness. As it was expected, the correlations of the three scales are relatively high (the correlation between subscales one and three was as high as .60, the other two coefficients were about .50). Internal consistency of the three scales was estimated satisfactorily with Alphas of .89, .82 and .79 respectively. (These first estimates of reliability were computed from the analysis sample data and are therefore likely to be slightly overestimated.)

The division of the pool of symptoms into three correlated but separate areas seems to have one major advantage. In contrast to unifactorial tests where all the heterogeneous symptoms are combined in only one total score our three scales provide a greater chance to reveal sex specific differences. In our sample girls, regardless of their age, had higher average scores in the dysphoria subscale, while boys tended to score higher in agitated behaviour. No sex differences were found in the third subscale. There were also some indications for age effects, in the sense that sixth graders had higher average scores than the younger children in both the subscales one and two.

Further information on aspects of validity and independent estimates of reliability of our questionnaire are not yet available but will soon be prepared. New data of a large Austrian norm sample have already been collected and will be processed during the next months. However, information on the clinical applicability of the questionnaire has still to be waited for.

DISCUSSION

Our empirically developed scale contains most items of the Weinberg et al. (1973) list of symptoms though they are embedded in a completely different methodological concept. Though the origins and the goals of the two assessment methods are clearly different, we have the impression that the concepts behind them are beginning to converge in some respects. We hope that the presented results can be seen as a further indication that the definition of a depressive syndrome in childhood is making some empirical sense.

However, a comparison between psychiatric symptom lists and psychological questionnaire data can only be made with great caution because of the differences that still exist between psychiatric and psychological concepts concerning the definition and the assessment of psychopathology.

The psychiatric approach is still characterized by expert defined syndromes with an *a priori* selection of symptoms. The symptoms are then described with regard to severity and duration thresholds in order to allow the formulation of a diagnosis, which means categorial assessment of a person's psychopathology. Diagnostic decisions are typically based on psychiatric interviews and expert ratings. One should not forget that even DSM-III is still the result of expert discussion in classificatory committees rather than the result of empirical studies. Of course that issue is by no means new and has already been discussed extensively more than a decade ago (e.g. Kendell 1975), but the discussion so far has not had a real and visible impact on scientific work in this area. Psychiatrists continued to define *a priori* the disorders of their interest instead of trying to empirically cluster together those psychopathological signs that apparently belong together. However, the advantage of operationally based classification systems like DSM-III is that the issue is raised as an empirical question, once the definition of disorders has been made.

Psychology in contrast has since its early years devoted a good deal of its efforts to the development of psychometrically based self-rating instruments. In

Psychology in contrast has since its early years devoted a good deal of its efforts to the development of psychometrically based self-rating instruments. In doing this, psychologists have adopted a completely different approach to the description of psychopathological phenomena, namely dimensional instead of categorial description. In this approach departures from "normal" are typically delineated on the basis of the deviation of a particular person's testscore from the statistical average in a reference group.

It should be stressed here for the sake of clearness, that because of these profound differences between the categorial diagnosis of depressive disorder and the dimensional assessment of the severity of depressive symptoms one assessment method is not necessarily the criterion for the other. However, signs of convergence are clearly encouraging for both sides.

REFERENCES

American Psychiatric Association (1987) *Diagnostic and statistical manual of mental disorders*. Third edition revised (DSM-III-R). Washington DC:

Cantwell, D. P. (1983) Depression in childhood: Clinical picture and diagnostic criteria. In: Cantwell, D. P., Carlson, G. A. (Eds.) *Affective disorders in childhood and adolescence: An update,* pp. 3-18, Jamaica, NY: Spectrum Publications.

Carlson, G. A., Cantwell, D. P. (1980) Unmasking masked depression in children and adolescents. *American Journal of Psychiatry, 137*, 445-449.

Carlson, G. A., Cantwell, D. P. (1982) Diagnosis of childhood depression: A comparison of Weinberg and DSM-III criteria. *Journal of the American Academy of Child Psychiatry, 21,* 247-250.

Cattell, R. B. (1988) The meaning and strategic use of factor analysis. In: Nesselroade, J. R., Cattell, R. B. (Eds.) *Handbook of multivariate experimental psychology*. Second edition, pp. 131-203, New York: Plenum.

Cytryn, L., McKnew, D. H. (1972) Proposed classification of childhood depression. *American Journal of Psychiatry, 129*, 149-155.

Glaser, K. (1968) Masked depression in children and adolescents. *Annual Progress in Child Psychiatry and Child Development, 1*, 345-355.

Harper, J., Kelly, E. M. (1985) Antisocial behaviour as a mask for depression in year 5 and 6 boys. *Mental Health in Australia, 1*,(14) 14-19.

Kazdin, A. E. (1988) Childhood depression. In: Witt, J. C., Elliot, S. N., Gresham, F. M. (Eds.) *Handbook of behavior therapy in education*, pp. 739-772, New York: Plenum.

Kendell, R. E. (1975) *The role of diagnosis in psychiatry*. Oxford: Blackwell

Kolvin, I., Berney, T. P., Bhate, S. R. (1984) Classification and diagnosis of depression in school phobia. *British Journal of Psychiatry, 145*, 347-357.

Rie, H. E. (1966) Depression in childhood. A survey of some pertinent contributions. *Journal of the American Academy of Child Psychiatry, 5*, 653-685.

Rochlin, G. (1959) The loss complex: A contribution to the etiology of depression. *Journal of the American Psychoanalytical Association, 7*, 299-316.

Vermilyea, J. A., Heimberg, R. G., Silverman, W. K. (1985) Selected issues in the study of childhood depression. In: Dean, A. (Ed.) *Depression in multidisciplinary perspective*, pp. 118-144, New York: Brunner/Mazel.

Weinberg, W. A., Rutman, J., Sullivan, L., Penick, E. C., Dietz, S. G. (1973) Depression in children referred to an educational diagnostic center: Diagnosis and treatment. *Journal of Pediatrics 83*, 1065-1072.

LATERALITY RESEARCH ON AFFECTIVE DISORDERS: SOME REMARKS ON THEORY, SYMPTOMS, AND THERAPY

G.H. Schulter

Department of Neuropsychology, Institute of Psychology, University of Graz, Austria

In research on psychopathology a lot of work has concentrated on the biological and neurochemical bases of the various mental disorders. Despite of the progress made, however, there is still much confusion, especially with respect to affective illness (Rothschild, 1988; Janowsy et al., 1988): the first and most prominent hypothesis stated that some, if not all, depressions are associated with a deficiency of catecholamines, particularly noradrenaline; and that elation, conversely, may be associated with an excess of such amines (Schildkraut, 1965). This notion, however, is not fully supported by existing data, and the same is true for the idea that reduced serotonin alone (Coppen et al., 1965), or in interaction with abnormalities in central noradrenergic transmission could lead to the emergence of depressive or manic episodes (the so-called 'permissive hypothesis'; Prange et al., 1974).

Reduced dopamine activity is also assumed to be involved in depression (Depue & Iacono, 1989), particularly in motor retardation (Van Praag & Korf, 1971), while increased dopaminergic transmission might be associated with mania (Randrup et al., 1975; Carney et al., 1989).

Furthermore, the central cholinergic system also is supposed to be related to affective illness: an imbalance, i.e. a relative predominance of cholinergic or adrenergic neurotransmitter activity is assumed to result in depressive or manic states, respectively (Janowsky et al., 1988). Additionally, even GABA-ergic theories of affective disorders have been proposed recently (Berrettini & Post, 1984).

This diversity of hypotheses with certain empirical evidence for each of the models proposed should have some impact on theorizing and research methodology itself:

The need for and the progress in establishing common diagnostic criteria has - beside its clear advantage as a common reference - several shortcomings. Each of the general diagnostic categories of affective disorders includes patients with a variety of different symptoms, i.e. different symptom patterns, for instance in major depression. Of course, there are some basic symptoms seen in almost all cases, namely a 'depressed mood' and a (severe) 'loss of interest'; the presence of at least one of them is defined by DSM-III-R as a necessary condition for the diagnosis of an episode of major depression. But even with these two fundamental symptoms there are, for instance, 3 and 7% of female and male patients without (at least mild) signs of 'depressed mood', as is shown in a recent study by Hamilton (1989). The same is true to a much greater extent with respect to any other symptom constituting the diagnosis of major depression; more than that, some inclusive criteria relate to deviations in different directions, for instance, insomnia or increased sleep, weight loss or a gain in weight, motor retardation or agitation, a symptom which seems especially important for the neurobiochemical differentiation of possible subtypes within the broad category of major depression. Furthermore, the presence or absence of anxiety is most likely an additionally important differentiating aspect of the disease.

That is to say that classifying patients according to DSM-III-R, for instance, with respect to a general diagnostic category like 'major depression' may be - at least partially - responsible for the inconsistencies in biochemical and psychological models of depression. Therefore, research activities should focus to a greater extent on identifying symptom patterns within a general category - within the category of major depression, for instance. Such an identification of subdimensions, factors, or axes should be approached not solely on a pure empirical basis, by factor analysis, for instance, but should be guided by what is already known about behavioral concomitants of certain biochemical subsystems (the Noradrenalin- or the Dopamine-System, for example), or what is known about the functionality of the two cerebral hemispheres, seen as large subsystems of the brain.

Let me illustrate this idea with reference to laterality research: Differences between the hemispheres in response to, or in contribution to, emotional states have been inferred from a number of observations - in normal subjects (Smith et al., 1987) and in patients with cerebral vascular disease, for instance (Starkstein & Robinson, 1989) - indicating that right hemisphere activity is stronger associated with emotional states or expressions, especially negative ones, while the left hemisphere - if at all - seems to be rather involved in the processing of positive affect.

In addition to these findings patients with affective disorders have been shown to differ from normal or schizophrenic patients with respect to hemispheric asymmetry:

Several studies analyzing EEG power spectra (Flor-Henry, 1976), electrodermal activity (Myslobodsky & Horesh, 1978), and lateral eye movements (Myslobodsky & Horesh, 1978) first led to the idea that depressive symptomatology may be correlated with a dysfunction of the non-dominant hemisphere. Since then, a lot of work has focussed on this issue; for instance, in dichotic listening tasks using musical tones or click stimuli which normally yield a left-ear advantage reflecting right-hemisphere dominance for processing nonverbal dichotic stimuli groups of depressed patients have failed to show the left-ear, i.e. right-hemisphere advantage seen for normal controls (Berger-Gross et al:, 1985; Johnson & Crockett, 1982; Yozawitz et al., 1979).

Similar but less consistent results concerning perceptual asymmetries for words and nonsense syllables indicate an abnormally large right-ear advantage in bipolar disorders with manic features (Yozawitz et al., 1979) and no right-ear advantage in patients having unipolar depressive disorder (Johnson & Crockett, 1982). In a very recent study such differences in perceptual asymmetries, compared to normal controls, have been shown among different diagnostic subtypes of depressive disorder. Using dichotic and visual halffield presentation, the authors were able to demonstrate differences in lateral asymmetry among major depressives with and without melancholia and among bipolar and unipolar depression (Bruder et al., 1989).

Essentially, then, laterality research has supported the usefulness of hemispheric specialization as a theoretical model for studying psychopathology; the details, however, require a lot of further clarifications. And there is again good reason to assume that a lot of inconsistencies and negative results in laterality research on affective disorders may be attributed to the diagnostic process, i.e. to the choice of and restriction to general diagnostic categories. Let me illustrate this by a first example: Perris and co-workers (Monakhov et al., 1979; Perris et al., 1978) did not find any differences in EEG characteristics between two groups of depressed patients classified as 'endogenous' or 'reactive'. However, when they divided the whole group (by means of clinical ratings) into subsamples with high or low 'anxiety-depression' scores and, in a similar way, into groups with high or low 'retardation' scores,they observed marked EEG differences concerning the activity between and within the hemispheres, i.e. between anterior and posterior leads. And furthermore, these same authors could demonstrate marked differences in hemispheric asymmetry by correlating EEG variables with type and extent of single symptoms in depressed patients (Monakhov & Perris, 1980). Such results give support to the notion that not taking into account the different symptomatological components of a syndrome may provide no or only very crude information on the issue (Perris, 1988. Or, as Gruzelier (1981) concluded in a critical review on fact and fiction in research on cerebral laterality and psychopathology, greater clarity may arise in using single symptoms rather than diagnostic categories.

Perris and co-workers had their patients divided by symptoms and sought for different EEG patterns; even more important - both as support for the validity and usefulness of the laterality model and from a methodological point of view - is a very recent approach which first divided patients by laterality tests and then looked for differences in symptoms and other biological parameters. This study done by Wexler and co-workers (Wexler et al., 1989) used two language-related dichotic listening tests of cerebral laterality, i.e. a word test and a test made of nonsense syllables. With these measures opposite changes relating to the course and recovery of major depression have been shown in previous studies (Wexler & Heninger, 1979; Wexler, 1986). The patient sample analyzed was a very heterogeneous mixture of diagnostic categories, i.e. major depression, bipolar manic and schizoaffective disorder. Furthermore, about half of the patients were not receiving any medication at time of testing. Despite this multiple heterogeneity laterality testing resulted in two equivalent patient subsamples (as diagnosis and medication was concerned) with high and low scores in a combined laterality variable. Additionally, testosterone level and severity of several clinical symptoms were assessed and intercorrelated separately within each laterality group; very remarkably, these correlations differed significantly between laterality groups, i.e. symptom severity was positively or negatively related to testosterone level depending on type and extension of laterality.

Beside the lack of replication and yet insufficient elaboration of or integration in a theoretical framework this study may initiate important new research activities in differentiating symptom patterns and disease subtypes on the basis of neuropsychological testing, especially by the assessment of distinct laterality patterns. This may be of special importance for both theory refinement and an increase in treatment efficiency, an approach which might be similar to the development and application of light therapy where a certain subtype of affective disorder has been identified, seen as a disturbance of seasonal and/or circadian rhythm, and, consequently, is treated by the special use of bright light under a special time schedule.

A first and yet crude consequence of laterality research is reflected in the use of unilateral electroconvulsive therapy in affective disorder, with available evidence for greater therapeutic effects of ECT to the right hemisphere in depression (Malitz & Sackeim, 1982) and with the presumption of both-sided or only left-sided ECT in mania (Small et al., 1984). And further support of the relevance of the laterality model for clinical problems and therapeutic approaches may be seen in the following: there is increasing evidence suggesting lateralization in neurobiochemical systems on cortical and subcortical levels (Mandell & Knapp, 1979; Oke et al., 1978; Wagner et al., 1983; Glick et al., 1982)

Further there is indication that alteration in laterality patterns are concomitant with the course and recovery of psychiatric illness (Wexler, 1986; Brumback et al., 1980), but also with mood alterations in normal subjects (Tucker et al., 1981).

This various pieces of evidence give some support to the idea that hemispheric asymmetry may be affected in a different way by different somatic intervention procedures, i.e. ECT on the left or right side of the brain, neuroleptics versus antidepressants, physical exercise versus meditation, for instance, but also by the application of different types of cognitive behavior therapy: a first test of this later idea was already done by Tucker and co-workers (Tucker et al., 1977; Tucker & Newman, 1981); the rationale is that some cognitive behavior therapy methods focus on verbal cognition and others place more emphasis upon (visual) imagery. These two modes of cognition are represented differently in the brain and, furthermore, individuals differ with respect to their lateral preference, i.e. a tendency for a person to rely more on one hemisphere than the other - a further and important aspect of laterality which was denoted as 'hemisphericity' by Bogen and co-workers (Bogen et al., 1972). Therefore, an interaction of therapeutic method and patients lateral preference should be existent; and exactly this was suggested by the studies cited above, i.e. treatment (of speech-anxious subjects) was most effective if it employed cognition of the subjects non-preferred hemisphere.

And if one considers that cognitive-behavioral approaches to the treatment of depression have been evaluated to be equally or even more efficient than pharmacotherapy (Dobson, 1989), then this interaction of individual laterality and type of therapeutical method might be of great importance in striving for a further increase in treatment efficiency.

Let me conclude with a short remark on what seems to me the most prominent goals in future clinical research, especially on affective disorders:

The first goal is a further elaboration of diagnostic methods and categories on a theory-oriented neuropsychological basis; and the second is the investigation of criteria for a differential application of the various treatment methods.

In my opinion, the findings of laterality research may contribute to these goals.

REFERENCES

Berger-Gross, P., Bruder, G.E., Quitkin, F., Goetz, R. (1985) Auditory laterality in depression: Relation to circadian patterns and EEG sleep. *Biological Psychiatry, 20*, 611-622.

Berrettini, W.H., Post, R.M. (1984) GABA in affective illness. In R. M Post & J. C. Ballenger (Eds.), *Neurobiology of mood disorders*. Baltimore/London: Williams & Wilkins.

Bogen, J.E., Dezure, R., Tenhouten, W.D., Marsh, J.F. (1972) The other side of the brain: IV. The A/P ratio. *Bulletin of the Los Angeles Neurological Societies, 37/2*, 49-61.

Bruder, G.E., Quitkin, F.M., Stewart, J.W., Martin, C., Voglmeier, M.M., Harrison, W.M. (1989) Cerebral laterality and depression differences in perceptual asymmetry among diagnostic subtypes. *Journal of Abnormal Psychology, 98/2*, 177-186.

Brumback, R.A., Staton, R.D. Wilson, H. (1980) Neuropsychological study of children during and after remission of endogenous depressive episodes. *Perceptual and Motor Skills, 50*, 1163-116.

Carney, M.W.P., Chary, T.K.N., Bottoglieri, T., Reynolds, E.H. (1989) The switch mechanism and the bipolar/unipolar dichotomy. *British Journal of Psychiatry, 154*, 48-51.

Coppen, A., Shaw, D.M., Malleson, A., Eccleston, E., Gundy, G. (1965) Tryptamine metabolism in depression. *British Journal of Psychiatry, 111*, 993-998.

Depue, R.A., Iacono, W.G. (1989) Neurobehavioral aspects of affective disorder. *Annual Review of Psychology, 40*, 457-492.

Dobson, K.S. (1989) A meta-analysis of the efficacy of cognitive therapy for depression. *Journal of Consulting and Clinical Psychology, 57/3*, 414-419.

Flor-Henry, P. (1976) Lateralized temporal-limbic dysfunction and psychopathology. *Annals of the New York Academy of Sciences, 280*, 777-795.

Glick, S.D., Ross, D.A., Hough, L.B. (1982) Lateral asymmetry of neurotransmitters in human brain. *Brain Research, 234*, 53-63.

Gruzelier, J.H. (1981) Cerebral laterality and psychopathology: Fact and fiction. *Psychological Medicine, 11*, 219-227.

Hamilton, M. (1989) Frequency of symptoms in melancholia (depressive illness). *British Journal of Psychiatry, 154*, 201-206.

Janowky, D.S., Golden, R.N., Rapaport, M., Cain, J.J., Gillin, J.C. (1988) Neurochemistry of depression and mania. In: Georgotas,A. & Cancro,R. (Eds). *Depression and Mania*. New York: Elsevier, 244-264.

Johnson, O., Crockett, D. (1982) Changes in perceptual asymmetries with clinical improvement of depression and schizophrenia. *Journal of Abnormal Psychology, 91/1*, 45-54.

Malitz, S., Sackeim, H. (1982) ECT in the treatment of major affectiv disorders: Clinical and basic research issues. *Psychiatric Journal of the University of Ottawa, 7*, 126-134.

Mandell, A.J., Knapp, S. (1979) Asymmetry and mood, emergent properties of serotonin regulation. *Archives of General Psychiatry, 36*, 909-916.

Monakhov, K., Perris, C., Botskarev, V.K., Knorring, L.von, Nikiforov,A.I. (1979) Functional interhemispheric differences in relation to various psychopathological components of the depressive syndromes. *Neuropsychobiology, 5*, 143-155.

Monakhov, K.K., Perris, C. (1980) Neurophysiological correlates of depressive symptomatology. *Neuropsychobiology, 6*, 268-279.

Myslobodsky, M.S., Horesh, N. (1978) Bilateral electrodermal activity in depressive patients. *Biological Psychology, 6*, 111-120.

Oke, A., Keller, R., Mefford, I., Adams, R. (1978) Lateralization of norepinephrine in human thalamus. *Science, 200*, 1411-141.

Perris, C. (1988) Neurophysiological and neuroanatomical studies of depression and mania. In: Georgotas,A. & Cancro,R. (Eds). *Depression and Mania*. New York: Elsevier, 213-243.

Perris, C., Monakhov, K., Knorring, L.von, Boskarev,V., Nikiforov, A. (1978) Systemic structural analysis of the electroencephalogram of depressed patients. *Neuropsychobiology, 4*, 207-228.

Prange, A.J., Wilson, I.C., Lynn, C.W., Alltop, L.B., Stikeleather, R.A. (1974) L-Tryptophan in mania contribution to a permissive hypothesis of affective disorders. *Archives of General Psychiatry, 30*, 56-62.

Randrup, A., Munkvad, J., Fog, R., Gerlach, J., Molander, L., Kjellberg, B., Scheel, Kruger, J. (1975). Mania, depression, and brain dopamine. In W. Essman & L. Valzelli (Eds.), *Current developments in psychopharmacology* (Vol. 2, pp. 206-248). New York: Spectrum.

Rothschild, A.J. (1988) Biology of depression. *Medical Clinics of North America, 72/4*, 765-790.

Schildkraut, J.J. (1965) The catecholamine hypothesis of affective disorders: A review of supporting evidence. *American Journal of Psychiatry, 122*, 509-522.

Small, J., Small, I., Milstein, V., Kellams, J., Klapper, M. (1984) Manic symptoms: An indication for bilateral ECT. *Biological Psychiatry, 20*, 125-134.

Smith, B.D., Meyers, M., Kline, R., Bozman, A. (1987) Hemispheric asymmetry and emotion: Lateralized parietal processing of affect and cognition. *Biological Psychology, 25*, 247-260.

Starkstein, S.E., Robinson, R.G. (1989) Affective disorders and cerebral vascular disease. *British Journal of Psychiatry, 154*, 170-182.

Tucker, D.M., Newman, J.P. (1981) Verbal versus imaginal cognitive strategies in the inhibition of emotional arousal. *Cognitive Therapy and Research, 5*, 197-202.

Tucker, D.M., Shearer, S.L., Murray, J.D. (1977) Hemispheric specialization and cognitive behavior therapy. *Cognitive Therapy and Research, 1/4*, 263-272.

Tucker, D.M., Stenslie, C.E., Roth, R.S., Shearer, S. (1981) Right frontal lobe activation and right hemisphere performance decrement during a depressed mood. *Archives of General Psychiatry, 38*, 169-174.

Van Praag, H.M., Korf, J. (1971) Retarded depression and the dopamine metabolism. *Psychopharmacology, 19*, 190-203.

Wagner, H.N., Burns, D.H., Dannals, R.F., Wong, D., Langstrom, B., Duelfer, T., Frost, J., Ravert, H., Links, J., Rosenbloom, S., Lukas, S., Kramer, A. (1983) Imaging dopamine receptors in the human brain by positron tomography. *Science, 221*, 1264-126.

Wexler, B.E. (1986) Alterations in cerebral laterality during acute psychotic illness. *The British Journal of Psychiatry, 149*, 202-209.

Wexler, B.E., Heninger, G.R. (1979) Alterations in cerebral laterality during acute psychotic illness. *Archives of General Psychiatry, 36*, 278-284.

Wexler, B.E., Mason, J.W., Giller, E.L. (1989) Possible subtypes of affective disorder suggested by differences in cerebral laterality andtestosterone: a preliminary report. *Archives of General Psychiatry, 46/5*, 429-436.

Yozawitz, A., Bruder, G., Sutton, S., Sharpe, L., Gurland, B., Fleiss, J., Costa, L. (1979) Dichotic perception: Evidence for right hemisphere dysfunction in affective psychosis. *The British Journal of Psychiatry, 135*, 224-237.

MARRIAGE AND DEPRESSION: A PRELIMINARY DESCRIPTION OF SPOUSES' PERSONALITY TRAITS (CORRELATIONAL ANALYSIS)

T.L. Tyra and L. Wandzel

Department of Psychiatry, Medical School, Bialystok, Poland

Many reports have dealt with various aspects of the relationship between depression and marital satisfaction (Briscoe, 1973; Gove, 1973; Hinchliffe, 1987; Weissman, 1971). One of the most comprehensive studies was made by Brown and co-workers (1978) who noted that a lack of a close, intimate relation with the partner is one of the main social factors responsible for depression.

In their investigations, Roberts and Hooper (1969) found that the spouses of depressed patients presented a number of abnormalities in their behaviour. Most of the papers describing the psychological characteristics and behaviour patterns concern chiefly depressed women and their husbands. The husbands of depressed women are described as dominating persons who use force and revenge more frequently and often react to their wives' problems with criticism and rejection (Birtchnell, 1983). At the same time, the spouses of the chronically depressed women describe themselves as being socially less attractive, more self-controlled and uncommunicative. This may indicate a relation between the uncommunicative and inhibited attitude of the spouse and an unfavourable course of the disease (Hell, 1982). On the other hand, men are more depressed if their wives are unfeeling, unprotective and unaffirmative (Birtchnell, 1983).

In the study presented here, we have analyzed the relationship between the personality traits and the behaviour patterns of the healthy spouses and the course of depression in their afflicted partners. This paper presents a preliminary evaluation of these relations and further studies are still being continued (Tyra, in press).

MATERIAL AND METHODS

30 married couples, in each of which one of the spouses had been hospitalized for neurotic depressive syndrome (ICD-9), were studied. In one half of these couples, the wife was ill and in the other half, the husband. The mean age of the patients was 41.6 years and of their spouses was 41.1. The mean duration of marriage was 16.2 years. Each of the spouses completed the Adjective Check List (ACL) of H.G. Gough and A.B. Heilbrun (1960). Severity of depression was measured by the Zung Depression Scale (1974). The results of the study were statistically analyzed by the routine mathematical methods.

RESULTS

The patients examined did not present a high level of depressive symptoms (the mean results in Zung's Scale were about 50 points). Naturally the results of the healthy spouses are markedly lower (about 35 points). The results obtained by the Zung's Scale from the men and women suffering from depression showed no statistically significant differences either.

A significant relation in the group of depressed men and their healthy wives is presented in Table I. The relations were very strong though of differing character. The various types of relations are reflected in the positive or negative values of the correlation coefficients.

Table 1. **Statistically significant correlation coefficients in the group of depressed men and their wives**

Depressed men	Their wives	r
Depression /Zung/	Need of changes /Ch/	-0.67
Depression /Zung/	Self-control /Cn/	0.66
Counseling readiness /Cr/	Counseling readiness	0.60
Need of succourance /Su/	Submission /De/	-0.62
Need of succourance /Su/	Self-control /Cn/	-0.61
Need of succourance /Su/	Need of changes /Ch/	0.63
Need of dominance /Do/	Lability /La/	-0.63
Need of dominance /Do/	Self-control /Cn/	0.61
Need of affiliation /Af/	Self-control /Cn/	-0.60
Need of affiliation /Af/	Self-abasement /Ab/	0.67
Self-confidence /Cf/	Lability /La/	-0.72
Aggression /Ag/	Need of succourance	-0.73

Considerably more relations between personality traits of the spouses were noted in the group of couples where the wife suffered from depression. They are presented in Table 2.

DISCUSSION

A higher level of depressive symptoms and behaviour in men is often related to outwardly good functioning and adjustment, self-sufficiency and an unsubmissive attitude of their wives. Women, on the other hand, react with a higher level of depressive symptoms and behaviour in the face of submissive, passive, withdrawn and emotionally unstable behaviour of their husbands.

Table 2. **Statistically significant correlation coefficients in the group of depressed women and their husbands**

Depressed women	Their husbands	r
Depression /Zung/	Need of achievement /Ac/-0.63	
Depression /Zung/	Need of endurance /En/	-0.63
Depression /Zung/	Need of succourance /Su/ .062	
Depression /Zung/	Lability /La/	0.65
Unfavourable self-esteem /Uf/	Need of order /Or/	-0.64
Unfavourable self-esteem /Uf/	Need of achievement /Ac/	-0.60
Counseling readiness /Cr/	Need of achievement /Ac/	-0.76
Counseling readiness /Cr/	Self-abasement /Ab/	0.64
Self-abasement /Ab/	Lability /La/	0.66
Need of sucourance /Su/	Need of achievement /Ac/	-0.63
Need of sucourance /Su/	Lability /La/	0.65
Defensiveness /Df/	Need of achievement /Ac/	0.63
Self-control /Cn/	Submission /De/	-0.62
Self-control /Cn/	Favourable self-esteem	0.75
Self-control /Cn/	Need of achievement /Ac/	0.64
Self-control /Cn/	Need of affiliataion /Af/	0.69
Self-control /Cn/	Self-control /Cn/	0.65
Self-confidence /Cf/	Need of endurance /En/	0.67
Self-confidence /Cf/	Need of order /Or/	0.68
Need of achievement /Ac/	Need of order /Or/	0.77
Need of achievement /Ac/	Need of endurance /En/	0.69
Need of achievement /Ac/	Need of achievement /Ac/	0.61
Need of dominance /Do/	Need of endurance /En/	0.67
Need of dominance /Do/	Ned of order /Or/	0.73
Need of dominance /Do/	Need of achievement /Ac/	0.62
Need of affiliation /Af/	Need of achievement /Ac/	0.72
Need of affiliation /Af/	Need of endurance /En/	0.71
Need of affiliation /Af/	Need of order /Or/	0.67
Aggression /Ag/	Favourable self-esteem	-0.60
Aggression /Ag/	Depression /Zung/	0.67
Aggression /Ag/	Counseling readiness /Cr/	0.60
Need of nurturance /Nu/	Depression /Zung/	-0.62

We accept that there is no type of spouse of depressed persons. The constellations of personality traits and the needs of the partners in a marriage show that men with an overt need of submission married women with an inclination to dominance. At the same time, in the group of men studied a covert need of dominance (possibly, it is related to a social stereotype of man's role) was observed. As regards needs, the opposite was often found to be characteristic of the partners of the male patients investigated (an evident need to dominate with a covert need to be cared for and submission). The overt needs in such a marriage can be satisfied and it is possible that they are factors which reinforce the marriage ties. At the same time, the covert needs of both partners are constantly frustrated. Frustration in the wife is the source of her negative attitude to her husband whereas he is double frustrated by 1) the unsatisfied covert need of dominance, 2) the negative emotions of his frustrated wife. Over a long period of time, this frustration may lead to the onset of depression.

In the case of women suffering from depression, it can be assumed that in choosing a partner they preferred rather weak persons with traits analogical to their own. In their case, only the covert need of dominance is satisfied, whereas the overt need of dependence is constantly frustrated. Here again, such a relationship must in time lead to the onset of depression.

It should be emphasized that the dynamisms presented here, although drawn from the results of the study, should be treated as a working hypotheses in view of the comparatively small number of observations made. They do, however allow us to accept the concept of a specific choice of partner in keeping with the structure of their needs whereas the interaction leading to depression is, as it were, secondary in view of the relationship of the partners originally existing. These investigations are still being continued and the increasing number of observations have confirmed the hypothetical dynamisms.

CONCLUSIONS

1. An analysis of the results indicates a relation between the severity of the depressive symptoms and behaviour of the ill person and the personality traits and behaviour patterns of the healthy spouse.
2. The relation observed permits the formulation of the following hypotheses:

a) There is no type of personality of the spouse which leads to depression in the other partner.

b) The occurrence of depression in one of the spouses is the effect of long term frustration of needs which in the early stage of marriage may have drawn partners together and united them.

c) Depression mainly arose from frustration of a need of dominance and dependence and the differences in this psychodynamism in women as compared with men may be a reflection of the social image of their roles.

REFERENCES

Birtchnell, J., Kennard, J. (1983) Marriage and mental illness. *British Journal of Psychiatry, 142,* 193-198.

Briscoe, C.W., Smith, J.B. (1973) Depression and marital turmoil. *Archives of General Psychiatry, 29,* 811-817.

Brown, G.W., Harris, T. (1978) *Social Origins of Depression: A Study of Psychiatric Disorder in Women.* New York: Free Press.

Gough, H.G. (1960) The Adjective Check List as a personality assessment research technique. *Psychological Reports, 6,* 100-122.

Gove, W.R., Tudor, J.F. (1973) Adult sex roles and mental illness. *American Journal of Sociology, 78,* 812-835.

Hell, D.(1982) The spouses of depressive and schizophrenic patients. *Archives für Psychiatrie und Nervenkrankheiten, 232,* 167-178.

Hinchliffe, M.K., Hooper, D., Roberts, F.J. (1987) *Melancholia Malzenska.* Warszawa: PWN.

Roberts, F.J., Hooper, D. (1969) The natural history of attempted suicide in Bristol. *British Journal of Medical Psychology, 42,* 303-312.

Tyra, T.L. Zwiazek cech osobowosci malzonkow w parach z partnerem depresyjnym. *Psychiatria Polska* (in press).

Vanfossen, B.E. (1981) Sex differences in the mental health effects of spouse support and equity. *Journal of Health and Social Behaviour, 22,* 130-143.

Weissman, M., Klerman, G.L., Paykel, E.S. (1971) Clinical evaluation of hostility in depression. *American Journal of Psychiatry, 128,* 41-46.

Zung, W.W.K. (1974) The measurement of affects: Depression and anxiety. *Modern Problems of Pharmacopsychiatry, 7,* 170-188.

PART III:

PROGRESS IN RESEARCH ON ANXIETY AND OBSESSIVE-COMPULSIVE DISORDER

COGNITIVE AND EXPOSURE INGREDIENTS IN THE TREATMENT OF PANIC DISORDER WITH AGORAPHOBIA: PRELIMINARY RESULTS

T. K. Bouman and P. M. G. Emmelkamp

Department of Clinical Psychology, University of Groningen, Oostersingel 59, 9713 EZ Groningen, The Netherlands

Behaviour therapy has a longstanding tradition in the treatment of phobic avoidance. Exposure in vivo is considered by many to be the treatment of choice for this group of disorders.

Table 1. **Studies comparing exposure and cognitive interventions in agoraphobia**

	n	Conditions	Results
Emmelkamp et al. (1978)*	20	(1)Exposure - Cognitive	
			Exp>Cogn
		(2)Cognitive - Exposure	
Emmelkamp & Mersch (1982)	27	(1)Exposure	(1=3)>2
		(2)RET + SIT**	
		(3)SIT + Exposure**	
Emmelkamp et al. (1986)*	39	(1)Exposure - Exposure	
			Exp>Cogn
		(2)RET - Exposure	
		(3)SIT - Exposure	
Marchione et al. (1987)	14	(1)Exposure	(2=3)>1
		(2)Cognitive+ Exposure**	
		(3)Relaxation+ Exposure**	
Mavissakalian et al. (1983)	24	(1)PI + Exposure**	1=2
		(2)SIT + Exposure**	
Michelson et al. (1988)	73	(1)Exposure	1=2=3
		(2)PI + Exposure**	
		(3)Relaxation + Exposure**	
Williams & Rappoport (1983)	20	(1)Exposure	1=2
		(2)SIT + Exposure**	

Note: RET: Rational Emotive Therapy; SIT: Self Instructional training; PI: Paradoxical Intention.
*: *Cross-over design;* **: *Combined treatment*

On the other hand, the effectiveness of cognitive therapy with agoraphobic Patients is still a controversial issue.

A number of researchers compared the effectiveness of exposure in vivo with one or more cognitive therapies, such as Rational Emotive Therapy (RET), Self-Instructional Training (SIT), or Paradoxical Intention (PI).

Generally, the results of the outcome studies are in favour of the exposure condition, as is shown in Table 1. Even studies using a large number of agoraphobics do not show that cognitive therapy enhances the effects of exposure in vivo.

Definite conclusions as to the specific effects of cognitive procedures are precluded, because exposure elements are included in many so called "cognitive" therapies.

Two recent developments have stimulated new studies into the feasibility of cognitive treatment of agoraphobia. One is the diagnostic reformulation of agoraphobia as part of the Panic Disorder, as it took place in the third revised version of the Diagnostic and Statistical Manual of Mental Disorders (DSM-III-R, APA, 1987).

Secondly, a cognitive model of panic as proposed by Clark and his colleagues in Oxford (Clark, 1986; Clark et al., 1985) states that panic is produced by catastrophic misinterpretations of relatively harmless autonomic bodily sensations, e.g., caused by hyperventilation. Other authors have also reported on the synergistic interaction between hyperventilation and fear (Ley, 1985; Rapee, 1987). A vicious circle between physiological arousal and anxiety is postulated that leads to a full-blown panic attack (e.g., Margraf, et al., 1986).

The treatment of panic attacks proposed by Clark and his colleagues consists of several elements, notably the demonstration and discussion of the way hyperventilation induces panic symptoms, subsequent breathing exercises, the relabeling of bodily symptoms as non-catastrophic, and also behavioural experiments to help patients test and disconfirm their catastrophic beliefs. This package produced a substantial and rapid reduction in panic attacks in several uncontrolled studies (e.g. Clark et al., 1985). Because various cognitive and behavioural techniques are used simultaneously, however, it is difficult to pin-point the active ingredients in this approach. It remains unclear to what extent either cognitive or behavioural elements are responsible for therapeutic improvement.

For instance, there may be other specific behavioural techniques that are beneficial in treating panic disorder with agoraphobia, as was shown by Bonn et al. (1984). They used exposure in vivo alone and in combination with respiratory control treatment. No significant differences were found immediately after treatment. At 6 month follow-up, however, a significant difference emerged in favour of the combined group. Their results show that breathing exercise without cognitive interventions may have something to offer to these patients.

The cognitive treatment model has been largely tested on panic patients without too much avoidance. In addition, it is of theoretical and practical interest to know what the cognitive approach offers panic patients with agoraphobia.

Therefore, the aim of the present outcome-study is to systematically vary the relevant therapeutic ingredients (i.e. breathing exercise, cognitive therapy, and exposure). We do not intend to evaluate the ultimate treatment for these patients, rather we attempt to unravel the treatment package of Clark in its essential components.

MATERIAL AND METHOD

Patients

Patients were randomly assigned to one of the four treatment conditions mentioned below if a Dutch abbreviated version of the Anxiety Disorder Interview Schedule (ADIS, DiNardo et al., 1983) yielded the primary diagnosis of Panic disorder with agoraphobia. In addition, the patients' score at intake had to exceed 16 on the Agoraphobia scale of the Fear Questionnaire (Marks & Mathews, 1979), and exceed 23 on a Hyperventilation Syndrome scale (Garssen et al., 1983).

All patients had moderate to severe panic disorder with agoraphobia, implying that they had a considerably restricted life-style, and that they had experienced more than three panic attacks in the month preceding the intake interview. It should be noted that we also included patients who were free of attacks during the four week pre-treatment baseline period. Excluding them from our study would in fact inflate our results. Exclusion criteria were among others the use of tricyclics, previous behaviour therapy and other prominent Axis I pathology. Written informed consent was obtained in all cases.

Table 2. **Patients' characteristics in four treatment conditions**

	B (n=7)	BC (n=6)	BCE (n=6)	E (n=8)	Test
Sex (F / M)	6 / 1	3 / 3	5 / 1	8/0	X =5.86*
Mean age	30.3	33.0	36.8	30.7	X =3.14**
Mean duration of complaints (months)	21.7	16.2	62.0	52.5	X =3.83**
# Patients with previous treatment	3	4	4	5	X =2.10*
# Patients using minor tranquillizers	3	2	5	4	X =10.90*

*Note. B: Breathing exercises; BC: Breathing exercises plus cognitive therapy; BCE: Breathing exercises plus cognitive therapy and exposure in vivo; E: Exposure in vivo. *: X -test with df = 3; **: Kruskal-Wallis one-way ANOVA, corrected for ties. No significant differences were found between treatment conditions.*

Table 2 shows biographical and clinical characteristics of the patients in our preliminary report.

A total of 22 women and 5 men participated in our study so far, with a mean age of 32.5 years (SD = 10.1); mean duration of complaints was 38 months (median 24 months).

Treatment conditions did not differ significantly on any of these biographical or clinical variables. Patients using minor tranquillizers were instructed to take medication at predetermined hours in order to make its use time-contingent.

DESIGN

An ABA-design was applied with equally long periods of four weeks each. The first period of four weeks is the pretreatment baseline, with treatment itself consisting of eight one-hour sessions over four weeks. Finally, a posttreatment base-line of four weeks was observed. During these twelve weeks patients kept panic diaries and on four occasions (T1, Tg, T3, and T4 with four weeks apart) various clinical measures were taken.

Treatment conditions

The therapeutic agents are grouped into four treatment packages:

1) Breathing exercises (B). This approach consisted of regular hyperventilation provocations and breathing training. The latter was given on audiotape as daily homework. An explicit non-exposure instruction was given.
2) Breathing exercise plus cognitive therapy (BC). Hyperventilation provocation plus cognitive therapy was based on the procedures described by Clark and Salkovskis (1988). Particular attention was paid to the construction and discussion of the vicious circle, as well as to specific catastrophic interpretations. Homework consisted of breathing training mentioned previously, as well monitoring and challenging catastrophic thoughts, and non-exposure instructions.
3) Breathing exercise, cognitive therapy and exposure in vivo (BCE). This condition is very similar to the Clark and Salkovskis' (1988) programme consisting of breathing exercises, cognitive therapy and exposure in vivo. Exposure assignments are used as behavioural experiments to test the validity of the patient's catastrophic assumptions. Homework assignment consisted of breathing exercises, monitoring and challenging of catastrophic cognitions and as well as exposure to feared situations.
4) Exposure in vivo (E). Prolonged exposure in vivo (Emmelkamp, 1982) was applied in which patients were instructed to practice the items of a tailor-made hierarchy for about 90 minutes every day. No specific attention was paid to the occurrence of panic attacks.

Additional treatment

Since the treatment periods can be considered rather brief, we offered patients additional treatment, if they wanted. Seventy percent of them, about equally divided among conditions, accepted this offer.

Therapists

Therapy was carried out by advanced studentsof clinical psychology who had received intensive training in behaviour therapy and additional training in specific cognitive-behavioural techniques. Detailed treatment protocols were used, and therapists received group supervision by the first author for two hours twice a week. Sessions were recorded on audiotape in order to check treatment integrity.

MEASURES

A Panic Diary was used to provide daily monitoring of the panic symptoms, the number of panic attacks, and their specific symptoms according to DSM-III-R. Panic severity was rated for each panic attack on a 100 point scale. Furthermore, we used a behavioural test (at T1 and T4) and a number of self-report scales covering behavioural, cognitive and somatic aspects of panic and agoraphobia (at T1, T2, T3, and T4).

The Agoraphobic Cognitions Questionnaire (ACQ; Chambless et al., 1984) assesses catastrophic thoughts common to agoraphobics.
The Body Sensations Questionnaire (BSQ; Chambless et al., 1984) measures the occurrence of symptoms during exposure to feared stimuli.

The Fear Questionnaire (FQ; Marks & Mathews, 1979) contains an agoraphobia scale measuring the extent of avoidance in agoraphobic situations.

A standardized behavioural in vivo measure implied that patients had to walk a preestablished route until they started to feel uncomfortable, upon which they had to return to our clinic. The walk is divided into 20 segments, and the segment reached was recorded. (This measure was only obtained at T1. and T4.

RESULTS

The data were analyzed using a repeated measurement design with scores at intake as covariates. Table 3 displays the mean number of panic attacks in the four weeks preceding, during and following treatment.

The only significant difference found was a 'Time' effect on the 'Severity' rating, indicating that this severity of the panic attacks decreased over time.

Table 3. **MANOVA results on number and severity of panic attacks**

(Note. Results are based on the averaged number or severity, respectively, of panic attacks over the four week periods preceding, during and following treatment (i.e. Time). Condition: The four treatment packages.)

	Effect	F	df.	p
Number	Time	1.82	2	n.s
	Condition	1.82	3	n.s
	Time x Condition	1.17	6	n.s
Severity Time		14.80	2	<.001
	Condition	1.43	3	n.s
	Time x Condition	0.87	6	n.s

In Table 4 the results on the self-report measure and on the behavioural measure are presented.

Table 4. **MANOVA results on self-report scales and behavioural test**

(Note: ACQ: Agoraphobic Cognitions Questionnaire; BSQ: Body Sensations Questionnaire; F,Q-Ago: Agoraphobia subscale of the Fear Questionnaire; Walk: Behavioural test. Time: Two pre- and two post-tests; Condition:The four treatment packages.)

	Effect	F	df.	p
ACQ	Time	30.35	3	<.001
	Condition	2.31	3	n.s
	Time x Condition	1.72	9	n.s
BSQ	Time	9.05	3	<.001
	Condition	0.37	3	n.s
	Time x Condition	1.76	9	n.s
FQ-Ago	Time	30.06	3	<.001
	Condition	1.07	3	n.s
	Time x Condition	1.54	9	n.s
Walk	Time	13.66	1	<.002
	Condition	1.47	3	n.s
	Time x Condition	0.56	9	n.s

The overall picture in the self-report and behavioural measures yields main effects on 'Time'. Neither main effects on 'Treatment condition', nor interaction effects were observed.

DISCUSSION

No differential treatment effect was found in our groups, neither on panic diary data nor on self-report or behavioural measures. It is therefore concluded that cognitive treatment does not seem to improve the effect of exposure to external or internal stimuli in agoraphobic patients. There was no additive treatment effect, in the sense that a combination of interventions proved to be superior to single interventions.

It should be noted that our trial consisted of considerably affected agoraphobics, characterized by elaborate avoidance behaviours. In contrast, much research within the cognitive model of panic has been carried out with panic patients showing only little avoidance. It may well be the case that treatment according to the panic model does not hold for the entire array of panic psychopathology, ranging from hardly any avoidance to severe avoidance. To answer this question, though, more studies into the specific subtypes of panic disorder are needed, because at this moment no firm conclusions can be drawn on the active ingredients on the basis of the results reported thus far. However, if the disorder is characterized by a substantial amount of avoidance, exposure may well remain the major therapeutic agent.

REFERENCES

American Psychiatric Association (1987) *Diagnostic and Statistical manual of mental disorders (3rd revised edition)*. Washington, DC.

Aonn, J.A., Readhead, C.P.A., Timmons, B.H. (1984) Enhanced adaptive behavioural response in agoraphobic patients pretreated with breathing retraining. *The Lancet, 2*, 665-669.

Chambless, D.L., Caputo, G.C., Bright, P., Gallagher, R. (1984) Assessment of fear of fear in agoraphobics: The Body Sensations Questionnaire and the Agoraphobic Cognitions Questionnaire. *Journal of Consulting and Clinical Psychology, 6*, 1090-1097.

Clark, D.M. (1986) A cognitive approach to panic. *Behaviour Research and Therapy, 24*, 461-470.

Clark, D.M., Salkovskis, P.M., (1987) *Cognitive Treatment for Panic Attacks: Therapist's Manual*. Department of Psychiatry, University of Oxford,UK.

Clark, D.M., Salkovskis, P.M., Chalkley, A.J. (1985) Respiratory control as a treatment for panic attacks. *Journal of Behaviour Therapy & Experimental Psychiatry, 16*, 23-30.

DiNardo, P.A., O'Brien, G.T., Barlow, D.H., Waddell, M.T., Blanchard, E.B. (1983) Reliability of DSM-III anxiety disorder categories using a new structured interview. *Archives of General Psychiatry, 40*, 1070-1075.

Emmelkamp, P.M.G. (1982) *Phobic and obsessive-compulsive disorders: Theory, research and practice*. New York: Plenum.

Emmelkamp, P.M.G., Brilman, E., Kuiper, H., Mersch, P.P. (1986) The treatment of agoraphobia: A comparison of self-instructional training, rational emotive therapy and exposure in vivo. *Behavior Modification, 10*, 37-53.

Emmelkamp, P.M.G., Kuipers, A., Eggeraat, J. (1978) Cognitive modification versus prolonged exposure in vivo: A comparison with agoraphobics. *Behaviour Research and Therapy, 16*, 33-41.

Emmelkamp, P.M.G., Mersch, P.P. (1982) Cognition and exposure in vivo in the treatment of agoraphobia: Short-term and delayed effects. *Cognitive Therapy and Research, 6*, 77-90.

Garssen, B., Van Veenendaal, W., Bloemink, R. (1983) Agoraphobia and the Hyperventilation Syndrome. *Behaviour Research and Therapy, 21*, 643-649.

Ley, R. (1985) Blood, breath and fears: A hyperventilation theory of panic attacks and agoraphobia. *Clinical Psychology Review, 5*, 271-285.

Marchione, K.E., Michelson, L., Greenwald, M., Dancu, C. (1987) Cognitive behavioral treatment of agoraphobia. *Behaviour Research and Therapy, 25*, 319-328.

Margraf, J., Ehlers, A. Roth, W.T. (1986) Biological models of panic disorder and agoraphobia - a review. *Behaviour Research & Therapy, 24*, 553-567.

Marks, I.M., Mathews, A.M. (1979) Brief standard self-rating for phobic patients. *Behaviour Research and Therapy, 17*, 59-68.

Mavissakalian, M., Michelson, L., Greenwald, D., Kornblith, S., Greenwald, M. (1983) Cognitive-behavioral treatment of agoraphobia: Paradoxical ittention vs self-statement training. *Behaviour Research and Therapy, 21*, 75-86.

Michelson, L., Mavissakalian, M., Marchione, K. (1988) Cognitive, behavioral and psychophysiological treatments of agoraphobia: A comparative outcome investigation. *Behavior Therapy, 19*, 97-120.

Rapee, R.M. (1987) The psychological treatment of panic attacks: Theoretical conceptualization and review of evidence. *Clinical Psychology Review, 7*, 427-438.

Williams, S.L., Rappoport, A. (1983) Cognitive treatment in the natural environment for agoraphobics. *Behavior Therapy, 14*, 299-313.

SOMATIC SYMPTOMS IN PANIC ATTACKS: INTEROCEPTION, FEAR OF FEAR, AND LEARNING EXPERIENCES

A. Ehlers

Fachbereich Psychologie, Gutenbergstr. 18, 3550 Marburg, West Germany

Panic disorder is characterized by recurrent attacks of anxiety accompanied by many somatic symptoms such as palpitations, breathlessness or dizziness (American Psychiatric Association, 1987). Panic attack symptoms are very distressing, partly because they occur "spontaneously" without any cause that is obvious to the patient. Although no organic dysfunction can be identified, panic patients are worried about their health and repeatedly seek professional help for their symptoms. Boyd (1986) found that among patients with psychiatric disorders panic disorder patients consulted health professionals most frequently. Furthermore, many patients start avoiding situations in which panic symptoms are likely to occur or in which such symptoms might be embarrassing or dangerous. This "agoraphobic" avoidance can be so pronounced that patients become housebound.

Why do patients with panic disorder complain more often about somatic symptoms such as palpitations, dizziness or dyspnea than other people? Why do panic patients find these symptoms frightening, seek professional help, or develop agoraphobic avoidance behavior? Why do many panic patients live in the permanent fear of a heart attack although their heart is healthy whereas many patients with cardiaQ disease report very few symptoms and tend to ignore the first signs of their disorder?

In this chapter, I am going to focus on three aspects of the perception of somatic symptoms in panic disorder that may be involved in this behavioral pattern:

-Interoception: Do panic patients differ from other subjects in their ability to perceive their physiological processes?

-Fear of fear symptoms: Do panic patients differ from other subjects in their cognitive evaluation of somatic symptoms associated with anxiety?

-Learning history: Do panic patients differ from other subjects in their learning experiences concerning somatic anxiety symptoms?

Interoception

Panic patients may be more likely to experience somatic symptoms than other people because of a more accurate interoception (Tyrer, 1976). Our own studies of interoception in panic disorder focussed on cardiac perception since palpitations are the most common symptom of panic attacks. To assess cardiac awareness, we used the mental tracking paradigm developed by Schandry (1981). Subjects were asked to silently count their heart beats during signalled intervals of 35,

25, and 45 seconds. In our first study, we found a more accurate cardiac perception in panic disorder subjects (N=65) than in infrequent panickers (N=50), patients with specific phobias (N=27), or normal controls (N=46, Ehlers, in press a). In a second study, patients with panic disorder (N=13) showed a higher cardiac awareness than patients with depression (N=16). Patients with generalized anxiety disorder (N=15) resembled panic patients in their cardiac perception (Ehlers, in press a). Figure 1 illustrates the results of the second study.

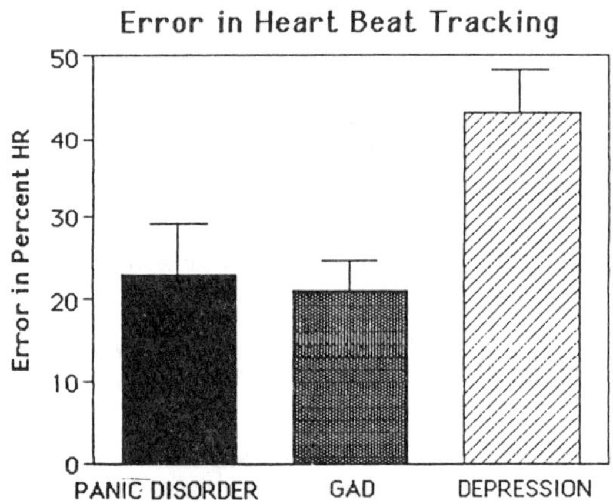

Figure 1. **Error in heart beat tracking (in percent rate) for patients with panic disorder, generalized anxiety disorder, or depression**

Thus, an enhanced cardiac awareness seems to be a specific characteristic of patients with anxiety states, i.e. panic disorder and generalized anxiety disorder. Both conditions have in common that the patients suffer from many somatic symptoms. An enhanced cardiac awareness may increase the probability that patients experience sensations from their heart, develop anxiety and worries about their heart function, or avoid situations in which they feel their heart. All of these possible consequences of good cardiac perception may be involved in the development or maintenance of panic disorder. Consistent with this hypothesis is our preliminary finding that a good cardiac perception is related to an increased risk for relapse in remitted panic patients (Ehlers, in press a).

Fear of Fear

It has been suggested that panic attacks are not spontaneous in the sense that no trigger can be identified, but that they represent a response to perceived physiological changes that are associated with danger (e.g., Clark, 1986; Ehlers, Margraf, & Roth, 1988). Several previous studies found that panic patients report to be more afraid of somatic symptoms associated with anxiety than controls (e.g., Chambless, Caputo, Bright, & Gallagher, 1984; Reiss, Peterson, Gursky, and McNally, 1986). We recently replicated these findings and extended them by including subjects with infrequent panic attacks in our design. This group might represent a possible risk group for panic disorder. We compared 27 patients with panic disorder, 21 subjects with infrequent panic attacks, and 26 normal controls on three measures of "fear of fear": the Agoraphobic Cognitions Questionnaire and the Body Sensations Questionnaire developed by Chambless et al. (1984) and the Anxiety Sensitivity Index developed by Reiss et al. (1986). On all scales, panic patients and infrequent panickers differed significantly from controls. Differences between the panic groups were only found for the Anxiety Sensitivity Index.

	Panic Disorder	Infrequent Panic	Controls
Agoraphobic Cognitions Questionnaire	1.92 (0.54)	1.70 (0.35)	1.22 (0.17)
Body Sensations Questionnaire	2.60 (0.68)	2.29 (0.45)	1.48 (0.39)
Anxiety Sensitivity Index	28.1 (11.0)	21.6 (4.7)	13.8 (4.7)

Table 1. **"Fear of Fear" Measures (Means and Standard Deviations)**

In another study, we had subjects rate the dangerousness of various somatic symptoms (Ehlers, in press b). The symptom list included general anxiety symptoms (e.g., sweating,accelerated heart rate), panic symptoms (e.g., dizziness, dyspnea), and control symptoms not associated with anxiety (e.g., itching, toothache). We compared 110 patients with panic disorder, 81 subjects with infrequent panic attacks, 37 patients with other anxiety disorders, and 61 normal controls. Table 2 shows the results for panic and control symptoms, respectively. For panic symptoms, but not for control symptoms, significant group differences were found.

	Panic Disorder	Infrequent Panic	Other Anxiety Disorders	Normal Controls
Panic Symptoms	5.9 (2.3)	4.9 (2.3)	3.9 (2.5)	3.0 (2.7)
Control Symptoms	2.0 (2.0)	2.8 (2.5)	2.7 (2.3)	2.3 (2.5)

Table 2. **Ratings of Dangerousness (Scale 0 to 10, Means and Standard Deviations)**

Panic disorder patients found panic symptoms more dangerous than all the other groups. Infrequent panickers gave higher ratings of dangerousness than patients with other anxiety disorders or normal controls.

The results of these studies are consistent with the hypothesis that panic patients - and to a lesser extent infrequent panickers - report to be afraid of body

The results of these studies are consistent with the hypothesis that panic patients - and to a lesser extent infrequent panickers - report to be afraid of body sensations associated with anxiety. The second study provided evidence that this fear is specific to anxiety symptoms.

Learning Experiences

Several studies found a connection between illness behavior and learning experiences during childhood and adolescence (Feuerstein, Labbé, & Kuczmierczyk, 1986; Turkat, 1982; Whitehead, Bush, Heller, & Costa, 1986). Subjects who received special attention or who were encouraged to avoid strain when having symptoms at a young age subsequently consulted health professionals more often and reported more symptoms than subjects whose parents did not encourage illness behavior.

We conducted an exploratory study of learning experiences concerning anxiety symptoms in subjects with panic attacks. We used a modified version of a questionnaire developed by Whitehead et al. (1986) to assess social learning influences on menstrual symptoms and illness behavior. In our version of the questionnaire subjects are asked how often they experienced symptoms such as palpitations, breathlessness, dizziness, or severe nausea during their childhood or adolescence. They are then asked to rate how frequently their parents brought them special food, encouraged them to skip school, homework, or household chores. As shown in Table 3,patients with panic disorder (N=121), infrequent panickers (N=86), and patients with other anxiety disorders (N=38) reached higher scores on this scale assessing encouragement of illness behavior when having anxiety symptoms than normal controls (N=61). In contrast, no differences were found on a similar scale assessing encouragement of sick role behavior when having colds.

Another scale assessed whether the subjects' parents had shown illness behavior when having anxiety symptoms during the subjects' childhood or adolescence. On this scale, only subjects with panic attacks differed significantly from normal controls. Similarly, patients with panic disorder and infrequent panickers, but not patients with other anxiety disorders stated that they had lived together with a larger number of relatives who suffered from chronic diseases lasting more than six months.

Because of the retrospective nature of the data, the results remain preliminary and need to be substantiated by further research, preferably prospective studies. However, the findings point to a possible specificity in that subjects with panic attacks, but not patients with other anxiety disorders, seem to have observed more illness behavior related to anxiety symptoms or chronic disorders in their homes than controls. These experiences may contribute to the panickers' evaluation that body sensations are harmful. Interestingly, subjects with infrequent panic attacks did not differ in their learning history from patients with panic disorder. This might point to a common vulnerability.

	Panic Disorder	Infrequent Panic	Other Anxiety Disorders	Normal Controls
Encouragement of Illness Behavior/ Subject's Anxiety Symptoms	1.1 (1.8)	1.0 (1.6)	0.8 (1.4)	0.1 (0.3)
Observation of Illness Behavior/ Parents' Anxiety Symptoms	2.8 (2.9)	2.8 (2.9)	1.8 (2.3)	0.9 (1.6)

Table 3. **Social learning Experiences and Anxiety Symptoms (Scale 0 t0 9, Means and Standard Deviations)**

DISCUSSION

Somatic sensations represent both a symptom and a possible trigger of panic attacks. The research described in this chapter has identified two factors that may contribute to the experience of somatic symptoms and symptom-related anxiety in panic disorder. First, panic disorder patients demonstrated a better cardiac perception than clinical and nonclinical control groups. Second, these patients rated panic symptoms as more dangerous and reported a higher fear of these symptoms than normal controls and patients with other anxiety disorders. Whether a relatively good cardiac awareness and a fear of body sensations develop prior or secondary to panic disorder remains open and can only be determined in prospective longitudinal studies.

Regardless of this question, both factors may be involved in the maintenance of panic disorder.

The results of our retrospective questionnaire study suggest that subjects with panic attacks may have different learning experiences concerning somatic symptoms than clinical and nonclinical controls. They may have learned that it is appropriate to show illness behavior when having somatic symptoms typical of panic attacks.

Acknowledgements

The studies described in this chapter were supported by German Research Society grant Eh 97/1-3. The help of Peter Breuer is gratefully acknowledged.

REFERENCES

American Psychiatric Association (1987) *Diagnostic and Statistical Manual of Mental Disorders*. Third edition - revised. Washington, D.C.: American Psychiatric Press.

Boyd, J.H. (1986) Use of mental health services for the treatment of panic disorder. *American Journal of Psychiatry, 143*, 1569-1574.

Chambless, D.L., Caputo, G.C., Bright, P., Gallagher, R. (1984) Assessment of fear of fear in agoraphobics: The Body Sensations Questionnaire and the Agoraphobic Cognitions Questionnaire. *Journal of Consulting and Clinical Psychology, 52*, 1090-1097.

Clark, D.M. (1986) A cognitive approach to panic. *Behaviour Research and Therapy, 24*, 461-470.

Ehlers, A. (in press a) Cardiac perception, panic attacks, and phobias. In D. Vaitl & R. Schandry (Eds.), *Interoception and Cardiovascular Processes*. Chicester: Wiley.

Ehlers, A. (in press b) Cognitive factors in panic attacks: Symptom probability and sensitivity. *Journal of Cognitive Psychotherapy*.

Ehlers, A., Margraf, J., Roth, W.T. (1988) Selective information processing, interoception, and panic attacks. In I.Hand & H.U. Wittchen (Eds.), *Panic and Phobias 2* (pp. 129-148). Berlin: Springer.

Feuerstein, M. Labbé, E.E., Kuczmierczyk, A.R. (1986) *Health Psychology: A Psychobiological Perspective*. New York: Plenum Press.

Reiss, S., Peterson, R.A., Gursky, D.M., McNally, R.J. (1986) Anxiety sensitivity, anxiety frequency, and the prediction of fearfulness. *Behaviour Research and Therapy, 24*, 1-8.

Schandry, R. (1981) Heart beat perception and emotional experience. *Psychophysiology, 18*, 483-488.

Turkat, I.D. (1982) An investigation of parental modeling in the etiology of diabetic illness behavior. *Behaviour Research and Therapy, 20*, 547-552.

Tyrer, P.J. (1976) *The Role of Bodily Feelings in Anxiety*. London: Oxford University Press.

Whitehead, W.E., Bush, C.M., Heller, B.R., Costa, P.T. (1986) Social learning influences on menstrual symptoms and illness behavior. *Health Psychology, 5*, 13-23.

THE ROLE OF CARDIOCEPTION IN ANXIETY DISORDERS

L. Hartl, D. O. Nutzinger, and F.Strian

Max-Planck-Institut für Psychiatrie, Munich, F.R.G. and Psychiatrische Universitätsklinik, Vienna, Austria

INTRODUCTION

Cardiac complaints and anxiety are the most frequent symptoms reported in medical as well as in psychiatric practice, and they are the items most frequently scored on psychiatric self-rating scales. As diagnosis in medicine and psychiatry is based largely on symptom reports and cardiac complaints and anxiety have a vital significance representing basic bodily functions and warning signals, it becomes clear that it is of importance to study the psycho-cardiac interactions.

Bodily symptoms have an adaptive and functional base as a source of feedback for the self-regulation of bodily and environmental states (Pennebaker, 1982; Pennebaker, Gonder-Frederick, Cox, & Hoover, 1985). But as bodily symptoms and their report are subjective, they are error-prone in three different ways: perception or report of bodily symptoms may be lacking, bodily symptoms may be misinterpreted, or overestimated. In psychophysiological models of the etiopathology of anxiety disorders the importance of physical and cognitive changes and their perception is emphasized. They ar supposed to play a role as internal stimuli of panic attacks as well as for the maintenance of panic disorder. It has been postulated that the perception of bodily sensations can trigger the development of panic disorder (Clark, 1986; Clark, 1988; Ehlers, Margraf, & Roth, 1988). A two-stage process is thought to be involved. In the first stage bodily sensations (such as palpitations or dizziness) are perceived and misinterpreted as signs of disturbed bodily activity (e.g., as evidence of an impending heart attack). These sensations are increasingly perceived with anxiety. During this stage the sensations can intensify anxiety and vice versa. This process rounds up in a vicious circle which culminates in a panic attack. In the second stage abnormal forms of coping behaviour (such as avoidance of stressful situatins) are observed.

Pathological anxiety always results from the interaction of physiological and psychological factors. Even normal, i.e. adequate, anxiety goes along with autonomous activation and unpleasant bodily sensations. Because of the very pronounced character of perception of anxiety syndromes, one can assume that cardiac perception disturbances play an important part in these syndromes. Until now, however, psycho-cardiac interactions have been studied almost exclusively under the aspect of psychological influences. There is hardly any information about the process of perception itself and its neurophysiological substrates. Cardiac perception can be understood as a complex visceral information processing system including receptor structures, ascending pathways to the lower brainstem and limbic midbrain, and cortical projections. The different levels interact with efferent mechanisms analogous to sensory perception systems (Hartl & Strian, 1989; Strian, 1989; Strian & Hartl, 1988). To study cardiac perception, we chose different perceptual modalities (like the perception of the regular heart beat and cardiac arrhythmias), different perceptual levels (disturbance of peripheral stimulus generation, disturbance of afferent neuronal pathways, and disturbance on the CNS-level), and used investigation strategies according to the lesion model paradigm.

The existence of cardiac perception could be demonstrated by our findings in patients with autonomous diabetic neuropathy as a clinical paradigm for the visceral afferent blockade (Hartl & Strian, 1989; Lautenbacher, Stalmann, Haslbeck, & Strian, 1987; Pauli, Hartl, Marquardt, Stalmann, & Strian, 1989). These patients proved to suffer from an impairment of cardioception regarding the regular heart beat as well as cardiac arrhythmias due to cardiac deafferentation. The impaired perception of visceral activity also reduced the frequency of bodily symptom report and affected the emotional state of these patients (Pauli, Strian, Lautenbacher, Karlbauer, & Hölzl, 1989).

If patients with anxiety disorders suffer from a disturbance of visceral perception in the sense of an inadequate, emotionally exaggerated perception of bodily sensations, this can originate from three different causes:

1. abnormal organic sensations
2. disturbed organic perception
3. inadequate appraisal of perception.

METHOD

Our experimental approach was a combined laboratory-field-design to assess heart activity and the perception of regular and pathological cardiac events. Heart activity and the perception of the regular heart beat (mental tracking method; Schandry, 1981) were assessed under laboratory conditions by means of various physical and psychological manipulations. Heart activity and the perception of spontaneous cardiac arrhythmias (ventricular extrasystoles and tachycardias) were assessed by means of ambulatory 24h-ECG-monitoring in natural setting together with concomittant subjective and emotional reactions. Additionally, all persons filled out several self-rating scales (regarding anxiety, well-being, bodily complaints, and cognitions).

We included 58 patients with panic disorder (diagnosed by DSM-III-R criteria) and 20 healthy control persons in our study about cardiac perception processes (Hartl, Nutzinger, Marquardt, Strian, & Pauli, 1990). The clinical group specified palpitations and fear of getting a heart attack as the most frequent symptoms in connection with anxiety.

RESULTS

Regarding the heart activity as well as the spontaneous arrhythmias, we didn't find any differences between the panic group and the controls during the laboratory and the field part of the study. This is supported by the findings of Taylor et al. (1986) who reported no heart rate differences between panic patients and healthy controls during non-panic periods. Regarding the perceptual performance, panic patients were slightly worse heart beat perceivers according to the peception score of the mental tracking method in all experimental situations. To our surprise they did not overestimate their heart rate. Instead, they demonstrated heart rate imperceptivity significantly more often than the controls, were more uncertain in judgements about their perception, and showed an increase in baseline anxiety. Under everyday conditions they tended to mark cardiac sensations more frequently and had a trend to mark without preceding cardiac irregularities as compared to the controls. Overall, on the perceptional level panic patients turned out to have an inconsistent cardioceptive performance. On the one hand they were able to discriminate their cardiac signals equally well as the control subjects, but with the same frequency they reported total imperceptability of their heart beat combined with a subjective uncertainty about their judgement. These findings correspond with the results of arrhythmia perception in the field study. Overall, correct perceptions seldom occurred in both groups. Panic patients, however, reported changes in cardiac activity without preceding cardiac events more frequently and had a higher baseline anxiety under laboratory and everyday conditions, whereas there were no group differences in reported motoric activity and strain during the day.

DISCUSSION

These findings confirm our results from a preceding field study with cardiac phobics and patients with mitral valve prolapse as a model of increased cardiac signal input without any other disturbance of cardiac functioning (Strian, Hartl, Pauli, Stalmann, & Hölzl, 1989). We found differences on the level of cardiac irregularities as well as on the level of cardiac perception and related emotional reactions. The cardiac phobics had a perceptual structure characterized by a predisposition to anxiety and phobias. Although they did not show a higher incidence of abnormal cardiac events, the increased anxious focussing of attention on rare and unpredictable events may have contributed to the persistence and generalization of cardiac anxiety. In contrast, mitral valve prolapse subjects had a higher incidence of arrhythmias, but did not evaluate these events in an anxious manner. By analysing the heart rate intervals in which cardiac perceptions were reported, we found that cardiac perceptions related to anxiety are followed by an additional heart rate increase with a delayed compensatory decrease in cardiac phobics (Pauli, Marquardt, Hartl, Strian, & Nutzinger, 1990). This heart rate course in connection with cardiac perceptions can be interpreted as a positive feedback process between perception, increase of cardiac activity, and the development of anxiety. These results demonstrate that perception of abnormal visceral signals by itself does not provoke anxiety.

CONCLUSION

Summing up, these findings in patients with anxiety disorders can be interpreted as cardioceptive inconsistency with distortion and uncertainty not caused peripherally by disturbed cardiac signals. Interestingly, it is known from sensoric systems that contradictory sensoric perceptions without a plausible model of explanation always are evaluated negatively, and frequently are experienced as anxiety provoking (Birbaumer & Schmidt, 1990; Hartl & Strian, 1990). Thus, there is some evidence that patients with panic disorder suffer from a disturbance of central nervous information processing with the following three components: abnormal anxiety disposition, incorrect cardiac perception, and dysregulation on the central nervous level in the perception and emotion processing brain structures. Thus, uncertainty and distortion of visceral stimuli could prompt the development and maintenance of anxiety.

REFERENCES

Birbaumer, N., Schmidt, R. F. (1990) *Biologische Psychologie*. Berlin: Springer.

Clark, D. M. (1986) A cognitive approach to panic. *Behaviour Research and Therapy, 24*, 461-470.

Clark, D. M. (1988) A cognitive model of panic attacks. In S. Rachman & J. D. Maser (Eds.), *Panic: Psychological perspectives* (pp. 71-89), Hillsdale: Erlbaum.

Ehlers, A., Margraf, J., Roth, W. T. (1988) Selective information processing, interoception, and panic attacks. In I. Hand & H.-U. Wittchen (Eds.), *Panic and phobias 2* (pp. 123-148). Berlin: Springer.

Hartl, L., Nutzinger, D. O., Marquardt, C., Strian, F., Pauli, P. (1990) *The role of cardioception and heart activity in panic disorder*. Manuscript submitted for publication.

Hartl, L., Strian, F. (1989) A clinical approach to cardiac perception. In D. Vaitl & R. Schandry (Eds.), *Interoception and cardiovascular processes*. Manuscript accepted for publication.

Lautenbacher, S., Stalmann, H., Haslbeck, M., Strian, F. (1987) Neuroendokrine Einflüsse auf die Wahrnehmung der Herzaktion. *Deutsche Medizinische Wochenschrift, 112*, 1492-1497.

Pauli, P., Hartl, L., Marquardt, C., Stalmann, H., & Strian, F. (1989) *Cardiac perception in autonomous diabetic neuropathy*. Manuscript submitted for publication.

Pauli, P., Marquardt, C., Hartl, L., Strian, F., & Nutzinger, D. O. (1990) *The influence of anxiety on heart rate in cardiac phobia*. Manuscript submitted for publication.

Pauli, P. Strian, F., Lautenbacher, S., Karlbauer, G., & Hölzl, R. (1989) Emotionale Auswirkungen der autonomen Deafferentierung bei Diabetes-Neuropathie. *Zeitschrift für Klinische Psychologie, 3*, 268-277.

Pennebaker, J. W. (1982) *The psychology of physical symptoms*. New York: Springer.

Pennebaker, J. W., Gonder-Frederick, L., Cox, D., & Hoover, C. W. (1985) The perception of general vs. specific visceral activation and the regulation of health related behavior. In E. S. Katkin & S. B. Manuck (Eds.), *Advances in behavioral medicine*, (Vol. 1, pp. 165-198). Greenwich, CT: JAI Press.

Schandry, R. (1981) Heart beat perception and emotional experience. *Psychophysiology, 18*, 483-488.

Strian, F. (1989) A neuropsychological approach to cardiac anxiety. In D. Vaitl & R. Schandry (Eds.), *Interoception and cardiovascular processes*. Manuscript accepted for publication.

Strian, F., & Hartl, L. (1988) Anxiety and sensitization: a neuropsychological approach. In I. Hand & H.-U. Wittchen (Eds.), *Panic and Phobias 2* (pp. 186-192). Berlin: Springer.

Strian, F., Hartl, L., Pauli, P. Stalmann, H., & Hölzl, R. (1989) *Perception of arrhythmias in mitral valve prolapse syndrome and cardiac phobia*. Manuscript submitted for publication.

Taylor, C. B., Sheikh, J., Agras, W. S., Roth, W. T., Margraf, J., Ehlers, A., Maddock, R. J., & Gossard, D. (1986) Ambulatory heart rate changes in patients with panic attacks. *American Journal of Psychiatry, 143*, 478-482.

BEHAVIOUR THERAPY IN PATIENTS WITH OBSESSIONS ONLY

C.A.L. Hoogduin, E. de Haan, C. Schaap and W. Arts

Psychologisch Laboratorium, Katholieke Universiteit Nijmegen, Postbus 9104, 6500 HE Nijmegen

INTRODUCTION

In recent years research has been reported claiming considerable success in the treatment of obsessive-compulsives. The success rate is around 75% (Emmelkamp, 1982; Foa et al, 1985; Hoogduin et al., 1989).

Patients with obsessions only, are not included in most of these outcome studies. The impression is that obsessions are more difficult to treat in comparison with compulsions (Rachman, 1983; Foa et al,1985). However, no research findings to support that suggestion are available.

In this article, a study is reported on patients with obsessive symptoms only, that will furnish some data regarding this issue. The treatment procedure, applied in this outcome study, is based on Rachman's work on obsessions (Rachman, 1976a). Rachman suggested that obsessions produce both discomfort as well as attempts to put 'matters right'. These attempts are construed as being functionally equivalent to compulsive rituals. He suggested the same treatment procedure as used with patients having both obsessions and compulsions, consisting of exposure and prevention of the neutralizing rituals (Rachman, 1976a). It is likely that the patient will attempt to rid himself of the obsession by eliciting reassuring answers from members of the family. It may be assumed then that not only the neutralizing thoughts and the cognitive rituals will lead to a reduction in the level of anxiety and discomfort, but the answer to repetitive questioning given by those close to the patient can also have this result. (Hoogduin, 1986).

Obsessions are often accompanied by anxiety and depression (Marks,1973; Rachman & Hodgson, 1980; Foa et al., 1982; Hoogduin, 1986). Improvement in patients is indexed in terms of the reduction of the specific obsessions, but a concomitant reduction in anxiety and depression can also be expected (Hoogduin et al., 1989).

In this study the research question is formulated as follows: "Does behavioural treatment of patients with obsessions only have an effect on obsessions, anxiety and depression?"

METHOD

Patients

In order to be included in the study the patients had to satisfy the DSM III-R diagnostic criteria for obsessive-compulsive neurosis. Patients with compulsions were excluded from the study.

Instruments of measurement

Self-monitoring: since the patients were suffering from obsessional thoughts the only possible way of measuring the symptoms was asking the patients to monitor their thoughts.

The degree of *depression* was determined by using the Dutch version of Zung's Self-rating Depression Scale (S.D.S.) (Zung, 1965).

Anxiety was measured by using the Dutch version of the Spielberger State-Trait Anxiety Inventory (S.T.A.I. DY) (Spielberger et al, 1970).

The *severity of the obsessive complaints* was measured using a Dutch version of the Leyton Obsessional Inventory (L.O.I.).

Treatment

The treatment consisted of the following:

1. Self-observation and self-monitoring.
2. Exposure: the patient exposes him/herself to anxiety-provoking situations; the patient is required to evoke certain obsessional thoughts on purpose and to concentrate on them at a given time each day; the patient is to regard the recurrence of spontaneous obsessional thoughts as an indication of the need for additional training in the above mentioned procedure, instead of resisting them.
3. Response prevention: the patient is required to put an end to the neutralizing thoughts and cognitive rituals (cf. Rachman, 1976a; 1976b); people close to the patient should no longer reply to his/her persisting questioning.

The treatment program is designed by the therapist in collaboration with the patient, but the actual procedure is performed by the patient without supervision. The outpatient treatment utilizes a self-control procedure which enables the patient to refrain from cognitive rituals and to gradually expose him/herself to threatening situations (see also Hoogduin & Hoogduin, 1984).

Failure criteria

Emmelkamp et al. (1983) and Foa et al. (1983a; 1983b), in their studies on success and failure in the treatment of obsessive-compulsives, determined an improvement of 30% or less to be a failure. It was decided to follow Emmelkamp and Foa, and to regard an improvement of less than 30% as the failure criterion.

Procedure

Twenty-six patients with the diagnosis obsessive-compulsive disorder with obsessions only, were, upon intake, psychologically examined by an independent assessor. The variables depression, anxiety and severity of obsessional complaints were measured. The patients were then randomly assigned to one of four therapists. After ten sessions, which roughly corresponded to a period of twenty weeks, a second measurement (the post measurement) was taken by the independent assessor. If necessary, treatment was continued. During the intake procedure the patient was administered the self-monitoring assignment. He/she was asked to keep a detailed record of the obsessions. Frequency and sometimes duration of complaints were recorded on special registration forms.

A follow-up examination was carried out a minimum of one year after the post measurement. The patient was asked once again to record the obsessions during the week preceding the follow-up assessment. Again, the assessment consisted of the measurements of depression, anxiety and severity of obsessional complaints.

RESULTS

Patients

Twenty-six patients, consecutively referred to the psychiatric outpatient department of a general hospital, were accepted in the study.

General information

Sex: the group of 26 patients included in the study consisted of 16 (62%) women and 10 (38%) men. Marital status: twenty-three (88%) patients were either married or living with someone in a long-standing relationship.

Age at onset of the complaints: the mean age at onset of the complaints was 30,4 years. Duration of complaints: the mean duration of complaints was 9,3 years. Previous treatment: nineteen (73%) had had previous outpatient treatment.

Self-monitoring: seven (27%) of the patients showed an improvement of 30% or less (failure group: F-group). Nineteen (73%) benefited from the treatment (success group: S-group). The failure group consisted of five patients who dropped out of the treatment program before the tenth treatment session and two who, after the tenth session, appeared not to have benefited from treatment.

Depression: the mean score on the S.D.S. showed a significant decrease for patients in the S-group (Mann-Whitney-U-test: $p < 0.001$).

Anxiety: the mean, combined score on the S.T.A.I.-DY 1 and 2 showed a significant reduction for the patients in the S-group (Mann-Whitney-U-test: $p < 0.005$).

The *severity of the obsessive complaints*: the mean score on the L.O.I.showed a notable reduction in the S-group. This improvement is significant (Mann-Whitney-

Figure 1. **Pre, post, and follow-up measurement of the success group**

S.D.S. "Zung's Self-rating Depression Scale", S.T.A.I.-DY 1 "State anxiety (Spielberger's Anxiety Inventory)", S.T.A.I.-DY 2 "Trait anxiety (Spielberger's Anxiety Inventory)", L.O.I. "Leyton Obsessional Inventory".

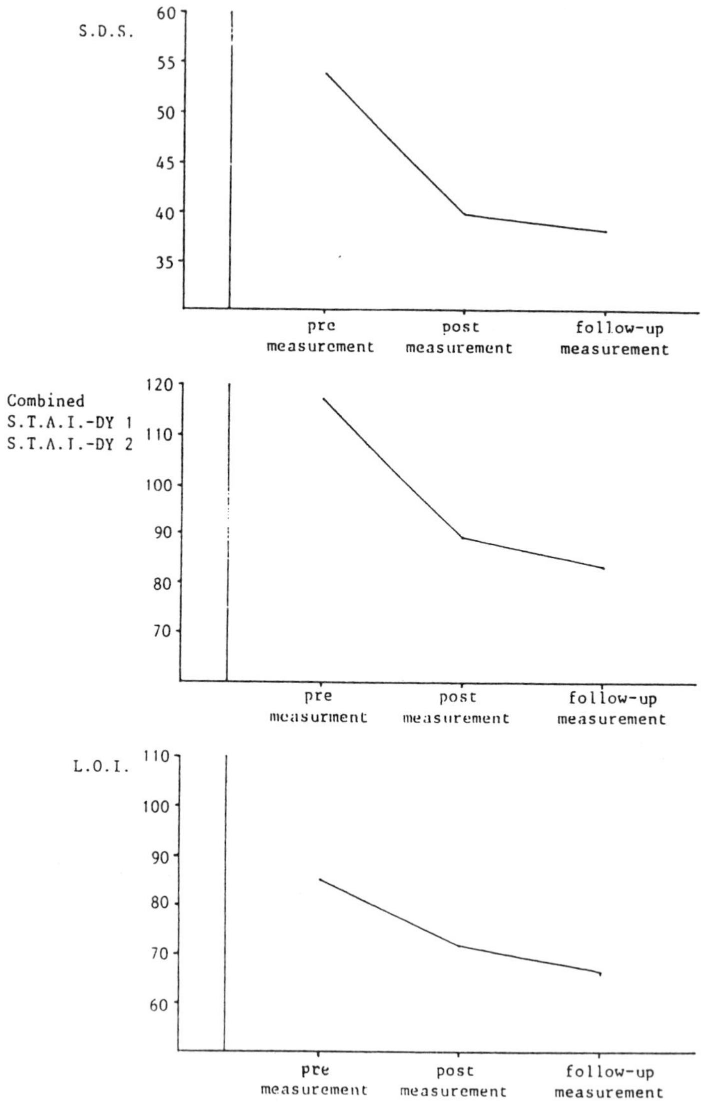

U-test: $p < 0.005$). Only two patients in the F-group could be re-assessed after the tenth session, making a correct comparison between the S-group and the F-group impossible.

Follow-up assessment

The patients in the S-group were re-assessed at least 12 months (12 - 36) after the post measurement. Three of the 19 patients had had a relapse. Improvement appeared to have been maintained or to have increased in 16 of the 26 patients (61,5%). The scores for these patients are presented in figure 1. The mean scores on the S.D.S., combined S.T.A.I.-DY 1 and 2 and the L.O.I., have further decreased.

CLOSING REMARKS

It is a striking fact that obsessive-compulsives are often without a partner. From a study of the available literature Black (1974) found this to be true of 40 - 50% of patients with obsessions and compulsions. In this study 12% of the patients with obsessions only are unpartnered.

Seventy-three percent of the patients benefited from treatment based on exposure and response prevention. The percentage remained relatively favourable on follow-up. This results concur with the findings of Kirk (1983). In this study, 16 patients with obsessions only, were treated on an outpatient basis with thought-stopping, exposure, relaxation and imaginary desensitization. Eighty-one percent of these patients were successfully treated. These and our findings support Rachman's suggestion to apply exposure and response prevention not only in patients with compulsive rituals, but also in patients with obsessional complaints only.

REFERENCES

Black, A. (1974) The natural history of obsessional neurosis. In: H.R.Beech (Ed.) *Obsessional States*. London, Methuen.

Emmelkamp, P.M.G. (1982) *Phobic and Obsessive-Compulsive Disorders*. New York, Plenum Press.

Emmelkamp, P.M.G., Hoekstra, R.J., Visser, S. (1983) The behavioral treatment of obsessive-compulsive disorder, prediction of outcome at 3,5 year follow-up. In: H. Brenner (Ed.), *Psychiatry, Current States*. New York, Wiley.

Foa, E.B., Grayson, J.B., Steketee, G.S. (1982) Depressions, habituation and treatment outcome in obsessive-compulsives. In: J.C. Boulougouris (Ed.), *Learning Theory Approaches to Psychiatry*. New York, Wiley.

Foa, E.B., Grayson, J.B., Steketee, G.S. , Doppelt, H.G., Turner, R.M., Latimer, P.R. (1983a) Success and failure in the behavioral treatment of obsessive-compulsives. *Journal of Consulting and Clinical Psychology, 51,* 287 - 297.

Foa, E.B., Steketee, G.S., Grayson, J.B., Doppelt, H.G. (1983b), Treatment of obsessive-compulsives: When do we fail? In: E.B. Foa & P.M.G. Emmelkamp (Eds.) *Failures in Behavior Therapy.* New York, Wiley.

Foa, E.B., Steketee, G.S., Ozarow, B.J. (1985) Behavior therapy with obsessive-compulsives: From theory to treatment. In: M. Mavissakalion,S.M. Turner & L. Michelson (Eds.) *Obsessive-Compulsive Disorder: Psychological and Pharmacological Treatment.* New York, Plenum Press.

Hoogduin, C.A.L. (1986) On the diagnosis of obsessive-compulsive disorder. *American Journal of Psychotherapy, Vol. XL (1),* 36 - 51.

Hoogduin, C.A.L., Duivenvoorden, H., Schaap, C., Haan, E. de (1989), Outpatient treatment of obsessive-compulsives: outcome, prediction of outcome and follow-up. In: P.M.G. Emmelkamp, W.T.A.M. Everaerd, F. Kraaimaat & M.J.M. van Son (Edt.), *Fresh Perspectives on Anxiety Disorders.* Amsterdam, Swets & Zeitlinger.

Hoogduin, C.A.L., Hoogduin, W.A. (1984) The outpatient treatment of patients with an obsessive-compulsive disorder. *Behav. Res. & Ther. 22*, 455 - 459.

Kirk, J.W. (1983) Behavioral treatment of obsessional-compulsive patients in routine clinical practice. *Behav. Res. & Ther. 21* , 57 - 62.

Marks, I.M. (1973) New approaches to the treatment of obsessive-compulsive disorders. *Journal of Nervous and Mental Diseases, 156*, 421 - 426.

Rachman, S. (1976a) Obsessional-compulsive checking. *Behav. Res. & Ther. 14*, 269 - 277.

Rachman, S. (1976b) Obsessional-compulsive checking. *Behav. Res. & Ther.,* 14, 437 - 443.

Rachman, S. & Hodgson, R.J. (1980) *Obsessions and Compulsions.* New Yersey, Prentice Hall.

Rachman, S. (1983) Obstacles to the successful treatment of obsessions. In: E.B. Foa & P.M.G. Emmelkamp (Eds.), *Failure in Behavior Therapy* (pp. 35 - 57). New York, Wiley.

Spielberger, C.D., Borsuch, R.L., Lushene, R.E. (1970) *STAI - Manual of the State-Trait Anxiety Inventory.* Palo Alto, Consulting Psychologists Press.

Zung, W.W.K. (1965) A self-rating depression scale. *Arch. Gen. Psychiatry, 12*, 63 - 70

ANXIETY AND BRAINSTEM AUDITORY EVOKED POTENTIALS (BAEP) IN PATIENTS WITH SCHIZOPHRENIA AND DEPRESSION

J. Jakitowicz, R. Hebel and M. Majkowicz

I Department of Psychiatry and Department of Neurology, Medical Academy in Gdansk, Poland

INTRODUCTION

Several authors have made attempts to find correlations between evoked potentials and the clinical state of patients suffering from psychiatric disorders (Ashton, 1988; Bolz, 1979; Buchsbaum, 1976; Dimond, 1976; Patterson, 1988; Shagass, 1985; Szelenberger, 1982). Some of the EEG parameters (event-related potentials) appear to be correlated with cognitive processes (as stimulus registration and evaluation, attention, memory) and with behaviour of patients (Buchsbaum, 1976; Donchin, 1979; Dongier, 1973; Picton, 1974). Brainstem auditory evoked potentials (BAEP), as a functional measure of brain activity (Fabiani, 1979), could also correlate with behaviour.

In the present study we try to estimate the state of higher levels of the central nervous system in the patients with behavioral symptoms of so called "endogenic" anxiety, as seen clinically .

MATERIAL

The examinations comprised 38 patients hospitalized in the I Clinic of Mental Diseases in the Medical Academy in Gdansk. In 27 patients (21 male and 6 female) a schizophrenic process was diagnosed, in 11 patients (only men) - a primary affective disorders was found. Mean age in the schizophrenic group was 28.96 + 8.61, in the depression group - 43.45 + 14.06 and did not significantly differ from mean age in the control group (28.65 + 7.85, F = 0.017, n.s.). The control group was made of 23 healthy volunteers, in that number 7 women and 16 men (mean age: 32.6 + 11.3 and 26.9 + 5.4).

METHODS

The examinations of brainstem auditory evoked potentials (BAEP) were performed at the Clinic of Neurology for Adults in the Medical Academy in Gdansk. BAEP were averaged on-line (2000 times) by a Neuromatic - 2000 C, according to the routine rules illustrated in the table 1. The latency of each wave in the evoked response was estimated.

Table 1. **Stimulation and recording parameters for BAEP**

SITE:	Right or left ear with headphones
INTENSITY:	60 dB above normal hearing level
STIMULI FREQUENCY:	10 Hz
DURATION:	100 microseconds
MASKING:	Yes
ELECTRODE PLACEMENT:	Both ear mastoid and forehead (Fz)
ELECTRODE IMPEDANCE:	3 k
SWEEP SPEED:	10 milliseconds
UPPER FREQUENCY:	2 kHz
LOWER FREQUENCY:	100 Hz

On the same day patients were subjected to psychiatric and neurologic examinations, also the estimation by means of BPRS according to Overal was carried out. The anxiety level in the scale was defined as arithmetical sum of the scores in the items: 2 - timidity, 6 - emotional tension, 11 - suspicious and 13 - psychomotor retardation.

The analysis of the results obtained was performed by SPSS analysis system (analysis of variance, median test, Pearson's correlation test).

RESULTS

The latencies of BAEP waves in both tested groups compared with the control group are presented in Table 2.

Table 2.

LEFT SIDE	MEANS LATENCIES OF THE BAEP PEAKS						
	I	II	III	IV	V	VI	VII
SCHIZO-PHRENIA	1.7	2.29	**4.05**	**5.33**	**6.05**	7.52	**8.68**
DEPRESSION	1.94	3.04	4.09	5.12	5.80	7.31	8.81
CONTROL	1.66	2.88	**3.87**	**5.05**	**5.78**	7.42	**9.10**
P =	0.320	0.620	**0.047**	**0.002**	**0.01**	0.430	0.005
RIGHT SIDE	MEANS LATENCIES OF THE BAEP PEAKS						
	I	II	III	IV	V	VI	VII
SCHIZO-PHRENIA	1.73	2.87	3.99	5.30	5.94	7.38	**8.62**
DEPRESSION	1.89	2.95	3.97	5.16	5.85	7.29	9.05
CONTROL	1.70	2.83	3.88	5.09	5.83	7.40	**8.97**
P =	0.660	0.460	0.060	0.090	0.400	0.920	**0.004**

As shown in Table 2 schizophrenics have on the left side a statistically significant prolongation of the III-wave latency ($p < 0.05$), IV-wave latency ($p = 0.002$), V-wave latency ($p = 0.01$) and shortening of the VII-wave latency ($p = 0.005$). On the right side - significant shortening of the VII-wave latency was also obtained ($p = 0.004$). In some patients we didn't find IV and/or VII peaks, distinctly (it was most characteristic for depression group). In the rest of patients shortening of IV - VII interval in comparison with the control group was observed (means on the left side: 3.39 + 0.56 in schizophrenics, n = 17, 3.50 + 1.06 in depressives, n = 4,4.05 + 0.30 in the control group , n = 16).

These differences between schizophrenic group and control one on the left side had a high statistical significance in the Median test (M = 3.76, $p = 0.003$). This dependence is pictured in table 3.

Table 3. **Interwave IV - VII On the Left Side in Schizoprenics and Control (median of interval IV-VII = 3.76)**

		SCHIZOPHRENIC	CONTROL	TOTAL
	> 3.76	4	12	16
Me = 3.76				
	< 3.76	13	4	17
	N =	17	16	33
	missing cases:	10	7	
Chi-Square = 8.742			p = 0.003	

In the group of patients suffering from the affective disorders no statistically significant differences in the latencies of several waves in comparison to the control group were observed. We found however a statistically significant negative correlation between anxiety level (in the BPRS Scale) and the shortening of the interwave IV - VII, present in the whole population (n = 37, r = 0.27, $p = 0.03$) and in the schizophrenic + control group (n = 33, r = -0.561, $p = 0.01$).

DISCUSSION

The data presented suggest, that in schizophrenia sufferers a disturbed regulation of the stimuli conduction may be manifested (Szelenberger, 1982). Initial waves of brainstem potentials have prolonged values whereas later waves have shorter latency than in the healthy. That regulation is affected also by the state of the central nervous system perceived and manifested in behaviour as anxiety. It was seen more distinctly and was more statistically significant on the left side of the brainstem. This is in accordance with the suggestion that there is a different emotional response from left and right hemispheres.

CONCLUSIONS

1. The changes in the latencies of some waves (III, IV, V, VII) of auditory brainstem evoked potentials seem to differentiate schizophrenia sufferers from the control group. Particular characteristic seem to be the shortening of the interval between IV and VII wave on the left side.

2. In the affected with a higher anxiety level, the shortening of the interval between IV and VII waves was found significantly more often.

REFERENCES

Ashton, H., Golding, J.F., Marsh, V.R., Thompson, J.W., Hassanyeh, F., Tyrer, S.P. (1988) Cortical evoked potentials and clinical rating scales as measures of depressive illness. *Psychological Medicine, 18,* 305-317.

Bolz, J., Giedke, H., Heimann, H. (1979) GSR, AEP and CNV in depressed patients and healthy controls. In Lehmann, D., & Callaway, E. (Eds.) *Human Evoked Potentials - Applications and Problems.* New York: Plenum Press (p. 448).

Buchsbaum, M.S., Coppola, R. (1976) Signal-to-noise ratio and response variability in affective disorders and schizophrenia. In Begleiter, H. (Ed.) *Evoked Potentials and Behavior.* Plenum Press (p. 447-465).

Dimond, S.I., Farrington, L., Gohnson, P. (1976) Differing emotional response from right and left hemispheres. *Nature, 261,* 690.

Donchin, E. (1979) Event-related brain potentials: A tool in the study of human information processing. In Begleiter, H. (Ed.) *Evoked Brain Potentials and Behavior.* New York: Plenum Press (p. 13-88).

Dongier, M., Dubrowsky, B., Engelmann, F. (1973) Event-related slow potentials of the brain: Their relations to behaviour. *Electroencephal. Clinical. Neurophysiology, 35, Suppl. 33,* 309-315.

Fabiani, M., Sohmer, H., Tait, C., Gafni, M., Kinarti, R. (1979) A functional measure of brain activity: Brainstem transmission time. *Electroenceph. Clinical Neurophysiology, 47,* 438-491.

Patterson, J.V., Michalewsky, H.J., Starr, A. (1988) Latency variability of the components of auditory event-related potentials to infrequent stimuli in aging, Alzheimer-type dementia, and depression. *Electroenceph. Clinical Neurophysiology, 71,* 450-460.

Picton, T.W., Hillyard, S.A. (1974) Human auditory evoked potentials. I Effect of attention. *Electroenceph. Clinical Neurophysiology, 36,* 191-199.

Shagass, C., Roemer, R.A., Straumenis, J.J., Armadeo, M. (1985) Evoked potential correlates of psychosis. *Biological Psychiatry, 20,* 701-702.

Szelenberger, W. (1982) Brainstem Auditory Evoked Potentials. *Warsaw Medical Academy,* 100-102.

COGNITIVE-BEHAVIORAL TREATMENTS FOR PANIC DISORDER

J. Margraf, M. Göbel and S. Schneider

Fachbereich Psychologie, Philipps-Universität, Gutenbergstr. 18, D-3550 Marburg, West Germany

Anxiety attacks were already described by Freud (1895) as one cardinal feature of what he proposed to call "anxiety neurosis." Such attacks are frequent among agoraphobics, but also occur in patients without phobic avoidance. Especially interesting for behavioral and biological researchers alike is that the patients often cannot tell what exactly caused their anxiety attacks. Many patients report at least some instances where their anxiety came "out of the blue." Recent research, however, suggests that internal cues serve as triggers for anxiety in such patients. These cues are usually bodily sensations (e.g., palpitations, dyspnea, dizziness) that are associated with an immediately imminent bodily or mental catastrophe. This may explain, why panic patients seek professional help more often than patients with any other psychological disorder (Boyd, 1986).

In the past 20 years exposure based treatments were systematically developed and tested. This confirmed exposure in vivo as the method of choice for the treatment of avoidance behavior and panic attacks triggered by external stimuli (Marks, 1987). Attempts to treat agoraphobia with systematic desensitization have been less successful (Thorpe and Burns, 1983). The long-term efficacy of exposure treatments for agoraphobia has been clearly established by numerous studies with follow-ups of up to 9 years (Hand et al., 1974; Mathews et al., 1977; Emmelkamp & Kuipers, 1979; Goldstein, 1982; McPherson et al., 1980; Munby and Johnston, 1980; Burns et al.,1983; Michelson et al., 1985; Hand et al., 1986; Lelliott et al., 1987; Fiegenbaum, 1988). The success rate (proportion of patients rated as "improved" or "much improved") averages 75-80% at the end of treatment. Follow up results show that gains are usually maintained and that relapses are rare (Marks, 1987). An especially high success rate has been reported for a program using a massed flooding approach: 78% of 104 patients were totally symptom free and another 19% "moderately" to "highly" improved five years after treatment (Fiegenbaum, 1988). The emergence of new symptoms ("symptom substitution") is not more frequent after successful exposure treatment than in the general population (see reviews by Mathews et al., 1981; Marks,1987). An important practical problem of exposure therapy seems to be acceptance. In some studies up to 20 or 25% of the patients refused treatment or terminated it prematurely (see O'Brien and Barlow, 1984; Michelson, 1987). Barlow and Waddell (1985) point out that treatment refusal seems to be less frequent in graded exposure (under 5% in three studies).

While there is widespread agreement about the efficacy of exposure based methods for phobic avoidance behavior, the effects on "spontaneous" panic attacks have been neglected by researchers and therapists. Until recently, the direct treatment of panic attacks was not in thefocus of behavior therapy (Jacob and Rapport, 1984; Barlow and Waddell, 1985; Margraf et al.,1986; Margraf and Ehlers, 1986). Only a few treatment studies on agoraphobia reported results on panic attacks. Jacob and Rapport (1984) found eight such studies. Six of these obtained a reduction in panic attacks as a consequence of treatment focussing on avoidance behavior. Measures of panic were insufficient in these early studies. However, most recent investigations have confirmed the earlier findings of a positive effect of exposure with anxiety provoking situations on panic attack frequency and intensity in agoraphobics (Telch et al., 1985; Michelson et al., 1985; Chambless et al., 1986; Lelliott et al., 1987; cf. however, Arnow et al., 1986).

In the past few years a number of authors have reported success in the direct treatment of panic attacks using cognitive behavioral methods. Most programs combine exposure to internal cues (usually bodily sensations) with the teaching of anxiety management skills and cognitive methods that aim at changing the appraisal of anxiety symptoms. These programs were developed for patients whose main complaints were panic attacks and not phobic avoidance behavior. However, they are a useful addition to the treatment of agoraphobics that also suffer from "spontaneous" panic attacks since relapses sometimes seem to follow the reoccurrence of one or more panic attacks (Gelder and Marks, 1966). In a diagnostic phase information is gathered about possible triggers for panic attacks and other factors that influence the probability of their occurrence (e.g., cognitions, hyperventilation, interpersonal events, eating habits). The patients are then given a rationale for the development of their attacks based on psychophysiological or cognitive models (Clark, 1986; Margraf et al., 1986; Ehlers and Margraf, 1989). "Spontaneous" as well as "situational" panic attacks are explained as the result of a vicious circle involving the individually relevant bodily sensations (e.g., palpitations, dizziness), cognitions (e.g., "I am losing control"), and behaviors (e.g., hyperventilation). Depending on the individual symptoms the appropriate techniques for exposure to anxiety symptoms, their management and reattribution are deduced as methods of breaking the vicious circle.

Respiration based methods should be used, if the patients consider the effects of voluntary hyperventilation as similar to their naturally occurring panic attacks. Exposure to the symptoms induced by hyperventilation can lead to habituation of feared bodily sensations. The patients repeatedly perform hyperventilation exercises. They are instructed to pay attention to their bodily sensations, cognitions, and level of anxiety. After a few repetitions the somatic symptoms are experienced as less dangerous and anxiety decreases to appropriate levels. Homework assignments using hyperventilation should only be given after the patients have acquired some sense of control over the exercise. Anxiety increasing thoughts (e.g., "I might faint") may be identified and replaced by more rational alternatives.

In addition, chronic hyperventilation can be treated by respiratory control approaches (Clark et al., 1985; Salkovskis et al., 1986a). Here, patients learn to use slow diaphragmatic breathing as a coping strategy that prevents or interrupts acute hyperventilation and the ensuing panicogenic symptoms. At first, the patients are lying on their bellies with their hands folded under their heads. In this position abdominal breathing is automatically used. The patients concentrate on the breathing movements of their abdomen and thus learn to perceive abdominal breathing. Subsequently, this is practiced while lying on the back, sitting, and eventually standing. Once the patients have mastered diaphragmatic breathing, they are instructed to imagine anxiety-inducing situations or sensations and to use correct breathing as a coping technique. Taperecordings may be useful for breathing exercises at home. A respiration rate of 8-12 cycles per minute has been favourable in most cases.

Palpitations are the most frequent symptom of panic attacks and consequently many patients are afraid of having a cardiac disease. Extreme cases of this fear have in the past been called "cardiac neurosis". Exposure to cardiac symptoms can be conducted using physical exercises such as climbing stairs, knee-bending, or running. Even mild degrees of exercise lead to increases in heart rate and stroke volume that are much stronger than those that usually accompany panic attacks (Taylor et al., 1986; Margraf et al., 1987). In addition, most patients show low physical fitness which makes them even more likely to experience palpitations subsequent to physical effort (Taylor et al., 1987). A comparison of the symptoms accompanying physical exercise and panic attacks facilitates the reappraisal of sensations that are otherwise interpreted catastrophically. In addition, exposure to an on-line display of the patient's own ECG is helpful in some cases.

There are numerous other methods to expose patients to their internal threat cues depending on the individual symptoms of the patients. For example, Griez and van den Hout (1986) had patients breathe high concentrations of carbon dioxide. This leads to symptoms similar to those of hyperventilation. Bonn et al. (1973) used lactate infusion to produce anxiety symptoms. Other examples are rowing on a remote lake, riding on a roller coaster, or going to the sauna (Bartling et al., 1980). Many patients fear catastrophic consequences of their panicattacks or symptoms that cannot be produced voluntarily or that are beyond the patient's or therapist's control (e.g., going crazy, being stared at by strangers, getting in trouble with the boss). In these cases, exposure in sensu is usually a helpful complement to exposure in vivo. Flooding in imagination has been used successfully by Foa and her colleagues (e.g. Steketee and Foa, 1985) in obsessive-compulsives and by Chambless et al. (1982) in agoraphobics. During these exercises it is attempted to induce a high level of anxiety and to keep the image vivid until anxiety decreases.

In patients that are especially frightened by tachycardias vagal innervation techniques have been shown to be clinically effective by Sartory and Olajide (1988). Patients are given a heart rate monitor that displays beat-by-beat heart rate. The therapist then instructs the patients about assessment of heart rate, the phenomenon of sinus arrhythmia and its relationship to breathing,and the effects of vagal and sympathetic innervation on cardiac activity. By pressure stimulation of baroreceptors vagal activity can be increased which results in decreased heart rate and stroke volume.

So far, there are fewer studies of the efficacy of behavioral treatment for patients that suffer primarily from panic attacks unrelated to external phobic stimuli than for agoraphobia. Many of these are case studies or uncontrolled studies of small samples (Clark et al., 1985; Gitlin et al., 1985; Griez and van den Hout, 1983; Rapee, 1985; Salkovskis et al., 1986; Shear et al., 1988; Waddell et al., 1984). However, there are some recent studies comparing several treatment conditions (Barlow et al., 1984; Bonn et al., 1984; Griez and van den Hout, 1986; Klosko et al., 1988; Ost, 1988; Sartory and Olajide, 1988). Patients in these studies in general met DSM-III criteria for panic disorder, sometimes also for agoraphobia with panic attacks. Duration of treatment was most often about 15 sessions although there was considerable variation across studies. The most important outcome measures were the frequency and intensity of panic attacks, usually assessed by standardized diaries. The most frequently used treatment components in addition to giving a detailed treatment rationale were exposure to anxiety symptoms, cognitive techniques, and respiratory control. In all studies strong and stable improvement or complete remission was obtained for the majority of patients. Gains made by the end of treatment on the average were retained or patients improved further during follow-up. In the great majority of patients panic attacks could be abolished completely. The direct treatment of panic attacks was superior to indirect approaches in the three studies that investigated this topic (Bonn et al., 1984;Griez and van den Hout, 1986; Sartory and Olajide, 1988).

Further information on possible active ingredients of cognitive-behavioral treatments for panic disorder comes from an ongoing study conducted by our group. We compare the efficacy of a pure cognitive therapy with a combined cognitive-behavioral therapy in patients with panic disorder. Both therapies are based on the psychophysiological model of panic attacks (Margraf et al. 1986). The cognitive therapy aims at identifying and correcting, by means of reattribution techniques, the misinterpretation of anxiety provoking internal stimuli. In the combined treatment we additionally make behavioral experiments that involve exposure to internal and external fear stimuli. Preliminary results show that both treatments are similarly effective in reducing "spontaneous" panic attacks. After 15 therapy-sessions 84% of the patients were free of panic attacks in contrast to two attacks per week during a 4-week baseline prior to the beginning of the therapy. Furthermore, both treatment programs did not differ in their efficacy in reducing measures of anxiety, agoraphobic cognitions and fear of body sensations. The findings suggest that even a purely cognitive treatment without any exposure to anxiety provoking cues can be highly effective. Although further controlled studies of larger samples should investigate the active ingredients of the different treatment programs, the results available so far are encouraging in their consistency. They justify further research and the clinical application of the treatment methods presented above.

REFERENCES

Arnow, B.A., Taylor, C.B., Agras, W.S., and Telch, M.J. (1986) Enhancing agoraphobia treatment outcome by changing couple communication patterns. *Behavior Therapy, 16*, 452-467.

Barlow, D.H., Cohen, A.S., Waddell, M.T., Vermilyea, B.B., Klosko, J.S., Blanchard, E.B., and DiNardo, P.A. (1984) Panic and generalized anxiety disorders: Nature and treatment. *Behavior Therapy, 15*, 431-449.

Barlow, D.H., and Waddell, M.T. (1985) Agoraphobia. In D.H. Barlow (Ed.), *Clinical Handbook of Psychological Disorders*. New York: Guilford.

Bartling, G., Fiegenbaum, W., and Krause, R. (1980) *Reizüberflutung. Theorie und Praxis*. Stuttgart: Kohlhammer.

Bonn, J.A., Harrison, J., and Rees, W. (1973) Lactate-induced anxiety: Therapeutic application. *British Journal of Psychiatry, 119*, 468-470.

Bonn, J.A., Readhead, C.P.A., and Timmons, B.A. (1984) Enhanced adaptive behavioral response in agoraphobic patients pretreated with breathing retraining. *Lancet*, 665-669.

Boyd, J.H. (1986) Use of mental health services for treatment of panic disorder. *American Journal of Psychiatry, 143*, 1569-1574.

Burns, L.E., Thorpe, G.L., Cavallero, A., and Gosling, J. (1983) *Agoraphobia eight years after behavioral treatment: A follow-up study with interview, questionnaire and behavioral data.* Presented at the 17. Annual Meeting of the Association fo the Advancement of Behavior Therapy/World Congress of Behavior Therapy, Washington, D.C., November 1983.

Chambless, D.L., Foa, E.B., Groves, G.A., and Goldstein, A.J. (1982) Exposure and communication training in the treatment of agoraphobia. *Behaviour Research and Therapy, 20*, 219-231.

Chambless, D.L., Goldstein, A.J., Gallagher, R., and Bright, P. (1986) Integrating behavior therapy and psychotherapy in the treatment of agoraphobia. *Psychotherapy, 23*, 150-159.

Clark, D.M. (1986) A cognitive approach to panic. *Behaviour Research and Therapy, 24*, 461-470.

Clark, D.M., Salkovskis, P.M., and Chalkley, A.J. (1985) Respiratory control as a treatment for panic attacks. *Journal of Experimental Psychiatry and Behaviour Therapy, 16*, 23-30.

Ehlers, A. and Margraf, J. (1989) The psychophysiological model of panic. In P.M.G.Emmelkamp, W. Everaerd, F. Kraaymaat, M. an der Son (Eds.) *Anxiety disorders*. Amsterdam:Swets.

Emmelkamp, P.M.G., and Kuipers, A.C.M. (1979) Agoraphobia: A follow-up study four years after treatment. *British Journal of Psychiatry, 134*, 352-355.

Fiegenbaum, W. (1988) Longterm efficacy of graded and massed exposure in agoraphobics. In I. Hand, and H.U. Wittchen (Eds.), *Treatments of Panic and Phobias*. Berlin: Springer.

Freud, S. (1895) Über die Berechtigung, von der Neurasthenie einen bestimmten Symptomkomplex als "Angstneurose" abzutrennen. *Neurologisches Zentralblatt, 2*. In S. Freud (1947). Gesammelte Werke. Band I. London: Imago.

Gelder, M.G., and Marks, I. (1966) Severe agoraphobia: A controlled prospective trial of behaviour therapy. *British Journal of Psychiatry, 112*, 309-319.

Gitlin, B., Martin, J., Shear, M.K., Frances, A., Ball, G., and Josephson, S. (1985) Behaviour therapy for panic disorder. *Journal of Nervous and Mental Disease, 173*, 742-743.

Goldstein, A.J. (1982) Agoraphobia: Treatment successes, treatment failures, and theoretical implications. In D.L. Chambless, and A.J. Goldstein (Eds.), *Agoraphobia: Multiple Perspectives on Theory and Treatment.* New York: Wiley.

Griez, E., and van den Hout, M.A. (1983). Treatment of phobophobia by exposure to CO-2 induced anxiety symptoms. *Journal of Nervous and Mental Disease, 171*, 506-508.

Griez, E., and van den Hout, M.A. (1986) CO 2- inhalation in the treatment of panic attacks. *Behaviour Research and Therapy, 24*, 145-150.

Hand, I., Lamontagne, Y., and Marks, I. (1974) Group exposure (flooding) in vivo for agoraphobics. *British Journal of Psychiatry, 124*, 588-602.

Hand, I., Angenendt, J., Fischer, M., and Wilke, C. (1986) Exposure in vivo with panic management: Treatment rationale and longterm outcome. In I. Hand, and H.U. Wittchen (Eds.), *Panic and Phobias*. Berlin: Springer.

Jacob, R., and Rapport, M.D. (1984) Panic disorder: Medical and psychological parameters. In S.M. Turner (Ed.), *Behavioural Theories and Treatment of Anxiety*. New York: Plenum Press.

Klosko, J.S., Barlow, D.H., Tassinari, R.B., and Cerny, J.A. (1988) Comparison of alprazolam and cognitive behaviour therapy in the treatment of panic disorder. A preliminary report. In I.Hand, and H.U. Wittchen (Eds.), *Treatments of Panic and Phobias*. Berlin: Springer.

Lelliott, P.T., Marks, I.M., Monteiro, W.O., Tsakiris, F., and Noshirvani, H. (1987) Agoraphobia 5 years after imipramine and exposure. Outcome and predictors. *Journal of Nervous and Mental Disease*, 175, 599-605.

Margraf, J., and Ehlers, A. (1986) Erkennung und Behandlung von akuten Angstanfällen. In J.C.Brengelmann, and G. Böhringer (Eds.), *Therapieforschung für die Praxis 6*. München: Röttger.

Margraf, J., Ehlers, A., and Roth, W.T. (1986a) Biological models of panic disorder and agoraphobia - A review. *Behaviour Research and Therapy, 24*, 553-567.

Margraf, J., Taylor, C.B., Ehlers, A., Roth, W.T., and Agras, W.S. (1987). Panic attacks in the natural environment. *Journal of Nervous and Mental Disease, 175*, 558-565.

Marks, I. (1987) *Fears, Phobias, and Rituals. Panic, Anxiety, and Their Disorders*. New York:Oxford University Press.

Mathews, A.M., Gelder, M.G., and Johnston, D.W. (1981) *Agoraphobia: Nature and Treatment*. New York: Guilford Press.

Mathews, A.M., Teasdale, J., Munby, M., Johnston, D.W., and Shaw, P. (1977) A homebased treatment program for agoraphobia. *Behaviour Therapy, 8*, 915-924.

McPherson, F.M., Brougham, I., and McLaren, S. (1980) Maintenance of improvement of agoraphobic patients treated by behavioural methods - four year follow-up. *Behaviour Research and Therapy, 18*, 150-152.

Michelson, L. (1987). Cognitive behavioural assessment and treatment of agoraphobia. In L.Michelson, and L.M. Ascher (Eds.), *Anxiety and Stress Disorders*. New York: Guilford.

Michelson, L., Mavissakalian, M., and Marchione, K. (1985) Cognitive and behavioural treatments of agoraphobia: Clinical, behavioural, and psychophysiological outcomes. *Journal of Consulting and Clinical Psychology, 53*, 913-925.

Munby, M., and Johnston, D.W. (1980) Agoraphobia: The long-term follow-up of behavioural treatment. *British Journal of Psychiatry, 137*, 418-427.

O'Brien, G.T., and Barlow, D.H. (1984) Agoraphobia. In S.M. Turner (Ed.), *Behavioural Theories and Treatment of Anxiety*. New York: Plenum Press.

Ost, L.G. (1988) Applied relaxation vs. progressive relaxation in the treatment of panic disorder. *Behaviour Research and Therapy, 26*, 13-22.

Rapee, R.M. (1985). A case of panic disorder treated with breathing retraining. *Journal of Behavior Therapy and Experimental Psychiatry, 16*, 63-65.

Salkovskis, P.M., Jones, D.R.O., and Clark, D.M. (1986a) Respiratory control in the treatment of panic attacks: Replication and extension with concurrent measurement of behaviour and pCO2. *British Journal of Psychiatry, 148*, 526-532.

Salkovskis, P.M., Warwick, H.M.C., Clark, D.M., and Wessels, D.J. (1986b) A demonstration of acute hyperventilation during naturally occurring panic attacks. *Behaviour Research and Therapy,24*, 91-94.

Sartory, G., and Olajide, D. (1988) Vagal innervation techniques in the treatment of panic disorder. *Behaviour Research and Therapy, 26*, 431-434.

Shear, M.K., Ball, G.G., Josephson, S.C., and Gitlin, B.C. (1988) Behavioral therapy efficacy for panic. In I. Hand, and H.U. Wittchen (Eds.), *Treatments of Panic and Phobias*. Berlin: Springer.

Steketee, G., and Foa, E.B. (1985) Obsessive-compulsive disorder. In D.H. Barlow (Ed.), *Clinical Handbook of Psychological Disorders*. New York: Guilford.

Taylor, C.B., Sheikh, J., Agras, W.S., Roth, W.T., Margraf, J., Ehlers, A., Maddock, R.J., and Gossard, D. (1986) Ambulatory heart rate changes in patients with panic attacks. *American Journal of Psychiatry, 143*, 478-482.

Telch, M.J., Agras, W.S., Taylor, C.B., Roth, W.T., and Gallen, C.C. (1985) Combined pharmacological and behavioral treatment for agoraphobia. *Behaviour Research and Therapy, 23*, 325-335.

Thorpe, G.L., and Burns, L.E. (1983) *The Agoraphobic Syndrome*. Chichester: Wiley.

Waddell, M.T., Barlow, D.H., and O'Brien, G.T. (1984) A preliminary investigation of cognitive and relaxation treatment of panic disorder: Effects on intense anxiety vs. "background" anxiety. *Behaviour Research and Therapy, 22*, 393-402.

ANXIETY AND THE PERCEPTION OF THREAT-RELATED MATERIAL

M. Martin

University of Oxford, Department of Experimental Psychology, South Parks Road, Oxford, OX1 3UD

It has recently been proposed that higher levels of aaxiety are associated with selective processing of threat-related material. This idea fits well into the broader framework of the cognitive propagational model of emotion (Martin, 1988; in press; Martin & Williams, in press). According to this model, an emotion will influence cognitive processing in such a way that the particular emotion will be maintained or enhanced. For example, anxiety will increase,if the possibility of threat increases (see Martin, in press). That is to say, emotions tend to ensure preferential cognitive processing of information which is itself consonant with those emotions. Most of the empirical studies supporting this view, have compared anxious patients with normal subjects (e.g., Burgess et al., 1981; Foa & McNally, 1986; MacLeod,Mathews & Tata, 1986; Mathews & MacLeod, 1985, 1986; Watts et al., 1986). Although the results of these studies have been taken as evidence that anxiety level is the critical variable differentiating these two groups of subjects, it is possible that other differences account for the observed bias in selective attention, for example, whether a individuals see themselves as being in an emotional state or suffering from an emotional disorder.

One of the more popular paradigms for examining selective perception is the Stroop task where subjects are required to name the colour of the ink in which words are written while ignoring the meaning of the words. This paradigm has been widely investigated in cognitive psychology. The slowing down of ink colour naming times is usually attributed to interference arising from the meaning of words which is processed faster than ink colour, producing conflict probably at the response buffer (see Mastin, 1978, 1981). More interference occurs when the words are colour names such as green rather than words unrelated to colour. However, some interference occurs even for noncolour words compared with a control condition such as a row of coloured Xs. If highly anxious individuals selectively attend to threat-related words then in a Stroop task threat words may be more distracting to the highly anxious than the nonanxious. Thus it would be expected that the highly anxious will experience more Stroop interference from these threat words while colour naming than will nonanxious individuals. In support of this view, examination of the experimental literature reveals that, typically, anxious patients compared with non-anxious individuals show relatively slower colour naming when the words are threat-related than when they are not.

In order to evaluate the effects of anxiety per se on selective attention, three groups of nonpatients varying in anxiety level were selected from individuals in the community who were registered on the Oxford Subject Panel. Level of trait and state anxiety was assessed using the STAI (Spielberger, 1966). The high anxiety group had traitscores between 52 and 70 with a mean of 56. This sample had comparable trait anxiety scores to the Generalised Anxiety Disorder (GAD) patients presented later and those of anxiety patients in the studies by Mathewsand his colleagues. The rest of the normel sample was split at the median score to form two groups. The medium anxiety group had trait anxiety ranging from 38 to 49 and the low anxiety group had trait anxiety ranging from 20 to 32. There were 12 people in each group. The words used were the same as those used by Mathews and MacLeod (1985). If anxiety level is linked to selective processing of threat material then it would be expected that as anxiety increased there would be an increase in the time to name the ink colour of threat-related words in a Strooptask as shown in Figure 1.

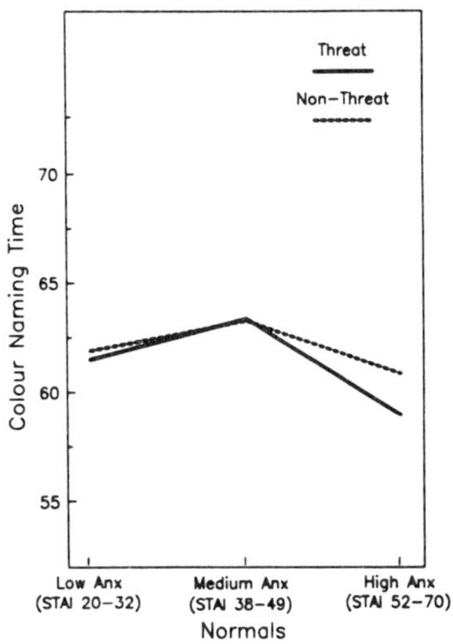

Figure 1. **Predicted mean colour naming times for threat and non-threatwords for normal subjects scoring low, medium and high on Spielberger Trait Anxiety Inventory**

It is more difficult to predict what will happen with the non-threatwords as they are positive to some degree, colour naming times may decrease with increasing anxiety. The obtained results from the Stroop task are shown in Figure 2. They provide no support for the anxiety hypothesis. Statistical analysis confirmed that there was no significant interaction between word type and level of anxiety as would be predicted by the anxiety hypothesis. The lack of an effect of anxiety in the predicted direction was surprising.

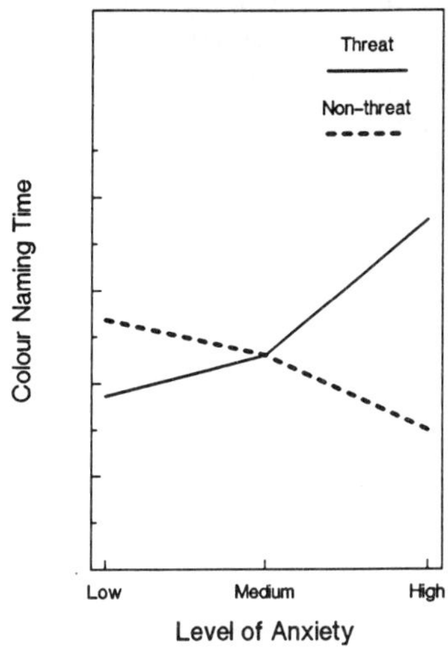

Figure 2. **Mean colour naming times for threat and non-threat words for normal subjects scoring low, medium and high on Spielberger Trait Anxiety Inventory.**

To test the hypothesis further, a group of 12 GAD patients were compared with a group of 12 people from the normal population who were matched on trait and state anxiety.

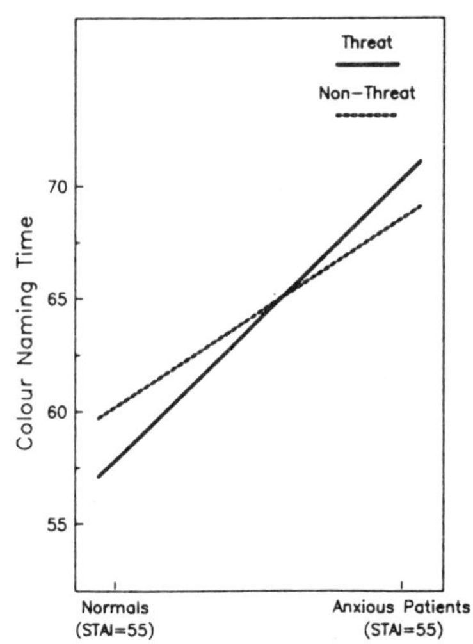

Figure 3. **Mean colour naming times for threat and nonthreat words for Generalised Anxiety Disorder patients and normal subjects matched on trait and state anxiety (STAI)**

If the hypothesis is correct, then there should be no difference between the two groups of subjects on the Stroop task as they are matched on anxiety level. If on the other hand,a variable other than anxiety such as viewing oneself as in emotional state or suffering from an emotional disorder is important, then the usual difference between patients and normals should reemerge. The obtained results shown in Figure 3 reveal that compared with normals, patients were slower at colour naming threat words than non-threat words.

The two groups did not differ in anxiety level. There was a significant interaction between materials and subject group. Thus it appears that anxiety is not the critical variable that differentiates those with selective bias from those without, but rather a characteristic of those who view themselves as suffering from an emotional disorder or being in an emotional state.

Although many studies (e.g., Burgess et al., 1981; Foa & McNally, 1986; MacLeod, Mathews & Tata, 1986; Mathews & MacLeod, 1985, 1986; Watts et al., 1986; Williams & Nulty, 1986; Williams & Broadbent, 1986) have demonstrated that anxiety or depression is associated with selective processing of threat-related material, several studies (e.g.,Clark, 1983; Clark et al., 1983; Segal, 1988) have failed to find such effects. Naturally, as experiments which fail to observe effects are considerably more difficult to publish this may lead to a bias in the literature. However, inspection of the control words used in previous studies led to the hypothesis that interference is observed when the stimuli differ in emotionality as well as degree of threat. Essentially, these studies have confounded emotionality and threat. In order to test this hypothesis, I conducted a study with David Clark and our graduate student, Rachel Williams. A group of twenty normal subjects rated the emotionality of the threat and non-threat words used in previous studies. The results supported the hypothesis as most studies which have observed a significant interference effect have confounded emotionality with threat since the control words used were significantly less emotional as well as less threatening than the threat words. (One exception was noted and that was an experiment by Watts et al. (1986) testing spider phobics on a Stroop task using spider related words. This will be returned to later.) In addition, none of the studies (Clark, 1983; Clark et al., 1983; Segal, 1988) which have used control words matched in emotionality to the threat words have found a significant interference effect.

To test the emotionality hypothesis further, an experiment manipulating emotionality and threat independently was conducted. Twelve new Generalised Anxiety Disorder patients and twelve new normal controls, named the colour of the ink in which threat words, neutral words and positive words were written. The stimulus words were selected so that the threat words and positive words were matched in emotionality and the neutral words were nonemotional. The results were clear cut. Analysis of variance revealed that there was a significant interaction between subject group and type of word. Tukey post hoc tests revealed that for the GAD group colour-naming times of threat and positive words were significantly slower than colour-naming of neutral words. Importantly, for the GAD group there was no significant difference between colournaming of the positive and threat words. In the normal group there were no significant differences in colour naming among the three types of words. These results suggest that anxious people selectively attend to emotional (positive and negative) material, not just threat material.

Altogether, the results of the studies reported here cast doubt on the interpretations of results of previous studies. It appears that it is not anxiety level per se which determines selective attention to threat material, but rather knowledge that a person is in an emotional state or suffering from an emotional disorder. It could be argued that anxious patients may have been anxious for longer than the matched anxious controls from the normal population. This is difficult to rule out, but trait anxiety is measured by asking subjects how they generally feel, so both groups will have experienced heightened anxiety over an extended period in time, making this type of explanation less plausible.

These results do not mean that anxiety is never associated with selective attention to threat. Most studies have used threat words (e.g., disease, fatal, hated, inadequate, mutilated, stupid), which would be considered highly threatening by both patients and normals. However, it could be argued that the key cognitive disturbance in anxiety disorders is the presence of a set of beliefs which lead patients to erroneously perceive certain predominately nonthreatening stimuli as threatening. Although this is also likely to happen to some extent in nonanxious individuals, such interpretations are quickly dismissed. Thus we should be able to observe, according to the emotionality hypothesis, enhanced processing of material which is judged by most people not to be threatening but may be idiosyncratically interpreted as threatening by a specific group of anxious individuals. For example, panic attacks are said to arise when certain benign body sensations are misinterpreted as potential catastrophies (Clark, 1986; Clark et al., 1988). Panic patients might be expected to experience selective attention to "breathless", but not to general threat words such as "dying". It is consistent with this view that the only study, Watts et al (1986), that has shown an interference effect in the absence of a difference in general emotionality between threat and non-threat words studied spider phobics and used their own idiosyncratic threat words (e.g., creepy, hairy, crawl, legs). It is probable that spider phobics would judge the spider-related words to be more emotional than the non-threat control words.

The implications for the cognitive propagational model are that it appears that individuals who view themselves as being in an emotional state or suffering from an emotional disorder selectively attend to emotional material irrespective of whether it is positive or negative. A stage of information processing sensitive to both positive and negative terms, which these results seem to suggest, could occur in at least two ways. First, it could be that some degree of emotional analysis may precede full semantic analysis. Second, it could be that the phenomenon is a consequence of morphemic decomposition. Many threat words are derivatives of positive lexemes (e.g., unkind-- from kind--, and disease-- from ease--), and it may be that at a preliminary stage of processing there is considerable cross-talk between the positive and negative terms.

Acknowledgements
The author wishes to thank the Leverhulme Trust and the Medical Research Council for their financial support.

REFERENCES

Burgess, I.S., Jones, L.M., Robertson, S.A., Radcliff, W.N., Emerson,E. (1981) The degree of control exerted by phobic and non-phobic verbal stimuli over the recognition behaviour of phobics and non-phobic subjects. *Behaviour Research and Therapy*, *19*, 233-243.

Clark, D.M. (1983) *Differential effects of mood on the accessibility of positive and negative information.* Unpublished Dr.phil thesis, University of Oxford. Chapters 5 and 6.

Clark, D.M. (1986) A cognitive approach to panic. *Behaviour Research and Therapy, 24*, 461-470.

Clark, D.M., Salkovskis, P.M., Gelder, M.G., Koehler, K., Martin, M.,Anastasiades, P., Hackman, A., Jeavons, A., Middleton, H. (1988) Tests of a cognitive theory of panic. In I. Hand, & U. Wittchen. *Panic and phobias*. Berlin: Springer Verlag.

Foa, E.B., McNally, R.J. (1986) Sensitivity to feared stimuli inobsessive-compulsives: A dichotic listening analysis. *Cognitive Therapy and Research*, *10*, 477-485.

Martin, M. (1978) Speech recoding in silent reading. *Memory & Cognition, 6*, 108-114.

Martin, M. (1981) Reverse Stroop effect with concurrent tasks. *Bulletin of the Sychonomic Society, 17*, 8-9.

Martin, M. (1988) Individual differences in imagery for emotionalevents. In C. Cornoldi (Ed.), *Imagery and Cognition*. University of Padua.

Martin M. (in press-a) Cognitive basis of anxiety. In R.J. Takens Ed.), *European Perspectives in Psychology*. New York: John Wiley.

Martin, M. (in press-b) *On the induction of mood.* Clinical Psychology Review.

Martin, M., Williams, R. (in press) Imagery and emotion: Clinical and experimental approaches In P.J. Hampson, D.F. Marks, & J.T.E.Richardson (Eds.), *Imagery - current Developments*. London: Routledge & Kegan Paul.

Mathews, A., MacLeod, C. (1985). Selective processing of threat cues in anxiety states. *Behaviour Research and Therapy*, *23*, 563-569.

Mathews, A., MacLeod, C. (1986) Discrimination of threat cues without awareness in anxiety states. *Journal of Abnormal Psychology,* 95 ,131-138.

MacLeoc C., Mathews, A., Tata, P. (1986) Attentional bias in emotional disorders. *Journal of Abnormal Psychology, 95*, 15-20.

Segal, Z.V. (1988) Appraisal of the self-schema construct in cognitive models of depression. *Psychological Bulletin, 103*, 1-16

Spielberger, C.D. (1966) The effects of anxiety on complex learning and academic achievement. In C.D. Spielberger (Ed.), *Anxiety and Behavior.* New York: Academic Press.

Watts, F.N. , McKenna, F.P., Sharrock, R., Trezise, L. (1986) Colournaming of phobia-related words. *British Journal of Psychology, 77*, 97-108.

Williams J.M.G., Nulty, D.D. (1986) Construct accessibility, depression and the emotional Stroop task: transient mood or stable structure? *Personality and Individual Differences*, 7, 485-491.

Williams, J.M.G., Broadbent, K. (1986) Distraction by emotional stimuli: use of the Stroop task with suicide attempters. *British Journal of Clinical Psychology, 25*, 101-110.

PREPAREDNESS, PREPOTENCY, AND FEAR ACQUISITION

H. Merckelbach, M.A. van den Hout and I. Lavy

University of Limburg, The Netherlands

INTRODUCTION

In the last two decades, several authors have argued that evolutionary considerations might be of relevance to learning models of phobias (Marks, 1969; Seligman, 1971). In this context, the notions of "preparedness" and "prepotency" are frequently cited. This chapter evaluates the empirical basis on which these notions rest. It presents a broad, overall review of the main findings in this area rather than an exhaustive summary of experimental and clinical studies on preparedness and prepotency. For a detailed description of these studies, the reader is referred to McNally (1987).

Preparedness and Conditioning

The conditioning approach that dominated behaviour therapy in the 50s and early 60s assumed that an object turns into a phobic stimulus (conditioned stimulus; CS) whenever that object is paired with a painful, traumatic event (unconditioned stimulus; UCS). In the 70s it gradually became clear that this assumption is untenable. Most importantly,]epidemiological studies (e.g., Agras et al., 1969) drew attention to the fact that there are numerous objects (e.g., cars, rifles) which seldom become phobic stimuli although they are regularly associated with traumatic events. These studies suggested that phobias are selectively distributed, that is to say, pertain to a relatively narrow class of stimuli (e.g., snakes, spiders, open spaces etc.). It is against this background that Seligman (1971) introduced his preparedness hypothesis. According to this hypothesis, the selectivity of phobic fears is due to an evolutionary predisposition ("preparedness") operating in fear conditioning. Briefly, the hypothesis states that, as a result of genetic transmission, modern man tends to react with fear to stimuli that have been survival-threatening in the course of human evolution. Even a mild, aversive UCS that accompanies these stimuli would activate this tendency.

Four important predictions can be derived from the preparedness hypothesis. The first prediction is that phobias are selectively distributed, because most of them are directed at stimuli that have been survival-relevant during man's phylogenesis. The second prediction is that, as a result of a genetically based predisposition, fear of survival-relevant stimuli is easily acquired. Finally, it is predicted that precisely, because fear of survival-relevant stimuli has a biological basis, it extinguishes slowly (third prediction) and is non-cognitive, i.e. is insensitive to verbal manipulation (fourth prediction). Table 1 shows to what extent these predictions have been confirmed by various research paradigms.

Some fear survey studies among normal populations report fear hierarchies that are difficult to reconcile with the idea that most fears are directed at survival-relevant stimuli. For example, in his community study, Kirkpatrick (1984) found that fear of roller-coasters and fear of untimely death were the top intense fears of women. For men the fear of being punished by God ranked highest. It has also been found that fear of such "prepared" animals as snakes and spiders probably originates from the strange appearance and the unpredictability of these animals rather than their survival-threatening nature (Merckelbach et al., 1987).

Table 1: **Predictions and results of preparedness research**

Predictions	Fear Surveys	Clinical studies	Conditioning studies	Animal studies
Selectivity of fears due to "preparedness"	-	?		+
Easy acquisition of "prepared" fears		-	-	
Resistance to extinction of "prepared" fears		?	?	+
Insensitivity to instructions of "prepared" fears			?	

A minus sign (-) indicates that, on the whole, research has yielded evidence that does not support the predictions. A plus sign (+) indicates that research has yielded mixed or inconclusive results. The absence of a sign indicates that no relevant data are available.

Clinical studies have yielded mixed results. Some researchers (de Silva et al., 1977) found that a majority of clinical fears are prepared in the sense that they involve stimuli that were probably survival-relevant to pretechnological man. Other researchers (Merckelbach et al., 1988) have failed to confirm this finding. Similarly, it is far from clear whether or not phobias that do pertain to survival-relevant stimuli ("prepared phobias") are characterized by a poor treatment outcome ("resistance to extinction"). However, all clinical studies agree in one respect:

None of them found any evidence to suggest that prepared phobias are associated with a sudden or quick onset ("easy acquisition"). If the preparedness hypothesis is correct, than one predicts that mild fear responses to survival-relevant cues can be easily elicited in normal, non-phobic subjects. A number of conditioning studies have examined this issue. In most of them, autonomic (skin conductance, heart rate) responses of normal subjects are conditioned to slides depicting survival-relevant (snakes, angry faces) or survival-irrelevant (flowers, happy faces) cues by means of an aversive, electric shock UCS. In such classical conditioning set-up, several parameters can be studied, e.g., the speed with which the conditioned autonomic response is acquired, the speed in which it extinguishes and the extent to which it can be modulated by instructions. Meanwhile, the results that have generated by this paradigm are confusing. Thus, studies carried out by the Öhman group claimed to have shown that responses conditioned to survival-relevant stimuli extinguish more slowly than responses conditioned to survival-irrelevant stimuli. Some of these studies also reported that responses conditioned to survival-relevant stimuli are non-cognitive, i.e., are not modulated by instructions (Öhman, 1986). Subsequent research conducted in other centers have largely failed to replicate or cross-validate these findings (McNally, 1987). Additionally, nearly all conditioning studies concerned with preparedness have concluded that conditioned responses to survival-relevant stimuli are not more readily acquired than those to survival-irrelevant stimuli.

In recent series of experiments, Mineka (1987) sought to illuminate the etiology of snake fears in rhesus monkeys. Mineka employed a vicarious conditioning paradigm during which laboratory-reared monkeys ("observers") with no prior fear of snakes observed wild-reared monkeys ("models") reacting fearfully in the presence of either a snake or a flower. With this paradigm it was repeatedly found that, after having viewed models reacting fearfully to a snake, observer monkeys acquired an extremely persistent fear of snakes. On the other hand, after having seen models reacting fearfully to a flower, observer animals did not develop a fear of flowers.

Prepotency and Agoraphobia

Whereas "preparedness" refers to a special type of conditioning (interaction between survival-relevant CS and aversive UCS), "prepotency" refers to a certain class of stimuli that are said to elicit strong and slowly habituating fear responses which are unlearned. In the animal literature, incidental illustrations of prepotent stimuli can be found. For example, pictures of threatening monkeys elicit fear in rhesus infants that have been reared in isolation. As for pathological fears in humans, it has been suggested that such stimuli as blood (resulting in the vasovagal collapse in blood phobics), eyes (related to social fears), and public territory (related to agoraphobia) have prepotent characteristics (see review by Marks, 1969; 1987). However, experimental evidence to support the notion of prepotency is scarce. In both animal and human studies, it is often impossible to differentiate between biological factors on the one hand and the complex learning history of subjects (which is often unknown) on the other hand (for examples see Delprato, 1980).

In a recent study, van den Hout et al. (1990) examined the hypothesis that extraterritorial surroundings are prepotent, i.e., that humans tend to be alert to possible danger in public places. Normal, non-phobic subjects (n=20) were exposed to 7 loud, aversive human screams (6 sec.,90 dB), presented through a walkman, while in a crowded department store (agoraphobic environment). Control subjects (n=15) were exposed to the same loud screams in a non-agoraphobic surrounding close to the subjects home. Agoraphobic and non-agoraphobic places were matched in terms of familiarity and self-rated pleasantness. After each scream, subjects were asked to indicate the amount of distress they had experienced. Results showed that during the later trials, screams elicited more

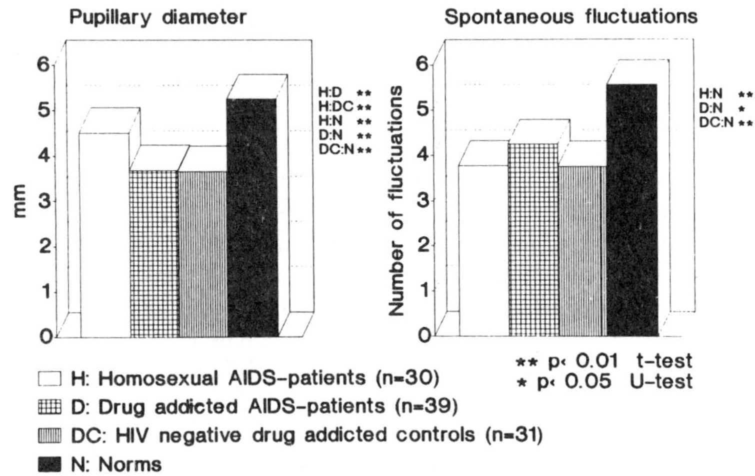

Figure 1. **Mean experienced distress reported immediately after each scream**

distress in agoraphobic than in non-agroaphobic places (see fig. 1). Furthermore, when retested with two mild screams (65 dB), subjects in the agoraphobic place reacted with cardioacceleration whereas control subjects reacted with mild deceleration. These findings are in line with the idea that agoraphobic places represent a prepotent background against which aversive events (e.g., panic attacks) evoke strong and slowly habituating fear responses.

Table 1 clearly shows that research concerned with prepared fears in humans is characterized by poor replicability and negative findings. So far, the most telling illustrations of prepared fears have been found in infrahuman subjects. However, as an evolutionary theory, the preparedness hypothesis stresses the particular characteristics of each species' niche. Consequently, it would be premature to base theories about prepared learning in humans on infrahuman evidence. The same holds for the notion of prepotency. The above presented data suggest that agoraphobic places are prepotent. Yet, earlier work in this field has taught us that one positive finding represents too small a basis for theorizing. Corroboration of these data by means of, for example, the startle probe methodology (see Lang et al., this volume) is called for.

REFERENCES

Agras, W.W., Sylvester, D., Oliveau, D. (1969) The epidemiology of common fears and phobias. *Comprehensive Psychiatry, 10*, 151-156.

Delprato, D.J. (1980) Hereditary determinants of fears and phobias: A critical review. *Behavior Therapy, 11*, 79-103.

De Silva, P. Rachman, S., Seligman, M.E.P. (1977) Prepared phobias and obsessions: Therapeutic outcome. *Behaviour Research and Therapy, 15*, 65-77.

Kirkpatrick, D.R. (1984) Age, gender, and patterns of common intense fear among adults. *Behaviour Research and Therapy, 19*, 109-115.

Marks, I.M. (1969): *Fears and Phobias*. New York, Academic Press.

Marks, I.M. (1987): *Fears, Phobias and Rituals. Panic, Anxiety, and their disorders*. New York, Oxford University Press.

McNally, R.J. (1987) Preparedness and phobias: A review. *Psychological Bulletin, 101*, 283-303.

Merckelbach, H., van den Hout, M.A., van der Molen, G.M. (1987) Fear of animals: Correlations between fear ratings and perceived characteristics. *Psychological Reports, 60*, 1203-1209.

Merckelbach, H., van den Hout, M.A., Jansen, A., van der Molen, G.M. (1988) Many stimuli are frightening, but some are more frightening than others: The contributions of preparedness, dangerousness, and unpredictability to making a stimulus fearful. *Journal of Psychopathology and Behavioral Assessment, 10*, 355-366.

Mineka, S. (1987) A primate model of phobic fears. In H.J. Eysenck & I.Martin (Eds.): *Theoretical Foundations of Behavior Therapy*. New York,Plenum Press, pp. 81-111.

Öhman, A. (1986) Face the beast and fear the face: Animal and social fears as prototypes for evolutionary analyses of emotion. *Psychophysiology, 23*, 123-145.

Seligman, M.E.P. (1971) Phobias and preparedness. *Behavior Therapy, 2*, 307-320.

van den Hout, M.A., Lavy, I. Boek, C. van Dieren, A., de Jong, P. Lulofs, R., Merckelbach, H. (1990) Aversive events in agoraphobic and non-agoraphobic places: Some indications of prepared responding. (*Submitted for Publication*).

DOES CONTROLLABILITY REDUCE PHOBIC ANXIETY?

G. Sartory and I. Daum

University of Wuppertal and University of Tübingen, F.R.G.

Controllability concerns the contingent relationship between a reaction (or the possibility of a reaction) and the subsequent event. If a reaction brings about a change in an event, then this event is seen or thought to be controllable. A number of studies have been carried out on perceived control over laboratory stressors or irritants (Gatchel, McKinney & Koebernick, 1977; Geer & Maisel, 1972; Davison & Gatchel, 1970; Bowers, 1968; Glass, Reim & Singer, 1971). Subjects were given the option of a reaction without their using it or they were told that previous reactions were leading to subsequent events. These studies showed virtually without exception that the aversiveness of the stressor decreases with perceived controllability. By contrast, studies on instrumental control with subjects executing a motor response to control, the laboratory stressors have not shown consistent results, some showing that instrumental control poses a strain on the cardiovascular system (Light & Obrist, 1983) others again showed it to be stress reducing (Seligman, 1968).

Mineka & Kihlstrom (1978) first associated controllability with phobic anxiety by suggesting that the acquisition of fear responses as found in animal research could be interpreted as loss of control over aversive events. It could be argued that establshing control over phobic stimuli should result in reduction of phobic anxiety. Rachman et al. (1986) have recently given agoraphobics the option of escaping from phobic situations during therapy sessions. Their phobic anxiety subsided more rapidly than that of controls without the option of escape although hardly any patients made use of it. It seems likely that the knowledge of the escape option conveyed a sense of controllability over the situation which in turn had a significant share in fear reduction.

The present study was designed to investigate whether or not instrumental control over phobic stimuli has a fear-reducing effect in phobics. Slides with phobic content constituted the stimuli and outcome measures were subjective fear ratings and the cardiac response to the slides. As HR responses can be affected by movement, the effect of the motor responses can be affected by movement, the effect of the motor response alone was compared with instrumental control. Furthermore, the effect of instrumental control was contrasted with that of knowledge of slide offset.

METHOD

Forty-eight snake and spider phobic Ss were allocated to one of four groups. All Ss viewed three different slides showing the phobic object. Each of the three slides was shown in a block of six trials and the order of the three slides was varied randomly between Ss. The condition under which Ss viewed the slides differed between the four groups. MOT-PRED: This group viewed the slide for 8 to 10 sec when a tone of moderate intensity was administered whereupon Ss could switch off the slide and the tone by pressing a button. Ss thus had instrumental control over the phobic stimulus conveyed by the availability of a motor response and predictability of offset. MOT-NOPRED:A tone was administered 5 to 7 sec after slide onset which Ss switched off without, however, switching off the slide. Ss had a motor response available without predictability of slide offset. NOMOT-PRED: The tone was administered prior to slide offset. Ss of this and the next group had no motor response available; NOMOT-NOPRED: The tone was administered during slide-display. Groups were yoked with regard to slide duration.

Outcome measures were subjective fear ratings at the end of each block of slide presentation and the phasic cardiac and electrodermal responses to slide onset EMG responses and reaction times were monitored in the two groups with motor option and respiration in all groups.

RESULTS AND DISCUSSION

Groups differed with regard to the subjective anxiety rating: The group with instrumental control yielded a lower fear rating throughout the experiment than the other three groups who did not differ from each other. So it can be said that instrumental control brings about a reduction in subjective fear but execution of a motor reaction or prediction of offset does not.

Averaging over all groups resulted in an accelerative cardiac response to the slide as it had been obtained previously in phobics. Groups did not differ during the first block which can be considered an acquisition block but their cardiac reactions differed during the following blocks. The groups executing a motor response showed a systematic decline of the cardiac acceleration over blocks whereas the lack of a motor option led to resensitization of the accelerative response by the third block. Similarly, spontaneous EDRs showed a more systematic decline in the motor option groups compared with those of groups without motor option. Motor responses thus appeared to have had a stabilizing effect on autonomic activity.

The interaction of motor response by predictability had a strong effect upon the cardiac response to the slide. The group with instrumental control (MOT-PRED) showed a change from an accelerative to a decelerative response from the 1st to the 2nd block and response attenuation by the 3rd block. By comparison, the group with a motor reaction during mid-display of the slide (MOT-NOPRED) maintained the accelerative response over the second block. By the third block the response had subsided. It could be argued that the HR response constituted motor preparation in this group since the motor response occurred soon after slide onset. It would, however, not explain why motor preparation ceased by the 3rd block. The EMG response showed no changes over blocks nor did reaction time, thus not substantiating the notion of greater response efficiency by the third block. There were, however, differences in tonic EMG between groups. The controlling group showed a clear quadratic decline over blocks whereas the non-controlling group showed a more linear decline thereby maintaining a higher EMG level during the second block. It is possible that the introduction of a phobic slide during a high level of EMG activity leads to a greater cardiac reaction than one introduced during a low level of muscle activity which in turn allows for the stimulus processing indicated by the cardiac deceleration. The effect was in any case due to controllability rather than motor preparation. The group with knowledge of offset and no motor option (NOMOT-PRED) showed no systematic response attenuation, but reinstatement of the response in the last block. It could be argued that additional information to a phobic stimulus without the option acting upon it prevents orderly processing in specific phobics. The group without motor option or knowledge of offset (NO-MOT-NOPRED) showed no remarkable course of cardiac responding.

Finally, it could have been argued that the EMG response and reaction time differed between motor response groups since the controlling group was able to switch off the slide. This was, however, not the case.

The results seem to indicate that instrumental control over the phobic stimulus has a fear-reducing effect as reflected in subjective ratings, the attenuation of the cardiac response to fear-inducing slides and spontaneous EDRs.

A full account of this study is being published elsewhere:
Sartory, G. & Daum, I. Effects of controllability on subjective and cardiac responses in phobics. Submitted to Journal of Psychophysiology.

REFERENCES

Bowers, K. (1968) Pain, anxiety, and perceived control. *Journal of Clinical and Consulting Psychology, 32,* 596-602.

Gatchel, R.J., McKinney, M.E., Koebernick, L.F. (1977) Learned helplessness depression, and physiological responding. *Psychophysiology, 14,* 25-31.

Geer, J.H., Davison, G.C., Gatchel, R.J. (1970) Reduction of stress in humans through nonveridical perceived control of aversive stimulation. *Journal of Personality and Social Psychology, 16,* 731-738.

Geer, J.H., Maisel, E. (1972) Evaluating the effects of the prediction-control confound. *Journal of Personality and Social Psychology, 23,* 314-319.

Glass, D.C., Reim, B., Singer, J.E. (1971) Behavioral consequences of adaptation to controllable and uncontrollable noise. *Journal of Experimental Social Psychology, 7,* 244-257.

Light, K.C., Obrist, P.A. (1983) Task difficulty, heart rate reactivity and cardiovascular responses to an appetitive reaction time task. *Psychophysiology, 20,* 301-312.

Mineka, S., Kihlstrom, J.F. (1978) Unpredictable and uncontrollable events: A new perspective on experimental neurosis. *Journal of Abnormal Psychology, 87,* 256-271.

Rachman, S., Craske, M., Tallman, K. (1986) Does escape behavior strengthen agoraphobic avoidance? A replication. *Behavior Therapy, 17,* 366-384.

Seligman, M.E.P. (1968) Chronic fear produced by unpredictable electric shock. *Journal of Comparative and Physiological Psychology, 66,* 402-411.

PART IV:

THE PRESENT STATUS OF RESEARCH ON EATING DISORDERS

THE MODIFICATION OF HUMAN FOOD AVERSIONS: NEW APPLICATION OF BEHAVIOUR THERAPY

P. de Silva

Institute of Psychiatry, Depatment of Psychology, University of London, de Crespigny Park, London SE5 8AF

INTRODUCTION

Several studies have shown that human food aversions are widespread (e.g. Garb and Stunkard, 1974; Logue, Ophir and Strauss, 1981), but they hardly ever present as a clinical problem. However, it is likely that many people will seek help to have their food aversions modified, if clinicians offered such a service and it came to be widely reported as a clinical problem. Furthermore, in those cases where widespread food aversions exist, like for example, in cancer patients who acquire strong dislikes for foods temporally associated with the unpleasant consequences of some of the treatments they receive (e.g. Bernstein and , Webster, 1980), it will be of significance, if these aversions can be modified. The same applies to all anorexia syndromes where food aversion learning may play a part (Bernstein and Borson, 1986).

A good proportion of food aversions in humans are instances of conditioned taste aversion learning. That is, they have been acquired by a process of classical conditioning through the association of food with an unpleasant consequence - gastrointestinal illness. This type of conditioning has been described as a particularly powerful form or learning =de Silva and Rachman, 1987; Logue, 1985). Certainly, taste aversion learning often occurs, both in humans and in animals, with only one pairing of the stimulus and the response. This can occur even with a time lag between the stimulus and the response. And this learning has been found to be quite resistant to extinction (e.g. Garcia and Koelling, 1966; Logue, 1979, 1985).

There is evidence that also this learning is very strong, it is not unmodifiable. The literature on animal food aversions shows that, despite of the robustness of taste aversion, learning is generally observed, some learned aversions remit with time (e.g. Gustavson and Gustavson, 1985). Similarly, the work with alcoholic patients using a taste aversion paradigm, where the intervention consists of paring alcoholic beverage consumption with strong nausea, shows that any aversion developed may not last long (Nathan, 1985). Finally, survey studies of human food aversions have consistently shown that some aversions undergo natural remission (e.g. Logue et al., 1981). Thus, despite the robustness of food aversions that many writers have commented on, it is clear that at least some of them are modifiable.

adult humans, using behaviour therapy techniques.

METHOD

Subjects

The subjects were volunteers who had indicated that they had at least one food aversion. The criteria for inclusion were: (a) the aversion had existed for at least one year; (b) the aversion was strong with a negative hedonic value rating of 7 or more (see below); (c) it was not related to any allergic reaction; and (d) the subject had totally avoided consuming the food in question for the past 6 months. There were seven subjects, three males and four females. The mean age was 27 years. Three of the subjects had a clear history of a conditioning experience that led to the acquisition of the aversion.

Treatment

All subjects were treated individually with an in vivo - graded exposure programme. A hierarchy was constructed for the target food aversion the top item being consuming a normal quantity of the food in a way it was normally consumed in the subject's culture. The items were ordered on the basis of the difficulty of the action as rated by the subject on a 0-100 scale. The subject was encouraged to start with as high a step on the hierarchy as he/she was willing to try. The therapist was present at all sessions, encouraging the subject verbally and modelling the target behaviour. Verbal reinforcement was given for every successful step. In each session, in most cases, more than one step in the hierarchy was attempted. The sessions were held at two-to-four day intervals. The subjects were also encouraged to consume the food outside the sessions, once consuming the food, however limited,was achieved within the sessions.

Assessment

The main measure was a subjective rating scale for the hedonic value of the food (de Silva and Rachman, 1987). It was a bi-polar scale from 10 ('strongly disliked') through 0 ('neither liked nor disliked') to +10 ('very much liked'). The pretreatment assessment also included a behavioural avoidance test, to ensure that the subjects had strong avoidance of the food concerned. The subjects were also asked to keep a record of all relevant instances outside the sessions once the food, in any form, began to be consumed in the sessions.

RESULTS

Five of the seven subjects were able to reach the top of the hierarchy within four sessions. All but one were willing to attempt a relatively high item on the four sessions. All but one were willing to attempt a relatively high item on the hierarchy as their first step, and were able to carry it out. One subject failed to complete the programme, and another failed to show any change. These subjects did not differ from the others on any relevant variable. In terms of the hedonic value ratings, the changes showed a clear shift from the 'dislike' end of the scale to the middle; there was little indication of the foods becoming 'liked'. These changes are summarized in Table 1.

Table 1. **Changes in hedonic value of target food**

Subject	Pre-treatment	Post-treatment	Follow-up (6 months)
1	-9	0	0
2	-10	+1	+2
3	-7	-1	+1
4	-8	0	0
5	-9	1	0
6	-10	-	-
7	-8	-7	-

The frequency of consumption, once started, was maintained at six months after the final session, as shown by the self-records.

DISCUSSION

This essentially exploratory study shows that human food aversions are modifiable through the use of behaviour therapy techniques. The key technique was graded in vivo exposure. The relative contribution of modelling, verbal prompting and verbal reinforcement to the effectiveness of the intervention is not clear. In the sessions, the subjects seemed to be persuaded to attempt their hierarchy steps by the therapist's verbal prompts and the reinforcement, more than by the modelling. It is perhaps relevant to note that the work of Birch shows both modelling and social-affective context to be important in a related phenomenon, the development of food preferences in young children (e.g. Birch, 1980; Birch, Zimmerman and Hind, 1980). There can not be a definite answer to this question from the present data.

The relative rapidity with which the results were achieved was surprising. It appeared that once the subject was willing to try, progress was fairly smooth. The fact that all the subjects who successfully completed the programme continued to consume the food after the intervention was over, indicates that the gains were conclusions about this. A further problem is that the subjects were probably a somewhat biased sample as they were all volunteers who were willing to have their aversions treated, rather than a random selection.

Definite answers to questions about the correlates of successful therapy for food aversions, the crucial ingredients of an effective therapy package, and the stability of gains over time, will clearly require more ambitious studies. What the present study has done is to demonstrate that human food aversions are subject to modification within a behaviour therapy framework and that a relatively simple in vivo exposure approach can lead to such modification in many cases. How this strategy compares with other possible approaches such as cognitive restructuring, the use of liked foods as reinforcers for the disliked ones etc. is a matter for future investigation.

REFERENCES

Bernstein I.L., Borson S. (1986) Learned food aversion: a component of anorexia syndromes. *Psychol. Rev. 33* , 462-472.

Bernstein I.M., Webster M. (1980) Learned taste aversions in humans. *Physiol. Behav., 25,* 363-366.

Birch L.L. (1980) Effects of peer models' food choices and eating behaviors on preschoolers' food preferences. *Child Devel., 51,* 489-496.

Birch L.L,Zimmerman S.I. and Hind H. (1980) The influence of social affective context on the formation of children's food preferences. *Child Devel., 51,* 856-861.

de Silva P., Rachman S. (1987) Human food aversions: nature and acquisition. *Behav. Res. Ther., 27,* 457-468.

Garb J.L., Stunkard A.J. (1974) Taste aversions in man. *Am. J. Psychiat., 131,* 1204-1207.

Garcia J., Koelling R.A. (1966) Relation of cue to consequence in avoidance l(arning. *Psychonom. Sci., 4,* 123-124.

Gustavson C.G. Gustavson J.C. (1985) Predation control using conditioned food aversion methodology theory, practice and implications. *Ann. NY Acad. Sci., 443,* 348-356.

Logue A.W. (1979) Taste aversion and the generality of the laws of learning. *Psychol. Bull., 86,* 276-296.

Logue A.W. (1985) Conditioned food aversion learning in humans. *Ann. NY Acad. Sci., 443,* 316-329.

Logue A.W., Ophir, I., Strauss K.E. (1981) The acquisition of taste aversion in humans. *Behav. Res. Ther., 19,* 319-333.

Nathan P.E. (1985) Aversion therapy in the treatment of alcoholism: success and failure. *Ann. NY Acad. Sci., 443,* 352-364.

TREATMENT OF OBESITY: A CRITICAL APPRAISAL

Martin Hautzinger

University of Konstanz, Department of Psychology, P.O.Box 5560, D-7750 Konstanz 1, F.R.G.

Obesity has been recognized as one of the most serious and prevalent health problems in the western world. Approximately 1/3 of the population in Europe and the USA is considered to be obese (Stunkard 1984). The prevalence tends to increase as age increases and social class decreases. About 9/10 of the obese population is mildly obese, while 9% are moderately obese (over 40% overweight), and only less than 1% are severely obese (above 100%).

Causes of obesity

Only about 5% of all obesity can be attributed to underlying physical disorders such as brain damage, endocrine dysfunction, and hereditary diseases (van Itallie 1979). The causes for the remaining 95% of obesity has not been conclusively established. However, various viewpoints on its pathogenesis have emerged. One school of thought holds that obesity develops from particular kinds of life-styles, including inactivity and chronic overingestion of food. In addition to the use of food for nutritive purposes, many individuals eat in response to various arousal states such as anger, anxiety, disappointment, or boredome (Rodin 1982). Much overeating may also be attributed to highly palatable foods, especially those high in fat and sugar content, which are readily accessible (Rodin 1981). If we feed rats a "supermarket diet", like chocolate chip cookies, salami, cheese, bananas, milk chocolate, peanut butter, etc., the animals will gain over a two month period 269% more weight than control animals (Sclafani and Springer 1976). Such a "supermarket diet" may similarly contribute to the development of obesity in humans. Another variable contributing to the onset of obesity may be the low level of physical activity. Obese men and women walk less and are not physically fit, therefore, a vicious cycle is created. Another school of thoughts regarding the pathogenesis of obesity holds that obese individuals are biologically programmed to be fat. Heredity and early nutritional experience determine the number and the size of the fat cells in the body (Stunkard, Sörenson, Hanis, Teasdale et al. 1986). Although each school of thought argues for a unique primary etiology, there is most likely a combination of factors influencing the development of obesity: Behavioural, social, environmental, biological, and genetic variables may all contribute to it's onset. However, given their interdependence, it is difficult to identify the relative influence of each component.

Maintenance of obesity

Once obesity is established in an individual, a variety of different mechanisms may operate to maintain the obese state. An intriguing fact is that the state of being fat is a characteristic that may perpetuate one's fatness. This occurs because obesity itself alter body chemistry, size and number of fat cells and metabolic activity, each contributing to the maintenance of obesity.

For example, as an individual accumulates fat in the body, the fat cells become larger and their capacity to store more fat becomes even greater. In addition, obese persons tend to have higher basal insulin levels than normal-weight individuals. This suggests that insulin may act as an appetite-inducing mechanism that can lead to a vicious cycle of hyperphagia and increasing obesity (Björntorp and Sjöström 1971).

Fat accumulation also effects the metabolic activity of obese individuals. Since fat tissue is more metabolically inert than lean tissue, the metabolic rate is lowered if lean body tissue is replaced by fat. When placed on a very low calory diet, both obese and nonobese humans lose not only fat, but also a great deal of lean tissue. This change in body composition among restricters may be one reason why some obese people require fewer calories to maintain their elevated body weight than normals.

In conclusion, an overaccumulation of fat in the body creates a physiological state that is highly resistant to weight change. Once obesity has developed, a number of biological, psychological, and behavioral factors, including body chemistry, size and number of fat cells, metabolic activity, adverse emotional reactions, bad eating habits, and sedentariness, all contribute to its maintenance.

Despite the variety of factors that have been found to produce and maintain obesity, it is still most commonly believed that obesity results from a period of overeating. However, whether or not obesity is caused by an increase in caloric intake, it can certainly be maintained without overeating. In fact, obese on the average do not eat any more than persons of normal weight.

Treatments of obesity

Despite this finding, one of the most popular weight reduction techniques is behavior therapy, which is based on the notion that eating patterns are maladaptive and need to be normalized. However, behavior therapy has often yield discouraging results. The majority of people can lose weight initially utilizing behavior therapy techniques, but very few can keep their weight off. Another development in the treatment of obesity is the use of low-calorie diets or/and drug treatments. Both can produce large weight losses initially, but as with behavior therapy, the weight losses achieved have been poorly maintained (Hautzinger 1989).

As a result of all these discouraging findings some raised an important question: "Should obesity be treated at all?" "Do the modest benefits of temporary weight loss outweigh the negative effects of repeated dieting and relapse?" (Wooley and Wooley 1984). Reports discovered that repeated dieting was a cause of atherosclerosis, leading to heart attacks and strokes. Other reports discovered that a high incidence of obesity was associated with levels of heart disease and diabetes below the average for slender Americans. Although overweight is generally considered to be a health risk, several studies suggest, that becoming thinner does not necessarily make one healthier (Keys 1980).

So far,a pessimistic picture has been painted regarding the weight loss literature. The numerous incidences of weight loss failures have created a near hopeless attitude among researchers and clinicians alike. Unfortunately, this attitude is defeating since it maintains the focus of attention on the dieting failures. A further examination of the literature shows that successful weight loss attempts with long-term maintenance exist (Schachter 1982).

To determine the weight loss strategies utilized by individuals who have been successful in their efforts, Colvin and Olson (1983) performed a descriptive analysis of people who had lost at least 20% of their body weight and had maintained that loss for at least two years. The principal strategies used by the subjects to achieve and maintain their weight losses were vigourous exercise, better nutrition, and self-monitoring of weight. In addition, many of the women who had been housewives sought business or professional jobs and became more involved in other activities outside of the home. Although an emphasis has often been placed on the weight loss failures in the obesity literature, successes do occur.

Predictors of weight loss

In reviewing the obesity literature (Garrow, Durrant, Mann et al. 1978, Stunkard 1984, Smith and Fremouw 1987), a number of variables emerge which seem to predict successful weight loss. The single most effective predictor of weight loss may be the rate of one's metabolism. For obese women placed on an 800 kcal/day diet for 3 weeks the best predictor of weight loss under these strictly controlled conditions was the patients' *resting metabolic rate*. In another dieting study, the only difference between "good losers" and "poor losers" was their resting metabolic rate. There were no differences with respect to age, relative weight, body fat or adipose tissue cellularity.

The best currently available method for facilitating weight loss by increasing metabolism is *vigorous and consistent exercise*. In fact, strict adherence to an exercise program may be another factor which is predictive of successful weight loss and maintenance. Dieting produces 15% to 30% decreases in basal metabolic rate, exercise counteracts this energy saving slowdown. Exercise also exerts effects on metabolism by altering body composition. Dieters typically lose muscle tissue as well as fat when restricting their food intake. Exercise in addition to dieting will increase fat loss while maintaining lean tissue. Furthermore, exercise does not increase hunger, actually it decreases one's appetite. A third predictor of successful weight loss may be a *very minimal history of repeated dieting attempts*. Obese patients who have a long history of dieting failure have a poor prognosis, making the unlikely candidates for future success. A fourth predictor is one's *developmental history*. Regardless of the cause of obesity, 80% of obese children become obese adults. In fact, if obese children have not reduced by the end of adolescence, the odds against them becoming normal-weight adults are 28 to 1. In addition, early-onset obesity which may be indicative of genetic influence, is much more resistant to change than is obesity acquired during adulthood. A final predictor is the *nutritional makeup* and caloric content of a diet. While most diets restrict calorie intake, all calories are not equal in terms of their uptake and usage by the body. There is evidence that through the involvement of brain serotonin, humans regulate the quantities of carbohydrates they consume. When obese persons are placed on low-carbohydrate diets, they become carbohydrate deprived and develop a craving. This process could contribute to the carbohydrate bingeing which is common among dieters. While a low-carbohydrate diet may contribute to the maintenance of obesity by eliciting dietary relapse, a high fat diet may promote obesity by improving the efficiency of food utilization. This has been attributed to the lower energy requirement of converting dietary fat to body fat. A calorically restricted diet that is low in fat and high in fiber containing complex carbohydrates thus appear to enhance weight loss by minimizing the "craving", decreasing the proportion of calories stored as fat, and accelerating the time to satiety.

Consequences and recommendations

The most common approach to treating obesity has been to modify patients maladaptive eating patterns and caloric intakes. However, all obese bring to treatment different genetic, biological, behavioral, and developmental backgrounds and, consequently, different probabilities for permanently maintaining a reduced weight. A more responsible approach to treating obesity would be to thoroughly assess each individual to determine his or her previous weight, exercise, and diet history, present lifestyle, and, if possible, metabolic rate. Based on this information and our current knowledge about predictors of weight loss, the clinician and patient can make an educated decision about the individual's probability of success.

REFERENCES

Björntorp, P., Sjöström, L. (1971) Number and size of adipose tissue fat cells in relation to metabolism in human obesity. *Metabolism, 20*, 445-452

Colvin, R.H., Olson, S.B. (1983) A descriptive analysis of men and women who have lost significant weight and are highly successful at maintaining the loss. *Addictive Behaviors*, *8*, 287-295

Garren, L., Giordano, F. (1985) Gastric Balloon implantation for weight loss in the morbidly obese. *American Journal of Gastroenterology*, *80*, 860-863

Garrow, J.S., Durrant, M.L., Mann, S., Stalley, S.F., Warwick, P.M. (1978) Factors determining weight loss in obese patients in a metabolic ward. *International Journal of Obesity*, *2*, 441-447

Hautzinger, M. (1989) Die Behandlung des Übergewichts. In: Jacobi, C., Paul, T., Brengelmann, J.C. (Eds.) *Therapie bei Eßstörungen*. München: Röttger Verlag

Keys, A. (1980) Overweight, obesity, coronary heart disease, and mortality. *Nutrition Review*, *38*, 297-307

Rodin, J. (1981) Current status of the internal-external hypothesis for obesity. *American Psychologist*, *42*, 361-372

Rodin, J. (1982) Obesity: Why losing the battle? In: Wolman, B. (Ed.) *Psychological aspects of obesity*. New York: Van Nostrand Reinhold

Ruderman, A.J., Wilson, G.T. (1979) Weight, restraint, cognitions, and counterregulation. *Behaviour Research and Therapy*, *17*, 581-590

Schachter, S. (1982) Recidivism and self-cure of smoking and obesity. *American Psychologist*, *37*, 436-444

Sclafani, A., Springer, D. (1976) Dietary obesity in adult rats: Similarities to hypothalamic and human obesity syndromes. *Physiology and Behavior*, *17*, 461-471

Smith, MM.E., Fremouw, W J. (1987) A realistic approach to treating obesity. *Clinical Psychology Review*, *7*, 449-465

Stunkard, A.J. (1984) The current status of treatment for obesity in adults. In: Stunkard, A.H., Stellar, E. (Eds.) *Eating and its disorders*. New York: Raven Press

Stunkard, A.H., Sorensen, T.I.A., Hanis, C., Teësdale, T.W., Chakraborty, R., Schull, W.J., Schulsinger, F. (1986) An adoption study of human obesity. *New England Journal of Medicine*, *314*, 193-198

Van Itallie, T.B. (1979) Obesity: Adverse effects on health and longevity. *American Journal of Clinical Nutrition*, *32*, 2723-2733

Wooley, S.C., Wooley, O.W. (1984) Should obesity be treated at all? In: Stunkard, A.J., Stellar, E. (Eds.) *Eating and its disorders*. New York: Raven Press

PART V:

PHARMACOTHERAPY IN BEHAVIORAL TREATMENT

THE COMBINATION OF COGNITIVE BEHAVIOUR THERAPY AND ANTI-DEPRESSANTS IN THE TREATMENT OF DEPRESSED PATIENTS- DOES IT SHARE THE ADDITIONAL OR DEPENDENT MODEL OF INTERACTION ?

S. Cayiroglu, U. Holub, and H.G. Zapotoczky

Psychiatric University Hospital, Vienna, Austria

INTRODUCTION

Recently more and more controlled studies have been published which give some evidence of the efficiency of cognitive-behavioural methods in the treatment of depressive patients in comparison with antidepressants (Beck et al., 1985; Blackborn et al.; Conte et al., 1986).

The present paper is concerned with a follow-up of depressive patients treated by cognitive behaviour therapy (CBT) in a group-therapy setting.

In the first study (Cayiroglu, 1986) 32 patients suffering from "major depression" (according to DSM-III diagnostic criteria) were examined, 19 female and 13 male, their average age being 35 years. 19 were in-patients at the ward for Behaviour Therapy, 13 were out-patients. The patients were divided into three groups. The first group of 11 patients was treated with a combination of cognitive therapy and reversible Mao-inhibitor (of a type with a short biological half-life, branch name 11-1163, Moclobemid).

The second group, also 11 patients , was treated with a combination of cognitive behaviour therapy and placebo. The third group consisting of 10 patients was treated with cognitive behaviour therapy only.

CBT was applied largely based on Beck's concept of cognitive therapy of depression. Groups consisted of five to seven patients and two therapists. The therapy continued six weeks with 18 sessions altogether. In the first session, using a double-blind randomized procedure, group 1 and 2 received two tablets of placebo or two tablets of Moclobemid 100 mg each. The aim of the first study was the evaluation of the efficiency of the different therapeutic methods.

The present study is a follow-up after 18 months. At this time only 22 patients participated in the study, 14 were women, 8 were men; 6 patients belonged to group 1, 9 to group 2 and 7 to group 3; 13 were inpatients and 9 were outpatients. 2 refused to participate, 8 could not be contacted.

METHOD

The same test battery as in the first study was administered. The psychopathology state was evaluated independently of the therapist using a clinical interview. Each of the 22 patients was asked to complete the following tests:
Beck-Depression-Inventory,
Self-perception-Scale (Fenigstein, Schleier and Buss, 1975) to measure the self-perception in personal and public aspects as well as social anxiety,
Depressive Attitudes Scale (DAS): A questionnaire for depressive, negative and irrational views of oneself, the environment and the future as described by Beck.
Additionally each patient was interviewed using a *life-event-questionnaire.*
The questions concerned:
- the continuation of treatment,
- taking psychopharmaca,
- alcohol consumption,
- diseases in the family,
- pregnancy,
- abortion/miscarriage,
- children,
- partnerrelationship,
- separation/divorce,
- death of family member or a friend,
- accidents,
- financial problems,
- law suits,
- employment,
- spare-time,
- social relationships,
- change of residence,
- housebuilding,
- self-contentment.

HYPOTHESIS

1. At follow-up (i.e. at time T4) the three groups will differ in the variables depression, self-perception, dysfunctional beliefs and drive.
2. There will be differences in all groups between the end of therapy (T3) and at follow-up (T4) regarding the measured variables.
3. There will be differences among in- and outpatients at T4 concerning the evaluated variables.
4. There will be sex differences in the results obtained.

5. At T4 group 1 and 2, 1 and 3 as well as 2 and 3 will differ in the evaluated variables.
6. Associations between life-events and the measured variables will be registered at T4.

RESULTS

1. There are no significant differences among the three groups at point T4, i.e. in the evaluation of depression, self-perception, dysfunctional beliefs and drive no group was better than the other one. This result supports the finding obtained in the first investigation.
2. However, a statistically significant progressive decline of depression over all groups for the majority of the patients was observed (17 patients out of 22). In-patients are less depressive than out-patients at T4. At point T3 there was no diference between in- and outpatients.
3. Concerning dysfunctional beliefs and drive there were no significant results.
4. There were no significant differences between sexes.
5. Also variables did not differ significantly between group 1 and 2, group 1 and 3, and group 2 and 3 at the point T4. But all patients showed a significant result related to self-perception, which could not be observed at point T3. An increase of self-attention and at the same time a decrease of the *environmental dependence* were found. In spite of these facts the social anxiety stayed approximately the same from T3 to T4.
6. Some life-events correlate significantly with the variables depression, dysfunctional beliefs and drive. The life-events related to depression are: "psychopharmaca", "employment", "spare-time", "case of death" and "self-contentment" are events related to drive.

DISCUSSION

Out of 32 patients of the first study only 22 came to follow-up. This means a drop-out rate of 31.2 percent after a period of 18 months.

13 out of the 17 patients, who are now significantly less depressed, belonged to group 1 and 2, i.e. CBT combined with Moclobemid - 5 patients - or CBT and placebo - 8 patients. We consider that this result is a consequence of the more "supporting" effect of pill-taking than an "additive" effect of antidepressant medication. In view of the results presented regarding self-perception at follow-up, we would like to stress the point that the patients exhibit more self-competence and self-respect. They are less dependent from their social environment and become more self-confident. These findings emphasize the relationship between depression and self-confidence.

The data support the importance and efficiency of in-patient treatment. Obviously, in-patients benefit more from the treatment than out-patients, which may be an effect of leaving the routine of every day life.

Finally, we want to emphasize that 17 patients have not taken psychopharmaca in the last one and a half years, which gives some significance to the long term effect of cognitive behaviour therapy.

SUMMARY

A group-treatment of patients suffering from major depression consisting of a combination of cognitive behaviour therapy and reversible mao-inhibitor (Moclobemid) versus placebo was followed up after 18 months. The results show a statistically significant progress in the sense of diminished depression in all groups. In-patients improved in the follow-up period more than out-patients. Also self-perception and self-attention increased at the same time, whereas the dependence on environmental factors decreased. The correlations between depression, dysfunctional beliefs and drive and some life-events have stressed this result.

REFERENCES

Beck A.T., Hollon S.D., Young J.E., Bedrosian R.C., Budenz D. (1985) Treatment of depression with cognitive therapy and amitriptyline. *Arch. Gen. Psychiatry, 42*, 142-148.

Blackburn J.M., Eunson K.M., Bishop S. (1986) A two-year naturalistic follow -up of depressed patients treated with cognitive therapy, pharmacotherapy and a combination of both. *Journal of Affective Disorders, 10*, 67-75.

Cayiroglu S., Merkel E., Zapotoczky H.G. (1988) A comparative evaluation of cognitive therapy and psychopharmaca in the treatment of depression. In: P.M.G. Emmelkamp, W.T.A.M. Everaerd, F. Kraaimaat and M.J.M van Son (Eds.): *Advances in Theory and Practice in Behaviour Therapy*, Swets & Zeitlinger, Amsterdam .

Conte H.R., Plutchik R., Wild K.V., Karasu T.B. (1986) Combined Psychotherapy and Pharmacotherapy for Depression. A Systematic Analysis of the Evidence. *Arch. Gen. Psychiatry, 43*, 471-479.

Simons A.D., Murphy G.E., Levine J.L, Wetzel R.D. (1986) Cognitive Therapy and Pharmacotherapy for Depression. Sustained Improvement Over One Year. *Arch. Gen. Psychiatry, 43*, 43-48.

PHARMACOTHERAPY IN BEHAVIORAL TREATMENT FOR DEPRESSED OBESE

M. de Zwaan, D.O. Nutzinger, G. Schönbeck, S. Cayiroglu, R. Macura, P. Berger, G. Aschauer-Treiber, A. Bugnar, A. Kiss, and S. Meryn

Department of Psychiatry, University of Vienna, Lazarettgasse 14, Vienna, Austria

INTRODUCTION

In a subgroup of obese patients weight reduction is accompanied by high incidence of emotional problems, and for a considerable amount of these patients an inpatient setting is the only possibility for a successful weight reduction.

Stunkard A.J., already in 1957 described what he called "Dieting Depression", meaning symptoms emerging or being aggravated during efforts of weight reduction leading to a high drop-out rate, small or no weight losses and rapid weight regain after the end of therapy. In our own earlier treatment studies (Nutzinger et al, 1985) in obese patients who suffered from discrete depressive symptoms before therapy, we could also find that dieting was often linked with deterioration of depressive symptoms; additional antidepressive medication helped to improve the symptoms and in the longterm had a positive effect on the rate of weight loss.

In this study, we investigated a rather difficult sample of overweight females, suffering from emotional disturbances and having a longlasting history of fruitless attempts to loose weight. We applied a combined treatment approach of cognitive behavior therapy and antidepressive pharmacotherapy (Fluvoxamine), which we expected to be aapted to the specific needs of these patients.

Until now only few studies have examined the combination of psychotherapy and psychopharmacotherapy in the treatment of obesity (Öst & Götestam, 1976, Brightwell & Naylor, 1979, Walker et al., 1977) and most of them applied anorectic drugs, which have shown to compromise the longterm results of behavior therapy (Craighead et al., 1981).

By adding Fluvoxamine to behavior therapy we expected that in our difficult subsample an outpatient setting will be possible and successful and that the weight loss will be larger with a combined treatment than with behavior therapy or pharmacotherapy alone (model of "additivity"); furthermore we expected a mood stabilizing effect, a low drop-out rate and a lack of negative longterm effects as described by the addition of anorectic drugs.

METHODS

Treatments

Four treatment conditions were compared:
-Cognitive-behavior therapy and Fluvoxamine
-Cognitive-behavior therapy and Placebo
-Dietary management and Fluvoxamine
-Dietary management and Placebo.

The control group for behavior therapy was not a waiting list but a widely used form of dietary management. Already in 1974 Jeffrey has stated that behavior therapy research has reached a level where it no longer would be necessary to include no-treatment or "pseudotreatment" control groups, but rather compare the behavioral treatment with some other treatment method (Brownell, 1987). Patients met weekly in groups to 10-11 subjects for 90 minutes, for a total of 13 sessions. There were 6 groups, 3 with behavior therapy and 3 with dietary management. A follow-up of at least 1 year was carried out.

Psychotherapy

Table 1. **The major parts of the group therapies**

COGNITIVE-BEHAVIOR THERAPY (by psychologist, semi-structured)		DIETARY MANAGEMENT (by dietitian)
	balanced diet 1000 kcal/day	
	exercise	
detailed self-monitoring		food-monitoring
modification of eating behavior		nutritional counselling
stimulus control (Hautzinger)		meal planning
cognitive change		
assertiveness training		
relapse prevention		

Pharmacotherapy

We applied Fluvoxamine, a new antidepressive drug (serotonin re-uptake inhibitor) with appetite and weight reducing properties (in contrast to tricyclic antidepressants). In an earlier study in normal weight depressed patients, treated for depression for 6 weeks, Fluvoxamine produced weight loss rather than weight gain (Schönbeck et al., 1989). Furthermore Fluvoxamine is well tolerated and has no drug dependence properties.

After 2 weeks on single-blind Placebo (to see if Dieting Depression occurs) patients received Fluvoxamine in a fixed dose of 100mg/day in a double-blind placebo-controlled procedure. In each of the 6 treatment groups 50% of the patients received Placebo and 50% Fluvoxamine in a randomized manner. Placebo-controlled drug administration was continued after the end of group therapy for additional 6 weeks followed by further 6 weeks of single-blind Placebo administration.

Patients

64 women aged between 19 and 54 years fulfilled the entry criteria and gave their informed consent to participate in the study.

A comparison of demographic and clinical characteristics of patients who completed treatment and of drop-outs as well as of the patients of the four treatment conditions revealed no significant differences at baseline.

The patients had to fulfil the following criteria:

1) Body Mass Index (BMI) > 27 kg/m^2 and < 40 kg/m^2.
2) A history of emotional problems associated with dieting ("Dieting Depression").
3) No severe psychiatric illness.
4) No antidepressant or neuroleptic medication in the previous 4 weeks.
5) No contraindication for reduced food intake or antidepressive medication.

Assessment

At baseline a physical check-up and the Structured Clinical Interview (SCID) for DSM III-R diagnoses were carried out. Weighb was measured weekly and all patients were assessed on a large number of dependent variables a various times during the course of the study, including the 17-item Hamilton Depression Rating Scale (HAMD), the Beck Depression Inventory (BDI), standard eating disorder inventories, self-rating scales of self-esteem and body image. In addition measurements of body image disturbances using a video monitor procedure were carried out. Blood samples for measurement of Fluvoxamine plasma levels were taken pre- mid and post-treatment. Side effects were evaluated with the Dosage Record and Treatment Emergency Symptom Scale (DOTES).

RESULTS

Diagnoses

The results of the Structured Clinical Interview (SCID) for psychiatric diagnoses according to DSM III-R were amazing. 68% of the obese fulfilled the criteria for current or past Major Depressive Episode, 79% reported about emotional problems during previous dieting ("Dieting Depression") and 42% cyclically experienced changes in appetite with increased food intake and at the same time mood changes during the luteal phase (Late Luteal Phase Dysphoric Disorder).

Drop outs

Of the 64 patients originally chosen for the study, 2 dropped out during baseline assessment. 62 patients entered the study and were randomized, 31 to behavior therapy and 31 to dietary management. 14 (23%) of these 62 patients dropped out of treatment.

The attrition rate was higher in the Fluvoxamine group than in the Placebo group, but this difference was not significant and was not related to depressivity or side effects. Only one patient dropped out because of intolerable adverse experiences (nausea). The attrition rate was equal in behavior therapy and dietary management with 6 patients in each group.

Body Weight

The mean weight of all patients at baseline was 97,3 kg (SD 14,39); the mean BMI was 36,4 kg/m^2 (SD 5,02). No weight changes could be observed during the baseline period of at least one week.

A preliminary analysis revealed a significant weight loss in each of the four treatment conditions during combined treatment, without a significant difference between them; however, there was a trend in Fluvoxamine treated patients to loose more weight than Placebo treated patients. The average weight loss of all patients who completed active treatment was 5,8 kg; this corresponds to a weekly weight loss of 0,5 kg. The maximum weight loss was 16,3 kg in one patient. The extent of weight loss per week decreased during treatment phase and was highest in the first weeks with an average of 1 kg/week.

During the succeeding 6 weeks of placebo-controlled drug treatment alone patients on the active drug continued to loose weight, whereas patients on Placebo showed mild weight gain, but this difference did not reach statistical significance. At the end of the one year follow-up period there was still a weight loss of 3,3 kg.

Depression

There was a rather low intensity of acute depression at baseline. Patients did not develop "Dieting Depression" during the first 2 weeks of single-blind placebo. A first analysis of the data shows a significant decrease in depression ratings (HAMD and BDI) during combined treatment, but no significant difference between the 4 treatment conditions. Nevertheless, Fluvoxamine treated patients showed larger improvement of depression ratings, especially when combined with behavior therapy.

The improvement was largely maintained during the follow-up period, but there are a lot of missing data.

Other outcome measures

We found the same pattern (overall reduction, but no difference between the 4 treatment conditions) in other outcome measures (ratings of body image and self-esteem), but these results are very preliminary.

DISCUSSION AND CONCLUSION

The results of this trial are preliminary; however, they suggest that all four treatment conditions are effective in significantly reducing depression and body weight. The amount of weight reduction of 5,8 kg, which corresponds to a weekly weight loss of 0,5 kg during combined 13 weeks treatment is in line with other studies of comparable treatment duration and treatment approach (Bennet, 1986) Keeping in mind that this was a difficult sample characterized by a long-lasting history of emotional problems and dieting attempts (a long history of dieting attempts is a negative predictor for weight loss), these results and the drop-out rate of 23% can be viewed as a success.

REFERENCES

American Psychiatric Association (1980) *Diagnostic and Statistical Manual of Mental Disorders,* third edition. American Psychiatric Association, Washington DC.

Bennett, G.A. (1986) Behavior therapy for obesity: A quantitative review of the effects of selected treatment characteristics on outcome. *Behavior Therapy, 17*, 554-562.

Brightwell, D.R. and Naylor, C.S. (1979) Effects of a combined behavioral and pharmacologic program on weight loss. *Int. J. Obes., 3*, 141-148.

Brownell, K.D. (1987) Improving long-term weight loss: Pushing the limits of treatment. *Behavior Therapy, 18*, 353-374.

Beck, A., Ward, C., Mendelson, M. et al. (1961) An inventory for measuring depression. *Archives of General Psychiatry, 4*, 561-571.

Craighead, L.W., Stunkard, A.J., O'Brien, R.M. (1981) Behavior therapy and pharmacotherapy for obesity. *Archives of General Psychiatry, 38*, 763-768.

Douglas, J.G. and Munro, J.F. (1982) Drug treatment and obesity. *Pharmac. Ther., 18*, 351-373.

Hamilton, A. (1960) A Rating Scale for Depression. *J. Neurol. Neurosurg. Psychiatry 23*, 56-61.

Hautzinger, M. (1978) *Verhaltenstraining bei Übergewicht*. Otto Müller Verlag, Salzburg.

Jeffrey, (1978) Behavioral treatment of obesity: The state of the art in 1976. *Behav. Ther., 9*, 189-199.

Nutzinger, D.O., Cayiroglu, S., Sachs, G., Zapotoczky, H.G. (1985) Emotional problems during weight reduction: advantages of a combined behavior therapy and antidepressive drug therapy for obesity. *J. Behav. Ther. Exp. Psychiatry 16*, 3, 217-221.

Öst, L.G. Götestam, K.G. (1976) Behavioral and pharmacological treatments for obesity: An experimental comparison. *Addict. Behav., 1*, 331-338.

Schönbeck, G. et al. (1989) *Fluvoxamine in depressed outpatients*. Draft.

Stunkard, A.J. (1957) The dieting depression: Incidence and clinical characteristics of untoward responses to weight reduction regimens. *Am. J. Med., 23*, 77-86.

Walker, B.R., Ballard, I.M., Gold, J.A. (1977) A multicentre study comparing Mazindol and placebo in obese patients. *J. Int. Med. Res., 5*, 85-90.

PART VI:

RESEARCH ON BEHAVIORAL MEDICINE

FUNCTIONAL DYSPHONIA: PERSONALITY AND COPING BEHAVIOR IN STRESSFUL SITUATIONS

J. Egger, W. Freidl, and G. Friedrich

University of Graz, Department of Behavioral Medicine, Institute of Medical Psychology and Psychotherapy, Auenbruggerplatz 28/II, A-8036 Graz

PROBLEM

Functional dysphonics can be characterized through the following aspects: specific changes in voice quality, height of sound and volume. These changes correspond with emotional or social stress and depression (Bauer 1975, 1973).

Anxiety neurosis and personality disorders are often to blame (Pfau 1973). Small knots in the vocal cords, contact ulcus etc. can lead to an aggravation of the disease. Some empirical researchers (Gundermann 1970, Pfau 1975) stated that with such patients an increase of the MMPI-scales "hypochondria", "depression", and "hysteria" - which means an increase of the neurotic trias - takes place.

Gundermann (1970) found these symptoms with 500 voice-disturbed persons and set up a hierarchy of frequency: nervousness, a pressure to clear one's throat, huskiness, cough stimulus, feeling of dryness, feeling of strain, thick voice, burning in the larynx, feeling of pressure, choke-feeling, interruption of voice, pain in larynx and tiredness. Quite often there are also less important psychic symptoms. Such feelings can result in psychic risk factors of dysphonia - a devil's circle - which is described by Gundermann (1970) as follows: appearance of voice disease as a simple disturbance of functions - fixation in the psychic area and release of emotional alterations - complicated disturbance of functions and beginning of organic changes.

Brodnitz (1976) established in his study that with 40% of his patients a severely psychically depressing incident was responsible for triggering off the disease. Other factors for triggering the disease can be nervousness, stress, and unpleasant conditions at work.

THE SETTING-UP OF THIS INVESTIGATION

According to the functioning of the human voice one can assume that there are aspects and facets of one's personality reflecting in every dysphonia. Etiological clear-up should be done on basis of preconditions of the disturbed functions of the voice and through the biography of the patient and his interactions in the psycho-social field. By this the larynx is seen as a "preferred area of projection of the human soul" (Habermann 1978).

This paper is to be designed according to the principles of a theory concept for the empirical stress research and the life event research. For this special problem of functional voice disturbance, a practical usage of these generally worded theoretical starts should be carried out. At the same time, however, a perhaps neurotic personality structure as a problematic background is to be taken in consideration through a multi-dimensional personality test. The following concepts have been regarded as possible models of explanations: individual mastering of unpleasant and undesired events (Katschnig 1980), stress susceptibility (Bösel 1987), state-trait-anxiety theory (Spielberger, Gorsch & Lustrene 1970) as well as a two-dimensional start of the repression-sensitization construct (Weinberger, Schwartz & Davidson 1979, Asendorpf, Walbott & Scherer 19839. It is supposed that people with functional voice disturbances show high values on the scales of FPI "nervousness", "depression", and "neuroticism" and lower values on the scale "openness" in comparison to the control group. Furthermore, we assumed that such persons name a higher number of events and a higher stress through live events and high state (= situationally caused fear) and trait-fear values (that is fear caused by, one's own personality) in comparison with the check group. Through a combined research of so far only singularly proofed influences and the adding of more hypothetical factors (for which there is still no empirical proof) an evaluation of these potentially etiopathogenetic effect factors should be made possible.

METHOD

1. Sample

3 samples were compared:

a) Patients with functional dysphonia (n=20, x=34 years, 15 female and 5 male) during their inpatient treatment at the HNO-Clinic Graz;

b) Patients with organic dysphonia (n=14, x=44.6 years, 4 female and 10 male) during their inpatient treatment at the HNO-Clinic Graz; all patients showed clear evidence for somatic reasons for their voice disease which - at that time - was not yet chronic;

c) 20 controls, all equal to the group of functional dysphonics regarding age, sex and occupation.

2. Instruments

(a)Paper-pencil-test:

FPI (Freiburger Persönlichkeitsinventar, Fahrenberg & Selg, 1970) for the assessment of the personality structure; ILE (Inventar zur Erfassung lebensverändernder Ereignisse, Siegrist & Dittmann, 1983) to measure the life stress during the last two years; STAI (State-Trait-Angst-Inventar, Laux, 1981) to detect anxiety depending on situations or personality; SDS (Social-

Desirability-Scale, Crowne & Marlowe, 1960) to get information about the social reactivity.

(b)Psychophysiological measurement: EDA (GSR, psychogalvanic skin response) data were collected during a baseline situation and a experimental evoked stressful situation (cognitive power test, mathematical achievement task while confronted with noise presented over earphones).

3. Statistical Procedures

Combining the trait-anxiety scores with the social-desirability scores 4 groups are resulting, representing the 4 coping styles "low anxious", "high anxious", "defensive high anxious" and "repressor". For the statistical analysis SPSS/PC was used.

RESULTS

As shown in picture 1 the group of patients suffering from functional dysphonia (Fstg) as well as those with organically based dysphonia (Ostg) showed a higher level of nervousness when compared with the control group (KG). The Fstg-Group also reported less aggressivity - in the sense of a personality trait - then controls do. Patients with Fstg were more socially involved than those with Ostg and both clinical groups were less open minded and authentical than the control group. There were no other significant differences in the FPI-scores between these 3 groups.

No information could have got by using 4 coping styles, therefore the hypothesis could not be verified that patients with Fstg would tend to high anxiousness and repression. Trait anxiety also produced no differences between the groups, but functional dysphonics showed a higher level of state anxiety in the experimental stress situation than controls do (picture 2).

The life event scores were the most discriminating: The frequency as well as the strain of life events were higher with Fst-patients, the Ostg-group laid between Fstg and control group (picture 3 and 4).

The statistical analysis of the psychophysiological GSR-data showed that there is no significant difference between all 3 groups, neither in the baseline scores nor in the stressful situation. Only the discrepancy scores between the verbal and the physiological state anxiety values showed a tendency for a higher physiological arousal compared to the verbal self report with repressors.

A finally computed simultaneous analysis of discriminance with the most leading variables enabled a successful grouping of 94%. 51 out of 54 dysphonics and all controls were correctly classified. The most powerful factors for the analysis of discriminance were: frequency of life events, evaluation of strain caused by life events, social involvement, furthermore spontaneous aggressiveness, nonchalance

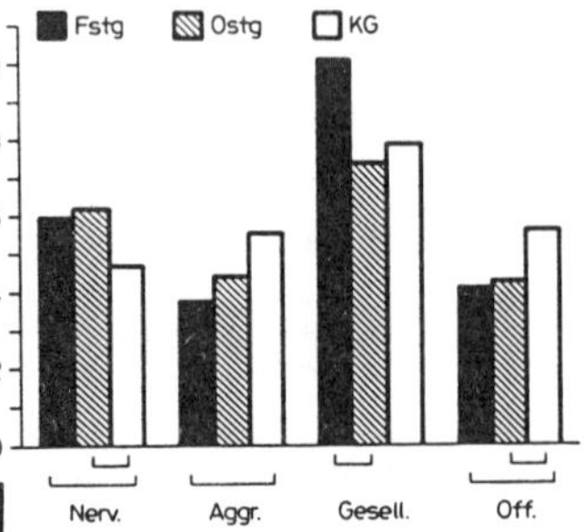

1

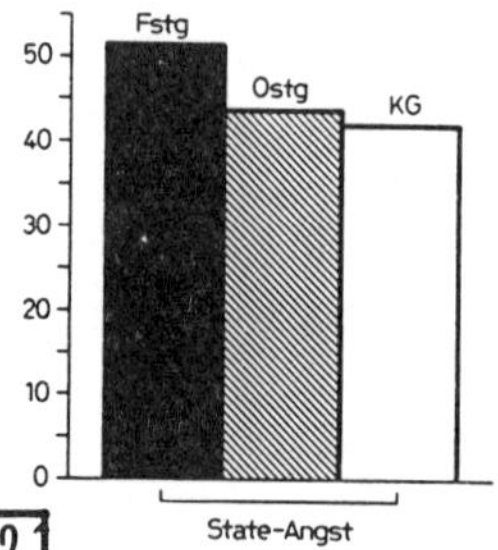

2

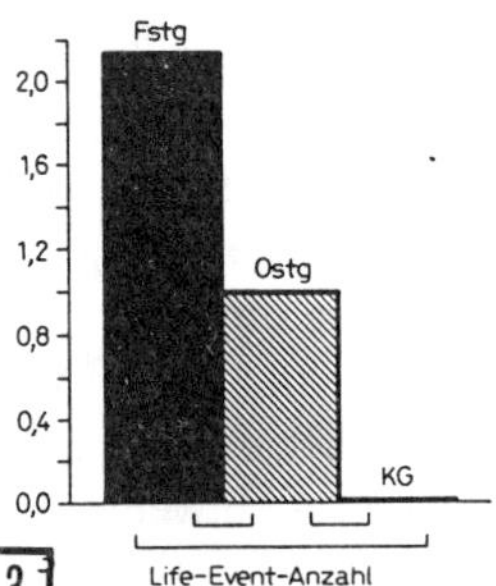

3

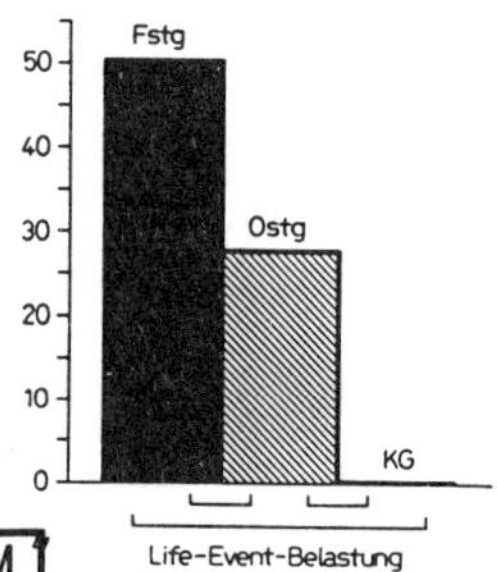

4

Legend

Fstg......	functional dysphonics
Ostg.....	organical (somatical) dysphonics
KG........	controls
Nerv.....	nervousness, psychosomatic disturbance (FPI)
Aggr.....	aggressivity (FPI)
Gesell...	social involvement (FPI)
Off..........	open minded, openness (FPI)
State-Angst.....................	state anxiety (STAI)
Life-Event-Anzahl..........	frequency of life events in the last 2 years (ILE)
Life-Event-Belastung...	strain caused by life events in the last two years (ILE)

└─┘ ... difference is statistically significant (at least $p < .05$)

and open mindedness/authenticity.

INTERPRETATION AND DISCUSSION

An increase of the neurotic trias for the group of functional dysphonics (high values on the MMPI scales hypochondria, hysteria, and depression) in comparison to people with a normal voice could not be proofed. The values of nervousness in this group, due to the suppositions, increased to a higher degree than those of people with organic voice disturbance. On the scale "depression" there was no difference among functional dysphonics, people with organic voice disturbance and the check group. Therefore, remarkable statements from theoretical and empirical papers by Gundermann (1970) and Pfau (1975) could not be proven.

On the openness scale there is, with respect to the hypothesis, a less openness by people with functional voice disturbance in comparison with the control group. The same is to say for people with organic voice disturbances. This viewpoint corresponds with findings by Frank and Schultze (1978). In their research, which was done with the personality-interest test (PIT by Mittenecker & Tomann 1972), they were unable to make use of the data, because the check scale A (self-criticism vs. lacking self-criticism) deviated from the standard data and displayed a clear falsification of the results.

A central point for the description of personality structure of functional dysphonics in this paper seems to be represented by the FPI openness scale. This could have led to falsifications on other scales, e.g. depression, neuroticism, which again would mean that this group of patients is unable to judge itself rightly and to take a critical standpoint towards itself. That could result in the conclusion that the ability of self-criticism is less present. In their verbal self-reports the functional dysphonics were displaying themselves in an absolutely positive way, e.g. less spontaneously aggressive and more social in comparison with the check group.

The people examined were - with regard to the effectiveness of coping style - divided into low-fearing, high-fearing, defensive high-fearing and repressive persons. The hypothesis that dysphonics would tend to rather higher fear and repression could not be proven statistically.

This assumption seemed to have pointed to the theoretical position of the life-event research. By the application of STAI (Laux 1981) both became two dimensions of anxiety researchable. In the field of state-anxiety - in contrast to trait-anxiety - there was a proof of a higher level of anxiety of functional dysphonics in comparison with voice disturbance and the check group. This shows that the functional dysphonics react with a distinct threat feeling and fear in stress situations.

It could be shown that functional dysphonics have to bear a greater number of life events and worries in the two years before the outbreak of the disease. The functional dysphonics were most, the people with organic voice disturbance less, and those with normal voice least affected. Both the importance of the number as well as the experienced worries of life events could be proofed well in this investigation. This theoretical assumption (e.g. Bauer 1975, Brodnitz 1976, Gundermann 1970) could now be demonstrated empirically. Life crises and life events seem to pace parallel with the etiopathogenesis of functional voice disorders. However, experienced strain through life events of people with organic voice disturbances are lower than those of functional dysphonics. This fact gives an interpretation that psychological factors are also responsible for the development of organic dysphonia.

It seems to be a striking aspect that the style of coping has no influence on the life-event strain. This is in contradiction to the hypothetical assumption that people with a high anxiety level should report more strain than those with less anxiety and repressors. The life-event research could lead to the expectation that the coping style was a decisive for the development of psycho-physiological pictures of disturbance.

Repressors showed - in comparison with people with high anxiety, defensive high anxiety and low anxiety - the greatest discrepancy between physiological and verbal anxiety report - although only in the sense of a statistical tendency. This would correspond with the expectation and the theoretical position (Carpeting 1973), whereafter repressors are unable to realize their state of emotion consciously.

The discrimination analysis must be seen as an important result. A higher number of life events and life strains, little spontaneous aggressivity, distinct social ability, tranquillity and little openness characterize the functional dysphonic.

In the sense of an optimized statistical charging it should be noted critically that the amount of spot-checks for multi-factorial analyses of variance was too small. As shown in other investigations, there are relatively few people being affected by this illness and at the same time go for hospital treatment for this reason. One possibility to solve this problem would be a multi-centre study carried out parallel with other specialized clinics (Throat-Nose-Ear clinics) or in surgeries of general practitioners.

REFERENCES

Asendorpf, J.B., Wallbot, H.G., Scherer, K.R. (1983) Ein empirisch begründeter Vorschlag zu einer zweidimensionalen Operationalisierung von Repression-Sensitization. *Zeitschrift für differentielle und diagnostische Psychologie, 2,* 113-128.

Bauer, H. (1973) Klinik der Stimmstörungen. In Biesalski, P. (Hrsg.) *Phoniatrie and Pädoaudiologie.* Stuttgart: Thieme Verlag (S. 165-193).

Bauer, H. (1975) Zur Notwendigkeit der ätiopathogenetischen Differenzierung funktioneller Stimmstörungen. *HNO, 23,* 165-167.

Bösel, R. (1978) *Streß, Einführung in die psychosomatische Belastungsforschung.* Hamburg: Hoffmann & Campe.

Brodnitz, F.S. (1976) Spastic dysphonia. *Annals of Otology, Rhinology and Larynology, 85,* 210-214.

Crowne, D.P., Marlowe, D. (1960) A new scale of social desireability independent of psychopathology. *Journal of Consulting Psychology, 66,* 547-555.

Fahrenberg, J., Selg, H. (1970) *Das Freiburger Persönlichkeitsinventar, (FPI).* Göttingen: Hogrefe.

Frank, F., Schultze, H. (1978) Psychogene Stimmstörungen im Testverfahren. *Stimme - Sprache - Gehör, 2,* 9-12.

Freidl, W. (1987) *Aspekte der Persönlichkeit und der Streßverarbeitung bei funktionellen Dysphonikern.* Philosophische Dissertation. Universität Graz.

Gundermann, H. (1970) *Die Berufsdysphonie.* Leipzig: Thieme.

Habermann, G. (1978) *Stimme und Sprache.* Stuttgart: Thieme.

Katschnig, H. (1980) *Sozialer Streß und psychische Erkrankungen.* München, Wien, Baltimore: Urban & Schwarzenberg.

Laux, L. (1981) *State-Trait-Anxiety Inventory (STAI).* Weinheim-Beltz.

Mittenecker, E., Tomann, W. (1972) *Persönlichkeitsinteressenstest (PIT)* Stuttgart, Wien: Hans Huber.

Pfau, E.-M. (1973) Zur Psychologie der funktionellen Dysphonie. (Eine Untersuchung der Persönlichkeitdiagnostik in Beziehung zur Stimmleistung). *Folia Phoniatrica, 25,* 251-269.

Pfau, E.-M. (1975). Psychologische Untersuchungsergebnisse zur Ätiologie der psychogenen Dysphonien. *Folia Phoniatrica, 25,* 298-306.

Scarpetti, W.L. (1973) The repression-sensitization dimension in relation to impending painful stimulation. *Journal of Consulting and Clinical Psychology, 40,* 377-382.

Siegrist, J., Dittmann, K.-H. (1983) *Inventar zur Erfassung lebensverändernder Ereignisse. ZUMA-Handbuch, Teil 2.* Mannheim.

Spielberger, Ch.D., Gorsch, R.L., Lustrene, R.E. (1970) *Manual for the State-Trait-Anxiety Inventory.* Palo Alto, CA: Consulting Psychologist.

Weinberger, D.A., Schwartz, G.E., Davidson, J.R. (1979) Low-anxious, high-anxious, and repressive coping styles: psychometric patterns and behavioral and psychological responses to stress. *Journal of Abnormal Psychology, 88,* 369-380.

ACTING ON THE BASIS OF INSUFFICIENT DATA - DECISION BEHAVIOUR IN BRAIN DAMAGED PATIENTS

E. Meier

Inselspital Bern, Abteilung für Neuropsychologische Rehabilitation

What does it mean to act on the basis of insufficient data? Imagine that you want to contact your doctor,because you have a fever. You find the name of your doctor in the telephone book,but you can hardly read the telephone number, because the page is dirty. What you read, might either be 567882 or 567892. You cannot decide, which of the two numbers is correct, because the numbers are distorted. That is, to say it in the terms of the signal detection theory, there is too much noise. The data base is not sufficient for a decision. However, even though it is hard to decide which number is the correct one, a decision has to be made. Even if you give no answer to the question at hand, this can be classified as one type of behaviour (giving up). The situation is quite different,if you own a new telephone book You can read the number clearly and you can dial it with confidence. In the language of the signal detection theory (e.g. Green & Swets, 1966; McNicol, 1972; Pachella, 1974) , this would mean that there is practically no "noise".

What has this to do with neuropsychological rehabilitation ? In my mind there is no doubt, that brain-damaged patients have difficulty in processing information. Visual field defects, deficits in contrast sensitivity and deficits in colour perception may lead to an incomplete representation of the surrounding world. However irrespective of these difficulties brain damaged patients must make decisions and act in a world that is only partially represented in their cognitive system.

Let me add one more aspect to that scenario. The costs and the benefits of a decision may be quite different in different situations. If you did not find the correct answer in the above mentioned example, the only consequence will be that you will have to dial for a second and maybe a third time. In other situations the costs may be much higher.

The example shows that a decision process consists at least of two components: one is the data-base or the representation of the situation, the other is the fact that you are willing to risk by falsely answering "yes" or "no" to a question. In our example, giving up would mean that you receive no medical care.

The signal detection theory can give answers - at least to some of the problems - that were raised in the questions above. But this theory has been largely ignored in neuropsychological research and rehabilitation. (Some of the rare exceptions are the papers by Howes (1966) Jenkins & Schuell (1966), and Kelter, Cohen, Engel, List & Strohner (1977).

Before discussing rehabilitation programs that include ideas from the signal detection theory, we have to proof that 1.) decision behaviour may be different in different neurological patients or groups of patients irrespective of sensitivity. 2.) That adequate or inadequate decision behaviour has consequences in everyday life.

In an experiment that Cohen, Glöckner-Rist and I developed (Meier, Cohen & Glöckner-Rist, in preparation), we tried to find out, whether aphasic patients are impaired in the spontaneous mnemonic processing of word and pictures. The question whether aphasic subjects have deficits in certain memory tasks is of no interest for the question at hand. What is important is the type of errors they make.

Let me explain the task : A total of 40 experimental stimuli were presented on slides, half of which showed words and the other half pictures - drawings of people in different occupations or of different animals. The drawings and the words referred to 20 different occupations and to 20 different animals. The pictures and words were drawn or written in either red or blue. The 40 stimuli were presented in two blocks.For half of the items patients were instructed to indicate as quickly as possible whether the information was given in blue or red ink (Sensory Task) for the other half they had to indicate whether the information referred to a human or to an animal subject (Semantic Task).

Immediately after the last slide and without any warning, a series of 60 recognition forms was presented, each with three frames arranged vertically. In one of the frames there was a picture, in another was a word referring to the same occupation or animal and in the third frame an "X". The patient had to decide by pointing to one of the frames whether he had previously seen the item as a word, as a picture or not at all ("X"). This recognition task consisted of the items presented earlier and 20 additional filler items.

Both groups of patients performed well above chance level. The percentage of correct decisions was M=70.6% for the aphasics and M=66.5% for the RH-controls. This difference is not significant. But for the error scores Scheffe' Tests revealed that aphasics incorrectly accepted as having previously seen words (M=23.7%) rather than pictures (M=11.4%). Moreover their mean percentage of incorrectly accepted words is higher than that of the RH-controls (M=8.0% for words and M=9.3% for pictures).

A speculative interpretation of this result might be : an aphasic subject knows that he has difficulties with words. When confronted with such a task he asks himself "When I do not know whether I have seen a word or not, this might be due to the fact that I have difficulties with words. So when in doubt it is better to accept a word as previously seen, as long as I have no clear evidence that I have not seen it before."

Group studies are not very popular nowadays and some of you might ask whether there is evidence, that clearly suggests that patients either respond "yes" or rather "no",if in doubt. In a first approach to that problem, I collected data from two patients that I tested with a "Sentence comprehension program". One of the patients had aphasic language problems, the other one had scanning problems due to a left visual field defect. In that experiment, a sentence was displayed on a computer screen for a very short time. Half of the sentences were incorrect (for example: "The policeman sings the cars".) the other half consisted of correct sentences (for example: "The teacher writes on the blackboard.") The patient had to decide whether the sentence was correct or not. Exposure duration was individually adjusted so that nearly 75% of the answers were correct. Both patients worked on the task on several occasions. The aphasic patient made more errors by saying "yes", if the opposite was correct, while the other patient made more errors by saying "no", if "yes" was the correct answer. What is important here is, that the decision behaviour of the two patients remained constant. Let us return to the theory of signal detection for one moment and try to explain what has had happened in these experiments. Within the theory of signal detection every decision process is based on the representation of sensory data within the cognitive system. At the same time there is "noise" within the system so that it is difficult to distinguish between signal and noise. On other occasions signals are quite clear. For illustration let us return to the second experiment. The answer that you give depends on how completely the sentence is represented in the cognitive system and on the criterion you have for answering "yes" and "no". Someone who is very cautious may answer "no" therefore trying to avoid false-alarm errors. However, is that really important for rehabilitation?

For a brain-damaged person the difference between signal and noise may be diminished. That means that the cognitive representation of the surrounding world is not as clear as it had been before. A naive researcher might think that this will result in more "no" responses (rejections) in certain tasks, but this is not necessarily the case. Let us speculate about a patient, who has not realized, that he is no longer able to detect signals with the same accuracy as before. He will continue to use the same criterion or cut-off value that he used before. The result will be a lot of "false negative" responses, which could be avoided by adjusting the criterion to the actual capabilities. This behaviour corresponds to what our naive researcher would expect. A second patient may have realized that he has difficulties with the given information, that means that the ratio between signal and noise is diminished. He therefore may adjust his decision criterion to the new situation meaning that he will often incorrectly reject the correct "no" answer and at the same time tends to accept something as being there when it is actually not (false acceptances).

Theoretical speculations about the criterion adjustments for decisions that might take place must be based on the theoretical assumptions about the signal- and noise-distribution and the parameters that can be derived.

While it is not possible to explain the theory of signal detection in this paper, I think that it is possible to explain some of the major assumptions and implications of this theory by looking at the decision and reaction behaviour that is demanded by video-games.

Video-games are very popular nowadays and everybody knows that the skills in playing these games and the resulting high-scores improve rapidly with practice. This cannot be explained with an improved speed in basic information processes. Even if reaction times in these complex situations decrease to a certain level, the improvements that normally occur cannot be explained on this basis alone. I think in many games one learns to avoid certain errors that are punished and at the same time take the risk to make other errors that only have minor consequences. So higher scores do not necessarily mean fewer errors,but may be due to a an optimal decision behaviour. To say it in other words: you learn to adjust your decision behaviour by the consequences it has.

The fundamental problem with signal detection experiments is that one has to collect a lot of data from one person under various feedback conditions. For neuropsychological research this means that signal detection experiments should be ideally training procedures, so that a lot of experimental/training sessions can be justified. A further problem in signal detection experiments is that a certain amount of errors must be made. Otherwise it would not be possible to differentiate between error types. In a two choice experiment there should be subtests with about 60, 70, 80 and 90% correct answers. Moreover when the patients performance gets better the parameters of the training procedure have to be adjusted so that error frequencies remain constant. This means that a patient never gets the feeling he really masters the task at hand.

I have tried to incorporate some of these ideas in a computer program - constructed as a game - that I have written. The aim of the program is to train visual scanning processes. Two types of figures appear on the screen for a very short time and then are masked by a flashing cross. The patient has to decide by pressing a button, whether it was one of his own figures or an "enemy" figures. The two basic parameters that can be manipulated are : time of presentation and the feedback conditions; meaning the cost for errors and the rewards for correct answers. The mean time of presentation can be chosen by the therapist. The itempool is then divided into 5 blocks with different exposure times.

The aim of the game is to eliminate the 40 enemies by correctly identifying their appearance on the screen. Making an error eliminates one or two of the patient's figures. The therapist decides whether both kinds of errors should be punished in the same way or whether one type of error "costs" more than the other does. Under all conditions the patient has a fair chance to win against the computer.

Presently we have not enough data to answer questions about response tendencies in brain damaged patients. But some of our patients trained their visual scanning abilities with the program and at the same time had fun playing the game, even though some of the items were too difficult. In further research we will try to systematically alter the decision behaviour of the patients.

REFERENCES

Green, D.M., Swets, J.A., (1966) *Signal detection theory and psychophysics.* New York: John Wiley

Howes, D. (1965) Comments on the so-called acquiescence set in aphasia. *J. Abnormal Psychol., 71,* 151-154, 1965

Jenkins, J.J., Shuell, H. (1965) Aquiescence response set in aphasics. *J. Abnormal Psychol., 70,* 111-113

Kelter, S., Cohen, R., Engel, D., List, G., Strohner, H. (1977) Verbal coding and visual memory in aphasics. *Neuropsychologia, 15,* 51-60

McNicol, D. (1972) *A primer of signal detection theory.* London: Allen & Unwin

Meier, E., Cohen, R., Glöckner-Rist, A., (in preparation) *Spontaneous mnemonic processing of pictorial and verbal stimuli in aphasia.*

Pachella, R.G. (1974) The interpretation of reaction time in information-processing research. In B.H.Kantowitz (Ed.) *Human Information Processing: Tutorials in Performance and Cognition.* Hillsdale, N.J.: John Wiley

PSYCHOPHYSIOLOGICAL STUDIES OF ATOPIC DERMATITIS

K. Münzel and R. Schandry

University of Munich, Institute of Psychology, Clinical Psychology

INTRODUCTION

The contribution of psychological factors is assumed for a number of dermatologic disorders. Among these atopic dermatitis (AD; synonyms: atopic eczema, Neurodermatitis constitutionalis, Prurigo Besnier) is the most frequently cited (Whitlock, 1976). While a large body of anecdotal literature attests to the importance of emotions, unconscious conflicts and personality constellations, a relatively small number of methodologically sound studies has so far investigated the influence of psychological stress on AD. A brief overview of these studies together with the dermatologic and epidemiological basics of AD will be presented in this paper.

Medical features and epidemiology

AD is an inflammatory skin disease of a mostly chronically relapsing course. In adults AD typically is characterized by a flexural distribution of the skin lesions which are dry and lichenified. A dominant feature is an easily provoked pruritus which induces scratching. Excessive scratching can lead to lichenification, excoriations, and serious skin infections thus worsening if not causing the skin lesions (Hanifin & Rajka, 1980).

AD is a common disease with a prevalence of 2-3 % in children and 0.7 % for all ages. It is influenced by heredity with roughly 70 % of patients having a positive family history of atopy, i.e. AD, allergic bronchial asthma, allergic rhinitis and/or allergic conjunctivitis. The natural course of AD is variable. Approximately 90 % of patients have onset in the first 5 years of life (Burgess et al., 1979). The figures reported for the long-term persistence of the disease vary considerably (10-83 %) which is probably due to methodolgical differences of the studies. According to a recent study (Rystedt, 1985) including nearly 1000 patients with a minimum follow-up time of 24 years the healing rate varies depending on a number of predictive factors, especially severe dermatitis in childhood, family history of AD and associated allergic rhinitis/bronchial asthma. Fewer than 20 % of individuals burdened with all of these were healed at the time of investigation as opposed to about 85 % without any of these.

The etiology of AD is not known. Pharmacological and immunological alterations assumed to be relevant for the development and maintenance of the disease are: elevation of humoral immunity, defects in cell-mediated immunity, disorders of the autonomous nervous system, diminished sebaceous secretion, and sweat disturbances (Braun-Falco, Plewig, & Wolff, 1984). The medical treatment of AD is symptomatic and not causal. Partial control of the disease can be achieved by the use of topical stereoids which due to undesirable side effects cannot be applied over a prolonged period of time. Furthermore the patient has to adhere to daily attention to general management measures, such as avoidance of skin irritants, overheating etc.

Psychological stress and AD

For a long time psychological stress has been considered a probable initiating or exacerbating factor of AD. However, this assumption is based almost exclusively on clinical observations and case studies. Only two controlled group studies have been published regarding the influence of life events on eczema in general. Brown (1972) found that 48 % of patients with eczema reported the experience of severe shock, upset, or worry within 6 months of the onset as opposed to only 15 % of a dental control group. The results of the second study (Edwards, Shellow, Wright, & Dignam, 1976) suggest that lowering of the itch threshold could be a crucial variable mediating between life stress and exacerbation of AD. Comparing itch thresholds of healthy individuals and eczema patients in remission who had experienced either a high or a low degree of life changes within the preceeding 3 months, it was found that the eczema patients had a lower itch threshold. Moreover individuals who had experienced a high degree of life changes had a lower itch threshold and this result was independent of the factor skin disease.

The first attempt to study the psychophysiological reactivity of AD patients during stressful situations was made by Graham and Wolf (1953). They measured forearm skin temperature and - in some cases - reactive hyperemia thresholds while discussing stressful or neutral topics with the patients who all had active lesions at the time of investigation. The patients responded with a lowering of hyperemia threshold, increases in skin temperature, and spontaneously complained of itching when stressful topics were discussed. Though no further physiological or subjective measures were recorded, it can be inferred from the description of the patients behaviour that they were in a state of high emotional arousal. Unfortunately, the interpretation of these interesting findings is hampered by the fact that no control subjects were included in the study. Amazingly, it took more than 30 years until the next study on this subject was published.

Faulstich, Williamson, Conerley, and Brantley (1985) compared 10 AD patients with active lesions and 10 healthy controls with regard to the following physiological measures: forearm electromyogram (EMG), peripheral vasomotor response (VMR), heart rate (HR), skin temperature (ST) of the left index finger, and skin resistance level (SRL). The stressors used were a series of intelligence quotient-type questions, imagination of the most vivid anxiety provoking event, and a cold pressor test. Although the patients scored significantly higher on an anxiety questionnaire they hardly differed from the controls in their physiological reactions to the stressors. During the cold pressor test their EMG activity was slightly higher and afterwards EMG and HR activity reduced more slowly. Considering the well known abnormal reactions of AD patients to temperature changes (Hanifin, 1986) this finding is not surprising but can hardly be interpreted as a sign of a stronger reaction to a psychological stressor. An attempt to replicate the results of this study with larger samples of 19 AD patients and 19 healthy controls was unsuccessful (Kirn, Morciozek, & Ehlers, 1989). The physiological measures assessed were VMR, HR, skin conductance level (SCL), blood pressure (BP), and respiration rate. All subjects responded with an elevation of arousal to all of the stressors, but there were no differential effects in the physiological measures. In addition, the authors included subjective ratings of the stressors. According to this measure the AD patients showed a tendency to experience the unpleasant imagery as more stressful. In a further study (Köhler, Weber, & Peters, 1989) HR, SCL, skin conductance response (SCR), BP, and the number of active sweat glands were assessed. Mental arithmetics and a distressing film served as stressors. Again no differences in reactivity between 20 AD patients and 20 healthy controls were found.

Contrary to these results a number of reaction differences became apparent in a study conducted by ourselves (Münzel & Schandry, 1990). Eighteen AD patients with active lesions were compared with 15 healthy controls with regard to the following measures: HR, VMR, SRL, SCR, forearm ST, subjective ratings of tension, state anxiety, and social anxiety. The stressors used were a mental arithmetic task, expectation of mental arithmetics under condition of divided attention, mental arithmetics under divided attention, and expectation of speaking in public. As in the studies reported above, reaction values were calculated as difference scores between stress and intermediate relaxation phases on one hand and the baseline phase on the other hand.

Table 1: **Summary of reaction differences between AD patients and controls**

Each of the stress induction and relaxation phases lasted 3 min. (X: $p <= .05$, one-tailed t-test; HR: heartrate, VMR: vasomotor response, SRL: skin resistance level, SCR: skin conductance response, FST: forearm skin temperature, ST: subjective tension).

	HR	VMR	SRL	SCR	FST	ST
Mental Arithmetic	X	X		X	X	X
Relaxation				X	X	
Expectation						
Mental Arithmethic + Divided Attentention		X		X	X	X
Ment. Arith. + Div. Attention					X	X
Relaxation				X	X	X
Expectation						
Speaking in public	X			X	X	X
Relaxation					X	

As can be seen in Table 1 there were reaction differences between the groups in all physiological measures except SRL. While HR and VMR differed in response to two of the stressors only, SCR and ST reactions were elevated during most of the phases. Furthermore, the patients reacted with higher subjective tension during most of the phases. However, there were no differences in state anxiety which was assessed after the baseline phase and social anxiety. An interesting finding resulted from subdividing (median split) the patients according to their ratings of how much they generally suffered from itch. It became apparent that the increase in ST for the patients on the whole was due solely to those patients who suffered extremely from itch while the others responded as the controls, i.e. with a slight decrease of ST in the course of the session. The two subgroups did not differ in any of the other measures. This finding seems of special importance as it is known that elevation of skin temperature can trigger itch in AD (Whitlock, 1976).

Each of the stress induction and relaxation phases lasted 3 min. (X: p .05, one-tailed t-test; HR: heartrate, VMR: vasomotor response, SRL: skin resistance level, SCR: skin conductance response, FST: forearm skin temperature, ST: subjective tension).

Summing up, in three of four group studies no remarkable differences could be found in the psychophysiological reactivity between AD patients and controls. On the other hand our own results suggest a heightened reactivity of the patients especially in skin related measures. These divergent findings could be due to a number of methodological differences between studies such as sampling procedures, stress induction methods, and type and/or location of measures assessed. Skin temperature which is known to be one of the variables that trigger itch was recorded in two of the studies only and from different locations. Furthermore, it has to be borne in mind that from a medical point of view the term AD comprises a very inhomogeneous group of patients. Thus, medical characteristics of the patients should be considered in more detail in further attempts to investigate the psychophysiology of AD. A more general point concerns the logic underlying the study of physiological reactivity to psychological stressors in AD. So far an elevated reactivity has been looked for. But it also seems feasible that even a normal reactivity to stressors is sufficient to trigger itch, for instance, in an especially vulnerable skin.

REFERENCES

Braun-Falco, O., Plewg, G., Wolff, H.H. (1984) *Dermatologie und Venerologie* (3. Aufl.). Berlin: Springer.

Brown, D.G. (1972) Stress as a precipitant factor of eczema. *Journal of Psychosomatic Research, 16*, 321-327.

Burgess, P.R., Dubson, R.L., Herndon, J.H., Botero, F., Chapman, R.C., Dimond, R.L., Tucket, R. (1979) Eczematous and immunologic diseases. *Journal of Investigative Dermatology, 73*, 414-433.

Edwards, A.E., Shellow, W.V.R., Wright, E.T., Dignam, T.F. (1976) Pruritic skin disease, psychological stress, and the itch sensation. *Archives of Dermatology, 112*, 339-343.

Faulstich, M.E., Williamson, D.A., Duchmann, E.G., Conerly, S.L., Branley, P.J. (1985) Psychophysiological analysis of atopic dermatitis. *Journal of Psychosomatic Research, 29*, 415-417.

Graham, D.T., Wolf, S. (1953) The relation of eczema to attitude and to vascular reactions of the human skin. *Journal of Laboratory and Clinical Medicine, 42*, 238-254.

Hanifin, J.M. (1986) Pharmacophysiology of atopic dermatitis. *Clinical Reviews in Allergy, 4*, 43-65.

Hanifin, J.M., Rajka, G. (1980) Diagnostic feature in atopic dermatitis. *Acta Dermato-Venerologica, Suppl. 92*, 52-56.

Kirn, U., Morciozek, M., Ehlers, A. (1989) *Atopische Dermatitis: Erhöhte Reaktionsbereitschaft auf Stressoren?* Paper presented at the 2nd Congress of the German Society for Behavioral Medicine, Munich, FRG.

Köhler, T., Weber, D., Peters, G. (1989) *Streßreaktionen von Neurodermitispatientinnen.* Paper presented at the 31. Conference of the German Collegium of Psychosomatic Medicine, Gießen, FRG.

Münzel, K., Schandry, R. (1990) *Atopisches Ekzem: Psychophysiologische Reagibilität unter standardisierter Belastung.* Manuscript submitted for publication.

Rystedt, I. (1985) Long term follow-up in atopic dermatitis. *Acta Dermato-Vernerologica, Suppl. 114*, 117-120.

Whitlock, F.A. (1976) *Psychophysiological aspects of skin disease.* London: Saunders.

RELAXATION, BIOFEEDBACK, AND INTERACTIONAL FEEDBACK IN THE PSYCHOLOGICAL TREATMENT OF ESSENTIAL HYPERTENSION

G. Näring, C. Schaap and H. de Mey

Department of Clinical Psychology and Personality, University of Nijmegen,P.O. Box 9104, 6500 HE Nijmegen, The Netherlands

INTRODUCTION

High blood pressure (BP) is one of the most important risk factors for the development of cardiovascular diseases and contributes substantially to heart insufficiency, cerebrovascular accidents (CVA's) and kidney diseases (van der Feen, 1978; Kaplan & Lieberman, 1986; van Ree, 1983). In the etiology and treatment of high BP, a distinction is made between primary or Essential Hypertension (EHT) and secondary hypertension. In the case of secondary hypertension a (organic) cause is known and a causal treatment is possible. However, for over 95% of the patients with high BP the cause is unknown and a symptomatic therapy is decided upon. By way of changes in living habits and/or medication, the physician attempts to decrease and control the BP. From a diastolic blood pressure (DBP) of > 105 mmHg the use of antihypertensive pharmaca is advised (Fodor, 1985). The antihypertensive pharmaca have considerable side-effects, amongst others, impotence. Another problem is the fact that EHT cannot be cured as yet. Patients have to take their medication in principle during their whole life or, in any case, remain under the control of the physician. The search for more effective psychological intervention strategies is therefore of the utmost importance.

The most effective psychological treatment consists mostly of relaxation, biofeedback or a combination of these two. However, these treatment packages typically focus on acquiring the skill to reduce BP levels while being alone, or at least while not in interaction with other persons. We do however spend most of our life interacting with others and this influences our BP. In a recently published review (Näring, De Mey & Schaap, 1988) we have listed the variables in dyadic interactions that do play a role in determining BP levels. These studies successively stress the role of the content of the conversation, the emotions of anger and anxiety, transactional involvement, and the act of speaking itself.

We designed a treatment procedure where excessive reactions of BP to one or more of the above mentioned variables are being reduced. If we call the classical combination of relaxation and biofeedback an 'in vitro' treatment, one might call the new treatment package an 'in vivo' treatment. The aim is to learn the patient to relax while interacting with others. The therapist gives the patient feedback on specific behaviours that raise BP levels. This information is gathered on the basis of coupling a continuous BP measurement device (called Finapres) to a video recording of the interaction between patient and therapist. In a series of replicated single-case designs, the impact of the 'in vivo' and 'in vitro' treatment is compared. Moreover, the characteristics of the subjects that improve and for whom treatment was a success (S-group) is assessed and compared to the characteristics of the subjects that do not improve, an for whom treatment apparently constituted a failure (F-group).

METHOD

Subjects

A newspaper advertisement offered a new treatment procedure free of charge to patients who were diagnosed as having essential hypertension. The following inclusion criteria were used:

- essential hypertension for at least three months
- age between 25 and 50
- either taking antihypertensive medication
- or diastolic BP at our laboratory of > 95 mmHg
  systolic BP of > 160 mmHg

Therapists

Three therapists: two women, one man; two interns, one psychologist.

Treatment

IN VIVO TREATMENT. The 'in vivo' treatment consisted of:

1st Session: Self Confrontation Method (Hermans, 1987). Establishment of the impact of a range of personal topics on BP. The two topics with highest absolute systolic BP levels were selected for further discussions.

2nd Session: Feedback while the topic with the highest absolute systolic BP was being discussed. Aim: instant feedback through red and green light, gathering material for interaction feedback in a later session, plus topic-relaxation.

All subjects received session 1 and 2. The sessions described below were optional, but most of the subjects received them all.

3d and 4th Session (optional): instructions and practice for lowering speech rate and decreasing speech volume. All subjects who exhibited a very high speech rate received instructions to lower this rate. Subjects practiced initially with the topic second in rank of mean absolute systolic BP level. During practice biofeedback was given. In the *4th Session* the topic to be discussed was : "'What do you think yourself caused and/or maintains your hypertension?" If the speech rate of the client was already in the normal range, the above-mentioned two topics were discussed while biofeedback was given. No specific instructions were given, except to pay attention to the feedback lights.

5th Session: The LSV formula: Listen, Summarize, Validate what other people say before responding. We introduced this session for two reasons. Firstly this formula helps people to relax while interacting with others: it forces them to listen before responding. While the technique from Sessions 3 and 4 helps the subject to relax while speaking, this technique additionally helps them to relax while listening. The second reason to introduce this formula is to provide the patient with a tool to handle interpersonal conflicts.

6th Session: Interactional feedback. From Session 2 onwards, video-recordings were made of the interactions of therapist and client, while BP was recorded simultaneously. With a computer program those segments of the recording were selected, in which BP increased. The program calculated difference scores of consecutive measures and counted the number of positive difference scores in eleven consecutive difference scores. A fragment was called a 'rise' when at least seven positive difference scores were present. Only occasionally this criterion had to be adjusted. Via a remote control the computer program automatically showed the segments of the interaction in which the blood pressure rose. At first the author and the therapist viewed all fragments while paying attention to speech rate, speech volume, involvement, recurrent topics, and recurrent emotions.

IN VITRO TREATMENT. The in vitro treatment consisted of 4 to 6 sessions that all had the same format. All sessions started with relaxation (15 min), followed by biofeedback (20 min). Subjects practiced relaxation in our laboratory. Additionally, they received an audiocassette with a recording of the first session. They were instructed to practice once every day. After three sessions they were encouraged to try and practice without the tape. In a later stage attention was paid to generalization, mostly to the situation at work. For the biofeedback procedure, the subject sat in a chair in front of a table on which a red and a green lamp were placed. The subject was instructed to try and keep the green light on as long as possible, and was then left alone. Feedback was given according to the same criterion that was used to select fragments from the interaction. In the first four sessions, systolic BP was monitored. In the last two sessions diastolic BP was monitored and displayed graphically on a TV set.

Baseline Procedure

In consultation with their general practitioner, a wash-out period of three weeks for patients on antihypertensive medication was used.

Directly after intake, all subjects received a BOSO or TAKEDA BP measurement device. They were instructed to monitor their BP at home twice a day (three measurements each time) during 2 to 4 weeks before treatment started. During treatment they continued measuring their BP. The three week baseline was included since it has been demonstrated (Laughlin, Fisher, & Sherrard, 1979) that BP measures, when taken at home, initially tend to decrease. A possible explanation for this initial fall in blood pressure is probably another feedback the differential influence of work, sleep, sports and food (alcohol) on BP.

DESIGN

A total of 16 patients was included in this study. Eight subjects started with the in vivo treatment, eight others with the in vitro treatment. Sessions were scheduled once every week. After four to eight weeks subjects received the other treatment condition. The in vitro treatment was terminated when BP showed so little variation around a normal level that feedback could not be provided.

Figure 1. **Design of the two treatments**

In vitro treatment
Session number

1	2	3	4	5	6
relaxation biofeedback	relaxation biofeedback	relaxation biofeedback	relaxation biofeedback	relaxation biofeedback	relaxation biofeedback

In vivo treatment
Session number

1	2	3	4	5	6
Self Confrontation Method	biofeedback on discussing topic with highest SBP	lowering speech rate	lowering speech rate	Listen Summarize Validate	Interactional Feedback with video fragments

MEASUREMENT INSTRUMENTS

BP Measures. Before and during the treatment program, BP was measured daily at home by the patient. In our laboratory it was measured at intake, at the start of each session in a baseline procedure, and at a follow-up, two to three months after termination of the treatment. Continuous BP measures were taken during baseline, during relaxation practice and biofeedback, and also during sessions with a focus on lowering the speech rate.

Questionnaire. All subjects completed a Symptom Check List (SCL-90; Arrindell & Ettema, 1986) several weeks before the start of the treatment and at the end of the treatment.

Behavioural Measures. Compliance to the practice of relaxation at home, as well as the speech rate could be estimated on the basis of the timing of the BP measurements. Each measurement consisted in reality of three measurements. In between measurement 2 and 3 they had to practice their relaxation training. A clock in the BP device registered the exact timing of the measurements.

Apparatus

Centered around the Finapres TM (1), an instrument that measures BP continuously and non-invasively, a system and a procedure was developed in which the 'in vivo' treatment could be given. This system contains a videocassetterecorder (VCR) and a Finapres TM, both linked to a microcomputer. Using this system the therapist is also capable of providing classical biofeedback treatment.

RESULTS AND DISCUSSION

For this paper we will present the results of the treatment of four patients. Since the data-analysis for the comparison between the treatment conditions is still under progress, we will not focus on the differences between the treatment modalities, but on the differences between the patients who were obvious successes (the S-group) and patients who did not improve during treatment (F-group). Four of these patients will be presented and their results discussed.

Patient 15, female, age = 40; weight = 80 kg; length = 160 cm, EHT since about three years, after sudden increase in weight. No antihypertensive medication; BP at intake 175/115; SCL-90 = 152 (high). SCL-90 at post-measurement = 148 (above average). First treatment condition: in vitro. Reported difficulties in practicing the relaxation training. Found it unpleasant that she couldn't talk about her problems during the first treatment condition. Second condition: in vivo. Main topics: (1) divorce, (2) suicide of son. Result: Moderate result with at home no diastolic measurements above 110 mmHg during the last 5 weeks. The laboratory measures do not show clear results. Treatment effect seems to be blocked by her overweight (impulse control problem). Because of clear signs of unresolved grief, she was referred for grief therapy. A self-control weight reduction program will then follow.

Patient 09, male, age = 40; weight = 85 kg; length = 180 cm eht since about four years. No antihypertensive medication; BP (with medication) at intake 150/100; SCL-90 = 112 (normal). SCL-90 at post-measurement = 101 (low). First treatment condition: in vivo. Main opics are relational: (1) mother (dementia), (2) children of his 2nd wife practiced enthusiastically the lowering of speech rate. Second condition: in vitro. Result: Good result. At home SBP from 137.5 to 127.5, DBP from 105 to 95. At laboratory a smaller decrease.

Patient 12, male, age = 38; weight = 60 kg; length = 170 cm. EHT since about four years. Used a ß-blocker; BP (with medication) at intake 150/90; SCL-90 = 112 (normal). SCL-90 at post-measurement = 94 (low). First treatment condition: in vivo. Main topics: (1) parents, (2) work. Results laboratory: already rather low after 3 week baseline: 140/85; lowering to 122/80 in last session. At home: Following withdrawal of medication, diastolic BP rose very slowly to levels above 95 mmHg in three weeks. Only after 7 weeks treatment these values returned to values below 95 mmHg. Systolic BP was in the normotensive range throughout the experiment.

Patient 20, male, age = 49; weight = 72 kg; length = 174 cm. EHT since about two years. No antihypertensive medication; BP at intake 167/110; SCL-90 = 181 (extremely high). SCL-90 at post-measurement: 127 (above average). First treatment condition: in vivo. Main topics: (1) parents, (2) work. Results laboratory: Systolic BP from 170 to 160, Diastolic BP from 108 to 98. At home: Systolic BP from 150 to 140, Diastolic BP from 100 to 90.

Since the relatively complicated data-analysis is still under way, it is impossible to draw firm conclusions from the results presented so far. What is clear, however, is that in the failure group a number of complicating factors seem to be responsible, particularly other problems in the lives of the patients (such as the suicide of her son and her divorce of Case 15) and compliance to the treatment regimen.

With two out of the original 16 EHT patients that started measuring their BP at home, treatment was not started at all. After three weeks of BP monitoring one patient concluded, and we agreed, that he was not hypertensive at all. The other one, who had been using ß-blockers for more than three years, could not believe that his BP did not rise after he stopped taking medication. He then measured for another four weeks and also took his BP device to work. Only after seven weeks measuring did he agree not to start treatment. These two "patients" have taught us that a baseline procedure, so common in research projects, should also be a standard element in every treatment of hypertensive patients.

That a baseline should preferably be determined at different locations is illustrated by the following case. Patient 12 showed a slow rise in BP at home to levels above 95 mmHg diastolic after stopping to take his medication. At our laboratory we once registered a diastolic value of 91 (with medication). However, from session two onwards values never exceeded 89 mmHg. Together with his wife this man ran a paramedical practice. Either he or she had to be available 24 hours a day. In effect, our laboratory was the only place were he didn't carry his beeper. It was also the only place where he felt really at ease. This observation motivated the patient very much to try and change his working life, with success.

Patient 03 described herself as a workaholic and drastically limited the time she spent working. Her BP subsequently became lower when measured at home, but kept showing hypertensive values in our laboratory. As with the previously described patient, we asked her to bring her blood pressure device to our laboratory for a check-up of the way in which she used it. It appeared that she was indeed only hypertensive in our laboratory. At work, values were also in the normal range. So, apparently for this patient, in contrast to the previously described case 12, the laboratory was a stressful setting.

Before this experiment started, we had studied the feasibility of decreasing speech rate and speech volume in a pilot with one patient. Since the knowledge about the effect of speaking itself on BP is not widespread, we anticipated that patients would not expect that speaking would be a target behaviour, and might even be hard to convince. This appeared not to be the case at all. All patients considered it a very credible rationale and, although practicing was not without problems, all experienced a relaxing effect and reported to continue practicing after the sessions were stopped.

A final comment about the experimental set-up: The system can easily be adapted for other applications. For future research we included a mini key-board to couple up to five different codes to BP measurements. This facility was designed to enable subjects to encode, while reviewing a recording of an interaction, the degree to which the experienced a specific emotion. Self-report affective data obtained in a video-recall procedure of a marital interaction appear to be valid measures of the actual affects during the interaction (Gottman & Levenson, 1985). The validity in other dyadic interactions has yet to be established.

To enable comparisons with earlier phases in our study when continuous BP measurement was not yet possible, the system was linked to discontinuous measurements of a Dinamap. The relationship between the two types of BP measures appears to be idiosyncratic, and has thus to be reestablished for every subject. Actually, if our study has shown anything so far, it is certainly, that in BP studies, the subject should be considered a world on his or her own.

(1) FinapresTM is a registered trademark of Ohmeda, Madison WI, USA.

REFERENCES

Feen, J.A.W.E. van der (1978). Opsporing en begeleiding van hypertensiepatienten: Een taak voor de huisarts. *Nederlands Tijdschrift voor Geneeskunde, 122*, 754-759.

Fodor, J.G. (1985). Mild hypertension: Should it be treated? *Canadian Family Physician, 31*, 303-304.

Gottman, J.M., Levenson, R.W. (1985). A valid procedure for obtaining self-report of affect in marital interaction. *Journal of Consulting and Clinical Psychology, 53*, 151-160.

Hermans, H.J.M. (1987). Self as an organized system of valuations: Toward a dialogue with the person. *Journal of Counseling Psychology, 34*, 10-19.

Kaplan, H.M., Lieberman, E. (1986). *Clinical jhypertension*. Fourth Edition. Baltimore: Williams & Wilkins.

Laughlin, K.D., Fisher, L., Sherrard, D.J. (1979), Blood pressure reductions during self-recording of home blood pressure. *American Heart Journal, 98*, 629-634.

Näring, G., DeMey, H., Schaap, C. (1988). Blood pressure response during verbal interaction: Review and Prospect. *Current Psychology: Research and Reviews, 7*, 3, 187-198.

Ree, W.J. van (1983). Assistente en hypertensiebeschrijding. *Huisarts en Wetenschap, 26*, 49-53.

Sime, W.E., Buell, J.C., Eliot R.S. (1980). Cardiovascular responses during emotional stress (quiz interview) in post-myocardial infarction patients and matched control subjects. *Journal of Human Stress, 6*, 39-46.

PSYCHOSOCIAL INTERVENTION WITH POST-MYOCARDIAL INFARCTION PATIENTS: RESULTS FROM A 2-YEAR FOLLOW-UP

A. Sardo , G.F. Goldwurm and E. Sanavio

Behavioral Medicine Center, Niguarda Hospital, Milano, Italy, and General Psychology Department, University of Padua, Padua, Italy

In cooperation with De Gasperis Cardiac department of Niguarda Hospital, we are carrying out a program of cognitive-behavioral intervention with coronary heart disease (CHD) patients.

There is scientific evidence that Type "A" Behavior Pattern (TABP) can be altered after intervention. We refer to the Recurrent Coronary Prevention Project (RCPP), the first large-scale, long-term attempt to explore the feasibility of altering the Type "A" style of life and to evaluate the effectiveness of such alteration on the incidence of CHD. The RCPP lasted 4.5 years and interested about 1,000 post-infarction male no-smoking volunteers.

Our study aims at investigating whether:

1) changes in the intensity of TABP can be achieved also after a shorter intervention (2 to 4 month treatment),
2) such an intervention can be effective in improving the outcome of coronary heart disease.

METHODOLOGY

Table 1. **Methodology**

*	ASSESSMENT	
	J.A.S.	(Jenkins Activity Survey)
	S.I.	(Structered Interview by R. Rosenman)
	C.B.A.	(Cognitive Behavioral Assessment)
*	GROUP FORMATION	
	4 - 7 Ss	grouped on the basis of education
*	TREATMENT	
	8 - 12	weekly sessions based on
		- Education about CHD and TABP
		- Jacobson Progressive Muscle Relaxation Training (reduced form)
		- Cognitive Restructuring aimed at the identification and modification of cognition linked to TABP
		- Behavior Modification focused on coping abilities
*	FOLLOW-UP	
	At 6, 12 and 24 months after treatment	

We give just a brief outline of our methodology, as it has already been reported elsewhere (Table 1).

Subjects

As shown in Table 2, our sample consists of 45 subjects, 39 men and 6 women, mean age 55.9 SD 8.7, range 37-73, mean level of education, most with a working activity before cardiac event.The main standard CHD risk factors at entry were familiarity, with a mean number of risk factors per person of 1.9. Most participants in our study suffered a recent myocardial infarction or had undergone cardiac bypass surgery.

Table 2. **Socio-Demographic and Clinical Data at entrance**

*	SUBJECTS	45	
*	SEX	39 M - 6 F	
*	AGE (years)	55.9 Mean 8.7 SD 37 -73 Range	
*	EDUCATION		
	Less than high school		30 Ss
	High school		11 Ss
	College graduate		4 Ss
*	WORKING ACTIVITY		
	White collars		20 Ss
	Blue collars		8 Ss
	Housewifes		4 Ss
	Retired		13 Ss
*	CHD STANDARD RISK FACTORS		
	Cigarette smoking		31 Ss
	Lipid disorder		19 Ss
	Familiarity		15 Ss
	Hypertension		13 Ss
	Obesity/Overweight		7 Ss
	Diabetes		3 Ss
*	NUMBER OF CHD STANDARD RISK FACTOR		
	2 Ss		Nil
	10 SS		1
	20 Ss		2
	10 Ss		3
	2 Ss		4
*	CARDIAC PATHOLOGY		
	Myocardial Infarction		34 Ss
	M.I. + Bypass		7 Ss
	Bypass surgery		3 Ss
	Valve substitution		1 Ss

Analysis of Psychometric Data

Table 3 shows psychometric data collected through CBA battery of tests. At Spielberger's State Anxiety Scale a reduction was obtained at 12 and 24 months. Eysenck's Extroversion Scale showed an increase at 6 month; reduction in neuroticism reached a statistical significance after treatment and at 24 month follow-up. Psychophysiological Questionnaire showed reduction at 12 and 24 months. Scores at the Depression Scale decreased after treatment and at 24 months.

Table 3. **Test Results: C.B.A.**

Variables	Pre-treat.	Post-treat.	6 months	12 months	24
STAI X2	52.3	48.9	48.4	47.9**	45.9****
Mean	11.8	10.5	12.1	12.3	9.4
EPQ E					
Mean	52.7	55.8*	56.1**	54.8	54.6
SD	12.7	13.0	13.6	15.6	14.0
EPQ N					
Mean	46.2	41.6****	43.3	43.3*	39.1*****
SD	12.8	10.8	12.1	12.9	11.8
EPQ P					
Mean	49.1	48.0	45.7	55.5	46.3
SD	13.1	11.5	13.6	28.2	10.8
EPQ L					
Mean	49.6	49.1	48.0	46.5	47.5
SD	8.6	8.9	11.6	11.9	10.6
QPF					
Mean	57.5	54.8*	56.2	54.1***	53.4****
SD	9.0	9.6	12.8	11.8	10.8
IP F					
Mean	50.1	51.4	51.5	49.5	48.5
SD	8.8	10.1	10.8	10.0	11.0
D					
Mean	49.0	45.4**	48.5	46.5	45.3****
SD	6.7	5.7	9.3	9.7	7.7
MOCQ					
Mean	51.1	48.7	47.8	47.5	48.0
SD	13.9	11.5	11.9	12.3	11.4

*Ss = 22, T-Student for pairs samples (df 21), *****= p < .001, ****= p < .01, ***= p < .02, **= p < .05, *= p < .10*

Psychometric Analysis of Type "A" Instruments

As for the Structured Interview proposed by Rosenman, the whole sample tested on entry (29 SS) met the criteria of Type "A", namely 18 subjects were rated A1 (strong type), and 11 A2 (weak type). At 12 and 24 month follow-up, only a few variations were registered on TABP (Ss = 29).

Table 4. **Test Results: S.I. Structured Interview by R. Rosenman**

TABP	Pre-treatment	12 months	24 months
A1	18 Ss	15 Ss	18 Ss
A2	11 Ss	13 Ss	9 Ss
X	-	1 Ss	2 Ss
B	-	-	-

Jenkins Activity Survey Form C shows a significant reduction at 6 and 24 months in Type "A" global construct, while the decrease in factor S (speed and impatience) at 6 months was not confirmed later .

Table 5. **Test Results : JAS FORM C**

Scales	Pre-treat.	Post-treat.	6 months	12 months	24 months
TYPE A					
Mean	304.8	282.1*	268.0***	277.3*	265.8***
SD	60.5	86.1	86.2	60.4	78.2
FACTOR S					
Mean	239.3	234.4	216.3**	223.8	221.3
SD	81.1	76.5	71.5	71.8	74.3
FACTOR J					
Mean	142.9	148.8	156.3	152.1	147.6
SD	38.6	40.0	45.1	46.3	41.7
FACTOR H					
Mean	140.1	147.3	142.0	135.3	141.1
SD	37.6	46.1	41.5	30.3	37.8

Ss = 16, Raw scores, T-Student for paired samples (df 15)
* $= p < .10$, ** $= p < .05$, *** $= p < .02$

Analysis of Social and Clinical Findings

As shown in Table 6, cigarette smoking was resumed by 6 subjects out of 32 at 2-year follow-up.

Hypertension was corrected in nearly all 13 subjects. Obesity persisted in 2 out of the 3 subjects. Weight in general showed a little variation with a mean value at entry of kilos 73.7 SD 11.4 and 74.6 kilos SD 11.5 at 2-year follow-up for the whole sample of 45 subjects. Serum Cholesterol remained unchanged in the average: 36 subjects presented at entry a total content above 200 mg/100ml, with a mean value of 229 SD 42, while at 24 months 31 subjects presented a mean value of 222 SD 35. As for working activity, it was resumed by 27 subjects out of 28 at 24 month follow-up.

The analysis of cardiac recurrence rate shows that myocardial infarction occurred to one subject, and angina episodes to 9 subjects by the end of the second year follow-up.

Table 6. **Clinical Data**

* CIGARETTE SMOKING			
	31 Ss	Before M.I. or Bypass	
	5 Ss	6	months after treatment
	4 Ss	12	months after treatment
	6 Ss	24	months after treatment
* HYPERTENSION			
	13 Ss	Before M.I. or Bypass	
	2 Ss	6	months after treatment
	1 Ss	12	months after treatment
	2 Ss	24	months after treatment
* OBESITY			
	3 Ss	Before treatment	
	2 Ss	6	months after treatment
	2 Ss	12	months after treatment
	2 Ss	24	months after treatment

* SERUM CHOLESTEROL > 200 mg/100 ml			
36 ss	Before treatment	Mean 229	SD 42
37 Ss	6 months after treatment		
33 Ss	12 months after treatment	Mean 223	SD 43
31 Ss	24 months after treatment	Mean 222	SD 35
* WORKING ACTIVITY			
28 Ss	Before M.I. or Bypass		
28 Ss	6 months after treatment		
28 Ss	12 months after treatment		
27 Ss	24 months after treatment		
* CARDIAC RECURRENCIES			
1 Ss	Myocardial infarction	6 Months	
4 Ss	Angina Pectoris	6 Months	
3 Ss	Angina Pectoris	12 Months	
2 Ss	Angina Pectoris	24 Months	

DISCUSSION

Variations in psychometric variables appear in line with expectation; similarly positive results were achieved in some clinical areas which were an indirect target of our intervention mainly addressed to TABP modification.

In this area results do not seem to cast a clear light on our hypothesis. In fact on one hand TABP appeared modified with statistical significance with JAS assessment, but on the other hand the Structered Interview showed only minor changes.

JAS is a questionnaire that relies upon subjective perception; the Structured Interview, on the contrary, offers a potentially more objective assessment because it relies primarily upon the direct observation of behavioral indices of excess adrenergic arousal, and it has been shown to be more potent as a predictor of CHD than a questionnaire. Because of its categorical classification system (A/B or A1, A2, X, B), anyway, the subtle changes expected to result from intervention.

Together with the University of Pavia and Veruno Centre we are testing the possibility of adopting Friedman's numeric scoring. The 28 questions of Friedman's Interview detect 38 indicators of Type "A" speech style, motor behavior and attitudes. Any indicator observed is weighted on a scale from 1 to 3, reflecting its intensity. The total Type "A" score is the sum of the weights of all indicators observed (scale rang 0-114).

With such scoring system available, we would probably have got results at the S.I. in line with JAS as well as consistent with our clinical observation and the subjects self-reports.

In fact most participants reported that they had experienced modifications in their life-style and/or cognitions and they tended to attribute such a change to our intervention rather than to myocardial infarction alone. They reported they could better control irritability and impatience, maintain more objective attitude towards illness and cope more adequately with time urgency and competitive drive.

As for the second hypothesis, the recurrence rate of infarction in our sample was 2.2% (1 subject out of 45). This percentage is consistent with data from the RCPP, at 2-year follow-up.

According to this study, participants who were exposed to Type "A"/cardiac counselling had the lowest recurrence rate (2.76%), but it was significantly lower than participants in the comparison section only (3.4%). A more direct test of the relationship between Type "A" reduction and recurrence was conducted by re-grouping participants according to the magnitude of TABP reduction (i.e. at least 1 SD reduction on two Type "A" measures) had the lowest recurrence rate, although again these differences were not statistically different. Thus the early results of RCPP suggest, but do not demonstrate that TABP reduction influenced recurrent cardiac events. Recent studies have reported contrasting results, casting a shadow on the utility of a modification of Type "A" behavior pattern in order to improve the outcome of CHD. A negative correlation in fact has been reported by some researchers between Type "A" and cardiovascular invalidity and mortality.

As for angina episodes, they do not seem to be affected by TABP modification, in out study as already reported in literature.

CONCLUSIONS

The limitations of our study (small size of sample, lack of data from control group, TABP instruments with limited sensitivity) make it useful and even necessary to further investigate on the effectiveness of a short intervention aimed at TABP modification.

As we said before, results did not confirm nor disconfirm our hypothesis, while showing some collateral positive outcomes in some clinical areas.

We can't but agree with Friedman's comment on the difficulty associated with conducting Type "A" interventions: "It is unclear what to change, how to change, and how to measure the change produced".

REFERENCES

Caracciolo, S., Baserga Marchetti, M.A., De Leo, D., Molinari, S. (1988) Comportamento die Tipo A e rischio coronarico. *Liviana Editrice.*

De Leo, D., Caracciolo, S., Berto, F., Mauro, P., Magni, G., Miraglia, G. (1986) Type A behavior pattern and mortality after recurrent myocardial infarction: Preliminary results from a follow-up study of 5 years. *Psychotherapy & Pschosomatics, 46,* 132-137.

Friedmann, M., Thoresen, C.E., et al. (1986) Alteration of Type A behavior and its effects on cardiac recurrences in post myocardial infarction patients: Summary results of the recurrent coronary prevention project. *American Heart Journal, 112,* 653-665.

Nunes, E., Franck, K.A., et al. (1987) Psychological treatment for the Type A behavior pattern and for coronary heart disease: A meta-analysis of the literature. *Psychosomatic Medicine, 48,* 159-173.

Yakubovich, I.S., Ragland, D.R., Brand, R.J., Syme, S.L.(1988) Type A behavior pattern and health status after 22 years of follow-up in the Western Collaborative Group Study. *American Journal of Epidemiology, 128,* 3.

IS SUCCESS IN SMOKING CESSATION TREATMENT PREDICTABLE?

H. Unland

Psychiatric Hospital of the University of Münster, Albert-Schweitzer-Strasse 11, 4400 Münster, FRG

In the literature relating to smoking cessation, many authors (Devins & Edwards, 1988; Benfari & Eaker, 1984; Mothersill et al., 1988; Pomerleau et al., 1978; Schneider, 1984; West et al., 1977 etc.) make statements on correlations between variables recorded prior to therapy and the success after completion of therapy.

According to Mothersill et al. (1988), most predictor studies have three essential disadvantages: they are carried out on small samples, only univariate methods of analysis are used, and the number of variables investigated is low. The question therefore arises of whether the therapeutic success of the specific smoking cessation method can be predicted by taking a larger number of different predictor variables into account in larger samples.

Should this be the case, then specific intervention strategies suitable for selective targetting on participants with high risk of failure could be derived from the results. The effectiveness of the therapy could be increased while the time and financial expenditure involved could be reduced.

METHOD

In our Münster smoking cessation studies, a total of 403 persons participated, 208 female and 195 male. Their average age was 40 years, and their average cigarette consumption 28 per day. The connection between 139 different variables on smoking behavior, personality, and person-related data and successful abstinence 6 month after therapy had been calculated by Kendall's correlations separately for each sex because men and women have different predictors, as has been confirmed by various authors (Minneker & Buchkremer, 1989; Stevens et al., 1982; Swan et al., 1988; Unland & Stögbauer, 1989).

Only with the significant variables discriminant analyses were performed. The six-month follow-up was selected as measuring time for therapeutic success because the relapse curve runs relatively flat from that time onwards; in other words, the proportion of long-term successful participants is more or less attained by then (Hunt et al., 1971).

RESULTS

For male subjects there was a canonical correlation of r=.49 between the discriminating variables and successful abstinence. Wether or not a smoker became a long-term non-smoker thus is clarified by roughly one-quarter with the variables measured prior to therapy.

Table 1. **Discriminant strength of the individual variables according to rank for the male subjects n=195)** *(Correlations between the discriminating variables and the canonical discriminant function. Positive correlation means a higher than random probability to be abstinant 6 months after cessation therapy*

Variable	Correlation
1. Expression of self-satisfaction in autocommunication	.426
2. Positive autocommunication	.392
3. Expression of self-discouragement in autocommunication	-.387
4. Nicotine dependence	-.346
5. Dysfunctional attitudes	-.343
6. Positive emotional well-being	.339
7. Search for recognition under stress	.312
8. Negative autocommunication	-.306
9. Smoking with intervals between inhalations	.275
10. External control conviction	-.267
11. Friends are smokers	-.266
12. Medical advice to give up smoking	-.256
13. Expectation of success	.250
14. Reacts to stress with self-pity	-.234
15. Length of maximum period of smoking abstinence	.233
16. Internal control conviction	.192
17. Body weight prior to cessation therapy	-.111

The proportion of male subjects correctly classified (accuracy) on the basis of discriminant analysis was 75.9%, corresponding to an improvement of 16.4% over the randomly correctly classified group (59,5%). Whereas the correct prediction rate for male non-smokers (specificity) was 64.6%, the rate for male smokers (sensitivity) was 83.6%.

Among the female participants the canonical correlation attained a value of r=.55. Whether or not a female smoker was still abstinent 6 month after treatment is thus clarified by one-third with the discriminating variables. The accuracy of the classification (78.8%) was 15.8% above what could be correctly determined according to random probability (63.0%).

64.9% and a sensitivity of 87.0%. Relapse within six month can thus be predicted with greater accuracy in general than long-term therapeutic success.

Among male participants, the 'autocommunication' variables were the best discriminating factors (Table 1). Positive self-verbalisation with a strong expression of self-satisfaction and a low degree of self-discouragement prove conducive to abstinence. Other factors contributing to discriminant strength are a low degree of nicotine dependence and a low measure of dysfunctional thoughts as defined by Ellis (1978).

Among women too, the 'autocommunication' variable was the best discriminating factor (Table 2). The avoidance of negative self-verbalisation in favour of self-satisfied thoughts has positive effect on the probability of abstinence.

Table 2. **Discriminant stregth of the individual variables according to rank for female subjects (n=208)**

Variable	Correlation
1. Expression of self-dissatisfaction in autocommunication	-.405
2. Negative autocommunication	-.301
3. Expression of self-satisfaction in autocommunication	.261
4. Occasional bad conscience about smoking	.252
5. Physical complaints	-.252
6. Self-accusation in stress situations	-.252
7. Length of maximum period of smoking abstinence	.247
8. Body weight prior to cessation therapy	-.229
9. Medical advice to give up smoking	-.212
10. Parents are smokers	-.267
11. Self-pity in stress situations	-.205
12. External control conviction	-.201
13. No. of ex-smokers in household	.193
14. Smokes with low, deep inhalation	-.189
15. Positive autocommunication	.183
16. Smokes to facilitate social contacts	.182
17. Nicotine dependence	-.175

The 'bad conscience' variable had the next highest discriminating strength. Women who claimed prior to therapy that they sometimes had a bad conscience about smoking had better-than-average chances of being a long-term non-smoker. Next in discriminating strength was the 'physical complaints' variable, indicating that minor physical complaints correlates to higher probability of treatment success.

Striking is the fact, that nicotine dependence ranked only seventeenth among the female subjects, whereas it ranked fourth among the male subjects.

CONCLUSIONS

According to the results obtained in this study, the question posed in the title of this paper has to be answered as follows: Even with relatively complex pre-treatment diagnosis, as carried out in our study, therapeutic success is not adequately predictable. A reliable prediction on smoker or non-smoker status can be made only about three-quarter of all participants.

Success in smoking cessation six month after therapy is less than one third determined by those factors measured prior to therapy. Two-thirds of the therapeutic success are due to factors not covered by our questionnaire, and it is doubtful whether they could be measured at all.

Nevertheless a discriminant analysis provides valuable information for the implementation of smoking cessation programs. In the first place, the finding that success correlates with different factors for men and women implies using different therapeutic strategies for the two groups.

The significance of the 'autocommunication' variable suggests that more attention should be paid to the cognitive process of the participants. It might be conceivable, for instance, for self-instruction training adapted to the needs of smokers to be given within the concept put forward by Meichenbaum (1977).

The fact that, among men, success in smoking cessation has strong correlation with the degree of nicotine dependence can be applied for targetting interventions in this group by emphasizing the benefit of nicotine substitution and recommending its use especially among strongly dependent male smokers.

Among female smokers, on the other hand, different factors have to be taken into account. Although the type of autocommunication is of very great importance among these participants too, psychosocial factors such as the attitude of parents and family doctor to smoking (Table 2, rank 9 and 10) also correlates to the treatment outcome, as does physical well-being (rank 5) prior to cessation therapy. For female smokers therefore other factors as for male smokers ought to be incorporated in the therapeutic strategies.

Taking account of sex-specific predictors of success is one step towards individualization in the therapy of smokers. If further variables correlating with success in cessation therapy were to be differentiated too, then specific therapeutic strategies directed towards a desired change in these variables could be developed. The therapeutic strategies diagnosed as relevant in a preliminary test could then be combined for each single smoker into one individual course of cessation therapy.

This procedure would increase the prospects of success for the individual as well as the efficiency of the therapy per se. This would result simultaneously in a reduction in the time and the financial expenditure involved, as the therapy would be compacted to the strategies needed for each individual case.

REFERENCES

Benfari, R.C., Eaker, E. (1984) Cigarette smoking outcomes at four years of follow-up, psychosocial factors and reactions to group intervention. *J. Clin. Psychol. 40*, 4, 1089-1097

Devins, G.M., Edwards, P.J. (1988) Self-efficacy and smoking reduction in chronic obstructive pulmonary disease. *Beh. Res. Ther., 26*, 2, 127-135

Ellis, A. (1978): *Die rational-emotive Therapie*. Pfeiffer, München

Hunt, W.A., Barnett, L.W., Branch, L.G. (1971) Relapse rates in addiction programmes. *J. Clin. Psychol., 27*, 455-456

Meichenbaum, D. (1977) *Cognitive-behavioral modification*. Plenum, New York

Minneker, E., Buchkremer, G. (1989) Relapse prevention in a multimodal smoking cessation therapy: In: Waahlberg, R.B. (Ed.): *Proceedings of the 35th ICAA, Oslo, July 31 - August 6, 1988, Volume III*, 217-228

Mothersill, K.J., McDowell, I., Rosser, W. (1988) Subject characteristics and long-term post-program smoking cessation. *Add. Beh., 13*, 1, 29-36

Pomerleau, D., Adkins, D., Pertschuk, M. (1978) Predictors of outcome and recidivism in smoking cessation treatment. *Add. Beh., 3*, 65-70

Schneider, S.J. (1984) Who quits smoking in a behavioral treatment program? *Add. Beh., 9*, 373-381

Stevens, P.A., Greissman Green, J., Primavera, L.H. (1982) Predicting successful smoking cessation. *J. Soc. Psychol., 118*, 235-241

Swan, G.E., Denk, C.E., Parker, S.D., Carmelli, D., Furze, C.T., Rosenman, R.H. (1988) Risk factors for late relapse in male and female ex-smokers. *Add. Beh., 13*, 253-266

Unland, H., Stögbauer, E. (1989) Prädiktoren erfolgreicher Raucherentwöhnung. In Buchkremer, G. (Ed.): *Fortschritte in der Raucherentwöhnung*. Thieme, Stuttgart, 103-109

West, G., Graham, S., Swanson, M., Wilkinson, G. (1977) Five-year follow-up of smoking withdrawal clinical population. *Am. J. Publ. Health, 67*, 536-554

PREDICTION OF LONG-TERM EFFCTS OF RELAXATION TRAINING ON BORDERLINE HYPERTENSION : THE ROLE OF PHYSIOLOGICAL AND PSYCHOLOGICAL FACTORS

J. Vinck, M. Arickh and A. Props

Limburgs Universitair Centrum, B-3610 Diepenbeek Belgium

Stress is supposed to play a role in the etiology of (at least some cases of) essential hypertension (EHT). Insofar as this is true, it is logical to use relaxation training (RT) as a treatment for EHT. Group mean blood pressure (BP) decreases after RT are, however, generally moderate (Vaitl, 1982; Cottier et al., 1984; Adsett et al., 1989). One possible reason for this relative failure is, that RT helps for some and not for other patients (maybe because the experience of stress is a more important etiological factor for some and is less important for others) and that mean group results mask large individual differences. At least the latter possibility is supported by research data : generally a large variability of the effect of RT is found (Cottier, et al., 1984; Vinck, in press). It would thus be good if one could select suitable candidates for RT or, in other words, if one could predict the effect of RT on BP.

This is what we and many other investigators have tried. Our first approach to this problem was to find out what predicted BP decrease after RT in students. This led to the construction of some regression equations (RE) that permitted to predict systolic (SBP) as well as diastolic blood pressure (DBP) (Vinck et al., 1987).

Next we turned to groups of subjects with borderline HT. In these groups, we investigated the predictive power of these RE, and of some additional predictors :

- cardiovascular reactivity (CVR) : one can expect that stronger CVR to stressors increases the risk for the development of stress-related HT (McCaffrey & Blanchard, 1985). RT should then be particularly helpful with subjects with stronger CVR. We distinguished task reactivity (TR) from situation reactivity (SR) : TR being the BP reaction to a mildly stressful task (Stroop Colour Word Interference Test) and SR being the difference between BP readings in a clinical and in a non-clinical situation. The problem with TR is that repeatedly negative correlations have been found with the effect of RT (Godaert, 1986; Larkin, 1988). This is difficult to understand.
- The representation of his/her condition by the subject (Nerenz & Leventhal, 1983) : RT can only be expected to reduce BP, if the technique is properly and regularly used. This, in turn, can only be expected when to do so is, in the mind of the subject, a reasonable thing to do, for example, because the subject attributes his high BP to stress. Such compliance will, furthermore, be

reinforced when the subject directly feels the effect of RT on his/her BP - and we know, that some subjects feel their high BP while others do not. In this paper, we examine the possibility to predict the 12 month follow up results of RT in a group of borderline hypertensives, using the described predictors.

METHOD

Subjects were recruited from a large administrative company : those having repeated BP readings over 140/90 mm Hg at medical screening in the company were invited to participate in the study; 80 % of the group accepted. The groups consists of 36 subjects (4 female, 31 male) with a mean age of 50 years and a pre-therapy mean BP of 143/97 mm Hg.

Before and after the training and after 6 and 12 months follow up, their BP was measured by the staff of the medical department of the company, using standard sphygmomanometer ("clinical" reading). A pre-therapy BP ("laboratory") reading was also taken during the irst RT session by the trainers using a semi-automated BP measuring device (Sphygmo-digital 4000).

Training consisted of 9 weekly one hour sessions of progressive relaxation, given in groups of 5 to 10 subjects.

The effect of RT was calculated, using clinical readings, as the difference between the initial BP and BP after 6 and 12 months follow up.

Regression equations used are : for SBP : 101.185 - .828 initial BP + 5.811 male; and for DBP : 59.222 - .757 initial BP + .33 BP change during first RT session (Vinck et al., 1987).

TR was measured as BP change during the Stroop Colour Word Interference test; SR as the difference between the pre-therapy clinical and laboratory BP readings.

Before RT subjects indicated (1), which of a number of possible factors they considered to be important as a cause for their HT and (2) whether or not they could feel when their BP was elevated.

After 12 month follow up the mean BP of the group was 134/89 mm Hg; we did, however, not include a control group and this reduction therefore cannot be attributed to the training with certainty.

RESULTS

1. Regression equations

The regression equations, that were found to predict BP changes after RT in students, were used to predict BP changes in the group of borderline hypertensives under consideration. As can be seen from Table 1, correlations between predicted are larger and significant for SBP.

2. Cardiovascular reactivity

The most striking results were obtained with TR : here we find systematically negative correlations with the effect of RT; most of these correlations are significant. This means that, contrary to logic, but consistent with other reported data, smaller amounts of reactivity before the training go with larger decreases of BP.

For SR we see that initially there is a relation in the logically expected direction, but this has disappeared after 12 months.

Table 1. **Correlations Between Changes Predicted By Regression Equations, Task Reactivity, Situation Reactivity And Observed BP Changes After 6 And 12 Months (n = 36)**

		6 MONTH FU	12 MONTH FU
REGRESSION EQUATIONS			
	SBP	+.25	+.72 **
	DBP	-.10	+.39
TASK REACTIVITY			
	SBP	-.53 **	-.41
	DBP	-.37 *	-.61 **
SITUATION REACTIVITY			
	SBP	+.38 *	-.07
	DBP	+.38 *	+.18

*$p<.05$, **$p<.01$

3. Attribution and symptom perception

We expected larger effects of RT in subjects that attribute their HT to stress. 69% of our subjects did so and from Table 2 we see that in this subgroup DBP decreases significantly after 12 months, whereas this decrease is not significant for the non-stress-attributing subgroup. For SBP results are less clear.

Table 2. **P Values For Differences Pre - 12 Month FU BP In Subgroups**

	WITH	WITHOUT	WITH	WITHOUT
	STRESS-ATTRIBUTION		SYMPTOM PERCEPTION	
SBP	NS	NS	.03	NS
DBP	.003	NS	.04	NS

NS = not significant

As far as symptom percption is concerned, we see that pre-training to 12 month follow up differences are significant for SBP and for DBP in the group with symptom perception and that these differences are not significant in the group without symptom perception.

DISCUSSION

To a certain extent, prediction of the effect of RT on the BP of borderline hypertensives appears to be possible. The regression equations, task reactivity and symptom perception appear to be useful in this respect.

The direction of the relation between BP change and TR is unexpected. It has been signaled, however, that other authors report similar findings. Also this finding is consistent with other unexpected data showing that TR increases in successfully trained subjects (Blanchard et al., 1988; Vinck, in press). The role of task reactivity in the etiology and maintenance of HT has clearly to be reconsidered.

The more psychological predictors (symptom perception and attribution) are most probably having their effect through compliance : in a self-regulation perspective, it can be understood, that subjects act according to their representation of the problem and RT will be readily considered to be a suitable strategy when a subject thinks of his problem as a stress-problem and when he directly feels the effect.

It seems to us, that we can set up a controlled clinical trial now, where groups of subjects are formed on the basis of the predictors which have been found to be useful and to see, whether groups with positive prediction achieve larger and clinically more significant BP reductions than have been found in earlier studies with unselected groups. In doing so, autonomic over-activity should be included as a potential predictor (McGrady & Higgins, 1989; Cottier et al., 1984). Also, the possible interaction of these psychological variables with biological variables (Gorkin, 1987) has to be taken into consideration.

REFERENCES

Adsett, C.A., et al. (1989) Behavioral and physiological effects of a beta blocker and relaxation therapy on mild hypertensives. *Psychosomatic Medicine*, *51*, 523-536

Blanchard, E.B., et al. (1988) The effects of thermal biofeedback and autogenic training of cardiovascular reactivity : The Joint USSR-USA Behavioral Hypertension Treatment Project. *Biofeedback and Self-regulation, 13*, 1, 25-38

Cottier, C., Shapiro, K., Julius, S. (1984) Treatment of mild hypertension with progressive muscle relaxation. Predictive value of indexes of sympathetic tone. *Archives of Internal Medicine, 144*, 1954-1958

Godaert, G. (1986) *Hoge bloeddruk en relaxatie. Klinisch psychologische en psychofysiologische aspekten*. (Hypertension and relaxation). Doctoral dissertation, Free Univ. Amsterdam,

Gorkin, L (1987) Behavioral Medicine research in the etiology of essential hypertension : bridging the cardiovascular reactivity and renal dysfunction paradigms. *Behavioral Medicine Abstracts, 8*, 4, 159-162

Larkin, K.T., Knowlton, G., D'Alessandri, R. (1988) *Predicting treatment response to progressive relaxation training in borderline essential hypertensive patients*. Presented Annual Meeting AABT, New York, Nov. 1988

McCaffrey, R.J., Blanchard, E.B. (1985) Stress management approaches to the treatment of essential hypertension. *Annals of Behavioral Medicine, 7,* 1, 5-12

McGrady, A., Higgins, J.T. (1989) Prediction of response to biofeedback-assisted relaxation in hypertensives : Development of a Hypertensive Predictor Profile (HYPP). *Psychosomatic Medicine, 51*, 277-284

Nerenz, D.R., Leventhal, H. (1983) Self-regulation theory in chronic illness. In : T.G. Burish & L.A. Bradley (Eds). *Coping with chronic disease. Research and applications.* New York, Academic Press,

Vaitl, D. (1982) *Essentielle Hypertonie. Psychologisch- medizinische Aspekte.* Springer, Berlin.

Vinck, J, Arickx, M., Hongenaert, M. (1987) Predicting interindividual differences in blood pressure response to relaxation training in normotensives. *Journal of Behavioral Medicine, 10*, 395-410

Vinck, J. Borderline hypertension and relaxation training. In : Schmidt, L., Schwenkmetzger, P., Weinman, J. & Maes, S. (Eds), *Health Psychology : theoretical and applied aspects.* Harwood Academic Publishers, London ,(in press)

PART VII:

PATIENTS WITH HIV POSITIVE REACTION OR AIDS

THE "DENIVELLIERUNGSSYNDROM" - DECLINE OF THE LEVEL OF PERFORMANCE AND DETERMINATION OF PERSONALITY AND PSYCHO-PHYSIOLOGICAL VARIABLES IN AIDS-PATIENTS

J. Grünberger, L. Linzmayer, N. Loimer , G. Pakesch , D. Pfersmann , K. Guggenberger and B. Saletu

Department of Clinical Psychodiagnostics, Psychiatric University Clinic of Vienna

INTRODUCTION

Since the first reports in 1981 AIDS has become an expanding major public health problem. Currently, the major high risk group comprises homosexual and bisexual men with multiple sexual partners. The group with the next highest prevalence is users of illicit intravenous drugs. Acquired immune deficiency syndrome can present neuropsychiatric symptoms of major depressive disorder, adjustment disorder with depressed mood and organic brain syndromes with affective, delusional and demented features. However, different findings concerning the incidence of "AIDS-dementia-complex" have been reported (Navia et al., 1986). Therefore the aim of the present study was to search for deficits in performance of AIDS-patients. Furthermore we were interested in the changes of personality and in the psychophysiological parameters of these patients.

DESCRIPTION OF THE INVESTIGATED SUBJECTS

30 homosexual AIDS-patients (mean age 32,82; s = 9,09; belonging to stage III and IV) undergoing a treatment in the I. Dermatologic University Clinic of Vienna participated in the study voluntarily. They were compared to 37 drug addicted AIDS-patients, whose age ranged between 20 and 45 years (x = 29,85; s = 6,37; stage III and IV); to healthy normals and to 20 healthy controls (x = 31; s = 5,78) respectively. The drug addicted patient group was compared to a control group of 30 drug addicted HIV-negative patients to objectivate AIDS-specific deficits. A control group of patients with lethal diseases is planed for the comparison with homosexual AIDS-patients.

METHODS

The investigations were carried out in the department of clinical psychodiagnostics of the Psychiatric University Clinic of Vienna. Performance investigations included the "Mehrfachwahl-Wortschatz-Intelligenztest" (MWT) of Lehrl (1978) and the Raven progressive matrices test (1968) for assessment of crystallized intelligence and fluid intelligence respectively, the Benton test (Benton, 1968) for determination of visual retention, the alphabetic reaction test (Grünberger et al., 1984) measuring attention (total score of erased letters) and concentration (percents of correct letters), the numerical memory test (short term memory) for retention of numbers, a computerassisted rigidity test for determination of flexibility (in the standard condition the patient has to press 10 buttons according to the beat of a metronome at random, while in speed condition he has to work as fast as possible indicating personal speed).

Changes in personality were evaluated by MMPI (Spreen, 1963) and STAI (Laux et al., 1981). Psychophysiological parameters were examined by means of computerassisted "static and dynamic light evoked pupillometry" (measurements of pupillary diameter and pupillary reagibility), skin conductance level, reaction and habituation. Statistical analyses included the U-test of Mann and Whitney, ANOVA and the Duncan test.

RESULTS

Performance

The drug addicted AIDS-patients, the drug addicted HIV-negative patients and the homosexual AIDS-patients showed average intellectual abilities.

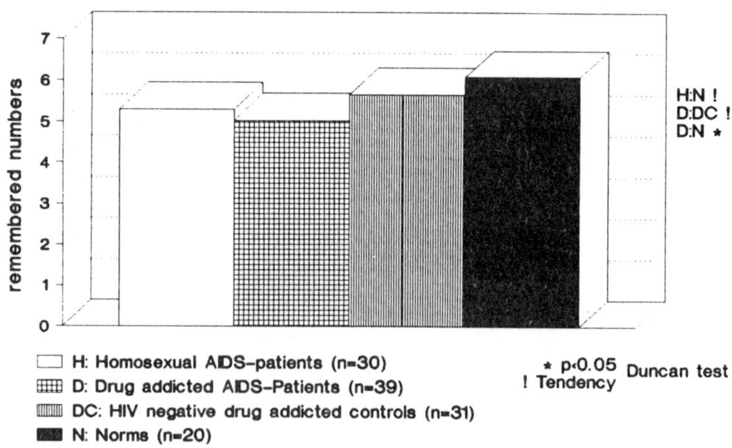

Figure 1. **Numerical memory in AIDS-Patients**

Considering numerical memory the drug addicted AIDS-patients differed from the normals but not from homosexual AIDS-patients ($p<0.05$, Duncan test). But only a small deficit to healthy normals ranging within the limits of standard deviation was obtained. As compared to drug addicted controls the drug addicted AIDS group tendencially showed a reduction in numerical memory.

Visual retention as evaluated by Benton test demonstrated following findings: The drug addicted AIDS-patients showed fewer correct reproductions and more errors than homosexual AIDS-patients and healthy normals ($p<0.01$; $p<0.05$). However,the performance of the drug addicted AIDS-patients only deviated from the norms within tolerable limits. In comparison to addicted controls the drug addicted AIDS-patients revealed significant differences ($p<0.05$, Duncan test).

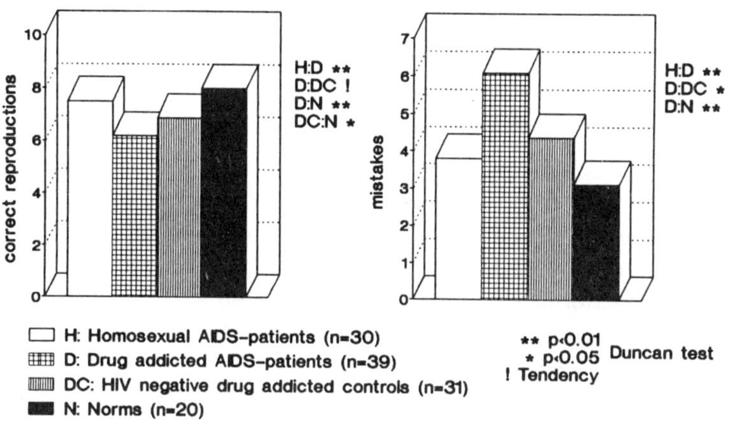

Figure 2. **Benton Test (visual retention) in AIDS-patients**

Differences in attention (global score in ARG test) between drug dependent AIDS-patients, homosexual AIDS-patients and normals did not reach the level of statistical significance. Only a slight impairment of attention could be observed in drug addicted AIDS-patients. Drug addicted controls demonstrated significant better attention than the addicted AIDS-patients ($p<0.05$, Duncan test). Assessment of concentration as evaluated by means of correct answers showed no significant differences between drug addicted and homosexual AIDS-patients. The difference between normals and drug dependent AIDS-patients reached the level of statistical significance ($p<0.01$; Duncan test). The latter demonstrated only a slight impairment of concentration. In comparison to the drug addicted controls concentration of the AIDS-patient group was reduced ($p<0.01$; Duncan test).

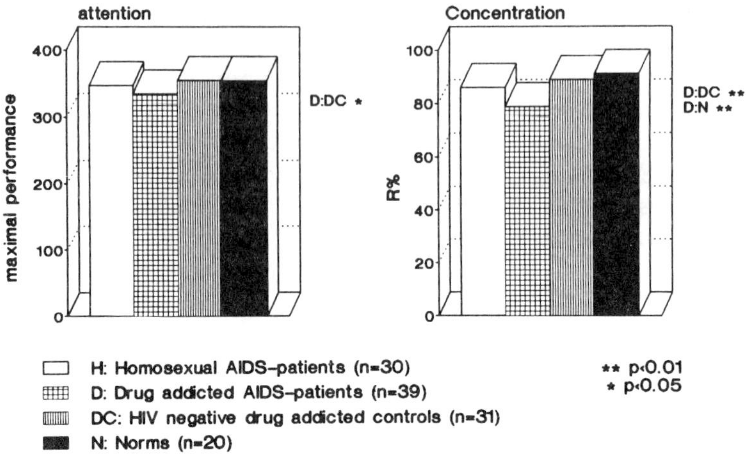

Figure 3. **ARG-Test (Attention and concentration) in AIDS-patients**

While no differences in rigidity between patients and normals could be found, all patients were characterized by a slight slowing of personal speed.

Summing up, the performance of the risk groups differed only slightly from the level of normals, therefore this observation is called "Denivellierungssyndrom" - that means decline of the level of performance. Our results are confirmed by the findings of Naber (1988) and Stieglitz et al. (1988). Both authors could not find marked deficits in performance of AIDS-patients.

Personality

The addicted AIDS-patients differed significantly from the homosexual AIDS-patients in all clinical dimensions of the MMPI, with exception of feminity-masculinity and social introversion ($p<0.01$; $p<0.05$; Duncan test). The AIDS-patients were characterized by higher loadings in clinical dimensions. Between drug dependent AIDS-patients and HIV-negative patients no differences could be observed. The homosexual AIDS-patients only revealed significant differences in the scales hypochondriasis, hysteria and feminity-masculinity, while AIDS-patients as well as the HIV-negative patients with exception of social introversion differed significantly from the norms in all clinical dimensions. In the drug dependent patient groups more psychopathological conspicuousness was observed, which might be caused by the addiction too.

Table 1. **Personality (MMPI) in AIDS-patients**

	H: Homo-sexual AIDS-patients	D: Drug addicted AIDS-patients	DC: HIV neg. Drug addicted controls	Healthy normals	Comparison Duncan test	Anova
Variable	$\bar{x}/s$	$\bar{x}/s$	$\bar{x}/s$	$\bar{x}/s$	$\bar{x}/s$	F
Hypochondriasis	9.91 4.00	13.01 4.45	13.05 3.67	7.90 3.00	H:D ** H:DC ** H:N * D:N ** DC:N **	18.62 **
Depression	6.10 3.54	11.10 4.98	10.55 4.43	5.40 2.10	H:D ** H:DC ** D:N ** DC:N **	23.44 **
Conversion hysteria	7.97 4.03	12.96 5.61	12.55 4.96	4.50 1.70	H:D ** H:DC ** H:N ** D:N ** DC:N **	39.06 **
Psychopathic Deviate	9.52 3.80	13.62 4.96	14.18 4.05	8.00 2.50	H:D ** H:DC ** D:N ** DC:N **	24.74 **
Masculinity/ Femininity	11.79 2.69	11.59 3.37	12.35 3.71	7.20 1.40	H:N ** D:N ** DC:N **	31.29 **
Paranoia	4.59 3.40	7.03 3.84	6.61 4.93	4.00 2.10	H:D * H:DC * D:N ** DC:N **	7.01 **
Psychasthenia	12.97 3.97	17.14 6.18	17.03 5.12	12.40 4.00	H:D ** H:DC ** D:N ** DC:N **	10.49 **
Schizophrenia	9.02 3.58	12.65 5.85	11.92 4.18	8.30 3.70	H:D ** H:DC * D:N ** DC:N **	9.21 **
Hypomania	8.47 3.16	13.69 4.29	12.80 3.74	9.20 3.00	H:D ** H:DC ** D:N ** DC:N **	19.18 **
Social Introversion	8.21 3.89	9.79 5.76	8.39 4.12	6.80 3.20	H:N **	3.54 *

** $p<0.01$ * $p<0.05$

Concerning state anxiety, the drug dependent AIDS-patients imposed more anxious than the homosexual AIDS-patients. The latter did not differ significantly from the healthy normals, while between the drug addicted patient groups and the normals the differences reached the level of statistical significance ($p<0.05$; 0.5; Duncan test). However, the anxiety of these patients ranged within the normal limits.

Trait anxiety of the drug dependent AIDS-patients only showed a small deviation from the normals ($p<0.01$; Duncan test). In the addicted AIDS-patient group higher trait anxiety was found than in the homosexual group ($p<0.01$; Duncan test). While no significant differences between the homosexual AIDS-patients and the healthy normals were obtained as compared to the normals the drug control group demonstrated a marked trait anxiety. The influence of addiction on anxiety should not be neglected.

Psychophysiological findings

The method of computerassisted static and dynamic light evoked pupillometry for determination of autonomous activation and pupillary reagibility is a very objective, reliable, valid and economical technique, which was developed in our department (Grünberger et al., 1984, 1987). As compared to homosexual AIDS-patients pupillary diameter of drug dependent AIDS-patients was smaller ($p<0.01$; Duncan test), indicating a lower vegetative activation, whereas central and emotional influences could not be excluded. No significant differences in diameter were found between AIDS-patients and the norms ($p<0.01$; 0.05; 0.01; Duncan test). Spontaneous fluctuations of the pupil (above 3 mm) are discussed as indicator of central activation. Both risk groups showed fewer fluctuations than healthy normals ($p<0.01$; U-test), reflecting lower central activation.

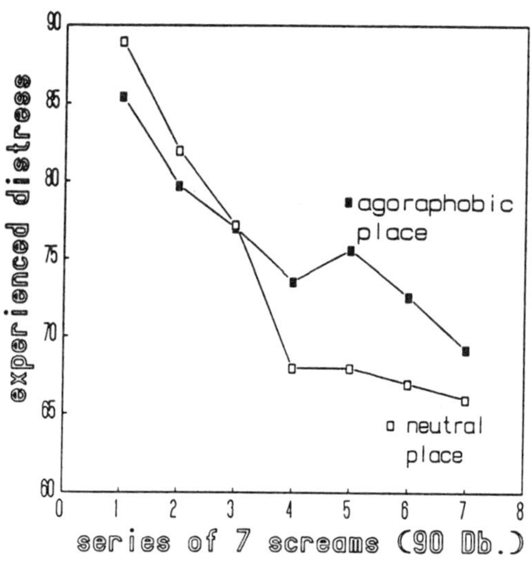

Figure 4. **Static pupillometry in AIDS-patients**

In comparison to healthy normals onset latency (dynamic pupillometry) of the patients did not differ, that means stimulus processing was not influenced. Significant differences concerning relative changes were found between homosexual AIDS-patients and drug dependent AIDS-patients ($p<0.01$; Duncan test). Pupillary reagibility of the latter showed a decrease, which could be caused by addiction. As compared to healthy normals in the patient groups a decrease of pupillary reagibility was observed ($p<0.01$; 0.01; Duncan test).

Skin conductance level was augmented in patients in comparison to normal controls, but the difference did not reach statistical significance. The patients demonstrated higher autonomous activation. This is not incompatible with the findings of static pupillometry, because another system was measured. While the secretory activity has only single innervation from the sympathetic nervous system the pupil is double innervated, having dilatator fibres with noradrenalin as transmitter and the constrictor fibres innervated by cholinergic nerves. The pupil offers the possibility of gaining access to a system showing the balance between the adrenergic and cholinergic activity. This is not possible with electrodermal activity. The drug addicted AIDS-patients group habituated earlier than the addicted HIV-negative group (n.s., U-test), the healthy controls and the homosexual patients (n.s., $p<0.01$). The drug dependent AIDS-patients were more psychovegetatively suppressed. As compared to addicted AIDS-patients the homosexual AIDS-patients differed in emotional reflection ($p<0.01$; 0.01; U-test); they showed a higher degree of excitement, while in drug dependent AIDS-patients a lower emotional reflection was found. Concerning emotional intensity similar results were obtained. Differences in the mean amplitudes did not reach the level of statistical significance between homosexual AIDS-patients, the healthy controls and addicted HIV-negative patients respectively.

CONCLUSION

Summarizing our findings AIDS-dementia could not be objectivated in AIDS-patients, but only a slight deficit in performance, which is called "Denivellierungssyndrom" - decline of the level of performance was observed.

AIDS-patients as well as the HIV-negative patients (the latter with exception of social introversion) differed significantly from the norms in all clinical dimensions.

Concerning state anxiety the drug dependent AIDS-patients showed more anxiety than the homosexual AIDS-patients. In the addicted AIDS-patient groups a higher trait anxiety was found than in the homosexual group, but only a small deviation from the healthy normals was observed.

Psychophysiological measurements in drug dependent AIDS-patient groups demonstrated autonomous desactivation, reduced pupillary reagibility and deficient psychovegetative resonance (Grünberger et al., 1989). Our reported findings could give some useful cues for pharmaco- and psychotherapeutical interventions in AIDS-patients to try to assuage the disease and if possible to prolong their survival.

SUMMARY

30 homosexual AIDS-patients (mean age 32,82; s =9,09; belonging to stage III and IV) undergoing a treatment in the I. Dermatologic University Clinic of Vienna participated in the study voluntarily. They were compared to 37 drug addicted AIDS-patients, whose age ranged between 20 and 45 years (x =29,85; s =6,37; stage III and IV), to healthy normals and to 20 healthy controls (x =31; s = 5,78) respectively.

Performance was measured by numerical memory test, Benton test, alphabetic reaction test and computerassisted rigidity test. Personality was assessed by means of MMPI and STAI.

Psychophysiological parameters were evaluated by computerassisted "static" and "dynamic" pupillometry, computerassisted measurements of skin conductance level, -reaction and its habituation. Performance in drug addicted AIDS-patients differed from controls and especially from healthy normals with a minimal range (Denivellierungssyndrom - decline of the level of performance). No AIDS-dementia could be objectivated. Personality profiles of drug addicted AIDS-patients differed significantly between homosexual AIDS-patients and healthy normals.

Furthermore drug dependent AIDS-patients demonstrated autonomous desactivation, reduced pupillary reagibility and deficient psychovegetative resonance.

REFERENCES

Benton A.L. (1968) *Der Benton-Test.* 3. Auflage. Bern-Stuttgart, Huber.

Grünberger J., Linzmayer L., Saletu B. (1984) Psychodiagnostik mit Hilfe psychophysiologischer Verfahren. *Wien. med. Wschr.*, 84, 29-35.

Grünberger J., Linzmayer L., Saletu B., Stöhr H. (1984) Zur Methodologie der Pupillenmessung. *Psychiatr. Clin.*, 3, 157-164.

Grünberger, J., Linzmayer, L., Wytek, R., Saletu, B. (1987) Faktorenanalytische Reliabilitätsbestimmung der statischen und dynamischen Pupillometrie bei Normalpersonen und psychopathologischen Gruppen. *Wien. med. Wschr.*, *7/8*, 135-139.

Grünberger, J., Linzmayer, L., Stöhr, H., Wytek, R., Saletu, B. (1989) Computerunterstützte Rigiditätsmessung zur Differenzierung psychopathologischer Gruppen. *Wien. med. Wschr.*, *9*, 206-212.

Grünberger, J., Linzmayer, L., Pakesch, G., Pfersmann, D., Saletu, B., Guggenberger, K. (1988) Das Denivellierungssyndrom und psychophysiologische Veränderungen bei AIDS-Patienten. *Fortschritte der Neurologie und Psychiatrie*, *1*, 13.

Grünberger, J., Linzmayer, L., Pakesch, G., Pfersmann, D., Guggenberger, K., Saletu, B. (1989, in press) Elektrodermale Aktivität - psychovegetative Resonanz bei AIDS-Patienten.

Laux, L., Glanzmann, P., Schaffner, P., Spielberger, C.D. (1981) *Das State-Trait-Angstinventar. Theoretische Grundlagen und Handanweisung.* Beltz Testgesellschaft, Weinheim .

Lehrl, S. (1978) *Mehrfachwahl-Wortschatz-Intelligenztest MWT-B*. Erlangen, Straube .

Naber, D., Bove, D., Erfurth, A., Perro, C., Sadri, J., Schick, U. (1988) Psychiatrische und neuropsychologische Auffälligkeiten bei HIV-Infizierten. *Fortschr. Neurol.-Psychiatr., 56* (Sonderheft), 5.

Navia, B.A., Price R.W. (1986) Dementia complicating AIDS. *Psychiatr. Ann., 16*, 158-166.

Raven, J.C. (1971) *Guide to Standard Progressive Matrices (Sets A, B, C, D,E)*. 13. Auflage. London, Lewis.

Sachs, L. (1972) *Statistische Auswertungsmethoden*. 3. Auflage. Wien-Berlin-Heidelberg-New York, Springer.

Spreen, O. (1963) *Manual zum MMPI*. Saarbrücken. Deutsche Bearbeitung des Minnesota Multiphasic Personality Inventory von S.R. Hathaway und J.C. Mc Kinley. Bern, Huber.

Stieglitz, R.D., Albrecht, J., Lundt, A., Pittik, V., Hedde, H.P. (1988) Psychopathometrie bei HIV-infizierten Patienten. *Nervenarzt, 59*, 330-336.

COPING WITH STRESS BY HIV-INFECTED PERSONS - AN ANALYSIS OF IT'S BUFFERING EFFECT

M. Perrez., M. Reicherts and B. Plancherel

University of Fribourg, Switzerland

INTRODUCTION

The study focuses on the relation of coping characteristics and psychological well being. We assume that not the global critical life event (to be HIV-affected) has major explicative value for the subjective well-being but rather the modalities of coping with the concrete consequences resulting from this critical life event. We are studying the question if there are coping tendencies moderating the relation of the stressful experience and psychological well-being of the HIV-infected persons.

HYPOTHESIS

The correlation of anxiety and depressive measures with HIV-related stressful experience may be strengthened 1) by a coping-characterized by low palliation probability, 2) by self-blaming tendency in stressful situations, 3) by evasion/avoidance and passivity (instead of instrumental behavior) in controllable situations.

Sample

HIV-positive persons were recruited from two information centres connected to two Swiss university hospitals. Persons consult these centers for medical check-ups.

The 31 subjects of this study are homosexual men. Their mean age is 36.3 years. The majority lives in town. One third of the group has a higher level education. All others with one exception had a professional education. At the time of our first contact all subjects worked full or part time.

Assessment of HIV-related stressful events, and coping with stress

For the assessment of coping with HIV-related stressful situations we constructed an S-R-questionnaire. The HIV-related stressful hypothetical situations were collected by interviewers. 12 prototypical situations were worked out as a situation sample for two different coping tasks: for aversive situation and for situations characterized by loss. The ratings concern stressor-perception variables, goals, and reaction variables. A prototype (UBV) of the questionnaire was evaluated in earlier studies (Reicherts, 1988; Reicherts & Perrez, 1986).

As negative indicators of mental well-being we used state anxiety, measured by the state-trait-inventory of Launx et al. (1981) and the depression scores measured by Beck's depression inventory (BDI).

The amount of HIV-related stressors the person experienced since their diagnosis is operationalized by the frequency they reported for the stressful situations of the UB-HIV questionnaire (familiarity of the described hypothetical situation).

RESULTS

Table 1. **Correlations between HIV-specific stress (frequency of the stressful situations of the UB-HIV) and mental well-being (state-anxiety, STAI, and depression, BDI) moderated by the coping tendencies in the UB-HIV-questionnaire (N= 31 HIV-positive men)**

coping tendency		correlation stress and depression	difference betw. corr. [1] $z_{r1}-z_{r2}$	correlation stress and state anxiety	difference betw. corr. [1] $z_{r1}-z_{r2}$
self-directed coping efforts:					
suppression of information	low	.61	1.70[b]	.40	
	high	.03		.09	
search for information	low	.19		.07	
	high	.39		.35	
palliation	low	.46		.53	2.37[c]
	high	.12		-.39	
reevaluation	low	-.23	2.95[c]	-.05	1.29[a]
	high	.74		.45	
other-blaming	low	-.42	2.67[c]	-.38	3.18[d]
	high	.55		.72	
self-blaming	low	-.34	2.32[b]	-.30	2.47[c]
	high	.52		.60	
environment-directed coping efforts:					
passivity (aversive sit.)	low	.25		-.18	1.74[b]
	high	.42		.49	
evasion/avoidance (aversive sit.)	low	.08	1.31[a]	-.04	
	high	.54		.29	
active influence on stressor av.)	low	.40		.27	
	high	.27		.07	
passivity (loss sit.)	low	.11	1.62[a]	.09	
	high	.64		.42	
acitve influence (loss sit.)	low	.34		.31	
	high	.48		.13	
active reorientation (loss sit.)	low	.43		.22	
	high	.32		.29	

a p<.10; b p<.05; c p<.01; d p<.001; 1) one-tailed tests

To study the moderating effects of different coping modalities on the correlation between the number of encountered stressful events and indicators of psychic well-being, we separated the sample at the mean in two subsamples of subjects with low resp. high probability of the given coping response.

Then correlation coefficients are calculated separately for the two groups, and their difference is compared using the critical ratio of the transformed coefficients according to Fisher. If there is a statistically significant difference of the correlation coefficients in the two coping subsamples, it can cautiously be interpreted as evidence for a moderating effect of the coping modality. (Conceptual and methodological aspects of moderator vs. mediator variables, and the possible shortcomings of the method used can not be discussed here; see for example Baron & Kenny (1986). Most of the conditions for the application of this method are given).

By this analysis we observed the following "moderating effects" of coping on the relation between stress and well-being: Concerning state anxiety, there is a moderating influence (a) of palliation, which seems to "buffer" the impact of stress, (b) of self- and other-blaming which seem to reinforce its impact, and (c) also a tendency of passivity in aversive but rather controllable situations to be positively related to state anxiety.

Concerning depression, the study reveals a moderating effect of (a) information suppression, which seem to "buffer" the relation between stressors and depression, (b) of self- and other-blaming strengthening the impact of stressors, and (c) also a moderating tendency of evasion (in aversive) and passivity (in loss episodes).

All results are in accord to our assumptions of effective coping, except the fact, that reevaluation seems to strengthen the impact of HIV-related stressors on depression and state anxiety.

DISCUSSION

We postulated that not only the fact to be HIV-infected as a critical life event plays a predictive or explicative role for the psychic well-being. We assumed that certain features of coping tendencies influence the relation between the amount of stressful encounters and the status of the psychic well-being. We formulated hypotheses concerning the question what the features of such coping competencies are.

The results of the presented study confirm the hypothesis with one exception (reevaluation) and are compatible to the results of other studies with normal (Perrez, 1988a) as well as with depressed persons (Perrez & Reicherts, 1986; Reicherts et al., 1987; Perrez, 1988b): The tendency to cope by palliating the stressful emotions, by avoiding self-blame and passive and evasive behavior in rather controllable situations can buffer the impact of stressful events on depression and anxiety as indicators of mental health. Therefore coping competencies can be considered as intrapersonal resources which can mitigate the psychosocial impact of the HIV-infection.

Acknowledgements
We thank Gebhard Hüsler and Eliane Gaspoz-Chevrier for their help in data collecting, Daniel Segmüller for his support in constructing the questionnaire. The study is part of a research project supported by the Swiss health department.

REFERENCES

Baron, R.M., Kenny, D.A. (1986) The Moderator-Mediator Variable Distinction in Social Psychological Research: Conceptual, Strategic, and Statistical Considerations. *Journal of Personality and Social Psychology, 51(6),* 1173-1182.

Laux, L., Glanzmann, P., Schaffner, P., Spielberger, C.D. (1981) *Das State-Trait-Angstinventar. Theoretische Grundlagen und Handanweisung.* Weinheim: Beltz.

Perrez, M. (1988a) Bewältigung von Alltagsbelastungen und seelische Gesundheit: Zusammenhänge auf der Grundlage computer-unterstützter Selbstbeobachtungs- und Fragebogendaten. *Zeitschrift für Klinische Psychologie, XVII(4),* 292-306.

Perrez, M. (1988b) Belastungsverarbeitung bei neurotisch und endogen Depressiven. *Psychotherapie, Psychosomatik, Medizinische Psychologie, 38(1),* 59-65.

Perrez, M., Reicherts, M. (1986) Appraisal, Coping, and Attribution Processes by Depressed Persons: An S-R-S-R Approach. *The German Journal of Psychology, 10(4),* 315-326.

Reicherts, M. (1988) *Diagnostik der Belastungsverarbeitung. Neue Zugänge zu Stress-Bewältigungs-Prozessen.* Freiburg/ Schweiz: Universitätsverlag und Bern: Hans Huber

Reicherts, M., Perrez, M. (1986) *UBV-Fragebogen zum Umgang mit belastenden Situationen im Verlauf.*Freiburg/Schweiz: Psychologisches Institut der Universität.

Reicherts, M., Käslin, S., Scheurer, F., Fleischhauer, J., Perrez, M. (1987) Belastungsverarbeitung bei endogen Depressiven. *Zeitschrift für Klinische Psychologie, Psychopathologie und Psychotherapie, 35(3),* 197-210.

PART VIII:

TREATMENT PROGRAMMS FOR SCHIZOPHRENIC PATIENTS

"SOTERIA BERN", TREATMENT AND PREVENTION OF SCHIZOPHRENIA WITHOUT NEUROLEPTIC DRUGS

J.P. Dauwalder

Institut de Psychologie, Universite de Lausanne, Lausanne

INTRODUCTION

Schizophrenia is often seen as a hopeless fate. Careful empirical research and behavioural data, however, prove the contrary. Nowadays there exists a lot of piecemeal scientific evidence that schizophrenia is no longer a hopeless fate. The problem is not to join another piece of evidence to this puzzle, but rather to integrate existing knowledge into a holistic and coherent view.

More than 15 years of clinical experience and research on schizophrenia have led to our conviction that monocausal and linear explanations, such as "double-bind", "schizophrenogenic mother", or more recently "high expressed emotions", would never be sufficient. This contribution presents our actual integrated and multicausal understanding of the evolution of psychotic behaviour and a related pilot experience for understanding of the evolution of psychotic behaviour and a related pilot experience for treatment and prevention of schizophrenia. The main concern will be to show the necessity of a multimodal approach in this field.

A COMPREHENSIVE EVOLUTIONARY MODEL OF PSYCHOTIC BEHAVIOUR

As the conceptual framework has been developed in extenso elsewhere (Ciompi, 1987; Dauwalder, 1989), our ideas will be summarized very shortly. Human behaviour results from a complex hierarchy of inseparable programmes for feeling, thinking and behaving (or cognitive and affective "systems of reference") built up in a continuous process of internalization from actions and experiences since early childhood. While relaying heavily on Piaget's notions about the origins of these inner "schemata" from actions through assimilation, accommodation and differentiation, this understanding seems compatible with biological, behavioural and even systemic views.

Our basic idea is that psychotic behaviour results from an individual and particular evolution of these "systems of reference":

1. During a first premorbid stage lasting from birth until outbreak of manifest psychotic behaviour, unfavourable genetic influences and/or prenatal damages interacting with unfavourable influences from the family or social environ-

ment lead in individually variable combinations to a vulnerable premorbid disposition. The exact nature of this vulnerability (Zubin & Spring, 1977) is not yet clear. Specific aspects of vulnerability consist in disorders of attention, categorisation and time-sequentiation, in a tendency to cognitive "overinclusion" and emotional oversensitivity and - consequently - in the blurring of boundaries between the inner and outside world (Nuechterlein et al., 1984; Patterson et al., 1986). The most obvious result of these deficiencies is an increased difficulty to cope with complex cognitive and emotional charges such as interpersonal conflicts and contradictions, complicated life situations or existential changes. But also everyday professional and social tasks certainly become more stressful. It is important to note that this premorbid vulnerability can, but must not result in psychotic behaviour.

2. During a second stage characterized by the outbreak of manifest psychotic behaviour this vulnerable information processing system is finally overtaxed by overwhelming stress, built-up through escalating processes between further critical stimulations from the environment and acquired coping deficits. Among the critical stressors from family and social environment identified so far, we find social overstimulation (Wing et al., 1970), high expressed emotions (Vaugn & Leff, 1976) or critical life-events and life-situations (Dorenwendt et al., 1981). But on the other hand, also the occurrence of unspecific prodromal symptoms (Herz & Melville, 1980; Mc Candless et al., 1986) or attentional deficits (Nuechterlein et al., 1984) may contribute to additional stress. The main point is, that once the acute psychotic behaviour has occurred, retroactive influences from accepting patient's role or being labelled as a psychiatric patient on the social and family environment or retroactive influences from dopaminergic dysfunctions on brain processes further enhance these escalating interactions in a sort of positive feedback- or "run away"-process. Again such psychotic experiences only can but must not in every case lead to chronic evolution subsequently.

3. During the third stage of chronic evolution, circular interactions between the fundamental vulnerability, acute psychotic episodes and unfavourable influences from the social and family environment might favour social withdrawal and pathological overcompensatory reactions, leading frequently to the so called "negative symptomatology" (Wing, 1987). It seems well established that different psychosocial factors can have a significant influence on the long-term course (Ciompi & Mueller, 1976; Harding et al., 1987). Particularly social understimulation (Wing et al. ,1970), family affective style and milieu (Tienary et al., 1985), but also resulting negative expectations by patients, families and therapists (Ciompi et al., 1979; Dauwalder et al., 1984) have to be mentioned. Our interpretation of these findings is that long-term course depends less on genetic and biological factors than on a multitude of situational influences in an endless loop. Choosing passive or withdrawn behaviour, for which at least the negative consequences would be predictable, may

thus become the only way to re-establish perceived self-efficacy (Badura, 1987) for chronic psychotic patients. If this understanding of psychotic behaviour is correct, it obviously implies a much more individual multicausal and circular reasoning and probably also quite a different therapeutic approach.

A MULTIMODAL TREATMENT FOR ACUTE SCHIZOPHRENIA

As no single event but a complex and circular interaction of many events over time may contribute to the outbreak of acute psychotic behaviour, our conviction is, that a MULTIMODAL TREATMENT will be needed. The main idea is, to restore an equilibrium (or negative feedback loops instead of the frequently occurring positive feedback loops) by avoiding further stressors, learning to cope with attentional deficits and prodromal signs and stabilizing retroactive stimulation from social and family environment and biological functioning.

As difficulties in processing complex informations are a crucial aspect of our understanding psychotic behaviour, and according to the vulnerability hypothesis, the most important principle for therapy and prevention should consist in trying to avoid overloads with confusing stimuli of every kind as much as possible. This speaks for instance strongly against the often highly confusing settings, in which acute schizophrenics are usually treated in psychiatric admissions wards. What would on the contrary be requested is restricted stimulation, in a small, quiet and human environment, providing stimulus-protective support, especially during acute psychotic behaviour. This is the first element of our multimodal treatment.

A second element concerns risk-management. According to the general idea of a stress inoculation programme (Meichenbaum, 1974), individual sensibilisation and coping with situations at risk and prodromal signs will help patients in avoiding stressful experiences.

The third element concerns psycho-educational training. Continuous collaborative problem-solving with relatives and significant others (Falloon et al., 1982), as well as clear and identical information about illness for patients, relatives and the therapeutic team (Leff et al., 1982; Hogarty & Anderson, 1986), have been identified as crucial elements in clarifying unclear and contradictory situations and helpful for preventing relapses.

The fourth element concerns coherent treatment. As patients and their families usually are in need of support for months or years. not just for weeks, avoiding multiple discontinuities of therapists and therapeutic concepts, too, appears as an important request. Concrete and collaborative goal-setting, favouring positive but realistic expectations, as well as continuous and systematic after-care and relapse prevention for at least two years seem therefore necessary.

The fifth element concerns drug-management. Neuroleptics are able to simplify the incoming information by filtering and narrowing the field of perception and by dampening emotional reactivity. However, apart from their well-known short and long-term side-effects, these sometimes rather knocking down effects are extremely undifferentiated. Therefore, attempts to replace them by approaches such as the no-medication, low-medication or targeted-medication strategies quite successfully explored by Matthews et al. (1979), Herz et al. (1982), Carpenter et al. (1983) and Kane et al. (1983) are certainly of interest. During treatment we give no or very low and targeted neuroleptic medication, whereas for after-care we prepare patients in medication management trainings, based on informed consent.

All these mentioned elements were included in a pilot experience for treatment of young acute schizophrenics, which will be described now.

SOTERIA BERN

"SOTERIA BERN" is a small and open therapeutic community, located in a very normally looking, nice, former hotel situated in town. It offers place for 6 to 8 patients and for two nurses at duty. Nursing staff consists of 8 specially selected and trained persons, four experienced professionals and four lay people in order to counterbalance possible professional biases. With overlapping shifts, nurses remain at duty for 48 hours continually. They meet once at week for an information exchanging and decision making round. Team-supervision is provided every two weeks. The costs are supported by Health Insurances and Rehabilitation Agencies.

Treatment is divided into four phases. During the first and acutest phase, patients usually live in the so-called "soft-room", that is in a pleasant, calm room with a minimum of sensory stimulation. The same nurse will almost continually be present during two days and two nights. Close and supportive interpersonal relations are usually built up during this often dramatic phase. The main task of the nurse consists in a warm, human support across the psychotic "trip" with the main aim of calming down the patient. Above all this includes calm "being with", almost as good mother would calm down her bewildered child awaking from a heavy nightmare. Background problems or attempts for behaviour modification are not actively searched, in order to avoid additional overstimulation. Usually no neuroleptics are given. Exceptions are emergency situations with acute danger for the patient himself or for the others.

The second phase of treatment, called activation-phase, follows after reduction of the most disturbing productive symptoms, usually after 1 to 4 weeks. Then the patient moves into another room and begins to participate at the normal life in the community. Social stimulation and behavioural training are gradually increased, first within the community itself through activities such as cooking, cleaning, gardening, painting walls and finally also by going to town for shopping. Simultaneously, through regular but informal contacts with two staff members assigned for each patient, continuous therapeutic efforts are made for risk management, psycho-educational training, collaborative goal setting and drug management.

The third phase consists in a gradual reintegration into normal social and professional life outside of the therapeutic community by reactivating external contacts, weekend-leaves, part-time work and other adequate arrangements. Simultaneously, discharge and the subsequent phase of relapse prevention are actively prepared by repeatedly exploring individual prodromal signs and individual situations at risk.

Finally the fourth phase, focused on consolidation and relapse prevention, begins with discharge and lasts for a minimum of two years. After a number of unsuccessful tentatives including formal prescriptions and control with private practitioners, after-care is now usually handled by our own community based teams consisting of social worker, a psychiatric nurse and a psychiatrist. In contrast to the private practitioner, this team is able to establish personal contacts with patients and relatives already during treatment and to intervene actively, for instance with visits at home or at work during critical moments before relapse. Drugs are used more extensively for prevention during this phase and consequently medication management training on informed consent is frequently introduced.

PROVISIONAL RESULTS

Outcome, costs and several other aspects of the described pilot experience are systematically evaluated in a simultaneous research programme. The main results are expected from matched-pairs comparisons of the 2 years outcome with four control groups in various more traditional settings (a psychiatric service within a general hospital, a private psychiatric clinic and two traditional hospital services). So far only partial results concerning the immediate outcomes are available.

Since the opening of "SOTERIA BERN" 53 patients have been admitted. 6 are still in treatment, 47 patients (20 males and 27 females) were discharged. 32 of them were diagnosed DSM-III schizophrenias, 14 schizophreniform psychoses, 1 unclear. Age ranges between 17 and 30 years, with an average of 23.4 years. Beginning of the illness dates back to 1.2 years in average, length of stay averaged 4.7 months (s=5.7). 23 patients were treated completely without neuroleptics, the remaining 24 patients got neuroleptics in average during 62 days (s=121.1), that is an average 27.7% of the whole period of treatment. Average doses of neuroleptics amounted to 80.9 mg Thorazin-aequivalents per day on medication and to 36.9 mg Thorazin-aequivalents per day of treatment.

Favourable or rather favourable overall results were obtained in 59.5% of the cases. There were no significant statistical differences at all between DSM-III schizophrenias and schizophreniform psychoses, nor between age groups. Concerning psychopathology favourable immediate outcome (complete remission or marked improvement) was observed in 26 cases (or 55.3%). 61.7% returned to a normal housing situation (among them about 2/5 to their parents). Immediate reinsertion into normal or close to normal work situations was possible in 42.5% of the cases.

Relapses were observed in about half of the cases. Comparison with control groups is under way.

So far, the provisional results seem quite encouraging, even if they are not overwhelming. In fact, certain patients (especially extremely autistic and non-collaborative paranoids) did not fit well into this programme. On the other hand our results clearly confirm the pioneering observations by Mosher, Menn, Carpenter, Cane, Herz and others, showing that similar strategies certainly are feasible and effective. On the level of subjective and human experience, according to the opinion of most of the involved patients, relatives and professionals however, this programme is clearly better than traditional drug centred methods.

IMPLICATIONS FOR BEHAVIOURAL RELAPSE PREVENTION

The major problem with acute psychotic behaviour is its discontinuous nature: Even the affected persons themselves seem frequently to be surprised by its sudden onset. However, some recent studies have attempted to describe the preceding processes in more details. In a retrospective study Docherty et al. (1978) identified five characteristic phases:

1. Affected persons first experience a global feeling of being overwhelmed.
2. They notice a restricted capacity for processing complex informations.
3. This might include impulsive and inefficient tentatives of coping.
4. The acute psychotic decompensation with loss of control occurs.
5. Affected persons search for a psychotic stabilization at the lower level, avoiding thereby fearful experiences.

Another interesting study by Herz and Melville (1980, recently confirmed by Mc Candless et al., 1986) revealed that 70% of the affected persons and 93% of their relatives were able to identify individual prodromal symptoms. While the most frequently identified symptoms in this study were not specific by nature (for instance tension and feeling nervous, loss of appetite, troubles with concentration, sleep or memories), tentatives of coping seem to be quite individualistic and problem-solving-oriented (Breier & Strauss, 1983; Boeker,1987).

Despite their promising orientation, these findings reflect again a linear and monocausal reasoning. That is why we suggest their integration at the higher level and a search for the multiple interactive processes that we would like to identify.

In our opinion the major aim for interventions is to avoid irreversible "programming" of stressful feeling and thinking as leading to escalating processes by favouring experiences of mastering difficult situations and perception of self-efficacy (Badura,1987). On the one hand, this means protecting the affected person by offering favourable physical and psycho-social environments, and on the other hand this means anticipatory coping with the risks of relapse.

In our experience, such behavioural training for anticipatory coping is not easy with first admitted young schizophrenics. In a first trial we explored the feasibility of risk management based upon a "checklist for prodromal signs". Comparing the evolution of warning signs between a normal premorbid situation and a situation at admission, we observed generally poor responses from first admitted patients. Patients having had several admissions responded fairly well. Furthermore, the affected persons attributed their own behaviour mainly to situational factors. A particular difficulty seemed to be the separation between observation of prodromal signs and coping with.

In a second trial we explored the feasibility of risk management based upon a "self-management diary". Again we observed a particular resistance to report situations at risk and furthermore quite aversive effects of this "paper-pencil" task. In fact this approach proved valid only for highly motivated patients.

In a third trial we explored the feasibility of risk management based on a "educational self-help group". Contrary to our expectations, we found only very poor modelling effects among this group of patients and furthermore strong tendencies to focus on group dynamics, what led to rapid burn-out of therapists.

So far, only the fourth trial of risk management based on "individual anticipatory coping" proved to be feasible. These individual interventions, based on patient's daily experiences, focused on observed situations at risk and how to cope with these situations in the future, on observed warning signs and how to cope with these in the future, on knowledge about schizophrenia and partially on other topics. Generally, this kind of intervention proved to be quite efficient. While at the descriptive level the relations between cumulative interventions and decrease of mean daily symptomatology seems quite evident, statistical interpretation proves to be more difficult. Traditional approaches, such as calculating simple correlations or performing time-series analysis corresponds to a linear and monocausal interpretation. Establishing cross-correlations among time-series already proved to be more effective. In fact, linear but multicausal relations could be identified. Particularly, we found some delayed effects of the different forms of intervention on daily symptomatology. But even this more sophisticated form of statistical analysis does not correspond to the identification of circular relationships and endless loops we are looking for.

Actually we are trying to analyse these data with new methods, looking for non-linear characteristics of complex dynamic systems, which have been explored in other scientific fields by Prigogine, Mandelbrot, Feigenbaum and others. This approach allows for identification of non-linear transformations and complex forms of equilibrium in dynamic systems (see Prigogine & Stengers, 1980; Gleick, 1987). We have good reasons to think that this kind of analysis might bring new insight in the complex dynamics and observed sudden shifts during the treatment of psychotic behaviour.

CONCLUSIONS

Schizophrenia is no longer a hopeless fate. The big problem is to integrate existing knowledge in a holistic and coherent view. We propose a comprehensive evolutionary model, describing the multicausal and circular growth and maintenance of psychotic behaviour. A multimodal treatment for acute schizophrenia, based on behavioural interventions, such as restricted stimulation, risk management, psycho-educational training, continuous and coherent treatment and drug management has been tested in a pilot experience. Favourable or rather favourable overall results have been found in about 60% of the cases without neuroleptics or very low doses. Finally, the feasibility of different forms of behavioural relapse prevention has been investigated, showing, that new methods of mathematical analysis for non-linear characteristics of complex dynamic systems need to be explored.

REFERENCES

Bandura, A.(1987) Perceived self-efficacy: Exercise of control through self-belief. In Dauwalder, J.P. et al. (Eds) *Controversial Issues in Behavior Modification.* Amsterdam: Swets & Zeitlinger (p. 27-60).

Boeker, W. (1987) On self-help among schizophrenics: problem analysis and empirical studies. In Strauss, J. et al. (Eds) *Psychosocial Treatment of Schizophrenia.* Berne: Huber (p. 136-151).

Breier, A., Strauss, J. (1983) Self-control in psychotic disorders. *Archives of General Psychiatry, 40,* 1141-1144.

Carpenter, W., Heinrichs, D. (1983) Early intervention, time limited, targeted pharmacotherapy in schizophrenia. *Schizophrenia Bulletin, 9,* 533-542.

Ciompi, L. (1987) Toward a coherent multidimensional understanding and therapy of schizophrenia: Converging new concepts. In Strauss, J. et al. (eds) *Psychosocial Treatment of Schizophrenia.* Berne: Huber (p. 48-62).

Ciompi, L., Dauwalder, J.P., Ague, C. (1979) Ein Forschungsprogramm zur Rehabilitation psychisch Kranker.III. Längsschnittuntersuchung zum Rehabilitationserfolg und zur Prognostik. *Nervenarzt, 50,* 366-378.

Ciompi, L., Mueller, C. (1976) *Lebenslauf und Alter der Schizophrenen.* Berlin: Springer.

Dauwalder, J.P. (1988) A comprehensive view on affect and logic: some implications for treatment and prevention of schizophrenia. *Psychopathology, 23,* 113-121.

Dauwalder, J.P., Ciompi, L., Aebi, E., Hubschmid, T. (1984) Ein Forschungsprogramm zur Rehabilitation psychisch Kranker. IV. Untersuchung zur Rolle von Zukunftserwartungen bei chronisch Schizophrenen. *Nervenarzt, 55,* 257-264.

Docherty, J.P., Van Kammen, D., Siris, S. (1978) Stages of schizophrenic psychosis. *American Journal of Psychiatry, 135,* 420-426.

Dohrenwendt, W., Egri, G. (1981) Recent stressful life-events and episodes of schizophrenia. *Schizophrenia Bulletin, 7,* 12-23.

Fallooni, I., Boyd, J., Mc Gill, C., Razani, J., Moss, H., Gilderman, A. (1982) Family management in the prevention of exacerbation of schizophrenia. A controlled study. *Journal of Medicine, 306*, 1437-1441.

Gleick, J. (1987) *Chaos: Making a Science.* New York: Wiking.

Harding, C., Brooks, G., Ashikaga, T. et al. (1987) The Vermont longitudinal study of persons with severe mental illness: II. Longterm outcome of subjects who retrospectively met DSM-III criteria for schizophrenia. *American Journal of Psychiatry, 144,* 727-735,.

Herz, M., Melville, C. (1980) Relapse in schizophrenia. *American Journal of Psychiatry, 137,* 801-805.

Herz, M., Stymansky, H., Simon, J. (1982) Intermitted medication for stable schizophrenic outpatients: An alternative to maintenance medication. *American Journal of Psychiatry, 139,* 918-922.

Hogarty, G., Anderson, C. (1987) A controlled study of family therapy, social skills training and maintenance chemotherapy in the aftercare treatment of schizophrenic patients. In Strauss, J. et al. (Eds.) *Psychosocial Treatment of Schizophrenia.* Berne: Huber (p. 73-66).

Kane, J., Rifkin, A., Woerner, M. et al. (1983) Low-dose neuroleptic treatment of outpatient schizophrenics. *Archives of General Psychiatry, 40,* 893-896.

Leff, J., Kuipers, L., Berkovitz, R., Eberlein-Fries, R., Sturgeon, D. (1982) A controlled trial of social intervention in the families of schizophrenic patients. *British Journal of Psychiatry, 141,* 121-134.

Matthews, S., Roper, M., Mosher, L., Menn, A. (1979) A non-neuroleptic treatment for schizophrenia. Analysis of the two-year postdischarge risk of relapse. *Schizophrenia Bulletin, 5,* 322-333.

Mc Candless, L., Mc Knight, S., Hamera, E. et al. (1986) Use of symptoms by schizophrenics to monitor and regulate their illness. *Hospital and Community Psychiatry, 37,* 929-935.

Meichenbaum, D. (1977) *Cognitive Behavior Modification: An Integrative Approach.* New York: Plenum Press..

Nuechterlein, K., Dawson, M. (1984) A heuristic vulnerability-stress model of schizophrenic episodes. *Schizophrenia Bulletin, 10,* 300-312.

Prigogine, I., Stengers, I. (1984) *Order Out of Chaos.* New York: Bantam.

Tienari, P., Sorri, A., Lathi, I. et al. (1985) Interaction of genetic and psychosocial factors in schizophrenia. *Acta Psychiatrica Scandinavica, 71*, 19-30.

Vaughn, C., Leff, J. (1976) The influence of family and social factors on the course of psychiatric illness. *British Journal of Psychiatry, 129,* 125-137.

Wing, J. (1987) Psychosocial factors affecting the long term course of schizophrenia. In Strauss, J. et al (Eds) *Psychosocial Treatment of Schizophrenia.* Berne: Huber (p. 13-29).

Wing, J., Brown, G (1970) *Institutionalism and Schizophrenia.* London: Cambridge University Press.

Zubin, J., Spring, B. (1977) Vulnerability: A new view on schizophrenia. *Journal of Abnormal Psychology, 86,* 103-123.

ZUBINS'S VULNERABILITY-STRESSOR MODEL FOR SCHIZOPHRENIC PATIENTS. TREATMENT PROCESS AND LONG-TERM OUTCOME OF A COMBINED IN- AND OUTPATIENT BEHAVIORAL TREATMENT

F. M. Stark

Psychiatric Clinic, University of Hamburg, Martinistr. 52, 2000 Hamburg 20, F.R.G.

The efficacy of behaviorally oriented treatment programs for schizophrenic patients has been investigated with promising results at various research centers (Wallace et al., 1980; Hogarty et al., 1986; Brady, 1984). This paper reports on the implemention of such research models in everyday care at a psychiatric department of a general hospital, where extensive research funds and highly trained academic staff usually were not available.

The general hospital has 85 beds and four units serving the needs of its surrounding rural catchment area of 150,000 inhabitants. Treatment was offered to patients with a broad range of psychiatric disorders. Schizophrenic patients comprised about 25% of all admissions. Treatment consisted mainly of neuroleptic medication and some supportive milieu treatment. Outpatients services were restricted to medication review.

Two years after the department was established, the psychiatric staff began to observe the classic revolving door phenomenon of psychotic patients (Strauss, 1987). Symptom relapses occurred on a regular basis and staff morale decreased as they became aware of their limited ability to provide effective treatment.

To alter this situation, a comprehensive treatment program for relapsing schizophrenic patients was implemented. The program was begun on one of the open wards comprising 23 beds.

TRAINING PROGRAM

The adoption of the training program included an initial intensive training phase involving all staff members including the psychiatric resident in charge. All the staff agreed on emphasizing self-management strategies for patients as an underlaying rationale of the treatment program based on the vulnerability-stressor model of illness (Zubin et al., 1983).

Promoting self-management requires that therapists impart to their patients an understanding of their illness and of related conditions. This implies the recognition that the interaction of individual organic and environmental variables affects the course of illness. The final treatment program was therefore comprised of three steps:

Step 1: Patient Information Group

The Information Group ran for four sessions and provided a rough overview on etiology, the course of illness, and factors influencing relapse. The vulnerability-stressor model (Figure 1) conceptualizing the interrelation of organic and environmental factors was explained. Basic information was given on the role of medication, and side-effects. Finally, the contents of the three month Core Training were introduced and patients were invited to join.

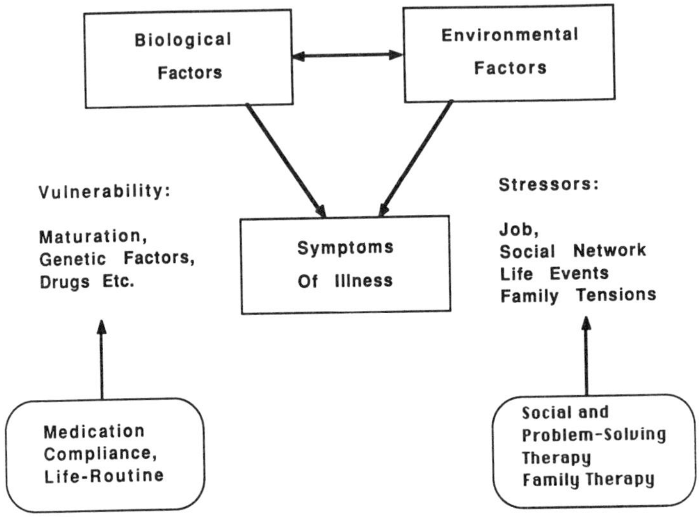

Figure 1. **Vulnerability-Stressor Model**

Step 2: Patient Core Training

The Core Training program ran for three months and focused on teaching and strengthening the application of self-management strategies to everyday problems. The actual training comprised of four different, though interrelated, components.

1) *Social Skills and Problem-Solving Training.*

The goal was to encourage patients to analyze their specific problems, then formulate their individual goals and self-assess alternate solutions. Problem situations were role-played with extensive video feedback. The training included patients expressing emotions and asserting themselves adequately, developing conversational friendship and dating skills and a broad range of other daily living skills (Feldhege & Krauthan, 1979; Wallace & Liberman, 1985). They were then able to seek consultation with peers, family members or professionals, if necessary.

2) *Medication Compliance.*

Medication problems were discussed in all three phases of therapy; in the Information Group, the Core Training and in the Long-Term Aftercare Groups. Patients received extensive information on psychotropic drugs, their effects and side-effects.

3) *Vocational Rehabilitation.*
Vocational Rehabilitation started with training the patients to expand their attention span. After showing that they could adhere to a structured daily routine, patients were increasingly involved in supervised tasks depending on their cognitive abilities. They then engaged in small tasks throughout the hospital supervised by ancillary staff. finally, patients went to part-time, supervised, on-the-job-training at various companies. Job-finding skills were trained if necessary.
4) Family Training.
Families and patients were invited to join a weekly group that lasted for two hours. Therapy started four weeks before discharge and continued for five more weeks. This time-frame provided continuous consultation during the patients' first critical weeks back with their families. Extensive information about the illness and the vulnerability-stressor model, and training in communication and problem-solving skills were provided in a non-blaming learning atmosphere (Fallon, Boyd & McGill, 1982).

Step 3: Long-Term Aftercare

After completing the Core Training, patients were asked to join the aftercare groups that ran biweekly up to two years. Group support and availability of crisis intervention helped to consolidate the patients' self-management skills in their daily routine. Staff interventions were decreased throughout the two-year period and medication was reduced or terminated on the basis of reduction of symptoms.

PATIENTS

After seven years, 14 groups totalling 71 patients had finished the training. At this time the first group was 7 years, the last group 2 years post treatment. 65 of the 71 patients could be retrieved. 51 patients agreed to be interviewed.

Demographic data showed that most patients included in the training belonged to those with less favourable outcome. Age ranged from 18 to 51 (mean = 30.9); years of illness before entry in the program, 2 to 24 years (mean = 7.3); age at first onset of illness was 12 to 43 (mean = 23.8).

In this study, data were collected on the course of illness, such as number of relapses and weeks spent as inpatients in psychiatric hospitals. Data on prestudy course of illness were obtained from hospital records. Patients served as their own controls by individually comparing data on prestudy course of illness with data on post study course until date of re-examination. The number of relapses decreased substantially, but could not be computed statistically because there was no equivalent time-frame before and after the training. Average days of hospitalization per relapse decreased significantly from 76.6 days to 30.3 (T-Test; $p < 0.001$), as shown in Figures 2 and 3.

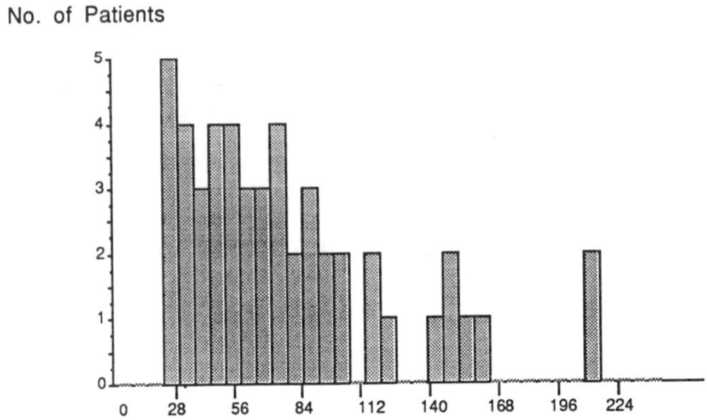

Figure 2. **Duration of Hospitalization before training**

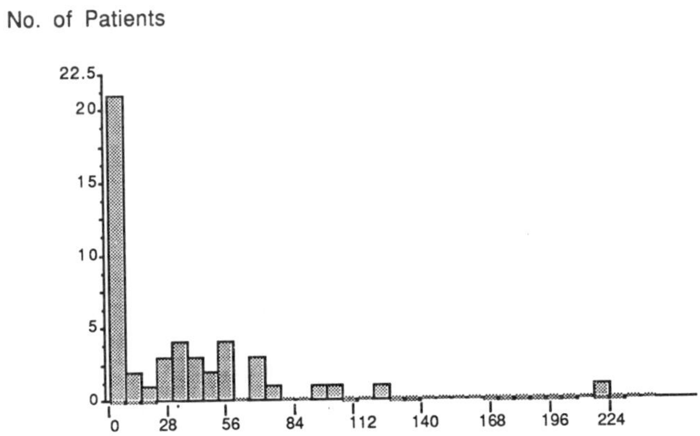

Figure 3. **Duration of Hospitalization after training**

In the semi-structured interview, 56% of the patients reported that they systematically use the principles of the vulnerability model. 66% stated that they watch for early warning signals of relapses. They differentiated up to 14 early warnning signals with an average of 7.6 different signals. In retrospect, they remembered up to 9 different components of the training program with an average of 4 distinct statements. 62 % stated that they needed medication and adhered to the regimen, which correlated positively ($p \leq .05$, Spearman rank) with the statement that they watch for early warning signals.

In addition, development of the individual's course of illness pre to post therapy was analyzed by independent clinical judgement. 42.9% had no relapse post treatment, another 30.8% had fewer relapses than pre training, 12.2% showed no change, and only 4.1% had a less favourable development.

Analysis of anecdotal evidence supported these results. Patients learned a lot about their illness and factors influencing the course of illness, were able to recognize early symptoms, thereby asked for professional help in time and accepted that an increase of neuroleptic medication might be necessary. Thus, re-admission was necessary only for short crisis interventions rather than for extensive treatment of symptom relapses.

DISCUSSION

The proper evaluation of the progress of this program was limited by two major factors. Statistical methods cannot sufficiently describe such a comprehensive rehabilitation program. Secondly, methodological evaluation in everyday mental health care is hampered by a generally negative attitude on the part of therapeutic staff.

In summary, we may conclude that patients benefited markedly from the program. Predictable deterioration of patients with less favourable prognoses could be interrupted or at least slowed down more efficiently than with the former standard treatment.

The program's success can be seen in significant improvements for patients. It also shows the feasibility of the cooperation of medication treatment and behavioral methods for psychotic patients in a standard psychiatric care facility.

REFERENCES

Brady, J.P (1984) Social skills training for psychiatric patients. *American Journal of Psychiatry, 141,* 491-498.

Falloon, I.R.H., Boyd, J.L., McGill, C.W. (1982) Behavioral family therapy for schizophrenia. In Curran, J.P., & Monti, P.M. (Eds.) *Social Skills Training: A Practical Handbook for Assessment and Treatment.* New York: Guilford Press.

Feldhege, F.J., Krauthan, G. (1979) *Ein Verhaltenstrainingsprogramm zum Aufbau sozialer Kompetenz (VTP).* München: Springer.

Hogarty, G.E., Anderson, C.M., Reiss, D.J., Kornblith, S.J., Greenwald, D.P., Javna, C.D., Madonia, M.J. (1986) Family psycho-education, social skills training and maintenance chemotherapy in the aftercare treatment of schizophrenia. *Archives of General Psychiatry, 43,* 633-642.

Strauss, J.S. (1987) Processes of healing and chronicity in schizophrenia. In Häfner, H., Gattaz, W.F., & Janzarik, W. (Eds.) *Search for the Causes of Schizophrenia.* Berlin: Springer.

Wallace, C.J. (1982) The social skills training project of the Mental Health Clinic Research Center for the Study of Schizophrenia. In Curran, J.P., & Monti, P.M. (Eds.) *Social Skills Training: A Practical Handbook for Assessment and Treatment*. New York: Guilford Press.

Wallace, C.J., Liberman, R.P. (1985) Social skills training for patients with schizophrenia: A controlled clinical trial. *Psychiatry Research, 15,* 239-247.

Zubin, J., Magaziner, J., Steinhauer, S.R. (1983) The metamorphosis of schizophrenia: From chronicity to vulnerability. *Psychological Medicine, 13,* 551-571.

PART IX:

CHILDREN'S AND OLD AGED PEOPLES' BEHAVIOURS AND THEIR TREATMENT

PARENTS' ATTRIBUTIONS ABOUT CHILDREN AND PARENTS' RESPONSES TO CHILDREN'S PROBLEM BEHAVIORS

L. Musun-Miller

University of Arkansas at Little Rock

Behavior therapists who work with families have often focused on the role of parents as the source of both antecedents and consequences for children's problem behavior and have taken great pains to describe parent-child behavioral contingencies. However, they have not generally tried as hard to explain why parents may behave as they do toward their children. Parents treat children within a family differently partly because they behave differently. However, how parents respond to children's behavior - including misbehavior - will also be influenced by what parents perceive to be the reasons for that behavior, how appropriate they perceive it to be in the situation, and how appropriate or important they think it is for them to intervene.

In this paper I will outline several factors that researchers have found, influence the attributions that parents form about their children. I would suggest that these are factors that behavior therapists should consider as possible mediators in how parents respond to the misbehavior of their children and should include in attempts to analyze the patterns of interaction in dysfunctional families.

When confronted with a child's misbehavior, parents may make attributions concerning the child's intent, level of self-control over the behavior, responsibility for the behavior, whether the behavior is a result of situational or constitutional factors, and the chances that the child will repeat the behavior. (see Figure 1). Researchers have found all of these to be factors in parents' decisions about how to respond to children's behavior. The more intentional parents perceive misbehavior to be and the more parents perceive the child as being able to control his or her behavior and understand that misbehavior is wrong, the more upset they are about the behavior and the more likely they are to intervene (Dix, Ruble, Grusec, & Nixon, 1986).

These attributions and judgments in turn will be influenced by characteristics of the situation, of the child, and of the parent him or herself. Parents will consider situational factors in explaining their child's behavior such as the context of the behavior, whether it occurred in public or in private, and the behavior of others present (see Figure 1).

However, in addition to the situation itself, there are several characteristics of children that seem to affect parental attribution. These include the age, sex, physical appearance, sibling status, handicapping conditions, perceived temperament, and perceived competence or the presence of other behavior problems.

Figure 1. **Model of Parental Attributions in Responding to Child Misbehavior**

When faced with:	Parent must make judgements concerning child's:
child misbehavior	intent
	self-control
	responsibility
	internal/external causes
	likelyhood will repeat behavior

Which may be influenced by:

situation	child characteristics	parent characteristics
context	age	sex
public versus private	sex	own sibling status
behavior of others	physical appearance	parenting experience
	behavior problems	pathology
	sibling status	affect/mood
	handicaps	stress
	perceived temperament	sense of control
	perceived competence	sense of responsibility
		developmental/ behavioral models
		conceptual level
		time thinking about child

These child characteristics may function as discriminative stimuli for certain parental expectations, beliefs and behaviors.

As children grow older, parents seem to assume that misconduct is more intentional and more under the child's control (Dix, Ruble, Grusec, & Nixon, 1986). The older the misbehaving child, the more negative the parents' affect and the more important they feel it is for them to respond. Misbehavior at older ages is seen as more the result of stable, internal factors and less the result of temporary, external factors - which may explain why mothers sometimes describe older children as more difficult to manage than younger ones (Gretarsson & Gelfand, 1988).

There is also a substantial body of developmental research that indicates that parents perceive and treat boys and girls differently (e.g., Maccoby, 1980). Parents generally ascribe more problem behaviors to boys than to girls (Lindholm & Touliatos, 1981). Mothers often see their sons as more responsible for their behavior than their daughters and they expect their sons' behavior to be more stable over childhood (Gretarsson & Gelfand, 1988). If a parent assumes misbehavior will persist, he or she is more likely to feel the need to "nip it in the bud". Active discouragement of misconduct then may come more swiftly and forcefully for boys than for girls for whom parents often believe the misbehavior to be a temporary aberration.

Another factor that has been shown to influence adults' perceptions of children is physical appearance (e.g., Dion, 1972). In the case of severe transgressions, less attractive children are seen as more antisocial while more attractive children are seen as misbehaving more as the result of temporary factors (Dion, 1972). The facial maturity of a child may also influence how others react to his or her misbehavior. Misbehavior by baby-faced young children is seen by parents to be less intentional and they tend to recommend less severe punishment for it (Zebrowitz-McArthur & Kendall-Tackett, 1989). Exactly the opposite seems to be true for older children. Perhaps parents find misbehavior more understandable in children who are younger and appear to be less mature. However, with older children, they may be surprised by misbehavior that seems out of character with the child's innocent appearance and thus recommend more serious punishment than for the more mature-appearing individual.

A child's sibling status also seems to be associated with some strong stereotypes on the part of adults. In my own work, I have found that most adults - parents and nonparents alike - tend to rate hypothetical oldest siblings as the most likely to be outgoing, obedient and unspoiled and only children as the most likely to be unlikable and spoiled (Baskett, 1985). I also have found that when rating their own children parents describe their oldest child more positively than their youngest - and more positively than do parents with only one child (Musun-Miller, 1988). In home observations I have also found that older children are more likely to experience negative consequences for their behavior than are children of the same age who are the youngest child in their families (Baskett, 1984).

It is also possible that parents may be influenced in their attributions about a child's misbehavior by the presence of certain handicapping conditions. Parents may judge children with physical or intellectual disabilities by different standards than their more able peers or siblings.

The temperament that parents have attributed to the child will also be a factor in how parents interpret and respond to the child's misbehavior. One of the problems with the current approach to measuring difficult temperament is its reliance upon parental report (Bates, 1980; Bates, 1983). Due to this frequent lack of external validity, it has been argued that such descriptive reports should be viewed as social perceptions rather than objective measures of constitutional differences. The temperament that parents have reported for a child does seem to be correlated with other aspects of parental perception. For example, Gretarsson and Gelfand (1988) found that the more difficult to manage they described their child to be, the more mothers tended to attribute those negative characteristics to inborn factors.

Finally, there could also be a "spill-over" effect from either perceived competence or the presence of other behavior problems. When presented with vignettes of a child acting in an appropriate, neutral or inappropriate way (Middlebrook & Forehand, 1984), clinic-referred mothers generally rated the child's neutral behavior as being more deviant than did non-referred mothers. Mothers with children with problem behaviors may become sensitized to the possibility of further misbehavior and start labelling even neutral behavior as deviant. This can quickly create a self-fulfilling prophecy, perhaps through the establishment of coercive interaction cycles. On the other hand, children who have established a reputation for competence may be given the benefit of the doubt and thus not seen as misbehaving in ambiguous situations.

Parental attributions are not the result of the situation or the characteristics of the child alone. Characteristics of the parents themselves will affect their attributions about their children's misbehavior. These factors could include parents' sex, their own sibling status, prior parenting experience, pathology, affect or mood, stress, sense of control over the parent-child interaction, sense of responsibility for the child's behavior, implicit models of child development and human behavior, their own level of conceptual development, and how often the parent actually thinks about the child (see Figure 1).

Some researchers have examined the effects of parents' sex, sibling status and years of experience on their perceptions of children. Several studies have reported significant differences in how mothers and fathers describe their children (e. g., Higbee, 1981; Lindholm & Touliatos, 1981; Pfeffer & Martin, 1981; Ventura & Stevenson, 1986), especially when rating problem behavior. Mothers in general tend to rate their children as having more problem behaviors than do fathers. When rating hypothetical children of different sibling status, I found that adults do tend to be somewhat biased in favour of their own sibling status (Baskett, 1985). Finally, the longer one has been a parent, the more one's attitudes about child misbehavior may change. So far, however, no relationship has been found between the number or age of one's own children - which can be thought of as measures of years of parenting experience - and parents' beliefs about the reasons for misbehavior (Dix, Ruble, Grusec, & Nixon, 1986) or about the degree to which they have influence on their child's development (Knight & Goodnow, 1988).

Much more attention has been given to the possible role of the pathology or level of dysfunctional behavior on the part of the parents in the development of child psychopathology. This has often been discussed in terms of the modeling of inappropriate behavior by parents, but could also be explained in terms of dysfunctional parents making inappropriate attributions about their children. Several studies have found that level of parental dysfunction - especially of mothers - may in many cases be more predictive of whether or not a child is referred to treatment than the level of deviant behavior of the child (e. g., Christensen, Phillips, Glasgow, & Johnson, 1983; Forehand, Wells, McMahon, Griest, & Rogers, 1982; Rickard, Forehand, Wells, Griest, & McMahon, 1981; Ventura & Stevenson, 1986). Highly stressed mothers have less confidence in their ability to resolve problems than do mothers who reported being under lower levels of stress (LaRose & Wolfe, 1987). There has also been a special interest in the relationships between depressed mothers and their children. The clinical literature has repeatedly found that children of depressed mothers are at greater risk for psychopathology, especially for depressive symptoms (e. g., Beardslee, Bemporad, Keller, & Klerman, 1983; Cytryn, McKnew, Zahn-Waxler, & Gershon, 1986; Hammen, Gordon, Burge, Adrian, Jaenicke,& Hiroto, 1987; Hops, Sherman & Biglan, in press; Lee & Gotlib, 1989; Zahn-Waxler, Cummings, McKnew, & Radke-Yarrow, 1984). Depressed mothers do tend to describe their children more negatively and as having more internalizing types of problems than either normal mothers or those with other sorts of psychiatric or medical diagnoses (Lee & Gotlib, 1989). Clinically depressed mothers of pre- school children tend to be less happy with their child's social and affective development than normal mothers (Kochanska, Radke-Yarrow, Kuczynski, & Friedman, 1987). They also were more likely to feel that their child's development was the result of uncontrollable factors, such as other people and luck. Thus the negative cognitive styles associated with depression may lead to more negative expectations about child-rearing outcomes, more negative perceptions of children, and a greater risk of inappropriate responding by mothers to problem situations.

It has also been argued that parents' mood or affect in general has not been given the attention it should, if one is to adequately understand parent-child interaction (Dix, Ruble, Grusec, & Nixon, 1986). Attributions regarding children's intent, control over and responsibility for their misbehavior are associated with various degrees of irritation or anger on the part of parents - and more negative emotion is in turn associated with a greater likelihood of punishment (e.g., Dix, Ruble, Grusec, & Nixon, 1986; Mills & Rubin, 1989). It is important to remember that parent-child relations are highly emotionally charged and that both memory and information-processing are influenced by one's affect and level of arousal (Dix, 1984).

How a parent responds to a child's misbehavior will also be a factor of the stress he or she is experiencing. In general, the more economic strain, the more negative the mother's emotional reaction to the child's misbehavior (Mills & Rubin, 1989). Mothers under high stress are more likely to attribute a child's social withdrawal to an internal factor and are less likely to intervene - perhaps as a way to reduce the demands upon herself by underreacting. However, when a child was portrayed as being aggressive toward a peer, highly stressed mothers are more likely to use a high power assertion technique - and thus possible overreacting.

Another factor that will influence how a parent responds to a child's misbehavior would be the adult's sense of control over the situation. Parents of children with behavior problems may feel that they are not able to deal effectively with their child and so may respond inappropriately to misbehavior. For example, parents of hyperactive children describe themselves as less skilled and knowledgeable about parenting than do parents of normal children (Mash & Johnston, 1983). Issues of control and perceived self-competence in parenting have been repeatedly implicated as contributing factors in cases of child abuse. Bugental and her colleagues (Bugental, 1987; Bugental, Blue, & Cruzcosa, 1989; Bugental & Shennum, 1984) have proposed a model in which the adult's self-perceived control over the parent-child interaction serves as a mediator in his or her response to the child's difficult behavior. Low self-perceived control may lead to higher arousal and more negative affect which is then followed by an aversive reaction, while high self-perceived control may simply lead to heightened attention and positive assertion in problem situations with children. Children at high risk for abuse, in that case, would be those, whose difficult behavior challenges and overwhelms the adult's capacity for maintaining low emotional arousal and a sense of control during problem situations. Bugental and her colleagues report that low perceived control over bad caregiving outcomes predicted whether a mother was abusive or not as well as her use of coercive techniques during an observed interaction with her children.

Parents will also be influenced by the ideas they hold about their responsibility for and influence on their child's development. Knight and Goodnow (1988) reported that parents believe they have considerable influence on children's development, and more so in the socioemotional than in the cognitive domain. Mothers were even more convinced of this opinion than fathers. If one feels responsible for a child's misbehavior, one will probably be more likely to intervene - or at least feel that one should.

Parental beliefs about what children of different ages ought to be able to do or ought to understand are part of implicit models of child development and human behavior. These may be partly the result of formal education, but more often they may be the result of cultural norms, standards and expectations. There seem to be significant relationships between parents' beliefs about how children learn and the strategies that they use to teach them (e.g., McGillicuddy-DeLisi, 1982; 1985).

Parents' own ability to conceptualize their relationship with their child will also influence how they interpret and react to children's misbehavior. Sameroff and Feil (1985) describe parents as operating at one of four levels. Those at the symbiotic level see their child's behavior as a direct result of their current action. At the Categorical level parents are able to perceive themselves and their child as separate entities with at least part of the child's behavior as the result of characteristics of the child him or herself. At the compensating level, parents can take into account developmental change as a factor in their child's behavior. Finally, perspectivistic parents are able to see that their child's behavior is the result of a variety of factors and that a different set of situations or experiences might have led to their child's developing different patterns of behavior. Bacon and Ashmore (1986) also discuss the importance of examining how parents cognitively categorize children's behavior. It is possible, for example, that parents may divide children's behavior into categories such as "things that make me angry and things that don't" or "things I need to do something about and things that I don't". Parental response would then depend on within which of these two categories parents perceived a particular child's action to fall. The ways in which behavior therapists categorize children's behavior may or may not match the ways parents do.

Finally, Dix and Grusec (1985) also make the point that parents may differ in how much thought they give to their child's behavior. Some parents may simply be more child-centered and thoughtful while others may show little concern about the reasons for their child's behavior and pay little attention to social information. The behavior of more child-centered parents may be more predicted by attributional style while the behavior of less child-oriented parents may be predicted more by transient states and immediate environmental conditions.

What are the implications of parents' attributions about children's misbehavior for the treatment of dysfunctional families? One immediate implication is the need for a more comprehensive approach to the assessment of families with reported problem behavior. The possibility that misbehavior may be more in the eye of the parent than in the action of the child must be more systematically addressed. And even when the parent's reports of problems are well-founded, why the parent thinks the child is behaving the way he or she is will be an important factor in understanding why the parent has responded the way he or she has and in predicting future parental response. The role of parental social cognition in mediating the parent-child interaction needs to be more fully assessed. Similarly for treatment, changes in the attributions of parents should be more formally considered for inclusion as treatment goals. Just as in the treatment of depression, continued dysfunctional attributions may serve to reinforce and maintain maladaptive behavior. Perhaps some of the techniques developed to deal with dysfunctional personal attribution should be evaluated as ways to deal with dysfunctional interpersonal attribution often found in disturbed families. I would argue that we need to extend the boundaries of behavioral family therapy to take more advantage of the insights gained from the cognitive evolution that is occurring in the fields of social and development psychology with regard to family relations.

REFERENCES

Bacon, M. K., Ashmore, R. D. (1986) A Consideration of the cognitive activities of parents and their role in the socialization process. In R. D. Ashmore & D. M. Brodzinsky (Ed.s), *Thinking about the family: Views of parents and children* (pp. 3-33). Hillsdale, NJ:Lawrence Erlbaum Associates.

Baskett, L. M. (1984) Ordinal position differences in children's family interactions. *Developmental Psychology, 20*, 1026-1031.

Baskett, L. M. (1985) Sibling status effects: Adult expectations. *Developmental Psychology, 21*, 441-445.

Bates, J. E. (1980) The concept of difficult temperament. *Merrill-Palmer Quarterly, 26*, 299-319.

Bates, J. E. (1983) Issues in the assessment of difficult temperament: A reply to Thomas, Chess, and Korn. *Merrill-Palmer Quarterly, 29*, 89-97.

Beardslee, W. R., Bemporad, J., Keller, M. B., Klerman, G. L. (1983) Children of parents with major affective disorder: A review. *American Journal of Psychiatry, 140*, 825-832.

Bugental, D. B. (1987, April) Caregiver attributions as moderators of child effects. In K. McCartney (Chair), *Bidirection of effects in parent-child interaction*. Symposium conducted at the biennial meeting of the Society for Research in Child Development, Baltimore, MD.

Bugental, D. B., Blue, J., Cruzcosa, M. (1989) Perceived control over caregiving outcomes: Implications for child abuse. *Developmental Psychology, 25*, 532-539.

Bugental, D. B., Shennum W. A. (1984) "Difficult" children as elicitors and targets of adult communication patterns: An attributional-behavioral transactional analysis. *Monographs of the Society for Research in Child Development, 49*(1, Serial No. 205).

Christensen, A., Phillips, S., Glasgow, R. E., Johnson, S. M. (1983) Parental characteristics and interactional dysfunction in families with child behavior problems: A preliminary investigation. *Journal of Abnormal Child Psychology, 11*, 153-166.

Cytryn, L., McKnew, D. H., Zahn-Waxler, C., Gershon, E. S. (1986) Developmental issues in risk research: The offspring of affectively ill parents. In M. Rutter, C. E. Izard, P. B. Read (Eds), *Depression in young people: Developmental and clinical perspectives* (pp. 163-188). New York: Guilford Press.

Dion, K. K. (1972) Physical attractiveness and evaluations of children's transgressions. *Journal of Personality and Social Psychology, 24*, 207-213.

Dix, T. (1984, August) *Social cognitive processes during parent-child disciplinary episodes*. Paper presented at the annual meeting of the American Psychological Association, Toronto.

Dix, T. H., Grusec, J. E. (1985) Parent attribution processes in the socialization of children. In I. Sigel, (Ed.), *Parental belief systems: Psychological consequences for children* (pp. 201-233). Hillsdale, NJ: Lawrence Erlbaum Associates.

Dix, T., Ruble, D. N., Grusec, J. E., Nixon, S. (1986) Social cognition in parents: Inferential and affective reactions to children of three age levels. *Child Development, 57*, 879-894.

Forehand, R., Wells, K. C., McMahon, R. J., Griest, D., Rogers T. (1982) Maternal perception of maladjustment in clinic-referred children: An extension of earlier research. *Journal of Behavioral Assessment, 4*, 145-151.

Gretarsson, S. J., Gelfand, D. M. (1988) Mothers' attributions regarding their children's social behavior and personality characteristics. *Developmental Psychology, 24*, 264-269.

Hammen, C., Gordon, D., Burge, D., Adrian, C., Jaenicke, C., Hiroto, D. (1987) Maternal affective disorders, illness, and stress: Risk for children's psychopathology. *American Journal of Psychiatry, 144*, 736-741.

Higbee, K. L. (1981) Parents' perceptions of their preschool children's obedience. *Psychological Reports, 49*, 209-210.

Hops, H., Sherman, L., Biglan, A. (in press) Maternal depression, marital discord, and children's behavior: A developmental perspective. In G. R. Patterson, Ed.), *Depression and aggression in family interactions* (pp.185-208). Hillsdale, NJ: Lawrence Erlbaum Associates.

Knight, R. A., Goodnow, J. J. (1988) Parents' beliefs about influence over cognitive and social development. *International Journal of Behavioral Development, 11*, 517-527.

Kochanska, G., Radke-Yarrow, M., Kuczynski, L., Friedman, S. L. (1987) Normal and affectively ill mothers' beliefs about their children. *American Journal of Orthopsychiatry, 57*, 345-350.

LaRose, L., Wolfe, D. A. (1987, April) *Determinants of stressful and non-stressful interpretations of parent-child interactions*. Paper presented at the biennial meeting of the Society for Research in Child Development, Baltimore, MD.

Lee, C. M., Gotlib, I. H. (1989) Maternal depression and child adjustment: A longitudinal analysis. *Journal of Abnormal Psychology, 98*, 78-85.

Lindholm, B. W., Touliatos, J. (1981) Mothers' and fathers' perceptions of their children's psychological adjustment. *Journal of Genetic Psychology, 139*, 245-255.

Maccoby, E. E. (1980) Social development: Psychological growth and the parent-child relationship. New York: Harcourt Brace Jovanovich.

Mash, E. J., Johnston, C. (1983) Parental perceptions of child behavior problems, parenting self-esteem, and mothers' reported stress in younger and older hyperactive and normal children. *Journal of Consulting and Clinical Psychology, 51*, 86-99.

McGillicuddy-De Lisi, A. V. (1982) The relationship between parents' beliefs about development and family constellation, socioeconomic status, and parents' teaching strategies. In L. M. Laosa & I. E. Sigel (Eds.), *Families as learning environments for children* (pp. 261-299). New York: Plenum Press.

McGillicuddy-De Lisi, A. V. (1985) The relationship between parental beliefs and children's cognitive level. In I. E. Sigel (Ed.), *Parental belief systems: Psychological consequences for children* (pp. 7-24). Hillsdale, N.J.: Lawrence Erlbaum Associates.

Mills, R. S. L., Rubin K. H. (1989, April) *Parental beliefs about children's maladaptive social behaviors*. Paper presented at the biennial meeting of the Society for Research in Child Development, Kansas City, MO.

Middlebrook, J. L., Forehand, R. (1984, November) *The effects of the interactions of child behavior with situational variables on parental perceptions of deviance*. Paper presented at the annual meeting of the Association for the Advancement of Behavior Therapy, Philadephia, PA.

Musun-Miller, L. (1988, March) *Parental perceptions of sibling status effects*. Paper presented at the biennial meeting of the Southwestern Society for Research in Human Development, New Orleans, LA.

Musun-Miller, L. (1988, March) *Parental perceptions of sibling status effects*. Paper presented at the biennial meeting of the Southwestern Society for Research in Human Development, New Orleans, LA.

Pfeffer, J., Martin, R. P. (1981) Comparison of mothers' and fathers' temperament ratings of referred and nonreferred preschool children. *Journal of Clinical Psychology, 39*, 1013-1020.

Rickard, K. M., Forehand, R., Wells, K. C., Griest, D. L., McMahon, R. J. (1981) Factors in the referral of children for behavioral treatment: A comparison of mothers of clinic-referred deviant, clinic-referred non-deviant and non-clinic children. *Behaviour Research & Therapy, 19*, 201-205.

Sameroff, A. J., Feil, L. A. (1985) Parental concepts of development. In I. Sigel (Ed.), *Parental belief systems: Psychological consequences for children* (pp. 83-105). Hillsdale, NJ: Lawrence Erlbaum Associates.

Ventura, J. N., Stevenson, M. B. (1986) Relations of mothers' and fathers' reports of infant temperament, parents' psychological functioning, and family characteristics. *Merrill-Palmer Quarterly, 32*, 275-289.

Zahn-Waxler, C., Cummings, E. M., McKnew, D. H., Radke-Yarrow, M. (1984) Altruism, aggression, and social interactions in young children with a manic-depressive parent. *Child Development, 55*, 112-122.

Zebrowitz-McArthur, L. A., Kendall-Tackett, K. A. (1989, April) *Parental reactions to transgressions by babyfaced and maturefaced 4 and 11 year old children*. Paper presented at the biennial meeting of the Society for Research in Child Development, Kansas City, MO.

EFFECTS OF COACHING, ROLE TAKING AND PROBLEM SOLVING ON SOCIAL COMPETENCE

P. Van Oost, M. Braem, H. De Ruyck and G. Mommerency

University of Gent, Department of Clinical Psychology, Henri Dunantlaan, 2, 9000 Gent , Belgium 1

INTRODUCTION

Sociometric status as an indicator variable for social incompetence

Several authors (f.i. Putallaz & Gottman, 1982, 1983; Coie, 1985 and Parker & Asher, 1978) reviewed the existing evidence on the relationship between negative sociometric status in elementary school children and mental health problems (academic problems, delinquency) in adolescence. In particular socially rejected children seem to be at risk. The two most widely used sociometric procedures are rating and nomination.

In the first procedure, all same-sex children of a given class contribute to the acceptance score of each child. In the nomination procedure, all children are asked to nominate three same-sex children with whom they prefer to play and three same-sex children with whom they do not want to play. Coie, Dodge & Coppotelli (1982) computed two different scores from the nomination data : a preference score (representing the degree to which a child is liked) and an impact score (representing the visibility of a child in the same-sex group). A combination of the two scores allows to identify four different status positions: popular, rejected, neglected and controversial children.

Some authors (f.i. Asher & Renshaw,1981, in Putallaz & Gottman, 1982) suggest that nomination and acceptance measure two distinct aspects of social functioning : nomination refers to the quality of the relationship (friendship), while acceptance refers to the general appreciation of a child in his social group. We have not been able to confirm this hypothesis . In a study on 508 children between 9 and 12 years old (Van Oost, Braem & Mommerency,1988) we found that : being engaged in a mutual friendship, receiving a positive evaluation from the teacher on both academic skills and social competence, and being able to differentiate between one's own and the other's point of view, were the main predictors of both popularity (nomination) and acceptance (rating).

We found in the same study that almost 25 % of the children in each class were rejected. There was a negative correlation between the level of acceptance and the grade: the younger the children were, the higher their acceptance of one another. The average acceptance score among boys was higher than among girls.

Busk, Ford & Schulman (1973) and Coie & Dodge (1983) reported that the sociometric status, in particular for popular and rejected children, appeared to be rather stable. Coie & Dodge found that 45 % of the rejected children were still socially rejected one year later and 30 % of the originally rejected remained in the same position four years later.

Lebon (1987) studied 107 Flemish children in third and fifth grade. He found that 47 % of the rejected children were still rejected one year later.

Differences in social cognitive functioning between socially competent and socially incompetent children

The theoretical models developed by Ford (1982,1984) and Dodge (1986) suggest that socially competent children (popular or well accepted children) differ from socially incompetent children (rejected or children with a low acceptance score) on several aspects of social cognitive functioning. More specifically : socially competent children obtain higher scores on both role taking and social problem solving.

METHOD

We investigated the differences in social cognitive functioning between rejected and popular, and between children with low and high acceptance scores and found slightly significant differences on both the role taking and problem solving measures.

We used the interpersonal dilemma and scoring system developed by Selman & Byrne (1974) as a measure of role taking skills. Selman 1 refers to the number of correct responses on the lowest level of role taking, e.g. being able to differentiate between one's own and the other's point of view. We were not able to find significant differences for the higher levels of role taking. We used the Means Ends Problem Solving Test (Spivack, Shure & Platt, 1981) to measure problem solving variables relevant for our age groups. Means ends problem solving refers to the process of specifying a sequence of possible means in order to solve the interpersonal problem at hand.

Table 1. **Acceptance / Role taking variables (Selman 1)**

		m	s.d.
50 % lowest		1,32	0,99
50 % highest		1,69	1,06
total		1,51	1,02
F (1)	$p<0,05$		

Table 2 : **Nomination / Role taking variables (Selman 1)**

Status		m	s.d.
popular		1,71	1,11
rejected		1,23	0,97
neglected		1,62	1,02
controversial		1,25	0,97
total		1,48	1,03
F (1)	p<0,10		

F(1): corrected for grade effects.

The total score is a summation of the number of relevant means, time indications and obstacles.

Table 3: **Acceptance / MEPS total score**

		MEPS	
Acceptance		m	s.d.
50% lowest		3,32	2,71
50% highest		4,35	3,24
total		3,83	2,99
F (1)	p<0,10		

Table 4: **Nomination/ MEPS total score**

		MEPS	
Status		m	s.d.
popular		4,45	3,16
rejected		2,90	2,23
neglected		4,23	3,38
controversial		3,46	3,16
total		3,77	3,03
F (1)	p<0,10		

Intervention study

Role taking and social problem solving are two social cognitive processes that were thought to differentiate between socially competent and socially incompetent children (Ford,1982,1984; Dodge, 1985,1986). We found in our study that rejected children differ from popular children on the 10% level on both variables. We also found that having reached at least a minimal level of role taking was an important predictor of positive sociometric status (popularity and acceptance).

Socially incompetent children benefit from both training programs in problem solving skills and in role taking skills. Chandler (1973) and Fesbach (1978, in Urbain & Kendall, 1980) reported that training in role taking resulted in a reduction of delinquent or aggressive acts. Murray & Ahammer (1977) found an increase in altruistic behavior. Shure & Spivack (1980) developed a training program including both role taking and problem solving skills and reported a positive effect on impulsiveness and popularity in 10 years old children. Weissberg and colleagues (1979,1981) combined cognitive strategies with skills training and monitoring and found positive results on both impulsiveness and popularity.

The program developed by Weissberg and others refers to the behavioral component in social competence. Asher & Oden experimented in 1977 with a training program called "coaching". They combined concept formation, a cognitive strategy , with behavioral rehearsal. The concepts they used were derived from the behavioral correlates of positive social status positions. Oden & Asher (1977) , Gresham & Nagle (1980), Siperstein & Gale (1983), and Bierman & Furman (1984) found a positive effect on acceptance. Other studies, such as those of La Greca & Santogrossi (1980) and Coie & Krehbiel (1984) failed to show any results on sociometric position.

We decided to experiment with three training conditions:

- a role taking program, developed by Gerris, Jansen & Badal,1980, - a problem solving program, adapted from Shure,1980, - a coaching program we based the coaching program on the literature concerning the behavioral correlates of positive as opposed to negative sociometric statuses.

We derived the concepts and skills from prospective and correlational studies in 10 to 12 years old children: cooperation, entry strategies, validation or helping, conflict resolution and referential communication.

We also decided to work with whole classes and not with specific clinical groups. As such, our approach is mainly preventive, and takes into account the social interaction conditions in the natural group.

Population

We included 183 children (8 classes, fifth grade) in the study. The classes were randomly assigned to four conditions : control, problem solving , role taking and coaching. Each program consisted of eight lesson and was spread over three months. The testing, by an independent research team, was scheduled three weeks before (pretest) and after (posttest) the training. At follow up, six months after the end of the training, the children had changed from fifth to sixth grade.

There were no significant differences between the four experimental conditions at the pretest (F test) in sociometrics, role taking, problem solving, self perceived social competence and anxiety.

HYPOTHESIS

We expect a strong and remaining positive effect of the coaching program on acceptance as was shown in the literature.- As rejected children learn to participate in a constructive way in dyads and small groups, we expect that they will have a chance to be experienced as positive and cooperative by their classmates. This could result in an increase in positive and eventually a decrease in negative nominations. We do not know however of any study that documents this effect, as all studies mentioned used the rating procedure. We expect, in line with the studies of Shure & Spivack (1980), a positive effect on popularity from the problem solving program.

RESULTS

Two statistical procedures were used :-an analysis of covariance (covariates: pretest level and school level) in order to appreciate the main effect of the programmes in relation to the control condition, both after the training (posttest) and at follow-up, -two-tailed T tests on the mean scores in each of the conditions, in order to appreciate the evolutions as compared to the pretest.

Acceptance

The pretest level was the main determinant of acceptance at both the posttest and the follow up test. The effect of the training conditions was significant; they explain 4,4% of the total variance of the acceptance score at the posttest ($p < 0.01$) and 4,7% at follow up ($p < 0.05$) when we compare the four conditions, children show more acceptance of one another in the role taking than in any other condition, both at the posttest and at follow up. Rejected children receive most inacceptance in the problem solving condition. In the coaching condition we find less differences between rejected children and the other status groups than in any other condition, both at posttest and follow up. The two-tailed T tests on the mean acceptance scores per condition show a general increase in acceptance for the role taking condition (posttest: $p < 0{,}005$; follow up: $p < 0{,}05$) and an increase in inacceptance for the coaching condition (both posttest and follow up: $p < 0{,}005$)

Nomination

We used an index of association (Cramer's V) in order to test the overall stability in each of the four conditions at post- and follow up test. We found that at the follow up , all three experimental conditions resulted in less stability than the control condition . At the posttest, only the coaching condition shows a lower stability :

Table 5

	pretest -posttest Cramer's V	pretest-follow up Cramer's V
Control	.417	.538
Role Taking	.435	.432
Probl. Solv.	.486	.470
Coaching	.368	.341

Coaching and role taking enabled more children to emigrate from the rejected position, both at posttest and at follow up. The number of mutual positive choices is significantly higher in coaching than in any other condition ($p< 0.001$).

We computed the number of children that remained in the rejected position at posttest and follow up, and the number of children that left the rejected position permanently (which means that they emigrated at the posttest and were still in a better sociometric position at follow up).

Table 6

number of children	**the rejected position**	
	remaining in	leaving permanently
Coaching	27,3% (3/11)	36,4% (4/11)
Probl.Solv.	57,1% (8/14)	21,4% (3/14)
Role Taking	31,3% (5/16)	31,3% (5/16)
Control	50,0% (4/8)	12,5% (1/8)

When we compare these results with those of Coie & Dodge (45%) and Lebon (47%), we can see that the problem solving condition seems to have a negative effect on the rejected children, whereas both coaching and role taking have a positive effect.

CONCLUSIONS AND DISCUSSION

All three experimental conditions have an effect on the stability of sociometric positions: they all result in more global migration at follow up .

Both coaching and role taking enable more rejected children to leave their negative position. This result was expected for coaching but not for role taking . As the main difference between the coaching and the role taking condition is the behavioral approach, this result seems to suggest that modeling and behavioral rehearsal do not appear to be a necessity for positive social evaluation. Rejected children are less differentiated from the other status positions in the coaching condition than in any other condition. Together with the positive effect of coaching on nomination, this suggests that coaching might be the most favourable program for rejected children.

It is not at all clear why problem solving has a negative effect on sociometrics. It has to be mentioned however that Shure 's program consisted of 55 lessons of 30 to 40 minutes each. We restricted all programs to 8 sessions of 60 minutes each. This duration is more in line with the coaching programs, but not with the role taking program (19 sessions). Another reason could be found in the complexity of the program, as problem solving requires role taking skills .Still another reason could be the absence of extreme groups : the studies of Spivack , Shure and others demonstrate a clear positive effect for clinical groups.

REFERENCES

Bierman, K.L., Furman, W. (1984) The effects of social skills training and peer involvement on the social adjustment of preadolescents. *Child Development, 55*, 151-163.

Busk, P.L., Ford, R.C., Schulman, J.L. (1973) Stability of sociometric responses in classrooms. *The Journal of Genetic Psychology, 10*, 546-553.

Chandler, M.L. (1973) Egocentrism and anti-social behavior : the assessment and training of social-perspective skills. *Developmental Psychology, 9*, 326-333.

Coie, J.D., Dodge, K.A., Coppotelli, H. (1982) Dimensions and types of social status. A crossage perspective. *Developmental Psychology, 18*, 557-570.

Coie, J.D., Dodge, K.A. (1983) Continuities and changes in children's social status: a five year longitudinal study. *Merrill-Palmer Quarterly, 29*, 261-282.

Coie, J.D., Krehbiel, G. (1984) Effects of academic tutoring on the social status of low-achieving, socially rejected children. *Child Development, 55*, 1465-1478.

Coie, J.D. (1985) Fitting social skills intervention to the target group. In B.H. Schneider, K.H. Rubin & J.E Ledingham (Eds.). *Children's peer relations: issues in assessment and intervention*. New York, Springer-Verlag, 141-156.

Dodge, K.A. (1985) Facets of social interaction and the assessment of social competence in children. In B.H. Schneider, K.H. Rubin & J.E . Ledingham, (Eds.). *Children's peer relations: issues in assessment and intervention*. New York, Springer-Verlag, 3-17.

Dodge, K.A. (1986) A social information process model of social competence in children. In M. Perlmutter (Ed). *Cognitive perspectives on children's social and behavioral development*. New Jersey, Erlbaum, 77-125.

Ford, M.E. (1982) Social cognition and social competence in adolescence. *Developmental Psychology, 18*, 3, 323-340.

Ford, M.E. (1984) Linking social cognitive processes with effective social behavior: A living-systems approach. In P.C. Kendall (Ed). *Advances in cognitive-behavioral research and therapy*. New York, Academic Press.

Gerris, J.R., Jansen, F., Badal, C.R. (1980) *Denken over jezelf en de ander.* Den Bosch, Malmberg.

Gresham, F.M., Nagle, R.J. (1980) Social skills training with children: responsiveness to modeling and coaching as a function of peer orientation. *Journal of Consulting and Clinical Psychology, 48,* 718-729.

La Greca, A., Santogrossi, D. (1980) Social skills training with elementary school students. A behavioral Group approach. *Journal of Consulting and Clinical Psychology, 48,* 220-228.

Lebon, B. (1987) : *Sociale kompetentie bij kinderen: longitudinaal onderzoek naar de stabiliteit van de sociale status bij lagere schoolkinderen*. Unpublished Dissertation. Gent, 105 p.

Murray, J.P., Ahammer, I.M. (1977) *Kindness in kindergarten: A multidimensional program for facilitating altruism.* Paper presented at the meeting of the society for research in child development. New Orleans.

Oden, S., Asher, S.R. (1977) Coaching children in social skills for friendship making. *Child development, 48,* 495-506.

Parker, J.G., Asher, S.R. (1987) Peer relations and later personal adjustment: are low-accepted children at risk. *Psychological Bulletin, 102,* 357-389.

Putallaz, M., Gottman, J.M. (1983) Social relationship problems in children. An approach to intervention. In B.B. Lahey en A.E. Kazdin (Eds.). *Advances in Clinical Child Psychology* , 6. New York, Plenum Press, 1-43.

Selman, R.L., Byrne, D.F. (1974) A structural-developmental analysis of levels of role taking in middle childhood. *Child Development, 45* , 803-806.

Shure, M.B., Spivack, G. (1980) Interpersonal problem solving as a mediator of behavioral adjustment in preschool and kindergarten children. *Journal of Applied Developmental Psychology, 1,* 29-43.

Shure, M.B. (1980) *Interpersonal problem solving in ten-year-olds*. Washington, National Institute of Mental Health.

Siperstein, G.N., Gale, M.E. (1983) *Improving peer relationship of rejected children*. Paper presented at the biannial meeting of the society for research in child development, Detroit.

Spivack, G., Shure, M.B., Platt, J.J. (1981) *Means-ends problem solving. Stimuli and scoring procedures supplement*. Philadelphia, Department of Mental Health Sciences.

Van Oost, P., Braem, M., Mommerency, G. (1988) Social competence: do social cognitive variables predict acceptance and preference scores. (Dutch). *Tijdschrift voor Klinische Psychologie , 18* , 1 - 20.

Urbain, E.S., Kendall, P.H. (1980) *Interpersonal problem solving, social perspective taking and behavioral contingencies: a comparison of group therapies with children*. Doctoral thesis.

Weissberg, R.P., Gesten, E.L., Liebenstein, N.L., Doherty-Schmid, K.D., Hutton (1979) *The Rochester social problem solving (SPS) program: a training manual for teachers of 2nd-4th grade children*. Rochester, Center for Community Study.

Weissberg, R.P., Gesten, E.L., Carnike, C.L., Torro, P.A., Rapkin, B.D., Davidson, E., Cowen, E.L. (1981) Social problem solving skills training: a competence-building intervention with second to fourth grade children. *American Journal of Community Psychology, 9,* 411-423.

PART X:

THE THERAPEUTIC RELATIONSHIP

THERAPEUTIC RELATIONSHIP ENHANCEMENT PROCEDURES AND THE SOCIALPOWER MODEL

G. Keijsers, C. Schaap and K. Hoogduin

Department of Clinical Psychology and Personality, University of Nijmegen, Nijmegen, The Netherlands

There is now considerable evidence for the impact of therapeutic relationship variables on the outcome of psychotherapy (Gurman, 1977; Orlinsky & Howard, 1987) and behaviour therapy (Sweet, 1984; Wilson & Evans,1977; Bennun, Hahlweg, Schindler, & Langlotz, 1986). Significant correlations have been reported in behaviour therapy research even when relationship variables were measured in an early treatment phase (LaCrosse, 1981; Bennun & Schindler, 1988; Hoogduin, de Haan & Schaap, 1989).

In 1973 Strong and Matross formulated a model that offers a plausible explanation for this relationship. The authors base their model on an extensive body of social psychological research: According to Strong and Matross, a characteristic feature of the therapeutic relationship is that clients seek help for complaints they are incapable of managing or enduring anymore. To the extent that they view the therapist as a person who can fulfil their personal and interpersonal needs, they are inclined to comply with the views and directives of the therapist. In other words: The therapist is able to influence the client to the extent that the client relates perceived qualities of the therapist to his personal needs. This is called "the social power of the therapist". Strong and Matross then distinguish between five themes, called power bases. Every power base describes a relationship between a specific need of the client and a specific perceived quality of the therapist that satisfies this need. The three most important power bases are called (1) Expert power base, (2) Referent power base, and (3) Legitimate power base.

Expert power base

Clients seek help for complaints they are incapable of managing or enduring anymore. Attempts to solve these problems appear to be too costly in terms of fear, stress, and discomfort. They decide to visit a therapist, because they believe the therapist has special knowledge and skills to help them reach goals they cannot reach themselves anymore. So, next to the need of help, the expert power base is a result of the degree to which the therapist is perceived as a helper with for example professional knowledge about psychological processes and interpersonal relationships, and with therapeutic skills.

Referent power base

The distress and discomfort that brings clients into therapy, is often the result of self-perceived inconsistency between actual behaviours and the way things should be. According to Strong and Matross, the experience of psychological inconsistency between behaviour and values is based on processes of social comparison, rather than on objective facts. As a consequence, persons seek other persons with whom to test this consistency. Therapists receive referent power (1) when they are found attractive, open, concerned and empathic, (2) when they are able to tune in to the experiences of the client, and (3) when they are experienced as similar in terms of values, opinions and experiences. Clients will destillate elements out of this personal contact that increasingly will help them to experience themselves as whole.

Legitimate power base

Therapists will gain legitimate power when clients approve of the therapeutic relationship and the definitions of client and therapist roles, inherent to the therapist's therapeutic system. Therapists can increase their legitimacy by explicitly obtaining clients' personal commitment to therapy and the process of change. By heightening clients' perception of their voluntary status in counselling and their commitment to achieving change, resistance to the therapist's suggestions becomes inconsistent with their own commitment (self-perception theory, cognitive dissonance-theory). Also, resistance can be diminished when client and therapist both explicitly agreeon the goals that are to be reached in treatment and the tasks that have to be carried out.

Resistance and opposition

Next to the social power of the therapist, Strong and Matross distinguish between two forces of the client that oppose the power of the therapist: resistance and opposition. Resistance is noncompliant behaviour of the client, being a result of the way the client and therapist interact. Resistance is generated by the therapist's characteristics and the way in which the therapist requests change. An influence attempt will appear illegitimate or improper, when it is founded on a power base not yet established in the relationship. For example, therapists with a strong expert power base and a minimal referent base increase the likelihood of noncompliant behaviour when they use a personal influence attempt like " According to me..." instead of an impersonal influence attempt like " To allow this treatment to be effective for you, it is necessary for you to....".

In contrast to the characteristic way of interaction between therapist and client, opposition refers to noncompliant behaviour that is generated by the content of the influence attempt of the therapist. Often it is difficult to change, even if the status quo is unbearable at the moment. In order to change their behaviour, clients have to change associated attitudes which often consists of critically balanced and long held views about oneself and others, and of oneself in relation to others (Strong, & Claiburn, 1982).

Although in the past fifteen years considerable evidence was found for the importance of the power bases, there are a number of methodological considerations which tend to affect the generalizability of these findings negatively. The research tended to be laboratory studies. The impact of increasing and decreasing influence cues in therapy-analogue settings were measured. But since subjects in these experimental investigations were no clients but volunteers for a research program, the content of the conversation was at best a personal topic and since, moreover, only one therapist-client contact was used, it is impossible to generalize the conclusions from these findings to an actual psychotherapy setting. The only field-study carried out to test the critical importance of the expert, referent and legitimate power base is the study by Lacrosse in 1981 (Corrigan, Dell, Lewis, & Schmidt, 1980; Heppner, & Dixon, 1981).

We intended to study the usefulness of the Social Power Model as a conceptual framework for enhancing the therapeutic relationship. As a first step we decided to gather motivating strategies and to study their structure. By investigating motivating behaviour of the therapist, we explore exactly the client-therapist interaction that is conceptualized by the Social Power Model. Therefore, we would expect that this structure in the motivating behaviour of the therapist would be comparable or identical to the classification of the Social Power Model.

Study 1

METHOD

Descriptions were gathered of interpersonal behaviour of the therapist from the literature on strategies to motivate people to change. We limited ourselves to the most important literature on directive behavioural therapy, the literature on compliance, on motivation for therapy, and on salesmanship (Keijsers & Kuijpers, 1988). Text units were collected out of these sources which met the following criteria:

1) Concrete therapist behaviour is described. Examples of these are: "offer information about treatment , take the client seriously" or "offer freedom of choice".
2) This behaviour has an influencing capacity, which is used or can be used to increase the probability that a client is going to start treatment, stays in treatment or participates actively in treatment to achievebeneficial treatment results.

These text units were rewritten in order to make them more readable, and were neglected, if the entries showed a great deal of overlap. At the end we had a collection of 396 descriptions of motivating therapist behaviour, which we called therapeutic relationship enhancement procedures (TREPs). Examples ofthese procedures are presented in Schaap and Hoogduin (1988).

The next step was to order and cluster the therapeutic relationship enhancement procedures. Because we had in mind to investigate these by means of pairwise cluster analysis, we sought for 10 to 18 categories. To cluster the TREPs was a difficult process. Some procedures such as "the therapist is courteous" or "the therapist is trustworthy" were quite easy to identify. Other similarities in content were harder to find. By means of defining and redefining the TREPs and by grouping and regrouping them, we were able to create 13 categories, each describing a different aspect of the motivating behaviour of the therapist. At the end, the definitions of the categories were stated in such a manner that a satisfactory discrimination between them was possible. Since descriptions of these categories are presented elsewhere (Schaap & Hoogduin, 1988) we simply list the final categories: The therapist (1) accepts the client unconditionally, (2) is courteous, (3) instils confidence in himself as a competent expert, (4) stays in the client's frame of reference, (5) sells the treatment procedures, (6) offers support, (7) offers help, (8) instils faith in the treatment, (9) gives information, (10) stimulates the client towards participation, (11) utilizes reactance, (12) puts pressure on the client, and (13) gets a third party involved.

The next step was to offer the 13 categories pairwise to therapists and instruct them to rate the similarity of each pair. A total of 38 therapists completed these questionnaires. The data were analyzed by multi-dimensionalscaling (ALLSCAL) and hierarchical clusteranalysis (HCA) (Keijsers, & Kuijpers, 1988).

RESULTS AND DISCUSSION

The results indicated (Figure 1) that twelve categories cluster into four groups and that the thirteenth category is dissimilar to all other categories.

The respondents see the categories "The therapist (3) instils confidence in himself as a competent expert", (8) "instils faith in the treatment ", and (9) "gives information" as one cluster, distinguishable from the other categories. Such interpersonal qualities of the therapist as expertise, credibility and trustworthiness, and therapist behaviours like offering credible explanations for the problems of the client, the strict conduction of therapeutic techniques, the explicit information about the treatmenttechniques, treatment process and client and therapist role, are all experienced as a separate group of influencing behaviours of the therapist. Unmistakably this expertise cluster is identical to the expert power base described in the Social Power Model of Strong and Matross.

The second cluster consists of the categories "The therapist (1) accepts the client unconditionally", (2) "is courteous", and (4) "stays in the client's frame of reference". This result strengthens the therapeutic truism of the important and distinguishable impact of the so called Rogerian conditions in psychotherapy. Unconditional positive regard, courteousness, respect, warmth, empathy and such therapist behaviours as tuning in to clients' language and use of expressions and metaphors, tuning in to clients'system of reference and preferences and expectancies with regard to treatment and treatment program are perceived by the respondents as a separate group of influencing behaviours. The similarity with the definition of the referent power base of Strong and Matross is clear.

Dendrogram: On the vertical axis are the categories, numbered from 1 to 13. On the horizontal axis is the degree of dissimilarity or Eucledean distance, coded from 0 (low) to 25 (high).

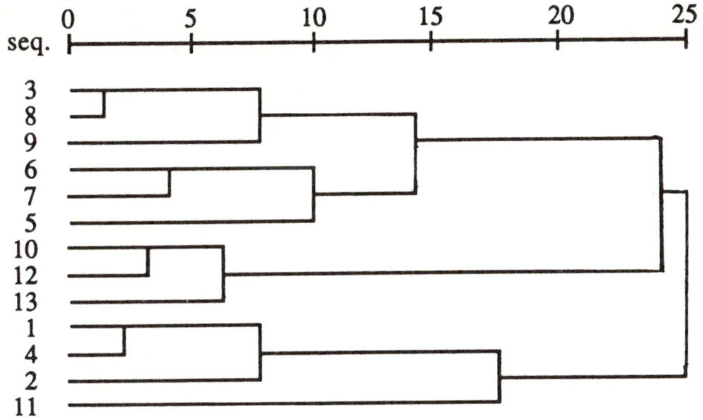

Figure 1. Results of the Hierarchical Cluster Analysis of the 13 categories (N=38) (Keijsers & Kuipers, 1988)

The third cluster consists of the categories "The therapist (10) stimulates the client towards participation", (12) "puts pressure on the client", and (13) "gets a third party involved". On the one hand this cluster refers to an active, directive and influencing therapist, at the other hand the therapist behaves in this manner together with and tuned in to the client. The working alliance of client and therapist is based on a division of tasks and responsibilities. Both invest according to their roles in the process of solving the problems of the client. The introduction of proposals, opportunities to choose between treatment alternatives and time schedules, responsibility and freedom all diminish client's resistance to influence attempts and increase the likelihood of change. Although this cluster, which we called the establishment of a working alliance, is rather typical for behaviour and directive therapy, it is by no means exclusive for these treatment forms. We see much resemblance with the legitimate power base as defined by Strong and Matross.

The last cluster from the analysis we called "Helping with the process of change". The categories belonging to this cluster are "The therapist (6) offers support", (7) "offers help", and (5) "sells the treatment procedures". They refer to therapist's effort to structure and guide the process of change of the client, i.e., the gradual relinquishing of ineffective coping behaviour and maladaptive attitudes, and the gradual incorporation of new attitudes and effective coping strategies. Such therapist's behaviours as structuring the change process, reinforcing effective behaviour, giving feedback, helping the client to clarify the problems and take a more objective stance, and choose and specify the treatment goals, stimulate the client to change. Often these activities are reassuring in nature. Desired changes are coming within reach of the client. Although this maybe less clear than the three clusters mentioned earlier, we can recognize here the concept of opposition as stated in the model of Strong and Matross.

We now turn to the thirteenth category (11) "The therapist utilizes resistance". This category is perceived by the respondents as relatively independent from the other categories. A possible explanation is the often indirect way the therapist deals with resistant behaviour of the client. Strategies like these are recommended, when the client uses a rather typical interaction style, for instance, when a personality disorder is diagnosed. The model of Strong and Matross does not provide for an analysis of typical interaction styles, but again this category can be linked to the concept of resistance (Keijsers, Schaap, Keijsers & Hoogduin, 1989)

The importance of the concordance between our inventory of TREPs and the Social Power Theory of Strong and Matross is that, apparently, every therapist behaviour, ranging from the Rogerian conditions to putting pressure on the client can be translated into social influence terms. This provides support for the contention that the concept of therapeutic relationship can be investigated successfully within a social psychological framework based on influence processes.

The next step now is to study, if these TREPs lead to improvements in the therapeutic relationship and to improvement of the outcome.

Study 2

METHOD

In this pilot study, therapists were instructed to explicitly employ therapeutic relationship enhancement procedures as described above. We decided to limit ourselves to the TREPs within the category of referent powerbase. This power base is quite similar to the traditional psychotherapeutic notion of the quality of the therapeutic relationship, i.e., the Rogerian conditions of unconditional acceptance, warmth, positive regard and accurate empathy. Additionally some TREPs out of the category ' The therapist offers support' were added to this selection.The descriptions of the TREPs from Study 1, were rewritten in such a way that they provided the therapist with clear and well-executable instructions. This investigation was carried out in a large psychiatric out-patient clinic. Thirty obsessive compulsive patients were included, but the results are only available of fourteen patients at this moment. The patients were treated by two therapists, using exposure and responseprevention. The patient-therapist relationship was measured by an independent assessor after the second and tenth session using the Dutch version of the Barrett-Lennard Relationship Inventory (RI), an inventory based on Rogerian assumptions (Lietaer, 1976). The RI consists of a client-form and a therapist-form. According to Lietaer (1976) four subscales of the RI, called the EPIN-scales, together offer a reliable indication of the quality of the therapeutic relationship. Each form consists of 28 statements which are to be confirmed or disconfirmed by client or therapist on a six point scale. Both forms have a theoretical minimum score of 28 (low quality) and a maximum score of 168 (high quality). At the end of the tenth session the percentage of symptom reduction was measured. Immediately after the second session, the scores on the EPIN-scale were inspected. If the client or therapist had a low score on one or more items, the therapist was instructed to use a specific set of TREPs in order to influence beneficially the aspect of the therapeutic relationship associated with this item or these items. Neither the therapist nor the patient was informed about the scores of the EPIN-scale. To illustrate the procedure we present item 3 of the EPIN-scale in figure 2. The item is: " Somehow I make him (therapist) feel nervous."

session:	3	4	5	6	7	8	9	10
-make carefully use of appreciating remarks								
-show the patient to be pleased about having him in treatment								
-tell the patient he's doing his best								
-emhasize his correct regristration assignment								
-emhasize his correct homework assignments								
-compliment the patient with his perseverance								

Figure 2. An illustration of instructions to enhance the therapeutic relationship used at a low score on EPIN (client version), item 3

The therapists were instructed to log after each session the frequency in which they made use of the instructions.

RESULTS

The average score of the EPIN-scale, filled in by the clients after the second and tenth session were 135 (sd=13) and 134 (sd=12.2), respectively. The average score of the therapists after the second and tenth session were 140 (sd=7.5) and 147 (sd=8.2),. respectively. Symptom reduction, measured after the tenth session was 33%.

If we compare these preliminary results with the earlier results on the EPIN-scale (Hoogduin et. al.,1989), some differences can be detected. First of all, in earlier research it was consistently found that both patients and clients had lower scores on the second measurement than on the first. Although this is an interesting finding in itself, we can only guess about the reason. It is possible that the first sessions are used mainly for establishing a relationship. At the tenth session, however, therapist and client are working together in the change process. In this phase, both become more demanding and, one may probably say, more realistic about each other's abilities. In this study, however, we did not find a lower average score on the second measurement. Although we ignore exactly how we manipulated the interaction and whom we did influence the most, according to the scores on the EPIN-scale, we enhanced the therapeutic relationship between session two and ten, compared to earlier studies. The average score of the clients remained almost the same and the average score of the therapists increased in the second measure. Apparently, the therapists experienced an improved relationship with the client when they are instructed to use pre-described TREPs. Secondly, the average symptom reduction in the earlier study, measured after the tenth session is less than the symptom reduction of 33% in this study.

DISCUSSION AND FUTURE DIRECTIONS

Of course, there are serious limitations to study 2. First, the results are based on a small sample. Second, the TREPs were based on the same instrument that we used to improve the therapeutic relationship in the first place. In further investigations we will have to use a parallel instrument to assess the quality of the relationship.

The third limitation is the most difficult one. For, how can we control the Hawthorne-effect of this type of manipulation research? Is it possible to use a control condition in which the therapists receive instructions that do not affect the quality of the relationship? We think this is possible. Clients could be assigned to two conditions at random. In both conditions clients are treated with the same behavioural techniques. In the experimental condition therapists receive TREPs, based on the EPIN-scale.In the control condition therapists receive instructions about the proper conduction of the treatment techniques. It can be expected that clients and therapists who are dissatisfied with the relationship in the beginning of therapy will profit more from TREPs than from instructions about treatment technique. But then we still face an important limitation in our research line, because we focused mainly on the traditional clinical-psychological concept of the quality of a therapeutic relationship. The interpersonal processes hypothesized as the expert and legitimate power base in the Social Power Model of Strong and Matross are left out of consideration. Concluding from the common factors literature and social psychological research of interpersonal perception, we can learn that expertness, trustworthiness and cooperation are important relationship variables as well, closely linked to the concept of motivation for psychotherapy (Corrigan et. al., 1980; Frank, 1973; Strong, & Matross, 1973; Strong, & Claiburn, 1982; Heppner, & Dixon,1981). This implies that we will have to incorporate these variables in further manipulation studies.

REFERENCES

Bennun, I., Hahlweg, K., Schindler, L., Langlotz, M. (1986) Therapist's and client's perceptions in behaviour therapy: The development and cross-cultural analysis of an assessment instrument. *ritish Journal of Clinical Psychology, 25*, 275-285

Bennun, I., Schindler, L. (1988) Therapist and patient factors in the behavioural treatment of phobic patients. *British Journal of Clinical Psychology, 27*, 145-150.

Corrigan, J.D., Dell, D.M., Lewis, K.N., Schmidt, L.D. (1980) Counselling as social influence process: A review. *Journal of Counselling Psychology, 27*, 395-441.

Frank, J.D. (1973) *"Persuasion and Healing: A comparative study of psychotherapy"*. New York: John Hopkins University Press.

Gurman, A.S. (1977) The patient's perception of the therapeutic relationship. In A. S. Gurman & A. Razin (Eds.). "Effective psychotherapy: A handbook of research" (pp. 503-543). New York: Pergamon Press.

Heppner, P.P., Dixon, D.N. (1981) A review of the interpersonal influence process in counselling. *Personnel and Guidance Journal, 59*, 542-550.

Hoogduin, C.A.L., de Haan, E., Schaap, C. (1989) The significance of patient-therapist relationship in the treatment of obsessive-compulsive neurosis. *British Journal of Clinical Psychology, 28*, 185-186.

Keijsers, G., Kuijpers, W. (1988) *"De motivatie verhogende aktiviteit van de therapeut: Een inventariserend onderzoek naar motiveringsstrategieën binnen psychotherapie"*. (The motivating behaviour of the therapist: An inventory of motivating strategies in psychotherapy.) unpublished.

Keijsers, L., Schaap, C., Keijsers, G., Hoogduin, C.A.L.(1989) *"De aanpak van lastige clienten"*. (Treatment of difficult clients.). in press.

LaCrosse, M.B. (1980) Perceived counsellor *social influence and counselli*ng outcomes: Validity of the Counsellor Rating Form. *Journal of Counselling Psychology, 27*, 4, 320-327.

Lietaer, G. (1976) *Nederlandstalige revisie van Barrett-Lennard's Relationship Inventory voor individueel-therapeutische relaties*. (Dutch revision of Barrett-Lennards's Relationship Inventory for individual-therapeutic relationships.) Psychologica Belgica, 16, (1), 73-94.

Orlinsky, D.E., Howard, K.I. (1987) Process and outcome in psychotherapy. In S. Garfield & E. Bergin (Eds.). *"Handbook of psychotherapy and behaviourchange"*. New York: Pergamon Press.

Schaap, C., Hoogduin, C.A.L. (1988) The therapeutic relationship in behaviour therapy: Enhancing the quality of the bond. In: P.M.G. Emmelkamp(Ed.). *"Advances in theory and practice in behaviour therapy"* (pp. 71-82).Lisse: Swets en Zeitlinger.

Strong, S.R., Claiburn, C.D. (1982) *"Change trough interaction: Social psychological process of counselling and psychotherapy"*. New York: John Wiley and Sons.

Strong, S.R. Matross, R.P. (1973) Change process in counselling and psychotherapy. *Journal of Counselling Psychotherapy, 20*, 25-37.

Sweet, A.A. (1984) The therapeutic relationship in behaviour therapy. *Clinical Psychology Review", 11*, 253-272.

Wilson, G.T., Evans, W.I.M. (1977) The therapist-client relationship in behaviour therapy. In A. S. Gurman & A. Razin (Eds.). *"Effective psychotherapy: A handbook of research."* (pp. 544-565). New York: Pergamon Press.

Erratum

Please note that the two figures below have changed places:

Figure 1 page 168 is Figure 4 page 256 — Figure 4 page 256 is Figure 1 page 168.

Please insert figures on the correct pages.

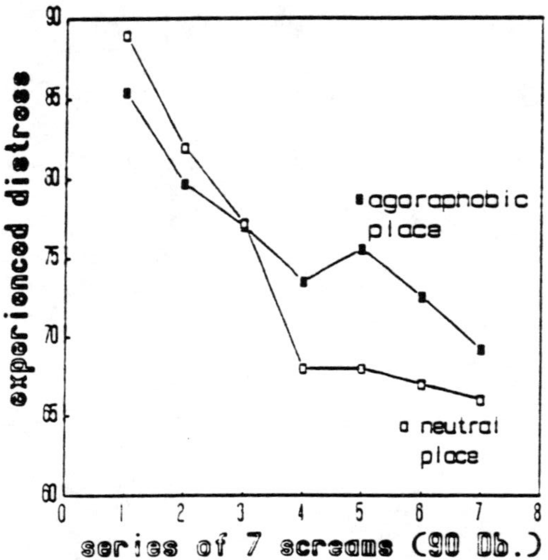

p. 168. Figure 1: Mean experienced distress reported immediately

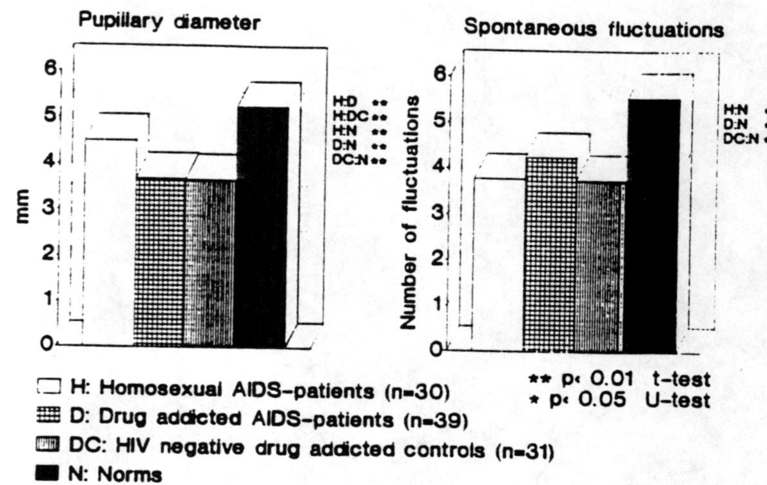

p. 256 Figure 4: Mean experienced Static pupillometry in AIDS-patients.